D1090368

HISPANIC
NOTES & MONOGRAPHS

ESSAYS, STUDIES, AND BRIEF BIOGRAPHIES ISSUED BY THE HISPANIC SOCIETY OF AMERICA

HISPANIC AMERICAN SERIES

I

OTHER BOOKS BY THE SAME AUTHOR ON THE COLONIAL PERIOD IN SOUTH AMERICA

The Establishment of Spanish Rule in America.

The Spanish Dependencies in South America, 2 vols.

Spain's Declining Power in South America.

South America on the Eve of Emancipation.

The Author of *La Araucana*

see page 158

SPANISH COLONIAL LITERATURE in South America

BY

BERNARD MOSES, Ph. D., LL.D.,

Professor Emeritus in the University of California,
Honorary Professor in the University of Chile

The Hispanic Society of America
LONDON : NEW YORK
1922

PRINTED AT THE
SHAKESPEARE HEAD PRESS
STRATFORD-UPON-AVON

PREFACE

No intelligent person is likely to deny the importance of official documents as the basis of a nation's history; but these documents do not tell the whole story. There are social activities, currents of national thought, and waves of popular sentiment, which are not fully described either in laws or governmental proclamations. Tradition sometimes conveys a knowledge of these aspects of society, but tradition undergoes such modifications in the course of time that it does not render the same account to all later generations or centuries. Only what is written remains fixed.

Each century writes the literature it reads. This is especially true of historical literature. It is also true that each century, in the various forms of its literature, writes its own history; and it is to this literature, not to the later critical writings that one must refer, who would know how any given period of the past appeared to those then living. It was once said of a distinguished modern historian of Rome that he knew more about the affairs of Rome than the Romans themselves knew; which was to say, that his works presented a view of Rome such as no Roman ever had. The critical history of the society of any given period of the past is so completely an artificial creation that it would hardly be recognized by a member of that society. It takes its character, in a considerable part, from knowledge, ideas, and emotions that were foreign to him. Therefore, in order to know a nation's life as known at any given epoch, or to visualise the worldly show that passed before the thoughtful contemporary mind, one should refer, not to the artificial creation of the modern historian, with its twentieth-century atmosphere, but to what men wrote of their own times or times near their own. Our ancestors' vision of the world and the reaction which the world produced in their minds are revealed in the various forms of their literature.

The material for an intellectual reconstitution of the view of their society entertained by the Spanish colonists of South America is much less abundant than that which the twenty-third-century historian will have for reproducing our view of our times. There were in the Spanish colonies no congressional or parliamentary debates, no popular orators describing social conditions and setting forth economic and political doctrines, no discussion of social programmes, and, more significant than all else, no periodical press recording from day to day and from month the events and ideas of the period in question. But in the books, the reports, and the relaciones there is a larger mass of written evidence than the comparatively rude state of colonial society would lead one to expect; and it is the purpose of this book to point out the principal documents of this colonial literature, and to introduce the reader to the men of letters in the colonies who wrote under the inspiration of their experience in the New World, whether their contributions were in the realm of poetry, history, geographical description, or ecclesiastical discussion. All this is brought together under a general title in which the term "literature" is consciously expanded from its narrower meaning to cover whatever was written on any of these general subjects; and by helping the reader to a knowledge of this literature it is believed that through it he will be enabled to acquire a more or less distinct view of the colonial society as it appeared in any period to men of that period.

It is presumed that copies of this book will fall into the hands of persons not completely versed in the Spanish language, and for this reason a somewhat broad view of Spanish accentuation has been carried out as an assistance in the pronunciation of such Spanish words and titles as it has been found advisable to introduce. It will, moreover, be noted that all titles and quotations from the texts of early colonial writers are given in modernized Spanish.

The portraits here presented help to show that the intellectual life of the colonies was not limited to a single class, but embraced friars, parish priests, and bishops; private soldiers and officers of the army; governors, judges, and viceroys.

It is not to be expected that a book covering the number and wide range of facts here included will be without errors; but there are fewer errors in this volume than would have appeared but for the valuable editorial assistance of Mr. A. H. Wykeham-George, who suggested and formed the Appendix, directed the preparation of the illustrations, and supervised the passing of the whole through the press. For that assistance I take this occasion to express my cordial appreciation; and at the same time I would gratefully acknowledge the important contribution to the undertaking rendered by Miss Janet Hunter Perry, Lecturer in Spanish at King's College, and the very friendly and helpful attention given by the authorities of the British Museum, particularly by Dr. Henry Thomas, Assistant Keeper of Printed Books.

BERNARD MOSES.

Paris, June 3rd, 1922.

CONTENTS

CHAPTER I

CHAPTER II

CHAPTER III

CHAPTER IX

Writers on Chilean History, 1600–1650

CHAPTER X

Writers of Peru and New Granada, 1600–1650

CHAPTER XI

The Last Half of the Seventeenth Century

CHAPTER XIV

SOME ECCLESIASTICS AND THEIR RELIGIOUS BOOKS

CHAPTER XV

GOVERNMENT AND LAW

CHAPTER XVI

Late Eighteenth Century Historians

CHAPTER XVII

Outlook towards Emancipation

APPENDIX

LIST OF ILLUSTRATIONS

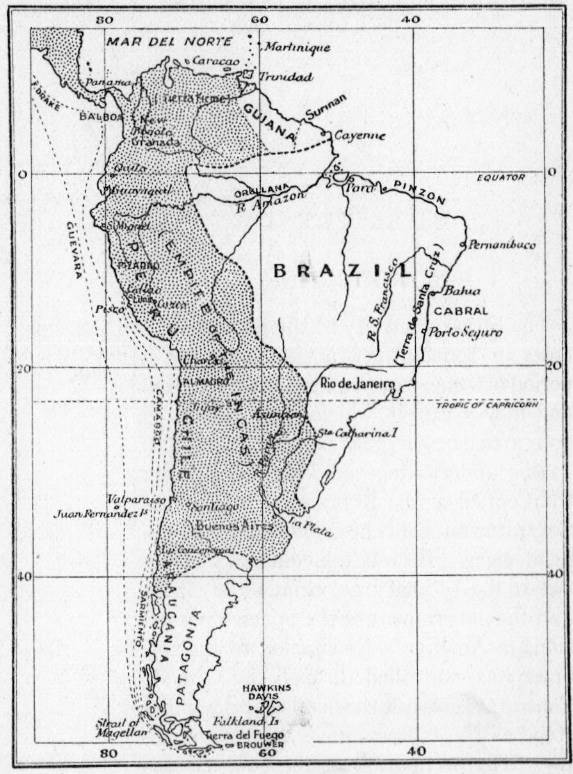

Map of South America, showing (shaded) the Spanish Colonial Possessions

CHAPTER I

INTRODUCTION

The Colonies and Spain

The literary activity of the Spanish Colonies in South America extended over a period of somewhat more than two hundred and fifty years, in which Spain organized and carried on her great colonial enterprise. In this undertaking the king, assisted by the Council of the Indies and the Casa de Contratación, held the colonies as royal dependencies. He was the common link between the ordinary government of Spain and the government of the Spanish possessions in America. Emigration to the colonies was controlled through the Casa de Contratación, while the Council of the Indies stood as the supreme governmental ministry. The occupation of the country was conducted largely as a material and spiri-

Spain's agencies of control

tual conquest, in which conspicuous parts were played by soldiers and priests, the soldiers giving to the process of colonisation the appearance of a military campaign, while the activity of the priests was supported by the idea that the acceptance of the Christian doctrine transferred the Indians from barbarism to the status of civilization.

The agencies of control in the colonial undertaking, whether military, ecclesiastical or civil, were directed from Spain. These agencies, in their final organization, were gathered into three important groups, or vice-royalties: Peru, New Granada, and Río de la Plata. The viceroy in each of these semi-independent states was assisted by a small body called an audiencia, which performed the functions both of a ministry and of a supreme court. In the several subdivisions of the territory local officers, known as corregidores, carried on a practically arbitrary administration, under which the Indians were oppressed and impoverished ; and in the larger town a cabildo, or municipal council, exercised a certain

The Inquisition

degree of control, when not impeded by a superior authority. Over the government and the inhabitants, in the course of time, the Inquisition extended its paralysing force; and in the presence of spies and malicious reporters men put off their intellectual independence, and either remained silent or conformed their utterances to the prescriptions of the Holy Office. This restraint naturally limited the range of ideas that found expression either orally or in writing. Authors had continually to face the possibility of seeing their manuscripts refused the privilege of publication. The subjects not liable to this embarrassment were the history of the colonies discreetly treated, the geography and natural history of the Indies, and the doctrines and history of the Church. Writings on these subjects, therefore, constitute the bulk of the colonial literature of South America.

Nature as displayed in the unspoiled wilderness of the New World attracted more attention than it had received in Spain, and writers of the history of the Indies gave much space to descriptions of their unfami-

Writings in verse

liar environment. Great writers of Italy had made verse a preferred form of literature in the sixteenth century, and there is no doubt that, in addition to their example, the exaltation of spirit maintained by the unaccustomed adventures of early colonial life contributed powerfully to the extensive adoption of this form of utterance. It was undoubtedly the new and inspiring scenes and events attending the campaigns against the Araucanians that moved Ercilla to give a poetic record of his experience. in *La Araucana.* When Barco Centenera under similar influences undertook to write an account of the Spanish occupation of the south eastern part of the continent, the result was an "historical poem" called *La Argentina;* and Peralta Barnuevo's extended history of the early development of Spanish society in Peru assumed the metrical form in *Lima fundada.* The form of Castellanos' chronicle was practically determined by the success of Ercilla's verses. And after these came a troop of chroniclers, whose verses were the product of imitation rather than the result of original inspiration.

The question of printing

Much that was written in the colonies has not been printed, sometimes because the manuscript was not approved by the censor, sometimes because the funds needed to cover the cost were not available, and sometimes because the manuscript was lost. The liability to loss was especially great during most of the colonial period, since manuscripts designed for printing had to be sent to Europe, and were exposed to dangers from shipwreck, the attacks of pirates, and the neglect of the persons to whom they were entrusted. It was only late that presses were established in the dependencies of South America; and even after they were provided, the quality of the work done was poor and the expense high. Printing was introduced into Mexico earlier than into South America, and it was from Mexico that Peru received its first printer. This was Antonio Ricardo, who had been a printer in Mexico for ten years. He decided to remove to Peru in 1579, but encountered serious obstacles to his proposed emigration, partly due to the fact that he was not a native of Spain. He encountered other ob-

Ricardo printer in Peru

stacles in seeking permission to undertake the business of printing in Peru after his arrival in that country. Finally, when the catechism prepared by the Jesuits at the request of the ecclesiastical council was completed, the audiencia,on February the thirteenth, 1584, decreed that Ricardo might be permitted to print it. But the work was interrupted in order to print instructions concerning corrections in the calendar, under the title *Pragmática sobre los diez días del año*. The authorization of this publication was given by the audiencia on the fourteenth of July, 1584, and this first product of the South American press appeared a little later. The catechism became the second publication.[1]

After this beginning the business of printing grew rapidly, in spite of the high cost of paper, receiving its principal impulse from a strong demand for primary books for schools and little manuals of devotion. News-sheets followed, issued at irregular intervals, and after twenty-five years, it be-

(1) It is entitled *Doctrina cristiana y catecismo para instrucción en nuestra santa fe, con un confesionario, y otras cosas necesarias para los que doctrinan.*

y confiar en el, y ſeruille con alma y cuerpo para ſiempre jamas. Amen Ieſus.

Q.	A.
yupaychaſpa muchácã chicpac, payman ſuya cuncanchicpac, animanchic huan, vcunchic huápas payta, viñaypac ſiruincanchicpac. Amen Ieſus.	chuymañaſſatáq, hupa ro huáqñaſſataq, hihua corpacàma animaſsápi háchiſſampiſa, hupá camachita áropa huacay chañaſſataqui yatiyáta cãcana. Amen Ieſus.

Fin del Catecíſmo mayor.

Page from the First Book to be printed in South America

Contreras Royal Printer

came customary to issue them on the arrival of ships bringing news from Spain. As early as 1621 Jerónimo de Contreras, who had been a printer in Seville, appeared as the publisher of these news-sheets; and for the next hundred years he and members of his family were the leading printers of Lima. His son, José de Contreras, succeeded him in 1641, and continued his business until 1688. Two years before this last date, in 1686, José de Contreras, a grandson of the founder of the house, organized an independent printing establishment, which held a practical monopoly of printing in Lima until 1712. The printing of books for primary instruction in the local schools brought to the head of this new establishment considerable profits, and by a decree of the crown José de Contreras acquired the title of Royal Printer. The Inquisition, the University of San Marcos, and various other institutions resorted to his press for the printing required. After the death of the Royal Printer his brother, Jerónimo de Contreras, carried on the business for a number of years, and the establishment maintained itself without essential change of character until 1779.

Printing by Jesuits

Early printing elsewhere in South America was almost exclusively the work of the Jesuits. They had a press at the mission station of Juli near Lake Titicaca, in the second decade of the seventeenth century, but it was only after about a hundred years that a press was set up in any other part of South America. In the missions of Paraguay the first book printed by the Jesuits appeared in 1705. This was entitled *De la diferencia entre lo temporal y eterno*, by Padre Juan Eusebio Nieremberg, translated into Guarani by Joseph Serrano.[2]

The Jesuits established a printing press at Córdoba in connexion with the college of Monserrat, but after the expulsion of the order from South America the press was transferred to Buenos Aires in 1780. About eight years later the authorities of the col-

(2) Other publications issued in the missions of Paraguay were the following: *Manuale ad usum patrum Societatis Jesu*, 1721; *Vocabulario de la lengua Guarani*, 1722; *Arte de la lengua Guarani*, by Padre Antonio Ruiz de Montoya, 1724; *Explicación del catecismo en lengua Guarani*, by Nicolás Yupaguay, 1724; *Sermones y ejemplos en lengua Guarani*, by Nicolás Yapuguay, 1727; *Carta de Antequera al obispo Palos*, 1727.

Press of Córdoba

lege felt the need of the press that had been removed, and sent Manuel Antonio Talavera to Buenos Aires to request that it might be replaced by another. The negotiations ended, however, without any immediate result.

Printing at Quito

In 1741 Alejandro Coronado, a resident of Quito, petitioned the Council of the Indies for permission to establish a printing press in that city, where previously no facilities for printing had existed. This petition was granted, and by a subsequent act of the Council this privilege was extended to his heirs, in case of Coronado's death before the projected press had been set up. Coronado's plan was not carried out, and nearly twenty years later the Jesuits, who had a press in Ambato, removed it to Quito at the beginning of 1760. The first printing in Quito was done on that press in the early part of that year.[3]

The beginning of printing in Bogotá is assigned to various dates. According to Vergara, the press was established there in

(3) Medina, José Toribio, *La imprenta en Quito*, Santiago de Chile, 1904, viii.

1740, but other statements maintain that there was no printing in Bogotá until 1789.[4]

The law and books

The development of literature in the Spanish dependencies of South America was hindered, not only by the very imperfect facilities for printing, but also by the extremely rigid restrictions on the publication and importation of books. These restrictions were, however, an after-thought of Spanish legislation. A law of 1480, relating to the introduction of books into Spain, provided that "no duties whatsoever shall be paid for the importation of foreign books into these kingdoms; considering how profitable and honourable it is that books from other countries should be brought to these kingdoms, in order that by them men men may become learned".[5]

But this wise and liberal law remained valid for only a few years. It was supplanted by legislation conceived in fear of foreign influences that might threaten the traditions of the nation and the accepted

(4) Quesada, Vicente G. *La vida intelectual en la América española durante los siglos xvi, xvii, y xviii*, p. 83.

(5) *Novísima recopilación de las leyes de España*, lib. viii, tit. xv, ley 1.

Blanco Núñez de Vela, 1st Viceroy of Peru
March to September, 1544

The Censorship

ecclesiastical doctrines. The new law, the law of July the eighth, 1502, was issued to prohibit the publication or sale of a book on any subject whatsoever without royal authorization, or the importation of any book except after submission to a rigorous censorship and on receipt of permission. In September, 1543, Charles V ordered the viceroys, the audiencia, sand the governors to prevent the printing, selling, holding, or the bringing into their districts, of books of fiction treating of profane subjects, and to provide that neither Spaniards nor Indians should read them. This legislation was designed to prevent the publication, sale, and reading of the romances of chivalry, which were held to have a demoralizing influence on the spirit of the Spaniards. A law of 1556 provided that the judges and justices "shall not permit any book to be printed or sold which treats of subjects relating to the Indies, without having a special licence issued by the Council of the Indies; and they shall cause to be collected and shall collect and send to that body all the books which they shall find, and no printer may

Sending manuscripts to Spain

print, hold, or sell them, under penalty of 200,000 maravedis and the loss of his printing office." Moreover, the sending of manuscripts to Spain to be examined by the Council of the Indies was attended with very great risks; and when an American author had secured the printing of his book in Spain or in any other European country, great difficulties were encountered in his attempts to have copies of it returned to America; for it was provided by law that no printed book treating of American subjects, whether issued in Spain or in a foreign country, could be taken to the Indies until it had been examined and approved by the Council of the Indies.[6]

The inconvenience of sending manuscripts to Spain to be examined and approved or disapproved by the Council of the Indies is illustrated by Bishop Villarroel's experience. He sent the manuscript of *El gobierno eclesiástico pacífico* to Spain, but the vessel carrying it was wrecked, and only by great good fortune was the manuscript saved. He sent another work in four vol-

(6) *Recopilación de leyes de los reinos de la sIndias*, lib. I, tit. xxiv, ley 2. Madrid 1681.

umes to Madrid, and solicited permission to publish it. The issuing of the licence was delayed three years, and in the meantime the manuscript was lost. The legal obstacles and the practical difficulties in the way of obtaining permission to print help to explain why many manuscripts, written in America or about America, remained unpublished until after the overthrow of Spanish rule in the Indies. Even after the establishment of presses in America, the great cost of paper furnished an obstacle to their extensive use, and except in Mexico and Lima there were few printing presses until late in the colonial period.

Obstacles to printing

While the Inquisition tended to destroy free intellectual activity in the Spanish colonies, the Church in other ways contributed to a certain cultivation along lines approved by itself. It helped to preserve old-world traditions in some departments of life. By the study of the Indian languages, which it encouraged, and the formation and the publication of grammars, it made public and preserved a knowledge of these languages. It, moreover, founded and supported schools, that maintained the light of learning, though a feeble and fluctuating light, within a narrow ecclesiastical horizon. But all efforts in favour of liberal enlightenment were counteracted by governmental measures in opposition to the importation of books, particularly secular books of all kinds.

The range of learning

But the range of learning was limited. Until near the end of the colonial period instruction in the colleges and universities retained its mediaeval character. The curriculum of studies embraced little, if anything, besides Latin, philosophy, and theology. Having attained proficiency in Latin the student was admitted to the courses on philosophy under the faculty of arts. After three years with this faculty he passed to the study of theology, which was continued for four, and later for five, years. The first enlargement of this curriculum was effected by the addition of jurisprudence, or Roman law. This change was not made until near the end of the eighteenth century.[7]

(7) See the author's *Spanish Dependencies in South America*, chaps. IX and XIII.

Teaching by Jesuits

The expulsion of the Jesuits in 1767 was a very severe blow to scholarly and literary activity in colonial society. The Jesuits had a school or a college in every important town of the dependencies, and their instruction was clearer and more effective than that of the other schools, although one is sometimes disposed to regard their employment of a rigid mould of predetermined form, in which to cast all minds, as the greatest educational error of history. But under conditions where, outside of the chief towns, the dominating influences made either for the roughness of the camp or the brutishness of semi-barbarism, a system of instruction that trained the mind to a definite standard was not without its merits, although that standard was the inelastic standard of the Jesuits.[8]

The universities presumed a more or less extensive group of cultivated persons in the towns where they were established; and when these towns were also the principal seats of government, as were Lima, Bogotá,

(8) For a general view of the expulsion of the Jesuits see the author's volume on *Spain's Declining Power in South America*, chap. IV.

The viceregal academy

Santiago de Chile, and Caracas, the officials of the administration formed another superior element in the population. Lima, as the viceroy's residence, was the social capital of the dependencies. The powers of the viceroy were practically those of an autocratic ruler, during the period of his incumbency, and there were brought to Lima from Spain many of the forms and ceremonies of the Spanish court. The viceroy appeared in public with much of the state affected by European monarchs of the seventeenth and eighteenth centuries. Sometimes he used the influence of his high position to encourage learning and literary activity. The viceregal palace, in the reign of the viceroy Casteldosrius, was the meeting-place of a society where authors assembled every Monday to present their writings and discuss subjects of interest to men of letters. Dr. Pedro Peralta Barnuevo, the author of *Lima fundada*, was a member of this academy. But the "high society" of Lima had a lower conception of literature and literary men than the learned viceroy, and expressed regret that the

El Marqúes de Casteldosríus, 24th Viceroy of Peru
1707–1710

Triunfos de amor y poder

ancient customs and dignity of the viceregal office had been violated by the participation of the head of the state in the proceedings of a literary society. The victory of the French under Vendome over the Austrians under Starhemberg was celebrated at the palace by the production of Barnuevo's comedy called *Triunfos de amor y poder;* and there were more regrets by the aristocracy that the palace of the viceroy had been turned into a theatre.

Lima at this time, the beginning of the eighteenth century, had about seventy thousand inhabitants, Europeans, mestizos, Indians, and negro slaves. Gold and silver flowed into the city from the mines, and the buildings that were constructed after the earthquake of 1687 were superior to those which had been destroyed; they gave Lima an appearance of prosperity; they suggested a degree of luxury that had not been evident earlier. The creoles, always fond of display, sought to avoid the simplicity and rudeness of the smaller towns. They made their wealth conspicuous by their possession of paintings from Italy and Spain, by their

Lima and the other capitals

extravagant dress, and by their abundant ornaments of gold, pearls, diamonds, and other precious stones; and it is said that the nobles of Lima exceeded in luxury the aristocracy of Spain. The Peruvian capital was enlivened not only by the presence of the fifteen hundred students of the University of San Marcos, but also by a large number of convents or monasteries, in which the conflicts attending the elections of their officers often ran so high that large sections of the population became involved, and the secular authorities were called upon forcefully to interfere.

Bogotá, Caracas, Quito, Santiago, Asunción, and Buenos Aires were capitals, like Lima, but on a smaller scale. Common fundamental characteristics prevailed in all, except as these were modified by the different material interests and opportunities of the several cities. In the very small towns and in the country the Indians and the mestizos predominated, suggesting barbarism rather than civilization.

The colonial society of Spanish South America had no notion of social or political

Colonial society

equality like that entertained by the British colonists in North America, and consequently recognized marked class distinctions as a phase of the normal social order. The authorities in Spain, charged with the government of the colonies, maintained the traditional view of social inequality, and encouraged its practical development by creating a titled nobility and conferring upon encomenderos a status of superiority over their dependents not greatly unlike the relation of superior and inferior that prevailed during the period of European feudalism. Under this social order the subdued Indians became an element, naturally a subordinate element, in the composite society of the colonies, instead of drifting into irreconcilable hostility to Europeans, as happened in British North America.

An analysis of Spanish colonial society in South America would reveal a body of officials composed almost exclusively of men born in Spain, and educated in accordance with the ideas and traditions of Spain's conservative administration. These were the viceroys, the judges of the audiencias,

Groups and classes

the royal treasurers, and the corregidores, or governors of small districts. Hardly less important than the civil officials were the ecclesiastics, who were sent to the colonies by the authorities in Spain, and paid out of the royal revenues of the colonies. These members of the clergy became teachers, missionaries, and parish priests, many of whom were friars belonging to the various religious orders. A third group was composed of soldiers, who were sent from Spain for a period of four or five years, and a more or less extensive body of militia. This military force was employed in putting down insurrections, defending the frontiers and extending the dominion of the Spaniards. And it was in this group that a number of the most noteworthy writers of South America appeared.

Some of the officials, in the exercise of their practically irresponsible authority, often made illegitimate appropriations from the public funds that passed under their control; and the parish priests, in many cases, and the petty governors almost universally, extorted whatever was to be had from the Indians by a systematic process of merciless oppression.

The Creoles

The dishonesty of officials, coupled with the fact that they were almost exclusively Spaniards, sent from Spain to occupy their posts for a few years, at length alienated the sympathies of the creoles and the mestizos from the Spanish administration. The creoles, persons of pure Spanish blood born in America, in many cases took advantage of the instruction offered in the colonial universities, and in some instances continued their studies in Spain. They became men of cultivation and sober judgment; they knew the circumstances and needs of the society of which they were members; they had a patriotic interest and an instinctive pride in their communities or commonwealths; yet they were practically barred from office, and their advice was seldom, or never, solicited. By this egoistical and stupid conduct of the government in Spain the creoles and the mestizos were thrown into an attitude of opposition; a rigid line was drawn between them and the Spaniards; and on the American side of this line the creoles and mestizos formed a new society, which increased in numbers and self-confidence with the passing decades. Finally, these two classes, merged into one and supported by the civilized Indians, asserted their determination to abolish Spanish domination and be independent. But throughout the two centuries and a half of colonial existence, under the influence of Spanish conservatism, the colonies remained, to a very great extent, in a state of social stagnation until near the end of the eighteenth century.

Social stagnation

The industrial and commercial life of the colonies suffered under restrictions quite as effective as those that burdened the cause of letters. Importation to the dependencies of South America was limited by positive laws, and the exportation of certain products was made practically impossible, because they could not successfully compete with similar commodities produced elsewhere, on account of the greater cost of transportation from the western ports of South America. Agriculture was limited by the prohibitory cost of transporting its

Restrictions on commerce

products, and by the fact that the small population offered only a restricted demand for them, a demand that was insufficient to bring into cultivation the available fertile land or to employ the available labourers. This limited domestic demand and the impossibility of exporting the products constituted an effective restriction on agricultural progress; and this restriction was intensified by arbitrary governmental prohibition affecting certain branches of cultivation, notably wine and sugar. But mining for gold and silver was free from all restrictions, and the fact that the crown received one-fifth of the products was a reason for governmental encouragement of the industry. This freedom in the development of mining and the hindrances encountered by other forms of industry caused the population and the appliances of civilization to increase more rapidly in the mining regions, in the inhospitable high lands of Upper Peru, than in the fertile valleys of Chile or on the rich Argentine plains. Potosí, for instance, became a bustling city of 150,000 inhabitants before Buenos Aires and the towns of Chile had emerged from the condition of dirty frontier villages.[9]

The spiritual inheritance

But the most effective factor in determining the character of colonial society was the spiritual inheritance from Spain. In government it was the spirit of autocracy, producing a political administration in no respect controlled by the popular will, an administration imposed by the king advised by the Council of the Indies. In matters of religion the spirit of the Spanish church passed to the colonies, and carried over to them the ecclesiastical traditions of the mother country, with no break, like that which appeared between the Puritans and the dominant Church of England. This was important for the aesthetic life of the colonies, for the artistic notions and sentiments entertained by the Church as a social body were transferred to Spanish America, and manifested their creative force in developing a somewhat original church architecture, and in elaborating the courts and interiors of secular

(9) An account of the rise of Potosí and some phases of its life as a mining town are given in the author's *Spanish Dependencies in South America*, II, chap. I.

Mediaevalism in the colonies

buildings. The aesthetic sense displayed in the Spanish colonies stands in interesting contrast with the Puritanic barrenness of the British colonies in artistic matters. The Spanish colonies, moreover, contained more abundant survivals of mediaeval ideas and traditions, and the lines of connexion with the European past tended to maintain the colonies for many decades in a state of social stagnation. This inheritance of conservatism helped to keep alive, in at least some part of the population, the sentiment of human dignity as a force counteracting the vulgarizing and brutalizing influences that attended life on the frontier of civilization. In this attitude the persons asserting their superiority were convinced of the value of their ideas and experience, and were moved to convey to posterity their opinions and a knowledge of the organization and growth of the colonial communities in which their lives were passed.

In considering the volume of literary production in the Spanish dependencies in comparison with the inferior amount produced in the British colonies, one must take ac-

Circumstances favouring literary production

count of two important facts bearing on this subject. In the first place, there was in the Spanish colonies a very large number of men, soldiers and priests, who derived their support from the state, and were thus relieved from the necessity of acquiring a livelihood by their personal efforts or by expending mental energy in forming plans, and in executing them by the employment of their time and force. In the second place, a relatively large number of men in the Spanish colonies were celibates, and consequently their time, their thoughts, and their energies were not absorbed in providing for the current wants of families, or in accumulating property to be passed as an inheritance to a succeeding generation. In the British colonies there was practically no subsidized class; and every man was interested in providing for a family and in accumulating property for the benefit of his heirs. This was the absorbing thought of the British colonists as they pressed back the aborigines and advanced upon the wilderness. They, moreover, conceived the affairs of the colonies as their own affairs and felt no need of sending elaborate reports to the king, or of writing geographical descriptions and historical narratives for the enlightenment of the nation they had abandoned. They were content with a minimum of communication with the mother country. The Spanish colonies, on the other hand, lived by their connexion with Spain and by action of the Spanish government.

Spanish interest in America

The intellectual class of Spain had more interest in the American possessions than was manifested by any class in Great Britain with respect to the British colonies; and this superior interest of Spaniards constitututed a demand for information concerning the New World, which encouraged persons in Spanish America by their writings to meet this demand.

These introductory suggestions help to explain the remarkable literary activity in the colonies during the period under consideration.

CHAPTER II

EARLY WRITERS OF TIERRA FIRME

I. *Bartolomé de las Casas.* II. *Gonzalo Fernández de Oviedo y Valdés.* III. *Pascual de Andagoya.*

I

Letters and reports from America

The letters and reports of the adventurers, the discoverers, and the early settlers, during the period of exploration and conquest, constitute a noteworthy introduction to the literary history of the Spanish colonies in America; and the intellectual vigour of some of these writers was quite in keeping with the practical energy and daring displayed by their Spanish contemporaries in exploring and subduing the wilderness.

The extension of the Spanish occupation from Santo Domingo, as an early seat of the administration, to the South American mainland, belongs to the first decades of the sixteenth century. During this period the Spaniards founded Santa Marta and Cartagena; explored and occupied the Isthmus; and Andagoya established his brief authority on the Pacific coast south of Panama.

Occupation of Tierra Firme

It was in this period, moreover, that the Spanish government granted to the German company of the Welsers a charter to an extensive region of Tierra Firme, where the agents of this company devoted their activity, almost exclusively to hunting Indians for the slave-market. On a part of the northern coast of South America Bartolomé de las Casas proposed to plant a proletariat colonial administration as the beginning of a practical reform of Spain's colonial policy. When this enterprise was wrecked by its internal weakness, Las Casas turned to the business of the Church and to unsparing criticism of the Spanish government. On its practical side the conduct of the government doubtless required modification, but the plan to introduce Spanish labourers and negroes to perform all the work of the colony, if it had been thoroughly

Indians under the British and the Spanish

and successfully carried out, would indeed have lifted the burden of labour from the Indians, but it would also have made it impossible for the Indians to have a place in the new society. The performance of a certain amount of work was an essential condition of the Indian's existence in regions occupied by the Spaniards. He had to work or disappear, as he disappeared before the British settlers in North America, who made no provision for incorporating him in the communities which they organized. The Spaniards had a very different plan for the social development of their American colonies. They proposed to form communities with important mediaeval features; they recognized distinct classes and feudal superiority and dependence. This method of social organization provided a place for the Indians, although a subordinate place, nevertheless a place where their continued existence would be assured on condition of performing a certain amount of labour. But when Las Casas faced the question of reforming the Spanish policy, he appears to have advocated, if not the worst possible solution, at least a project that could have had no happy outcome for the Indians.

Las Casas

The facts of Las Casas' life hardly need to be recited here. His prodigious defence of the Indian's right to liberty has made him widely known and given him an exalted position in the estimation of those in sympathy with his purposes. He was born in Seville about eighteen years before the discovery of America: the date of his birth is usually set down as 1474. His studies, begun in his native city, were continued at Salamanca, where he was graduated as "Licenciado". His first knowledge of the Indians appears to have been obtained through one who had been brought from America to Spain by his father, and was attached to Bartolomé at the University in the capacity of a servant. Las Casas went to the West Indies with Nicolás de Obando, governor of Santo Domingo. This was in 1502. In 1510 he became a priest, and a year later he accompanied Governor Velásquez to Cuba. In these nine years he witnessed certain acts of barbarity by the Spaniards, which seemed to presage the diminution of the native population, and intensified his sympathy for the oppressed race.

Brevísima relación

In the islands, on the mainland, or as Bishop of Chiapas, one dominating purpose controlled his actions, it was to ameliorate the condition of the Indians, and, in planning for their welfare, the welfare of no other race mattered. Las Casas' ideal of the Indians, which helped to inspire his zeal for their liberty is set forth in this passage from the *Brevisima relación*:

"All the territory that has been discovered down to the year forty-one is full of people, like a hive of bees, so that it seems as though God had placed all, or the greater part, of the entire human race, in these countries. God has created all these numberless peoples to be the simplest, without malice or duplicity, the most obedient, the most faithful to their natural Lords, and to the Christians, whom they serve, the most humble and patient, the most peaceful and calm, without strife or tumults, nor wrangling or querulous, as free from rancour, hate, and desire for revenge as any in the

Bartolomé de Las Casas

world. They are likewise the most delicate people, weak and of feeble constitution, and they are less able than any other to bear fatigue, and they succumb readily to whatever disease attacks them, so that not even the sons of our princes or nobles, brought up in luxury and effeminate ways, are weaker than they; although there are among them some who belong to the class of labourers. They are also very poor people, who have few worldly goods, nor wish to possess them."

Las Casas and Liberty

It was beings answering to this ideal that fascinated Las Casas, and a large part of the civilized world has been disposed to honour him for his marvellous service in the interest of an oppressed and outraged people; but when his eulogists announce him as the champion of universal human liberty, they make too large a claim. A champion of the liberty of the Indians he surely was, a champion of rare devotion and unflagging zeal, but with little concern as to the social cost of securing that liberty by his method. He was, moreover, so thoroughly absorbed in his own ideas and plans that he had no mind to consider the ideas and plans of others, or to deliberate with other persons in an attitude of possible compromise. He did not hesitate to seek with unslacking energy the execution of his plan, even when he was aware that it involved extending negro slavery, with all the horrors of the trans-oceanic shipment of slaves.

Encomenderos and liberty

Las Casas' project to introduce Spaniards into America to undertake the common work which the Indians were required to perform, or to throw the burden upon negroes, necessarily ran counter to the views of those Spaniards to whom Indians had been assigned by the government in Spain, and who depended upon the labour of the Indians to cultivate the lands that had been granted to them, to work their mines, and to carry on their manufacturing enterprises. The encomenderos had come to regard themselves as the foundation of the economic system of the colonies, and they naturally considered the government under obligation to defend them against attacks designed to destroy that system. But Las Casas had enthusiastic partisans, who praised extravagantly his devotion to the Indian and were apparently blind to the consequences of extending negro slavery with respect to the development of society in America. The intense hostility displayed towards Las Casas in the colonies did not proceed solely from his proposed interference with the interests of the encomenderos, but was in a large measure provoked by his reckless denuncia ion of opponents.

Reception of Las Casas' views

The views set forth in *Brevísima relación de la destrucción de las Indias* found an enthusiastic reception, particularly in England, promoted by the political friction existing between that country and Spain, and by the rage of militant Protestantism, which found in Las Casas' denunciation at least a partial expression of its own detestation of Catholicism and of all measures favoured by the Pope. The titles given to translations of the *Brevísima relación* are evidence of the force of that sentiment.[1]

(1) In 1646 a number of pamphlets that had been issued in 1552 at Seville, were reprinted at Barcelona. These were: 1. *Brevísima relación.* 2. *Treinta proposiciones pertenecientes al derecho que la iglesia y los príncipes cristianos tienen contra los infieles.* 3. *Una disputa entre el dicho obispo y el doctor Ginés de Sepulveda.* 4. *Un tratado* . . .

Vargas Machuca

This pamphlet was published in 1552, and aroused in the minds of some of the Spaniards an opposition only a little less marked than the favour with which it was received by the English. Bernardo de Vargas Machuca was one of those who rose to combat the views presented by Las Casas. His refutation appeared in *Apologías y discursos de las conquistas occidentales.* On the title-page of this pamphlet the author announces that it is written " in opposition to the treatise on the ruin of the Indies." [2]

sobre la materia de los indios que se han hecho . . . esclavos. 5. *Remedios . . . por la reformación de los indios.*

The following are titles of translation in point: *Tears of the Indians:* Being an Historical and true Account of the Cruel Massacres and Slaughters of above Twenty Millions of innocent People. Committed by the Spaniards in the Islands of Hispaniola, Cuba, Jamaica, etc. As also, in the Continent of Mexico, Peru and other Places of the West-Indies, To the total destruction of those countries. Written in Spanish by Casaus, an Eye-witness of those things. London, 1656. *Popery Truly Displayed in its Bloody Colours;* Or, a Faithful Narrative of the Horrid and Unexampled Massacres, Butcheries, and all manner of Cruelties, that Hell and Malice could invent, committed by the Popish Spanish Party on the Inhabitants of West-India. Together with the Devastations of several Kingdoms of America with Fire and Sword, for the Space of Forty and Two Years, from the time of the first Discovery by them. Composed first in Spanish by Bartholomew de Las Casas, a Bishop there, and an Eye-Witness of most of these Barbarous Cruelties. London, 1689.

(2) This is printed, together with the *Brevísima relación* and a number of other documents by Las Casas, in Fabié's

Opponents of Las Casas

The question concerning the servitude or the freedom of the Indians raised by Las Casas was discussed by a professor in the University of Córdoba, who wrote *Fasti novi orbis* under the nameof Cyriacus Morelli. His book was published in Venice in 1776. Dr. Juan Ginés de Sepúlveda, a distinguished Spanish theologian and jurist, opposed vigorously the ideas presented by Las Casas, and argued in support of the Spanish policy regarding the Indians. A similar attitude was assumed by Gonzalo Fernández de Oviedo, whose education at the Spanish court, and whose later service under appointment by the king naturally disposed him to justify the conduct of the government. This subject continued to engage the attention of writers as long as the Spanish régime lasted. A work by Giovanni Nuix translated from the Italian by Pedro Varela y Ulloa, entitled in Spanish *Reflexiones imparciales sobre la humanidad*

Vida y escritos de Don Fray Bartolomé de las Casas, vol. II. Vargas Muchuca's book on the militia was published in Madrid in 1599. The author was governor and captain-general of the island of Margarita. It is called *Milicia y descripción de las Indias*, and is in some sense the art of war as applied to affairs in the colonies.

de los españoles en las Indias, contra los pretendidos filósofos y políticos, was published in Madrid in 1782. The writer characterized the views of Las Casas as false or exaggerated, and defended the thesis that the conquests made by the Spaniards in America were just, or at least as just as those made by other nations; and he attributed whatever covetousness or cruelty was displayed by the Spaniards to the great distance of the colonies from the supreme authority, under which local officers served in the colonies without adequate supervision. He distinguished clearly, moreover, between the benevolent designs of the crown and the unjust and cruel acts of governmental subordinates and irresponsible private persons.

Las Casas' *Historia general*

Besides the *Brevísima relación* a number of other pamphlets were printed in 1552 and 1553, but the more important of Las Casas' writings remained in manuscript until long after the author's death. These are the *Historia general de las Indias* and *Historia apologética de las Indias*, apparently designed in the beginning to constitute a single work; but in the process of their composition, the character of each became more and more distinct, and they finally appeared in print as separate productions. The former is an account of the occupation of the West Indies and the mainland during the early years of Spanish rule, describing the condition of the native inhabitants, their mental state and their customs, with special emphasis on the treatment they received under the Spanish administration; the latter, the *Historia apologética de las Indias*, treats of the character of soil and climate of the occupied lands, of the natural and social position of the inhabitants, but does not contain a narrative of the events incident to the establishment and progress of Spanish settlements. Like other writers of his time, and even of later times, Las Casas faced the problem of the relation of the different races to one another, and of the capacity of the less developed race to rise to the highest form of civilization, and, like most of his countrymen, he regarded the fundamental difference between the races as consisting in the

Historia apologética

Conversion of Indians

fact that the Spaniards were Christians, while the Indians were pagans, and that the conversion and baptism of the Indians necessarily removed the main feature of difference, and transferred the Indian from the status of barbarism to civilization. But one-remedy reformers have not been found merely among Spanish missionaries. When the government of the United States conferred the right of suffrage upon the emancipated negro slaves, this action was supported by the extravagant expectation that the possession of this right would exercise a transforming influence on the quality of the subject. This hopeful view of the missionary's work was doubtless the principal source of Las Casas' inspiration; it was also the source of his intolerance.

Encomenderos

The King and the Council of the Indies, in granting lands to Spaniards establishing themselves in America, and distributing Indians among them to become labourers on these lands, had as one of their purposes an end not greatly different from the object of the missionary's striving. They hoped that by gathering the Indians on these estates to make them immediately subject to Christians who would be required to provide opportunities and facilities for the Indians to acquire a knowledge of Christian doctrine. Thus one of the features of the colonial organization against which Las Casas directed his vehement eloquence was in some part the product of a design formed to further the conversion of the Indians. If it did not attain its high aim or respond to the exalted purpose of Las Casas, it failed for the same reason that some of Las Casas' plans had failed: it was conceived in imperfect knowledge of American conditions, and was entrusted for execution to selfish, in other words, human agents.

II

Oviedo's early life

An attempt less radical than that of Las Casas to improve Spain's colonial administration was made by Gonzalo Fernández de Oviedo y Valdés, author of the *Historia general y natural de las Indias.* Although Oviedo's posthumous fame rests almost exclusively on his writings, his reputation during his lifetime was based chiefly on his practical activity. A contemporary of Las Casas, he was born in Madrid in 1478, and very early entered the service of Don Alfonso de Aragón, the second duke of Villahermosa, a nephew of King Ferdinand. Here his early years were spent under the influence of persons interested in literary cultivation, and where the circumstances tended to stimulate his natural intelligence. At the age of thirteen he became attached to the court of the Catholic Kings as a page. Two years later the sovereigns entered upon the campaign against Granada, and Gonzalo followed the Court to Santa Fe. There as a youth he saw some of Spain's most distinguished men of the time. He saw Columbus, whose distinction was yet to be won, and who appeared asking assistance to enable him to find a new world.

Oviedo in Italy

After the death of Prince Juan, on October the fourth, 1497, Oviedo visited Italy, where the art and literature of that country exerted a powerful influence on his intellectual development. In 1500, after three years of varied service, he appeared at Rome, claiming the jubilee indulgence granted to the faithful by the Pope. Subsequently he entered the service of the King of Naples, but in 1501 he left Naples in the train of Queen Juana for Palermo, and in May, 1502, he left Palermo for Valencia, where he took leave of the Queen's service and went to Madrid. In Madrid he married Margarita de Vergara, who died ten months later. Under the impression of this loss, he turned to service in the army, but he soon abandoned his plans for a military career, and became again attached to the court. Shortly after Oviedo's return to the court, preparations were made for the expedition of Pedrarias Dávila to Castilla de Oro, and he was appointed to inspect the production of gold in Tierra Firme.

Joins Pedrarias' expedition

The fleet sailed from San Lucar on April 11, 1514, and arrived at Santa Marta on the following 12th of June. At the end of June the company reached the gulf of Urabá, and proceeded to Santa María del Antigua, where they found the colony overwhelmed in misfortune, now rendered more distressing by the tyranny and cruelty of Pedrarias. Oviedo, out of favour with the authorities, returned to Spain to seek a remedy for the state of things he had observed. After years of waiting to have his memorial considered by the court, he encountered at Barcelona Bartolomé de las Casas, who was present on a somewhat similar mission. They both sought reform in the Indies, but with divergent views. Oviedo contemplated a reform in Darien through the efforts of a wise and just governor and a bishop devoid of covetousness, who would aim effectively at holding the clergy under proper regulations. Las Casas, on the other hand, a religious anarchist, advocated removing the governors, the captains, and the soldiers from the Indies, agreeing to maintain the territory of Cumaná in the power of the crown without other instrumentalities than a few hundred simple labourers and fifty knights of the cross.

Las Casas and Oviedo as reformers

In April, 1520, Oviedo embarked at Seville on his second voyage to America. Learning at Santo Domingo that Lope de Sosa, who had been appointed through his influence to supersede Pedrarias, had died on the outward voyage, Oviedo had little reason to expect that friendly relations would be established between himself and Pedrarias, and, in spite of the courteous reception extended to him, he discovered very early that his anticipations were realized. In fact, the governor's hostility appears to have been one of the influences that led Oviedo to abandon Antigua for Panama and to induce the colonists to remove to the new capital. Pedrarias' hostility and his desire to compromise and ruin the prestige of Oviedo, moreover, led the governor to appoint him to be his lieutenant or deputy.

Oviedo's return to Spain

The efforts of Oviedo to abate the evils of the colony only intensified the hostility of the governor and his supporters and led him to withdraw the deputy's appointment. Oviedo then, in 1523, returned to Spain to call the king's attention to the scandalous conduct of Pedrarias. The part of his voyage between Santo Domingo and the Peninsula was made in company with Diego Columbus. The charges presented specified with much detail the abuses and crimes of the governor; they were made not for the redress of personal wrongs Oviedo had suffered, but to preserve the colony from utter corruption and destruction; and, in spite of the vigorous attempt made to reply to them, Pedrarias was superseded by Pedro de los Ríos as governor of Castilla de Oro. Oviedo, not content to leave his proposed reform half accomplished, offered his services to the new governor, and embarked with him for America on the 30th of April, 1526. It was in this year, 1526, that he published by order of the emperor at Toledo his *Sumario de la natural historia de las Indias*, a work quite distinct from the larger work issued later under a similar title. Oviedo arrived at Nombre de Dios on the 20th of July. After four years of varying fortune in Castilla de Oro, Nicaragua, and Santo Domingo he returned again to Spain in 1530. Wishing to be relieved of the duties of his office as inspector of gold-smelting, he presented his resignation, and petitioned that his son might be appointed to succeed him. Not only was the petition granted, but the emperor appointed him General Chronicler of the Indies.

Sumario de la historia natural

After his experience in the warmer regions

of America, he no longer found the climate of Spain agreeable, and in the autumn of 1532 he returned to the New World, establishing himself in the city of Santo Domingo. Here the citizens showed their appreciation of his decision, and on the death of Francisco de Tapia, the alcaide, or governor of the fortress of the city, petitioned for the appointment of Oviedo to the vacant post. This petition was granted, and the appointment was confirmed by a decree dated October 25, 1533.

Oviedo made alcaide

In 1534 Oviedo went to Spain, published the first part of his *Historia general y natural de las Indias*, the printing of which was completed on September 30, 1535. In the following January he was once more in Santo Domingo. From this time forward the practical affairs of his office as alcaide engaged much of his attention. The fort had fallen into decay through neglect, and the increasing danger of pirates and the new wars into which Spain was plunged induced Oviedo to solicit from the King and the Council of the Indies more effective artillery and other means for making the defence

Historia general y natural

more complete. At the same time stories of Pizarro's exploits began to arrive from Peru, and the affairs of the island were thrown into confusion by emigration to that country. The tales of great wealth acquired by the invaders had the effect of news from newly discovered gold mines.

Final return to Spain

As Oviedo approached the end of life, he turned to Spain as his final residence, in spite of his lively interest in the New World. He therefore resigned his office of alcaide, retaining the post of honorary regidor of Santo Domingo. In June, 1556, he took final leave of America, where he had resided thirty-four years, and during this period had crossed the Atlantic at least twelve times.

During these last years his efforts were directed chiefly to giving to the world a complete and corrected edition of his *Historia general y natural de las Indias*. The printing was begun, but before it was finished the author succumbed to an acute fever at the age of seventy-nine. The undertaking was interrupted, and it was only after nearly three hundred years that the complete work appeared in print. The whole work was originally divided into three parts comprising fifty books. The first part published during his lifetime consisted of nineteen or nineteen and a half books. In 1557 the twentieth book was printed separately in Valladolid, but the rest of it remained in manuscript until the publication of the complete edition issued by the Academy of History in the middle of the nineteenth century. Oviedo wrote as the authorized chronicler of the Indies, and in this capacity he had access to official documents. His other works deal chiefly with the affairs of the Peninsula. Harrisse reports the existence of two collections of Oviedo's letters and diaries, and suggests the desirability of their publication. In referring to this principal work of Oviedo Las Casas manifests his ruling passion in affirming that Oviedo should have written at the top of his history: "This book was written by a conqueror, robber, and murderer of the Indians, whole populations of whom he consigned to the mines, where they perished."[3]

Oviedo's letters

(3) *Historia general y natural de las Indias*, cap. XXIII. A

Topics of the *Sumario*

The first chapter of the *Sumario* presents a description of the navigation between Seville and America. A number of the following chapters are devoted to the Indians of the islands and Tierra Firme, and these are followed by a series of chapters enumerating and describing the animals, birds, reptiles, trees, and other living things, succeeded by an account of mines and pearl-fishing. Of this latter business Oviedo gives a brief account:

Oviedo on pearl fishing

"It is off Cubagua and Cumaná that pearl fishing is chiefly carried on, as I have been fully informed by Indians and Christians, who say that many Indians go from the island of Cubagua. These belong to crews in the service of private persons, residents of Santo Domingo and San Juan. They go out in a boat or barge in the morning, in companies of four, five, six or more,

complete edition of the *Historia general* work was issued by the Royal Academy of History in Madrid in 1851. The *Sumario* is included in the first volume of *Historiadores primitivos de las Indias*, Madrid, 1849. An important account of Oviedo is found in *Vida y escritos de Gonzalo Fernández de Oviedo y Valdés*, by José Amador de los Ríos, prefixed to the Academy's edition of Oviedo's *Historia general*. Reference may also be made to Barros Arana's *Obras completas*, VIII, 3–11. See also Harrisse, *Biblioteca americana vetustísima*, 340.

and when it seems to them, or they know already, that there are pearls at the point they have reached, they stop there, and the Indians dive into the water and swim until they reach the bottom; one remains in the boat, which he holds in place as well as he can, waiting for those in the water to appear, and after the Indian has been down a long time, he comes to the surface and is taken into the boat, presenting and putting into it the oysters which he has brought up, for in the oysters are found the valuable pearls. He rests a little, eats a mouthful, and then enters the water again, and stays as long as he is able, and again comes up with the oysters which he has found this time and does as before, and in this manner all the rest proceed who are divers in this operat·on. And when night comes, and it appears to be time to rest, they go home to the island, and turn over the oysters to the major domo of the proprietor, who has charge of the Indians, and who gives them their supper, and places the oysters in a receptacle, and when he has a large number of them, he causes them to be opened, and in them are found pearls of two, three, four, five, six or more grains, as nature has placed them there."

Fate of fishers

This quotation from Oviedo's *Sumario* offers a glimpse of an occupation, which sooner or later proved fatal to immense numbers of the Indians forced into it. Many of those engaged in pearl-fishing were compelled to re-enter the water before they had recovered their normal condition after a previous descent, and either never returned to the surface alive, or returned hopelessly exhausted. But in connexion with this account our author makes no mention of the perilous and destructive character of the work, through which the population of the islands and the neighbouring coast was greatly depleted. Doubtless Oviedo wished to reform abuses in the colonies, but his relation to the court and his part in the public administration naturally rendered him reluctant to make conspicuous in his writings the abuses that were brought to his attention. The presence of these abuses produced in his mind a very different reaction from that observed in the fiery spirit of Las Casas.

The reference, in the *Brevisima relación*, to the pearl fishing described by Oviedo reveals the contrast between Las Casas' lively sympathy with the Indians and Oviedo's unconcern and official indifference:

Las Casas on pearl fishing

"The tyranny exercised by the Spaniard upon the Indians in fishing pearls is as cruel and damnable a thing as can be found in the world. On land there is no life so desperate and infernal in this century that may be compared with it, although that of digging gold in the mines is in its kind exceedingly severe and difficult. They let the Indians down into the sea, three and four and five fathoms deep, from the morning till sunset, where they are swimming under water without respite, gathering the oysters in which the pearls grow; they come up to breathe, bringing up little nets full of oysters. There is a very cruel Spaniard in a boat, and if they linger resting, he beats them with his fists, and, taking them by the hair, throws them into the water to go on fishing. . . . Their food is fish, and the fish that contain the pearls, and a little cazabi, or maize bread, which are kinds of native bread; the one gives very little sustenance, and the other is very difficult to make, so with such food they are never sufficiently nourished. Instead of giving them beds at night, they put them in stocks on the ground to prevent them from running away.

Dangers of the deep

"Many of the Indians throw themselves into the sea while fishing or hunting for pearls, and never come up again, because dolphins or sharks, which are two kinds of very cruel sea animals that swallow a man whole, kill and eat them. . . . With this insupportable toil, or rather infernal trade, the Spaniards completed the destruction of all the Indians of the Lucayan Islands, who were in the islands when they set themselves to making these gains."

III.

Companions of Pedrarias

A number of persons who became especially conspicuous in colonial affairs, besides Oviedo, accompanied Pedrarias on his expedition to the Isthmus. Among these were Bishop Quevedo; Enciso, some time governor of Darien and author of *Suma de*

Suma de geographia q̄
trata de todas las partidas ⁊ prouin-
cias del mundo: en eſpecial delas indias. ⁊ trata largamēte del arte del mare
ar: juntamēte con la eſpera en romāce:
con el regimiēto del ſol ⁊ del norte: nue
uamente hecha.

Con preuilegio real.

Title page of Fernández de Enciso's "Suma"

geografia; Benalcázar, who became governor of Popayán; Hernando de Soto; and Pascual de Andagoya, whose varied experience and the events associated with Pedrarias form the matter of a document which has been translated into English by Sir Clements R. Markham. The title of Markham's translation is *Narrative of the proceedings of Pedrarias Davila in the provinces of Tierra Firme, or Castilla del Oro, and of what happened in the discovery of the South Sea, and the coasts of Peru and Nicaragua.*[4]

Andagoya

Andagoya, the author of this narrative, was born in the valley of Cuartango in the province of Alava. The account of his life as narrated by himself begins with his departure from Spain. On the Isthmus and in regions lying north and south of Panama, he was engaged in various exploring expeditions, during which by observation he appears to have acquired much knowledge of the manners and customs of the Indians. A weaker and less positive character than Oviedo, he was consequently less

(4) *Relación de los sucesos de P.D. en las provincias de Tierra Firme* in Fernández de Navarrete's *Colección de los viajes y descubrimientos . . . del siglo xv*, vol. iii

disposed than Oviedo to revolt against the régime of Pedrarias; in fact, he went with him to Panama, and received from him an encomienda, and became one of the first regidores of Panama, after that settlement had been declared a city. In 1521 and 1522 he was inspector-general of the Indians on the Isthmus. He was the first to receive information concerning the Inca Kingdom of Peru, but, lacking the health, perhaps also the initiative, to become the leader of an expedition against it, he communicated his knowledge to Pizarro and his partners.

Failure of Andagoya's expedition

"In this province (Birú) I received accounts both from chiefs and from merchants and interpreters, concerning all the coast, and everything that has since been discovered, as far as Cuzco, especially with regard to the inhabitants of each province, for in their trading these people extend their wanderings over many lands. Taking new interpreters, and the principal chief of that land, who wished of his own accord to go with me, and show me other provinces of the coast that obeyed him, I descended to the sea. The ships followed the coast at some little distance from the land, while I went close in, in a canoe, discovering the ports. While thus employed, I fell into the water, and if it had not been for the chief, who took me in his arms and pulled me on to the canoe, I should have been drowned. I remained in this position until a ship came to succour me, and while they were helping the others, I remained for more than two hours wet through. What with the cold air and the quantity of water I had drunk, I was laid up next day, unable to turn. Seeing that I could not now conduct this discovery along the coast in person, and that the expedition would thus come to an end, I resolved to return to Panama with the chief and interpreters who accompanied me, and report the knowledge I had acquired of all that land.

News of Peru given to Pizarro

"The land had never been discovered either by Castilla de Oro, or by way of the gulf of San Miguel, and the province was called Pirú, because one of the letters of Birú has been corrupted, and so we call it Pirú, but in reality there is no country of that name.

"As soon as Pedrarias heard the great news which I had brought he was also told by the doctors that time alone could cure me, and in truth it was fully three years before I was able to ride on horseback. He therefore, asked me to hand over the undertaking to Pizarro, Almagro, and Father Luque, who were partners, in order that so great a discovery might be followed up, and he added that they would repay me what I had expended. I replied that, so far as the expedition was concerned, I must give it up, and that I did not wish to be paid, because if they paid me my expenses, they would not have sufficient to commence the business, for at that time they had not more than sixty dollars. Accordingly, these three, and Pedrarias, which made four, formed a company, each partner taking a fourth share." [5]

(5) Markham's translation of Andagoya's *Narrative.*

FRANCISCO PISARRO

CHAPTER III

CONTEMPORARY ACCOUNTS OF THE CONQUEST OF PERU

I. *Francisco de Xerés.* II. *Pedro Sancho.* III. *Tomás de San Martín; Benito Peñalosa Mondragón.* IV. *Pedro Pizarro; Cristóbal de Molina.* V. *Alonso Enríquez de Guzmán; Diego Fernández.* VI. *Agustín de Zárate.* VII. *Pedro Cieza de León.* VIII. *Girolamo Benzoni; Juan Fernandez.*

I

The story of Peru

The especially important event in South America in the first half of the sixteenth century was the conquest of Peru. If the story as it has been frequently told has exaggerated somewhat the magnificence of the kingdom destroyed, this presentation has only perpetuated the impression made on the Spanish mind by contemporary rumours and reports. These reports and rumours inspired and kept alive for many decades the hope of finding other kingdoms equally wealthy, by the spoils of which the conquerors might be enriched.

Effect of discovery

Until the discovery of the Pacific and the voyage along the western coast, knowledge of America had been only very slowly increased, and in this process no especially startling statements had been received in Europe. But reports that an empire had been discovered, that the emperor had been captured, and that his subjects had offered untold amounts of gold and silver as his ransom, fired the imagination of the Spaniards and appealed to their cupidity. After this the business of exploration and conquest moved with greater rapidity. The number of persons in Spain wishing to emigrate or to join expeditions bound for the New World increased, and the settlements already established in the islands lost a large part of their inhabitants, carried away to Peru by the desire for adventure and the wealth to be obtained; and the eagerness to get information from America was greatly intensified. Reports and letters sent from Peru to satisfy this demand tended to augment the popular excitement, and in so far as they have been preserved they constitute an important part of the historical record of Pizarro's enterprise in Peru. Those that were directed to the King or the Council of the Indies concerning the events of the conquest were usually deposited in the archives, and only a part of them have come to light. Among documents of this class belong some of the contemporary accounts of the conquest of Peru. Francisco de Xerés, the writer of such a document, was Pizarro's secretary, who left Spain in January, 1530. His account was written in Peru at the request or by the order of Pizarro. He returned to Spain in July, 1534, and his report was printed in Seville in that year. Three years later a second edition was printed in Salamanca. The edition most frequently referred to is that of 1749. Xerés was an actor in, or a witness of, the remarkable events which he describes, and his narrative has the freshness and vividness of a story by one writing of what he saw. The

Francisco de Xerés

Hakluyt Society included a translation of it into English in a volume entitled *Reports on the Discovery of Peru.* This volume contains also a translation of Hernando Pizarro's letter to the audiencia of Santo Domingo. This letter gives a summary of the events of the conquest prior to November, 1533. There is given here, moreover, a translation of Miguel de Astete's report on Hernando Pizarro's expedition to Pachacamac.[1]

The paragraph describing the capture of Atahualpa may serve as an illustration of Xerés' style of narration :

Capture of Atahualpa

"Then the Governor put on a jacket of cotton, took his sword and dagger, and, with the Spaniards who were with him, entered amongst the Indians most valliantly, and, with only four men who were able to follow him, he came to the litter where Atahualpa was, and fearlessly seized him by the arm, crying out 'Santiago.' Then the guns were fired off, the trumpets were sounded, and the troops, both horse and

(1) See *Historiadores primitivos de las Indias occidentales*, vol. III, 1749; Italian edition, Venice, 1556; English translation by Sir Clements R. Markham, London, 1872.

foot, sallied forth. On seeing the horses charge many of the Indians who were in the open space fled, and such was the force with which they ran that they broke down part of the wall surrounding it and many fell over one another. The horsemen rode them down, killing and wounding and following them in pursuit. The infantry made so good an assault upon those who remained that in a short time most of them were put to the sword. The governor still held Atahualpa by the arm, not being able to pull him out of the litter because he was raised so high. Then the Spaniards made such a slaughter among those who carried the litter that they fell to the ground, and, if the governor had not protected Atahualpa, that proud man would there have paid for all the cruelties he had committed. The governor, in protecting Atahualpa received a slight wound in the hand. During the whole time no Indian raised his arms against a Spaniard. So great was the terror of the Indians at seeing the governor force his way through them, at hearing the fire of the artillery and beholding the charg-

Xerés' story

ing of the horses, a thing never before heard of, that they thought more of flying to save their lives than of fighting. All those who bore the litter of Atahualpa appeared to be principal chiefs. They were all killed, as well as those who were carried in the other litters and hammocks. One of them was a page of Atahualpa and a great lord, and the others were lords of many vassals and his counsellors. The chief of Caxamalca was also killed, and others; but, the number being very great, no account was taken of them, for all who came in attendance on Atahualpa were great lords. The governor went to his lodging with his prisoner Atahualpa despoiled of his robes, which the Spaniards had torn off in pulling him out of the litter. It was a very wonderful thing to see so great a lord taken prisoner in so short a time, who came in such power."

II

Sancho's *Relación*

In his *Relación de la conquista del Perú* Pedro Sancho presented another contemporary account of the occupation of Peru. By reason of the writer's relation to Pizarro the narrative acquired a partisan bias; it was expected to contribute to restoring the governor to the emperor's favour. It was translated into Italian, and appeared in Ramusio's *Viaggi*, published in Venice about 1550. An edition in Spanish by Icazbalceta was issued in Mexico in 1849. A part of Sancho's document is included in the already mentioned volume called *Reports on the Discovery of Peru*. Sancho gives the following account of Pizarro's distribution of the gold and silver collected: "He caused all the gold which had been collected to be melted, which was in small pieces, an operation quickly performed by Indians skilled in the process. And when the sum total was weighed, it was found to contain five hundred and eight thousand, two hundred odd pounds of gold. The fifth for H.M. was taken out, and it was one hundred and sixteen thousand and seventy odd pesos of good gold. And the same smelting was performed for the silver, which was found to contain two hundred and fifteen thousand marks, a little more or less, and of them one hundred and seventy thousand or so were fine silver

Spoils of gold and silver

in vessels and plates, pure and good, and the rest was not so, because it was in plates and pieces mixed with other metals, from which the silver was extracted. And from all this, likewise, was taken the fifth for H.M. Truly it was a worthy thing to be seen, this house where the melting took place, all full of so much gold in plates of eight and ten pounds each, and in vessels and vases and pieces of various forms with which the lords of that land were served, and among other very sightly things were four llamas in fine gold and very large, and ten or twelve figures of women of the size of the women of that land all of fine gold and as beautiful and well-made as if they were alive. . . . There were, besides, other silver objects of like form. The seeing of great vases and pieces of burnished silver was certainly a matter of great satisfaction. The governor divided and distributed all this treasure among all the Spaniards who were at Cuzco and those who remained in the city of Jauja, giving to each one as much good silver, and as much impure, together with as much gold [as he deserved], and to each man who had a horse

Vases and figures

he gave according to the man's merit and that of the horse and in accordance with the services he had done; and to the peons he did the same according to what was posted up to his credit in the book of distributions, which was kept." [2]

III

Tomás de San Martín

An inquiry into the justice of the gains made by the conquistadores was undertaken by Tomás de San Martín, a Dominican, who played a conspicuous rôle in Peru during the troubled period covering the last years of Pizarro's rule, the introduction of the New Laws, the overthrow of the first viceroy, and the administration of President Gasca. While not much has come to light about the birth and parentage of San Mar-

(2) This quotation is from Means' translation, *An Account of the Conquest of Peru*, The Cortes Society, New York, 1917, 128–130. The Spanish title is *Relación de la conquista del Perú*, escrita por Pedro Sancho, secretario de Pizarro y escribano de su ejercito. On the distribution of the spoils of Peru, see *Libro primero de cabildos de Lima*, edited by Enrique Torres Saldamando, vol. III, 121–130 ; Mendiburu, *Dic. hist. biog. del Perú* vol. III ; See also Markham's *Reports on the Discovery of Peru*, 131–143. Oviedo, *Hist. gen. y nat. de las Indias*, lib. XLVI, cap. XV–XXII; *Bib. de aut. esp.* vol. XIX, 499–501; Zárate, *Hist. del Perú, in Bib. de aut. esp.*, vol. XXVI, 474–480.

tín, it is known that he took orders in the monastery of San Pablo in Córdoba in Spain: that he became a lecturer on arts and theology at Seville, in the college of Santo Tomás; and that he arrived very early in the island of Santo Domingo, where he laboured as a missionary among the Indians, exercising whatever influence he possessed to protect them from those who would reduce them to slavery. In this undertaking San Martín co-operated with Las Casas. Having returned to Spain, he was appointed by the king to be a member of the audiencia established at Santo Domingo. This post he later renounced, and joined a company of ecclesiastics going to Peru with Francisco Pizarro. He assisted at the founding of Piura and remained there, while Pizarro went on to Cajamarca, but after the murder of Atahualpa he rejoined Pizarro and went with him to Jauja. In 1534 he was sent to the province of Charcas, and thus became one of the first to preach Christianity in that region.

San Martín in Charcas & Lima

On the creation of the Dominican province in Peru San Martín became the Provincial, and from this time until he left America with President Gasca in 1550, he had part in the affairs of Lima. He was in the town when Pizarro was assassinated, June 26, 1541, was named by Cristóbal Vaca de Castro, who succeeded Pizarro, as a member of a commission appointed by Castro to take charge of the affairs of justice and administration in Lima, and was instrumental in the pacification of Peru, which was the object of Gasca's mission. His part in this work and his known interest in the affairs of the colonies assured for him an especially favourable reception by the king, and presentation in 1552 as the first bishop of Charcas. He returned to Lima two years later and died there in March, 1554. A memorial in which he discussed the acquisitions of the conquistadores was published in Madrid.[3] Among San Martín's writings we find also an account of the sacrifices made by the ancient Peruvians to their gods at seed-time and harvest, as well as on the occasion of undertaking public works.

(3) *Colección de documentos inéditos del Archivo de las Indias*, vol. VII, 348–362.

Like Las Casas and San Martín, other persons questioned the pretended right of the Spaniards to rob and destroy the Inca kingdom, and when these views were expressed they naturally provoked a reply. Such a reply was undertaken by Benito Peñalosa Mondragón, a Benedictine monk, in a book entitled *Libro de las cinco excelencias del español* (1629). One of his arguments consisted in showing that great riches were acquired by the Spaniards from the colonial possessions, from the mines of gold and silver and mercury, and from various other sources; but it is not conceived that men like Las Casas and San Martín would be greatly moved by Peñalosa's views.

Peñalosa on Spaniards

IV

Pedro Pizarro's book

Another account of the conquest of Peru is that by Pedro Pizarro, who went to America as a page to Francisco Pizarro in 1530, and remained with him until the governor's assassination. He afterwards settled in Arequipa, and, in 1571, completed his *Relación del descubrimiento y conquista de los reinos del Perú.* This work has been characterized as "the narration of a rough half-educated soldier, and occupies much the same place in the history of the conquest of Peru as the work of Bernal Díaz does in that of Mexico." [4]

Molina of Santiago

Cristóbal de Molina's narrative of the conquest long remained in manuscript, and the writer was confounded with another author of the same name. They are now distinguished by calling this one Molina of Santiago and the other Molina of Cuzco. Molina of Santiago was born in Spain, travelled in that country, Italy, and Flanders, and went to America at the age of forty-one. The circumstances of his education and entry upon the religious life are unknown; but we are informed that he was in Santo Domingo in 1532 and at Panama in April of the following year. While at Panama he joined an expedition designed to take reinforcements to Pizarro, but by ill fortune the expedition was obliged to halt at the river San Juan, whence after a period of forty days the members returned to Pan-

(4) *Life and Acts of Enriquez de Guzmán*, Markham's Introduction, xx.

ama. Molina went to Santo Domingo and later to Spain to carry news of Pizarro's discoveries. He remained only a short time in the Peninsula, and in 1535 he was again in America, where, in July of that year, he joined Almagro at the battle of Salinas. Molina went from Cuzco to Lima, and from the latter city he wrote to the king, on the twelfth of June, 1539, setting forth the dangers he had encountered and the losses he had suffered in the royal service. Twelve years afterwards he took part in the Chilean campaigns of García Hurtado de Mendoza. Later he became attached to the cathedral at Charcas, lived in Lima, and finally returned to Chile, where he died as a priest in Santiago.

Molina's *Conquista*

Molina's *Conquista y población del Perú* was written in Lima. It was printed for the first time in 1873 in *Sud-América*, of Santiago; it appeared later in Medina's *Colección de documentos inéditos para la historia de Chile* (vol. VII, 428). Besides his narrative of the conquest and settlement of Peru, Molina wrote a *Diario* of Almagro's expedition to Chile, in which he condemned the inhuman conduct of the conquistadores towards the Indians. He died in 1578 at the age of eighty-four, having many years before ceased to perform the duties of his priestly office on account of the failure of his mental faculties.

With respect to its style, the *Conquista y población del Perú* is superior to most of the writings of its time, and historians have found it sufficiently important to be carefully considered among their sources of information.

V

Enríquez de Guzmán

A part of the personal narrative of Alonso Enríquez de Guzmán belongs to the list of contemporary accounts of the conquest of Peru. Sections thirty-five to fifty-four treat of Guzmán's journey to Peru, which fell in the last part of 1533. He was absent from Spain between September, 1533, and the twenty-sixth of June, 1540, the date of his return to Madrid; and he was thus in Peru during the conflict between Pizarro and Almagro. The rest of the narrative is a record of his experience in Spain, chiefly in the Emperor's service in the islands of Majorca and Iviça. After his return he sent to the emperor an account of his observations during his absence from Spain, giving prominence to the conflicts between the two conquistadores.[5]

A glimpse of Guzmán's spirit may be had from the following statement at the end of his narrative:

Guzmán's confession

"In the year of our Lord, 1533, during Lent, I confessed and received the most holy sacrament, as every faithful Christian ought to do. Amongst other things which I then did, was to declare, as I now declare, that many things in this book, both to improve the style, and to give an appetite to him who reads it, are not related exactly as they happened, though the substance is true: I therefore desire that each reader may believe as much as he ought to believe, so that neither his conscience nor mine may be hurt."[6]

The part of Guzmán's narrative that relates to America may be accepted as true; in

(5) For this letter see *The Life and Acts of Don Alonso Enríquez de Guzmán*, London, 1862, pp. 140–153.
(6) *Ibid.* 78.

fact, as has been suggested, "Guzmán as an eyewitness may be considered as the most original authority for all events in Peruvian history from the commencement of the siege of Cuzco in 1534 to the execution of Almagro in 1538."

Diego Fernández

Diego Fernández, on the title-page of his *Primera y segunda parte de la historia del Perú,* identifies himself as "vecino de la ciudad de Palencia." He took part in the campaign against Francisco Girón in 1554, and the subject of his narrative was Peru in the most stormy period of its early history, the period of the introduction of the New Laws, the rebellion of Gonzalo Pizarro, the mission of President Gasca, and the labours of the Viceroy Hurtado de Mendoza (1555–1561) to bring order out of the social chaos. This volume was published in Seville in 1571, but its sale was prohibited for a time because it contained certain ideas and statements which it was desired should not be circulated in America. On questions relating to the civil wars and the conflicts growing out of the introduction of the New Laws, the population of Peru was still divided in 1571, and any discussion of these events by a person who had had an active part in them would inevitably have provoked antagonism and kept alive the hostility of the two parties.[7]

VI

To the later part of the period of the Pizarros belongs the account given by Agustín de Zárate, who was sent to Peru to take charge of the accounts of the "kingdoms and provinces of Peru," at the time

(7) Diego Fernández was known as Palentino. His history of Peru was reprinted by Odriozola in Lima in 1876. The second volume of the *Colección de libros y documentos referentes a la historia del Perú* contains a *Relación de la conquista del Perú y hechos del Inca Manco II* by Tito Cusi Yupangui, edited by Carlos A. Romero, Lima 1916. *De rebus Indicis*, by Cristóbal Calvete de Estrella, is one of the earliest writings in Latin on the Indies. Ercilla found it worthy of recommendation in these lines of *La Araucana*:

El coronista Estrella escribe al justo
De Chile y del Pirú en latín la historia,
Con tanta erudición, que será justo
Que dure eternamente su memoria ;
Canto IV, Oct. 70.

Barros Arana in his *Historia de Chile*, vol. II, 267, n., regarded it of so little value that even if it had been completed and corrected it would have been hardly worth printing. The manuscript in incomplete form is in possession of the Academy of History of Madrid.

In the thirteenth volume of the *Colección de libros españoles raros o curiosos* appeared in 1879 a number of narratives dealing with South American affairs. The first is an account of the siege of Cuzco, and the second is an account of Girón's rebellion.

that Blasco Núñez Vela was commissioned to become the first viceroy of the Spanish possessions in South America. Zárate had part in the conflicts occasioned by the arrival of Núñez Vela and the rebellion of Gonzalo Pizarro. He was one of the two commissioners sent by the oidores to order Pizarro to disband his army, which he held at Jauja, and enter Lima with only a small escort. Pizarro, however, sent out Captain Villegas, who met Zárate on the way, arrested him, took away his commission, confiscated his provisions, and imprisoned him at Huarochiri. Released after some days, he was persuaded to return to Lima, and it was suggested that in consideration of his release he should urge the audiencia to leave the government to Gonzalo Pizarro. Whatever may have been the influence of Zárate in this matter, Pizarro not long afterwards approached the capital and assumed the reins of government.

Agustín de Zárate

Having played his part in this turbulent period, a part regarding which writers venture a variety of opinions, Zárate returned to Spain, and, using notes made in America,

Zárate's *Historia del Perú*

wrote the *Historia del descubrimiento y conquista de la provincia del Perú.* His final plan for this work was to treat of the discovery and occupation of the country, and to narrate the principal events in the history of the colony until the pacification that followed the intervention of Pedro de la Gasca. The author is said to have intended that his work should remain in manuscript until after his death, but that under the persuasion, perhaps the orders, of Prince Philip, to whom he had presented it, he caused it to be printed in Antwerp in 1555.[8]

His style is less clear than that of some of his contemporaries, but his opportunities for gaining information enabled him to present abundant details of events within the period of his narrative. The following illustrative extract is from the thirteenth chapter of the second book. The person referred to as governor was, of course, Francisco Pizarro: "Diego de Almagro and

Pizarro pays Alvarado

(8) Zárate's *Historia* was reprinted in Seville in 1577, and again by Barcia in 1749. An English translation by T. Nicholas was issued in London in 1581; a Dutch translation at Amsterdam in 1596; a French translation at Paris in 1716.

Pedro de Alvarado[9] having arrived at Pachacamac, the governor, who had come there from Jauja, received them goodhumouredly, and paid to Don Pedro the one hundred thousand pesos which he had agreed to give him for his military equipment, although by many persons he was advised not to pay that sum, affirming that the equipment was not worth fifty thousand, and that Don Diego had made that agreement under the constraint of fear of breaking with Don Pedro, for whom it was very advantageous, and that it would be better to send him a prisoner to his Majesty; and although the governor might have done that very easily and without danger, he wished to carry out the promise of Don Diego de Almagro, his colleague, and he paid him freely the one hundred thousand pesos in good coins which he allowed him to take with him to his territory of Guatemala, and Pizarro remained in Peru estab-

Almagro goes to Cuzco

(9) Pedro de Alvarado had served under Cortes in Mexico; had been governor of Guatemala; went southward with five hundred men to take Quito, pretending to believe it was outside of Pizarro's territory; found Almagro in possession of the region; and agreed to withdraw on condition of receiving a payment of one hundred thousand pesos.

lishing the city of Lima, transferring thither the population that had been settled at Jauja, for the new site appeared to him more suitable and better adapted to all kinds of business, as it was a seaport. From there Don Diego went to Cuzco with a great number of persons, and the governor went down to Trujillo to reorganise the town and distribute the land. And there he learned that Don Diego de Almagro had wished to lead the city of Cuzco to revolt, for he had become aware that his majesty, with the news brought by Hernando Pizarro to him, had granted him a hundred leagues more of territory beyond the limits of Francisco Pizarro's territory, which it was said did not extend quite to the city of Cuzco. Against this view Juan Pizarro and Gonzalo Pizarro, brothers of the governor, with a large number of others who joined them, protested, and every day they were in conflict with Don Diego and with Captain Soto, who was one of his adherents; but at last he was not able to go out with him, for the majority of the cabildo took the side of the governor and his brothers.

Almagro-Pizarro compact

And when the governor was informed of the state of affairs he went immediately to Cuzco, and by his presence quieted everything, and pardoned Don Diego, who was greatly moved by what he had done without having either title or provision for it, save that they had told him it had been conceded to him. And they formed a new agreement and company in this manner, that Don Diego de Almagro should go on an expedition of discovery by land towards the south, and that if he should find a good country, he might ask the territory of His Majesty for himself, and, not succeeding in this, they should divide the territory of Don Francisco between them; and after this they swore on the consecrated Host not to oppose one another. And some say that Almagro swore to abandon all interest in Cuzco and in the region for a hundred and twenty leagues farther south although his Majesty might concede it to him, and he took a solemn oath, saying, 'If I shall break this oath, may it please thee, O Lord, to curse me body and soul.' Having made this agreement and taken this oath, Don

Almagro goes to Chile

Diego made his preparations and started on his expedition with more than five hundred men who followed him, and the governor returned to Lima."

VII

Cieza de León in the rush for America

In the third and fourth decades of the sixteenth century the desire for adventure in the New World moved many persons to emigrate from Spain. Well-founded reports that had been made public awakened a profound interest in America, and when to these reports there were added wildly extravagant tales of rich principalities there that might be plundered, a wave of excitement swept members of all classes towards the port of departure. Men of birth and cultivation were in the race with ignorant and rough adventurers. Diego de Alvarado, Garcilaso de la Vega, and Lorenzo de Aldana represented the first of these classes, but the majority of the other class were, in many cases, men of disappointed ambitions or such persons as usually yield to the allurements of newly discovered mines of gold. Among the emigrants of this time was Pedro

Cieza de León, a boy of thirteen or fourteen years of age. Like many others of his time, he left no record of his origin, save that he was born in the town of Llerena in Estremadura. Even the fleet with which he sailed is not positively known; but it is probable that he went with Rodrigo Durán, who left Cadiz in 1534, and entered the bay of Cartagena in November of that year. Three years later Cieza de León was at the town of San Sebastian on the gulf of Darien. In this year 1538, now nineteen years old, he was a private soldier in the force of four hundred Spaniards organized by Pedro Vadillo for the campaign up the valley of the Atrato.

Vadillo's Expedition

Juan de Vadillo, who led this expedition, was a member of the audiencia of Santo Domingo. He had been sent to San Sebastian to inquire into the conduct of Governor Heredia, and after the dismissal of that officer, he departed for the interior. This campaign, like many others of that time, was attended by serious obstacles: by the lack of food, by the loss of men by disease, and by the unrelenting hostility of the Indians. In view of the hardships they encountered the men were disposed to revolt, and asked to be led back to San Sebastian, but the determination of the leader to advance finally persuaded the soldiers to follow ; but on arriving at Cali they refused to proceed further, and Vadillo went on to Popayán without them. From that point he went to Panama, where he was arrested and taken to Spain by way of Cartagena.

Cieza de León at Cartago

The soldiers of Vadillo, who had been a year in the wilderness, now established themselves in the Cauca valley, where Robledo, under Benalcázar, had founded settlements. For about six years, ordinarily supposed to be critical years of a youth's education, Cieza de León had been in America,sharing the hardships, the dangers, and the demoralizing influences of expatriated soldiers and settlers in an inhospitable climate and in the presence of unfriendly Indians. He settled at Cartago, and remained in the valley five or six years. Here he gathered and set down important information concerning the Indians; he also described the progress of Vadillo's expedition across the "forest-covered plains," over the mountains, and along the Cauca river. In the dedication of one of his works to the king he thus made reference to his zeal: "Oftentimes when the other soldiers were reposing, I was tiring myself by writing. Neither fatigue nor the ruggedness of the country, nor the mountains and rivers, nor intolerable hunger and suffering, have ever been sufficient to obstruct my two duties, namely, writing and following my flag and my captain without fault."

President Gasca's call for loyal troops to assist in suppressing the rebellion led by Gonzalo Pizarro, offered to Cieza de León an opportunity for new adventures. The boy had grown to be a mature man of thirty, whose physical and intellectual faculties had been developed under the tuition of sixteen years of rough life. With other loyal soldiers he responded to the call, and marched from Popayán by way of Pasto, Quito, and Riobamba to the sea, and along the shore to Lima. From Lima he crossed the first ridge of the Andes to Jauja, thence proceeded southward through Gua-

Cieza de León joins Gasca's troops

manga to the valley of Andahuaylas, near the Apurimac, where the troop of which he was a member was taken into Gasca's army.

On this journey Cieza de León had an opportunity to see the Ecuadorian plateau, the western side of the Andes, and the sandy region of the coast, as well as some of the more important ruins of Inca buildings, the ancient roads, and the system of canals designed for irrigation under the Inca régime. He moreover witnessed the overthrow of Gonzalo Pizarro and was present at the execution of both Pizarro and Carbajal. Later he went to Cuzco. At this time Inca Garcilaso de la Vega, then eleven years of age, was at school in that city, and the two persons who were destined to become preeminent among the early historians of Peru were here either completing or beginning their training for the literary undertakings that were before them. Cieza de León had prepared himself for his work in the camp, and in extensive journeys over the country he was to describe. Garcilaso de la Vega was receiving such tuition as the Church of

Cieza de León at Cuzco

his day was accustomed to sanction. He was then studying Latin under the instruction of Canon Cuellar. In 1549 Cieza de León visited the province of Charcas, and in the ninety-fifth chapter of his Travels he wrote: "I went to see the cities in that region for which purpose the President Gasca gave me letters of introduction to the corregidores, that I might learn all that was worthy of notice."[10]

He passed along the eastern shore of Lake Titicaca, and visited the mines of Porco and Potosí. From Potosí he went to Arequipa, and thence by way of the coast to Lima. At Lima he completed the notes of his journey in September, 1550. From his observations he gives the following account of the fair of Potosí:

The fair at Potosí

"In all parts of this kingdom of Peru we who have travelled over it know that there are great fairs or markets, where the natives make their bargains. Among these the greatest and richest was formerly in the city of Cuzco, for even in the time of the Spani-

(10) See Markham's translation of Cieza de León's *Crónica del Perú*, Hakluyt Society.

ards its greatness was caused by the gold which was brought and sold there, and by the other things of all kinds that were sent into the city. But this market or fair at Cuzco did not equal the superb one at Potosí where the traffic was so great that, among the Indians alone, without including Christians, twenty-five or thirty thousand golden pesos exchanged hands daily. This is wonderful, and I believe that no fair in the world can be compared to it I saw this fair several times, and it is held in a plain near the town. In one place there were baskets of coca, the most valuable product in these parts. In another place there were bales of cloth and fine rich shirtings. Here were heaps of maize, dried potatoes, and other provisions, there great quantities of the best meat in the country. The fair continued from early morning until dusk, and as those Indians got silver every day, and are fond of eating and treating, especially those who have intercourse with Spaniards, they all spent what they got, so that people assembled from all parts with provisions and other necessaries for their sup-

Trading at the fair

port. Many Spaniards became rich in this settlement of Potosí by merely employing two or three Indian women to traffic in the fair. Great numbers of Yanaconas, who are free Indians with the right of serving whom they please, flocked to the fair, and the prettiest girls from Cuzco and all parts of the kingdom were to be met with there.

"I observed that many frauds were committed, and that there was little truth spoken. The value of articles was not great, and cloths, linens, and Hollands were sold almost as cheap as in Spain. Indeed, I saw things sold for so small a price that they would have been considered cheap in Seville." [11]

Crónica del Perú

Cieza de León returned to Spain after a sojourn of seventeen years in America. The first fruit of the experience and studies of these seventeen years was *Parte primera de la crónica del Perú*, which treats, according to the sub-title, "of the demarcation of the provinces, the description of them, the foundation of the new cities, the rites and customs of the Indians,

(11) Cieza de León, *La Crónica del Perú*, cap. 110.

and other strange things worthy of being known." This work was first published at Seville in 1553. The writer found interest in almost every phase of the country and its people, and scholars have accepted his views and conclusions as generally worthy of credence. Through the excellence of its style the book has proved to be one of the most attractive accounts of early Peru, and of the western part of the territory now claimed by the republic of Colombia.

Prescott on Cieza de León

Mr. Prescott refers to Cieza de León as "an author worthy of particular note. His *Crónica del Perú* should more properly be styled an itinerary, or rather geography of Peru. It gives a minute topographical view of the country at the time of the conquest; of its provinces and towns, both Indian and Spanish; its flourishing sea-coasts; its forests, valleys, and interminable ranges of mountains in the interior, with many interesting particulars of the existing population—while scattered here and there may be found notices of their early history and social policy. It is, in short, a lively picture of the country in its physical and moral relations, as it met the eye at the time of the conquest, and in that transition period when it was first subjected to European influences."[12]

Second & third parts of the *Crónica*

The second part of the *Crónica del Perú* was written, either completely or partially, before Cieza de León left Peru. In the prologue of his work the author announces the plan of this Part. He proposed to treat of the government of the Incas, of their great deeds and policy; to "describe the superb and magnificent temples which they built, the roads of wonderful size which they made, and other great things that were found in this kingdom. I shall also give an account in this book of what the Indians say concerning the deluge, and how the Incas magnify the grandeur of their origin." The subject of the third Part was the discovery and conquest of Peru by Pizarro, and the rebellion of the Indians; the fourth Part treats of the civil wars of Peru. Only certain sections of the third and fourth Parts have been printed.

The second Part remained in manuscript

(12) *Conquest of Peru*, vol II, 297.

until 1873, when it was printed by the Peruvian scholar, Dr. Manuel González de la Rosa. In 1880 it was edited by Marcos Jiménez de la Espada, and printed at Madrid. Three years later an English translation of it, by Sir Clements R. Markham, was issued by the Hakluyt Society. In collecting the information on which this Part is based, Cieza de León sought from the Indians what they knew concerning the inhabitants of Peru before the period of the Incas.

Preserving the unwritten history

After setting forth in this second Part what he was able to find out concerning the Indians before the period of the Incas, Cieza de León devotes his pages especially to the institutions and ceremonies of the monarchy, and to the history of the Incas in the line of their succession down to Atahualpa. The following passage from the twelfth chapter presents an account of the method employed to preserve the history of the kingdom, and also an illustration of the author's writing:

"Some of the most learned of the people were chosen to make known the lives of those lords in songs, and the events of their reigns, with the object I have already described. And it is also to be noted that besides this, it was the custom among them, and a law much kept and observed, for each king, during his reign, to select three or four old men, known for their intelligence and ability, who were instructed to retain in their memory all the events that happened in the provinces, whether they were prosperous or whether they were the reverse, and to compose songs to be handed down, so that the history of the reign might be had in remembrance in after times. But these songs could not be recited or made public, except in the presence of the lord, and those who were charged with this duty, during the reign of the king, were not allowed to say anything which referred to him. But after his death they spoke to his successor in the empire, almost in these very words: 'Oh, great and powerful Inca, the Sun, the Moon, the earth, the hills and the trees, the s ones, and thine ancestors, may they all preserve thee from misfortune and make thee prosperous, happy, and successful over

The narration

all that are born. Know that the events which occurred in the days of thy fathers are these.' Then in the narration, they stood in great humility, with eyes cast on the ground and hands lowered. They could very well do this for there were among them some men with very good memories, sound judgments, and subtle genius, and full of reasoning power, as we bear witness, who have heard them even in these our days.

"As soon as the king understood what was related to him, he caused other aged men to be called, and charged them with the duty of learning the songs which were handed down from memory, and to prepare others touching the events which might occur in his own reign."

Guerra de Quito

Besides these works dealing with his travels and the history and institutions of the Inca kingdom, Cieza de León wrote a history of the conquest and the civil wars of Peru. Only a part of this work has been published, the first part of the *Guerra de Quito,* edited by Jiménez de la Espada. This was printed in Madrid in 1877. The fate of the rest of the manuscript is un-

ERRATUM.

Page 94, 5th line from bottom, "only a part" to page 95, 5th line, "city of Quito" substitute:—

Of the five books of the *Guerras civiles del Perú* only the first three have been published, namely: *Guerra de las Salinas, Guerra de Chupas,* and *Guerra de Quito.* The MS. of books IV. and V., containing the guerras de *Huarina* y *Xaquixahuana,* is apparently lost. Perhaps the most interesting is the third book, which gives an account of the conflict between Gonzalo Pizarro and Blasco Núñez Vela near the city of Quito.

known. The part here published is the third book of the Civil Wars of Peru, and gives an account of the conflict between Gonzalo Pizarro and Blasco Núñez Vela near the city of Quito. It opens with the departure of Blasco Núñez Vela from San Lucar in Spain to assume his duties as the first viceroy of Peru. It describes the journey of the viceroy and his arrival in Peru, the effect of the introduction of the New Laws, the appeal to Gonzalo Pizarro to become the leader of the revolt against the viceroy, the reception of Núñez Vela at Lima, and the course of the rebellion until a short time before the triumph of Gonzalo Pizarro and the death of the viceroy near Quito.[13]

Cieza de León's plan

Cieza's work was designed to consist of four parts: 1. Geography and description of Peru; 2. History of the Incas and of the ancient civilization of Peru; 3. Discovery and conquest of Peru; 4. The civil wars of

(13) *Tercero libro de las guerras civiles del Perú, el cual se llama la guerra de Quito.* A translation of Cieza de León's *Guerra de Quito* into English was made by Sir Clements R. Markham, and published for the Hakluyt Society in London in 1913.

the conquistadores of Peru. In his *Obras completas* (VIII, 143–150) Barros Arana discusses the question as to what extent this programme was carried out by the author.

VIII

Girolamo Benzoni

Girolamo Benzoni, the author of *La Historia del mondo nuovo*, was a contemporary of Cieza de León. He was born at Milan about 1519, and at the age of twenty-one he undertook a voyage to America, moved by the marvellous stories of adventure and of quickly acquired wealth that were circulated in Europe. His route to the port of departure led him to Medina del Campo, thence to Seville and down the Guadalquivir to San Lucar. At this port he embarked for the Canary Islands, fearing that as a foreigner he would not be permitted to take passage directly from Spain to the Indies. After two months spent in the islands, he set out for America, and in the course of time we find him involved in the unfortunate enterprises of Governor Ortal in Venezuela, attracted by the governor's promise of riches. More fortunate, how-

Benzoni goes to America

ever, than many of the governor's followers, he escaped alive, although desperately ill. That he did not suffer a worse fate was due in a large measure to the care taken of him by Antonio de Castiglioni, a priest, who accompanied him to the island of Margarita. Later he embarked for Porto Rico, and sailed thence to Santo Domingo, where he was in 1544, and where he remained for eleven months. In the course of his subsequent wanderings he visited Cuba, Tierra Firme, Nombre de Dios, Panama, Cartagena, Nicaragua, Guatemala, and Peru. During some parts of these journeys, he suffered extremely from hunger, particularly in Nicaragua. Of his last years in America and his return to Italy, he gives the following account:

Leaves America on Gasca's order

"Three years after my arrival in Peru, I found myself possessed of some thousands of ducats, and quite tired of remaining in these countries. Moreover, President Gasca had ordered all foreigners to quit the country, in consequence of its having been reported to him by some Spaniards that the Levantines, that is that we, were false and cruel, and had caused the death of some of them. Therefore, when I was at Guayaquil, I availed myself of a large boat that arrived there laden with merchandise from Panama, to return to my own country. Accordingly, as soon as the master of it was ready, I embarked on the 8th of May, 1550. We sailed, and in the port of Zalaga we found President Gasca, who was going to Panama to cross over to Spain. He ordered our master to sail in company with him, for otherwise he was going alone. But as the bark had to take in a cargo of maize, the master requested to be left behind on ac-account of business. The President started, and we remained until the vessel was loaded. Sailing soon after this, we arrived at Manta, where the vessel struck a rock and sank, all the passengers and crew, however, were saved, with the greater part of their gold and silver.

Benzoni in Nicaragua

"The bark being wrecked, as here described, it became necessary to wait for another passage; and at the end of fifty days, a vessel arriving from Lima, we started on her and soon arrived at Panama.

Hearing there that the president had sailed from Nombre de Dios for Spain with all the ships, I went to Nicaragua. There I had a long and severe disease, so that at the end of four years, being then in Guatemala, and ships arriving from Spain, I went to Puerto de los Caballos, whence I sailed; but after navigating a few days, when we were near the island of Cuba, there arose a very severe storm, which drove the ship on shore, and almost all the specie on board was lost; scarcely could the crew be saved. After thirty-four days of hard labour and great dangers, we entered the port of Havana, expecting to find the fleet there; but it had sailed eight days before for Spain.

"I remained at Havana very discontented on two accounts: firstly, from having lost part of my small property in the wreck already mentioned; and, secondly, because we found that the fleet had sailed; but on hearing how it had been lost, I praised God for his divine grace that preserved me from it, and did not permit me to embark, for otherwise I should undoubtedly have been lost with the others. Ten months after

Benzoni's return to Spain

these events the Indian fleet arrived at Havana, consisting altogether of fourteen vessels, large and small. We soon sailed, with the help of Providence, and in thirty-nine days, though undergoing a frightful storm on the voyage, we reached a Portuguese island, commonly called Madera.

"Having taken on board there bread and wine and other provisions, we again set sail. At the end of eight days, on the 13th of September, 1556, we entered the port of San Lucar de Barameda, and thence proceeded to Seville. As soon as I was cleared, I went to Cadiz, and having embarked in an urca, at the end of two months I reached Genoa, where I rejoiced exceedingly, and soon afterwards arrived at Milan; always praising the Majesty of God, His power, and that of our Saviour, for having granted me the grace to see so many strange things, and so much of the world, and so many foreign countries; and for having liberated me out of so many serious trials. When I reflect, it seems to me impossible that a human body could have undergone so much—*che un corpo humano habbia potuto supportar tanto.*"

Fernández's *Relación*

Juan Fernández's *Relación*, dealing with the social disturbances of Peru, after the death of Viceroy Antonio de Mendoza (1551-1552) and the causes from which they proceeded is a clearly written and trustworthy document, which remained unpublished until 1865. It is especially valuable as a critical investigation of the principal causes and events of Girón's rebellion.[14] Its author was the fiscal of the audiencia of Lima, and arrived in Peru either with Pedro de la Gasca or with Viceroy Antonio de Mendoza, probably with the latter.

(14) The title of this work is: *Relación . . . de los desasosiegos sucedidos en Perú después de la muerte del Sr. Virrey D. Antonio de Mendoza . . . por el licenciado Juan Fernández.* It was published by J. F. Pacheco in his *Colección de documentos inéditos del Archivo de Indias*, vol. III, p. 246.

CHAPTER IV

PERUVIAN AND CHILEAN HISTORIANS, 1550–1600.

I. *José de Acosta.* II. *Garcilaso de la Vega.* III. *Pedro Sarmiento de Gamboa ; Polo de Ondegardo.* IV. *Cristóbal de Molina; Cabello de Balboa.* V. *Pedro de Valdivia.* VI. *Alonso de Góngora Marmolejo.* VII. *Pedro de Mariño de Lovera.*

I

Gasca's work

At the beginning of the second half of the sixteenth century a temporary calm brooded over the affairs of Peru. President Gasca had allayed the factional disturbances, but his administration, if it had produced peace, had nevertheless brought little satisfaction to the contending parties. A new attempt was now made to set up a viceroy. In the meantime the audiencia con-

Antonio de Mendoza & successors

trolled public affairs, but in 1551 Antonio de Mendoza arrived in Lima as the viceroy of Peru. With the prestige of his long reign in Mexico, he undertook the task of establishing order in the unorganized colony, but he died the following year, leaving the governmental authority again in the hands of the audiencia. In 1555 Andrés Hurtado de Mendoza accepted the vacant office, and a line of more or less distinguished successors continued the viceregal administration to the end of the century.[1]

During these decades the Peruvian government acquired its normal and stable character, largely through the legislative activity of Viceroy Francisco de Toledo. Lima gradually increased in population and acquired many of the institutions which later characterized its social life, such as the university, the tribunal of the Crusada, the inquisition, and various monasteries. In the meantime the mines of Upper Peru,

(1) Andrés Hurtado de Mendoza, 1556–1561; Diego López de Zúñiga y Velasco, 1561–1564; Lope García de Castro, 1564–1569; Francisco de Toledo, 1569–1581; Martín Enríquez, 1581–1583; Fernando de Torres y Portugal, 1585–1590; García Hurtado de Mendoza, 1590–1596; Luis de Velasco, 1597–1604.

State of Lima

particularly those of Potosí, continued to pour out their riches, making Lima the market at which the precious metals were exchanged for imported European wares. The increasing wealth was attended by a more elaborate style of living, by the growth of more formal and refined manners, by the multiplication of religious ceremonies, and by the rapid acquisition of property by the Church. At the same time, as the creoles in the population increased in numbers, they became conspicuous for their ostentation, and, by departing from the severe manners and customs of the Spaniards, added a certain lightness and freedom to social intercourse.

But in spite of the persistent call of these circumstances to practical affairs, a number of persons appeared in the colony during this period, who by their writings indicated that not all the world was absorbed in contemplating the output of the mines, the gains of trade, or in rivalling one another in the display of newly-acquired wealth. Some of these by their office in the Church were expected to stand aloof, and did stand aloof, from the ordinary economic activity of the community; in fact, this period and the half-century following were especially noteworthy for their literary production, both in Peru and in Chile.

Acosta

In Peru José de Acosta, Garcilaso de la Vega, and Pedro Sarmiento became especially prominent. These men were better equipped by education than most of the writers who had described the events of the conquest from personal observation. Acosta was a professor of theology in Lima, and the Church expected to have its influence extended by his eloquence as a preacher. His principal work is entitled *Historia natural y moral de las Indias*. The first book deals chiefly with Peruvian affairs, but the fifth, sixth and seventh books refer extensively to conditions and institutions in Mexico. The author was born in Spain in 1540, and his boyhood was passed with his parents in the town of Medina del Campo. He became a Jesuit in 1553 and went to America in 1570. The intervening years had been spent in study, so that when he set out for the Indies he had already acquired a vast amount of knowledge. He landed at Cartagena, went to Nombre de Dios and thence across the Isthmus to Panama. From Panama he proceeded to Peru, and arrived at Callao in 1571. Peru was then under the vigorous rule of Viceroy Francisco de Toledo (1569–1581), who at this time was absent from Lima, engaged in making an inspection of the viceroyalty. Acosta was ordered to join the viceroy's other assistants, particularly Polo de Ondegardo and Juan Matienzo. He accompanied Toledo, and was a member of the expedition directed against the Chiriguana Indians.

Acosta with Toledo

After his return to Lima he resumed his duties as professor of theology, and retained this post until the middle of 1575, when he became rector of the Colegio Máximo de San Pablo. The next year he was promoted to the office of provincial of the Jesuit province of Peru, succeeding the first provincial, Portillo. Acosta's term as provincial expired in 1580. He resided for some years at the missionary station of Juli, near Lake Titicaca, and during this period his time

Offices in Lima

was divided between missionary work and writing. The Jesuits had established a college at Juli to facilitate the study of the native languages. Holguín had resided there, and his Quichua grammar is an important contribution to knowledge of that language. Bertonio, also sometime a resident there, performed a similar service by his Aymara dictionary.

Acosta removed from Upper Peru to Lima near the end of Toledo's reign. The viceroy's administration, through his prolific and generally wise legislative activity, contributed greatly to the orderly establishment of the viceroyalty, but by his unjust condemnation and execution of the Inca he incurred the displeasure of the king, and died in disgrace. Under Martín Enríquez (1581–1586) Toledo's successor, was held the third ecclesiastical Council of Lima. At the last sitting Acosta delivered what has been characterized as "an elegant and learned oration"; he also wrote the history of the council. At this council he was theological adviser, and was appointed to edit the acts of the council.

Acosta at Council of Lima

A little later Acosta went to Mexico, where after a short sojourn, covering the year 1586, he returned to Spain in 1587 taking with him for publication various manuscripts written by him during the fifteen years of his residence in America. He was in Madrid in 1588, and in this year he began the publication of the work on which his reputation as a writer chiefly rests, his *Historia natural y moral de las Indias*. The complete work under this title was, however, not published until 1590, the date of the Seville edition.[2]

Historia natural y moral

The first four books treat of the natural history of the Indies. Of these the first and second were written in Latin, while Acosta was in Peru, and were translated into

(2) It was reprinted in Seville in 1591; at Barcelona the same year; at Madrid in 1608 and 1610; in Italian at Venice in 1596; in French at Paris in 1597; in Dutch at Haarlem in 1598; in Latin at Paris in 1598, and in 1600, 1606, and 1616; in Latin at Frankfort in 1602 and 1603; in German at Frankfort in 1601; in English at London in 1604. There is also reported a Flemish translation of 1617.

The following are some of his other works: *De natura novi orbis, . . . et de promulgatione evangelii apud barbaros, sive de procuranda Indorum salute*, Salamanca, 1589; *De vera Scripturae interpretandae ratione, ac de Christo in Scripturis revelato*, Rome, 1590; *Sumario del concilio provincial, que se celebró en la Ciudad de los Reyes, el año 1567*, Madrid, 1591; *Concilium limense celebratum anno 1583*, Madrid, 1591; *De temporibus novissimis*, Lyons, 1592.

Spanish by him after his return to Spain, where all the rest of the work was written. The fifth, sixth and seventh books contain what the author calls the moral history of the Indies, embracing such subjects as are involved in the organization and development of society.

The numerous editions of this work indicate somewhat the strength of the early demand for information regarding America. Large numbers of persons were solicitous to know about the climate and its fitness for securing human health; the metals, plants, and animals; the rites and ceremonies of the inhabitants; the laws and government; and the wars with the Indians. The nature of the contents of the work suggested the designation of the author as the Pliny of the New World.

After an extensive discussion of the views held by ancient writers, sacred and profane, concerning the geography and the natural phenomena of the Indies, Acosta touches on the project of cutting a canal across the Isthmus. He wrote:

"Some have discoursed and propounded

Acosta on a Panama canal

to cut through this passage of seven leagues, and to joyne one sea to the other, to make the passage from Peru more commodious and easie, for that those eighteen leagues of land betwixt Nombre de Dios and Panama is more painfull and chargeable than two thousand and three hundred by sea, whereupon some would say it were a means to drowne the land, one sea being lower than another. As in times past we finde it written, that for the same consideration they gave over the enterprise to win the Red Sea with the Nile, in the time of King Sesostris, and since, in the Empire of the Ottomans. But for my part, I hold such discourses and propositions for vaine, although this inconvenient should not happen, the which I will not hold for assured, I believe there is no humane power able to beat and breake downe those strong and impenetrable mountains, which God hath placed betwixt the two seas, and hath made them most hard rockes, to withstand the furie of two seas. And although it were possible to men, yet in my opinion they should feare punishment from heaven in seeking to correct the workes which the Creator by his great providence hath Ordained and disposed in the forming of this universall world."[3]

Food products

Among the food-products described Acosta makes mention of the potato, saying that "The Indians use another kinde of roote, which they call Papas. These rootes are like the ground nuttes; they are small rootes that cast out many leaves. They gather the Papas, and dry it well in the Sunne, then beating it they make that which they call *Chuñu*, which keeps many daies, and serves for bread. In this realme there is great trafficke of *Chuñu*, the which they carry to the mines of Potosí; they likewise eat of these Papas boyled or roasted. There is one sweete kinde which grows in hot places, whereof they do make certain sauces and minced meats which they call *Locro*."[4]

In writing of coca, Acosta calls attention to an article, the use of which under the

(3) From the translation by Edward Grimston, London, 1604, Book III, Chap. x; republished by the Hakluyt Society, London, 1880.
(4) *Ibid.* Book IV, ch. xvii.

Indian régime was subject to severe restrictions, enforced by a religious sanction, but since then these restrictions have been removed, with many of the evil consequences that were doubtless feared by the paternal government of the Incas:

Acosta on coca

"The Indians esteeme it much, and in time of their Kings Yncas it was not lawfull for any of the common people to use this coca without licence from the governor. Their use is to carry it in their mouthes, chawing it and sucking out the juyce, but they swallow it not. They say it gives them great courage, and is very pleasing unto them. Many grave men holde this as a superstition and a mere imagination; for my part, and to speak the truth, I perswade not my selfe that it is an imagination but contrariwise, I thinke it works and gives force and courage to the Indians; for we see the effects which cannot be attributed to imagination, as to go some daies without meat, but only a handfull of coca, and other like effects." [5]

(5) *Ib.* Book IV, chap. XXII. As to the traffic in coca in the single city of Potosí, our author makes the following

II

Garcilaso de la Vega

By his ancestry Garcilaso de la Vega was connected with some of the most distinguished families of Spain, the families of Mendoza and Vargas. His father was the son of Alonso de Hinestrosa de Vargas, whose wife was Blanca Suárez de Figueroa, a descendant of that Garcilaso de la Vega on whom the name was originally conferred for his famous duel with the gigantic Moor on the Vega of Granada. This name was adopted by the historian's father as that of a maternal ancestor. The son of Hinestrosa de Vargas thus became Garcilaso de la Vega. This Garcilaso de la Vega was born in the city of Badajoz in Estremadura in 1506. At the age of twenty-five, in 1531, he went to America as a captain of infantry, at the time of Pedro de Alvarado's return to resume the government of Guatemala. He became a member of Alvarado's ill-fated

statement: "The traffic of coca in Potosi doth yearly mount to above half a million of dollars, for that they use foure score and tenne or foure score and fifteen thousand baskets every year."

Parents of Garcilaso

expedition to Quito, that landed at Caraques in March, 1534. After Alvarado's surrender to Almagro, Garcilaso de la Vega entered the service of Pizarro, and was sent to subdue the natives about the port of Buenaventura. Owing to the difficulties of the march and the loss of a large part of his men he was obliged to abandon the undertaking. He then went to Lima, where he found Pizarro besieged by the Indians. His next service was in the campaign for the relief of Cuzco, that appeared to be in danger of falling into the hands of the insurgent natives.

During the conflict between Pizarro and Almagro that resulted in the death of Almagro, Garcilaso de la Vega was established at Cuzco. Chimpa Ocllo, a young Indian princess, baptized as Doña Isabel, was living at Cuzco at that time. She was a granddaughter of Inca Tupac Yupanqui. Her father was a brother of the distinguished king, Huayna Capac, the twelfth in the line as given by Cieza de León. She was thus a cousin of the unfortunate Atahualpa. In 1540 she gave birth to a child who became the historian, and whose father was Garcilaso de la Vega. The childhood and youth of the younger Garcilaso was spent in Cuzco, the capital from which members of his mother's family had ruled the famous Indian kingdom. During these early years his father was engaged in the civil wars that afflicted the unhappy country; at first on the side of Pizarro, and later taking part in the rebellion led by Gonzalo Pizarro against the first viceroy of Peru, Blasco Núñez de Vela. One of the earliest recollections of the historian was the triumphal entry of the forces into Cuzco after Gonzalo Pizarro had put down his enemies.

Garcilaso the elder

Garcilaso de la Vega, the elder, once more changed his allegiance; he deserted the cause of Gonzalo Pizarro, and fled from Cuzco to Lima. But the party of the viceroy, which he had hoped to join was overthrown, and the viceroy had departed.

Although pardoned by Gonzalo Pizarro, Garcilaso de la Vega went over to the forces of Gasca at the battle of Jaquijaguana in 1548. Between this event and the rebel-

Garcilaso at Cuzco

lion of Girón in 1553 he resided at Cuzco, and after the failure of this rebellion he was appointed corregidor and governor of that city and province. As the principal figure in the civil administration of the province, his house became the centre of the social activity of the city. Thus in the turmoil and rebellions and the quieter life that followed, the younger Garcilaso de la Vega, was in a more favourable position than any other historian had occupied for acquiring a correct view of the history and institutions of the two races here in conflict.

Garcilaso the younger

A suggestion of the opportunities the young Garcilaso de la Vega enjoyed for acquiring knowledge of the institutions and spirit of his mother's people is found in his statement that while she lived in Cuzco, her native town, "almost every week some of the male and female relations, who escaped the cruelty and tyranny of Atahualpa, came to visit her. On the occasion of these visits their usual conversation was on the subject of the origin of the Yncas, of their majesty, of the grandeur of their empire, of their greatness, of their mode of government in peace and war, and of the laws which they ordained for the good of their subjects. In short, they omitted nothing relating to the flourishing period of their history in the course of these conversations." [6]

As Garcilaso de la Vega advanced toward maturity, he became his father's agent in superintending his estates and acquired much information about Peru through journeys. After his father's death he determined to go to Spain. Here he was received with kindness by his father's relatives, and such generosity by others as might be accorded to one born in America. He entered the army of Philip II as a captain, and took part in the campaign against the Moriscos under Don Juan de Austria. On his retirement from active military service, he became a resident of Córdoba, where he was compelled by his poverty to adopt a very modest style of living. He was not only in debt when he left the army, but under a certain cloud of public disfavour by reason of his father's connexion with Gonzalo

Garcilaso in Spain

(6) *First Part of the Royal Commentaries of the Yncas*, Markham's translation, vol. 1, 62.

Pizarro's rebellion. It is quite possible that his consciousness of this prejudice deepened his piety for his native land and the kingly race from which he was descended and persuaded him to set forth their virtues and the nobler qualities of their rule, and not to omit the wrongs they had suffered at the hands of the Spaniards.

Los comentarios reales

Garcilaso de la Vega's principal work is *Los comentarios reales.* This was based not only on information acquired during his early life at Cuzco, but also on later contributions made by his former associates in Peru; for as soon as he decided to write this history, he communicated with his old schoolfellows and asked them to help him by sending accounts of the particular conquests which the Incas had made in the provinces of their families. They took up his project and caused to be brought out from the archives the accounts which their relatives possessed, and sent them to him; it was thus, he said, "that I obtained the records of the deeds and conquests of each Inca." [7]

(7) *Royal Commentaries*, Markham's translation, vol. 1, 77.

The first part of *Los comentarios reales del Perú* was published at Lisbon in 1609, and the second part was first published at Córdoba in 1617. The author died in 1617 and was buried in the cathedral of Córdoba. A second edition was published at Madrid in 1723, and a third edition at the same place in 1829.[8]

La Florida del Inca

An earlier work by Garcilaso de la Vega, *La Florida del Inca, historia del adelantado Hernando de Soto, gobernador y capitán-general del reino de la Florida, y de otros heroicos caballeros españoles e indios*, was published in Lisbon in 1605. Written in an agreeable style, it was received with great favour, and for it the writer would have been accorded distinction, even if he had not later produced a more important book. Much of the consideration enjoyed by Garcilaso and the popularity of his writings

He was, moreover, able to make use of earlier writings, such as those of Cieza de León, Zárate, López de Gómara, and Acosta, and also of the papers of the missionary, Blas Valera, that were afterwards destroyed in 1594 at the sacking of Cadiz by the English.

(8) A mutilated translation into English, by Sir Paul Rycaut, was published in 1688; a French translation, by M. J. Bardouin, in 1798; and a German translation, by G. C. Böttger, in 1798 at Nordhausen.

were due to the fact that he revealed to Europeans of his day a hitherto unknown kingdom, and set it before them idealized by the piety and patriotic emotions of an exile.[9]

Markham on Garcilaso

Sir Clements R. Markham, in his introduction to the *Narratives of the Rites and Laws of the Yncas*, makes this interesting note concerning Garcilaso's memory and the accuracy of his statements:

"Garcilaso wrote from memory, forty years after he had left Peru, with the aid of letters from correspondents. His main object was to publish a commentary, correcting the errors of Spanish authors who professed to give a history of the Yncas without being acquainted with their language. In doing this, he added much precious information from the store-house of his own memory, and the more his work is sifted and examined, the more clearly does it appear that he was scrupulously truthful,

(9) Barros Arana, *El Inca Garcilaso de la Vega*, in his *Obras completas*, vol. VIII, 151–158; Bancroft, *History of the United States*, ed. 1834, vol. I, 66; Winsor, *Narrative and Critical History* vol. II, 1921, 290; Julia Fitzmaurice-Kelly, *El Inca Garcilasso de la Vega*, published by The Hispanic Society of America, 1921.

and that, allowing for the disadvantage under which he laboured, his statements are wonderfully accurate. Perhaps the excellence of the Ynca's memory is best shown in the topographical details. He gives the conquests of each successive Ynca, mentioning the places through which the conquerors marched in the gradual acquisition of their vast empire. He enumerates three hundred and twenty places in Peru, yet, in describing the marches, he does not make a single mistake, nor give one of these places out of its order, or in the wrong position. When Garcilaso's routes of each of the conquering Yncas are placed on a map, they present convincing proofs of the remarkable accuracy of the author."

Garcilaso's accuracy

Another phase of Garcilaso's writing is presented by Prescott (*Conquest of Peru*, I, 469–473), where he affirms that Garcilaso de la Vega "wrote to effect a particular object. He stood forth as counsel for his unfortunate countrymen, pleading the cause of that degraded race before the tribunal of posterity. The exaggerated tone of panegyric consequent on this becomes apparent

Prescott on Garcilaso

in every page of the work. He pictures forth a state of society, such as an Utopian philosopher would hardly venture to depict." His work "is addressed to the imagination more than to sober reason. We are dazzled by the gorgeous spectacle it perpetually exhibits, and delighted by the variety of amusing details and animated gossip sprinkled over its pages. The story of the action is perpetually varied by discussions on topics illustrating its progress, so as to break up the monotony of the narrative, and afford an agreeable relief to the reader. This is true of the first part of his great work. In the second there was no longer room for such discussion. But he has supplied the place by garrulous reminiscences, personal anecdotes, incidental adventures, and a host of trivial details—trivial in the eyes of the pedant—which historians have been too willing to discard as below the dignity of history."

Referring to the edifices constructed at Cuzco by the Indians under the Incas, Garcilaso de la Vega gives expression to the astonishment which many persons since his day have experienced:

Ancient buildings at Cuzco

"The Yncas, kings of Peru, built wonderful edifices, whether fortresses, temples, gardens, palaces, store-houses, roads, or other works. All excited admiration, as may still be seen by their ruins, though these remains give but an inadequate idea of the complete edifice.

"The grandest and most superb work that they ordered to be built, to show their power and majesty, was the fortress of Cuzco. Its magnificence would be incredible to those who have not seen it, and even those who have gazed upon it with attention are induced to imagine, and even to believe, that such works must have been completed by enchantment, and that they were made by demons rather than by men. For the multitude of stones, so many and of such size, that are placed on the three circling lines (being more like rocks than stones), excite astonishment and wonder, as to how they could have been cut from the quarries whence they were brought. For these Indians had neither iron nor steel for cutting and working the stones.

"It is an equal wonder how the stones

could have been brought from the quarry; for the Indians had neither bullocks nor carts. Besides, no cart could bear the weight of such stones, neither could any bullocks draw them. They were drawn by the force of men's hands, hauling at stout cables passed round them." [10]

Destruction of Inca edifices

On a later page Garcilaso de la Vega expresses regret that the Spaniards did not preserve the fortress as they found it:

"The Spaniards should have preserved the fortress, and even repaired it at their own cost, that future ages might see how great had been the valour of those who took it, of which it would have been an eternal memorial. But not only have they not maintained it; they have themselves dismantled it to build the private houses they have now in Cuzco. In order to save the cost, delay, and trouble which the Indians expended on preparing dressed stones for building, the Spaniards pulled down all the masonry walls within the circle of the fortress, and there is not a house in the city

(10) *The Royal Commentaries*, Hakluyt Society, London. vol. II, 305.

which has not been partly built with those stones, at least among those that the Spaniards have erected."[11]

III

Sarmiento's career

A further contribution to the history of the Inca kingdom was made by Pedro Sarmiento, who not only held a high place among the Spanish navigators of the sixteenth century but also merits consideration among the writers of his time. He was born at Alcalá de Henares about 1532. His father was Bartolomé Sarmiento, a native of Pontevedra in Galicia, whose wife was of a Biscayan family named Gamboa. Pedro passed the period of his childhood and youth in his father's house at Pontevedra, near the little port of Bayona; but at the age of eighteen he entered the military service of Spain, and was a soldier from 1550 to 1555, when he succumbed to the desire to seek adventures and fortune in America. His sojourn in Mexico and Guatemala left no important record in the history of the period. In 1557 he arrived

(11) *Ibid.* vol. II, 317.

in Peru, then under the rule of Viceroy Andrés Hurtado de Mendoza, Marqués de Cañete, who had made his solemn entry into Lima on June 29, 1556.

Social unrest and sedition

The rebellions of Gonzalo Pizarro and Girón had been put down, but the spirit of discontent and hostility to the government was manifest in many quarters. The judges of the audiencia were leaders of opposing factions; the corregidores were supporting practically independent military forces, and their unlawful acts imposed intolerable burdens on persons subject to their authority. Everywhere there were smouldering embers of sedition. The viceroy faced this condition of affairs with a grim determination to bring peace to the troubled society. He gathered and held subject to his order the arms and munitions that were scattered among the corregidores. The prominent disturbers of the peace he disarmed and sent into exile. He caused Tomás Vásquez, the lieutenant of Girón, to be executed, and ordered the corregidores to impose the same punishment upon turbulent and dangerous persons within their districts. And to furnish a vent to the restlessness of adventurers, he encouraged the organization of exploring expeditions, of which the most notorious was that of Pedro de Ursúa, that finally fell under the control of the brutal Lope de Aguirre.

The viceregal court

Another phase of the viceroy's activity was the setting up of the viceregal establishment, where the vice-queen presided, and introduced much of the ceremonious life of a European Court. At this time the question of the aims and ambitions of the Incarial family began to excite inquiry if not alarm, and the prominence of this subject induced Sarmiento to study seriously the history of the Incas. This subject claimed his attention for a number of years after his arrival in Lima. But during his residence at the capital he was persecuted by the Inquisition. The charges against him were trivial, and for one alleged offence he was condemned to the absurd punishment of hearing mass in the cathedral at Lima, divested of his clothing and holding a candle in his hand. In addition to this penalty, it was ordered that he should be

Persecution of Sarmiento

perpetually banished from the Indies. But by appealing to the Pope he was released from the penalty of banishment, and permitted to reside in Cuzco and other parts of Peru until 1567. Still, this senseless persecution was continued until his public services obtained for him the protection of the government.

Segunda parte de la historia general

During these ten years he made various journeys throughout the country in pursuit of information concerning the Incas. Of the results of these investigations there remains *Segunda parte de la historia general llamada indica.* Other parts, if any others were written, have not come to light. The manuscript of this second part includes a dedication to the king that was written at Cuzco and signed by Sarmiento on March 4, 1572. The work as designed by the author was to consist of three parts. The second, and apparently the only part written, contains the history of the Incas. It treats of the early rulers of Peru and their principal officers, the settlement of Cuzco, the legends concerning the origin of the Incas, the entrance of Manco Capac into

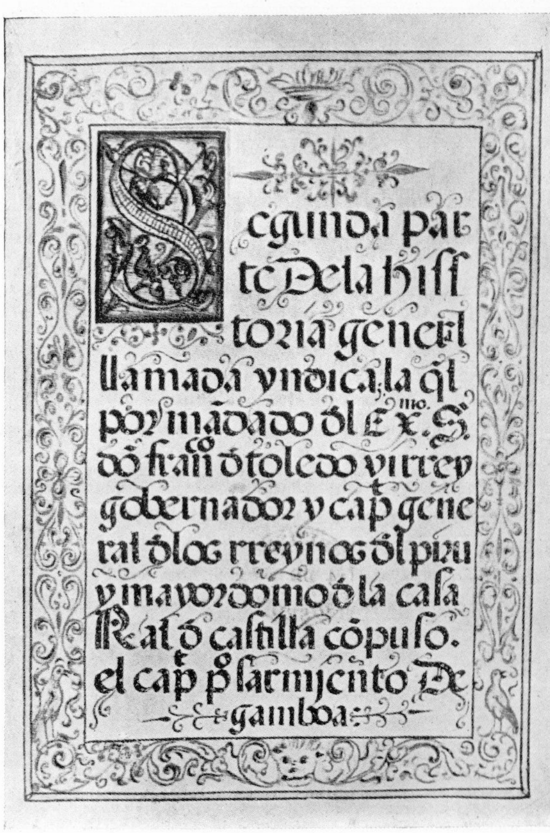

Segunda par
te dela hiss
toria general
llamada yndica, la ql
por mãdado dl Ex.mo S.r
dõ fran.co d toledo virrey
governador y cap. gene
ral d los rreynos dl piru
y mayordomo d la casa
Real d castilla cõpuso.
el cap. p.o sarmiento de
gamboa:

Page 2 of the MS. of Pedro Sarmiento de Gamboa

the region of Cuzco, the subsequent wars with other tribes, the reigns of Tupac Yupanqui and Huayna Capac, and the civil wars between Huascar and Atahualpa, of which the Spaniards took advantage on their arrival in Peru. Sarmiento fixes the beginning of the Inca dynasty at the year 565, thus making its continuance a little less than a thousand years.[12]

Continued persecution

In 1573 the Inquisition renewed its persecution of Sarmiento; it considered trivial charges brought against him; and finally reaffirmed its former sentence of banishment. The execution of this sentence was not then practicable, for Sarmiento was at that time engaged in a campaign against the Chiriguanos, eastward of the Andes, and after his return the civil authorities persuaded the inquisitors that the sentence should be revoked. But two years later they considered other equally trivial charges, and

(12) The full title of this part of Sarmiento's work is *Segunda parte de la historia general llamada índica la qual por mandado del Excelentísimo Francisco de Toledo, Virrey, Gobernador y Capitán General de los reinos del Perú y Mayordomo de la casa real de Castilla, compuso el Capitán Pedro Sarmiento de Gamboa*. See reproduction of 2nd title page of Sarmiento's MS. opposite.

Sarmiento pursues Drake

this time he was found guilty, imprisoned and sentenced again to be banished. At this time the viceroy, Francisco de Toledo (1569–1591), interfered, ordered that Sarmiento should be released, held him in the service of the government, and took him under his special protection. In 1579, when Drake appeared in Peruvian waters, Sarmiento led an expedition in pursuit of him, but failed to overtake him. On his return, he received the viceroy's orders to proceed to the Strait of Magellan, in order to intercept Drake there on his voyage back to England. At the same time he was under orders to fortify the strait so as to prevent the passage of explorers or pirates who might undertake to follow Drake. Other navigators had entered the strait before Sarmiento—Magellan in 1520, Loaysa and Cano in 1526, Alcazava in 1535, and Drake in 1578; but Sarmiento's account of his voyage virtually superseded all reports made by previous explorers. It, moreover, persuaded the king of Spain to fit out an extensive fleet for the purpose of transporting a considerable body of colonists, men with their families, to the inhospitable shores of the strait. Sarmiento was appointed to be the governor of the colony, but the command of the fleet was entrusted to the incompetent Diego Flores de Valdés, and his incompetence rather than the storms encountered caused the ruin of the enterprise. Sarmiento's narratives of his voyages, translated into English by Markham, have been issued as a volume of the Hakluyt Society's publications. This collection consists of five documents. The first is called *Voyage to the Strait of Magellan*, and gives an account of Sarmiento's passage through the strait, with such accuracy of detail as to elicit the commendation of later navigators and surveyors. The second document was written in Rio de Janeiro in 1583. It refers to the passage through the strait, the voyage to Spain, the preparation of the fleet under Flores de Valdés, and gives some account of what happened to the fleet. The third document enumerates the ships and their officers, while the fourth is a narrative of the equipment of the fleet, the

Voyage to the Strait

disasters it encountered, the disgraceful conduct of the officers, the settlements in the strait, and the captivity of Sarmiento. The last document gives some account of the tragic fate of the settlers, who waited in vain for the return of ships with provisions, and who distributed themselves along the shore, in order to support themselves with shell-fish picked up on the beach; but the supply was inadequate, and one after another they died of starvation and exposure. The appearance of the ships of Thomas Cavendish was the last hope of the survivors, and when these ships sailed away, taking only one man as a guide the remnant of the colony went speedily to its tragic end.

Thomas Cavendish

I quote Sarmiento's account of the manner in which Atahualpa was informed of the arrival of the Spaniards:

"Atahualpa was at Huamachuco celebrating great festivals for his victories, and he wished to proceed to Cuzco and assume the fringe[13] in the House of the Sun, where

(13) When one was acclaimed sovereign Inca, the *llantu*, or fringe, was placed on his head, this act forming part of a ceremony corresponding to a royal coronation. Other

all former Incas had received it. When he was about to set out there came to him two Tallanas Indians, sent by the Curacas—local governors under the Incas—of Payta and Túmbez, to report to him that there had arrived by sea, which they call 'cocha,' a people with different clothing and with beards, and that they brought animals like large sheep. The chief of them was believed to be Viracocha, which means the god of these people, and he brought with him many Viracochas, which is as much as to say 'gods.' They said this of the Governor Don Francisco Pizarro, who had arrived with one hundred and eighty men and some horses which they called sheep.

Spaniards reported to Atahualpa

"When this became known to Atahualpa he rejoiced greatly, believing it to be the Viracocha coming as he had promised when he departed, and as is recounted in the beginning of this history. Atahualpa gave thanks that he should have come in his time, and he sent back the messengers with

features of the ceremony were fastening over the Inca's shoulders the *yacolla*, or mantle, and clasping about his wrist the *chapana* or bracelet.—See Markham, *The Incas of Peru*, 292.

thanks to the Curacas for sending the news, and ordering them to keep him informed of what might happen. He resolved not to go to Cuzco until he had seen what this arrival was, and what the Viracochas intended to do." [14]

Incas in Conflict

In a subsequent chapter Sarmiento refers to Pizarro's project to inquire into the dispute between Huascar and Atahualpa: "Don Francisco Pizarro knew of the disputes there had been between Atahualpa and Huascar, and that Huascar was a prisoner in the hands of the captains of Atahualpa, and he urged Atahualpa to have his brother brought as quickly as possible. Huascar was being brought to Caxamarca by Atahualpa's order, as has already been said. Chalco Chima, obeying this order, set out with Huascar and the captains and relations who had escaped the butchery of Cusi Yupanqui. Atahualpa asked Don Francisco Pizarro why he wanted to see his brother. Pizarro replied that he had been informed that

(14) Sarmiento, *History of the Incas*, Hakluyt Society, London, 1907, chap. XVIII.

Huascar was the elder and principal lord of that land, and for that reason he wished to see him,and he desired that he should come. Atahualpa feared that if Huascar came alive, the Governor Don Francisco Pizarro would be informed of what had taken place, that Huascar would be made lord, and that he would lose his state. Being sagacious, he agreed to comply with Pizarro's demand, but sent off a messenger to the captain who was bringing Huascar with an order to kill him and all the prisoners. The messenger started and found Huascar at Atamarca, near Yana-mayu. He gave his message to the captain of the guard who was bringing Huascar as a prisoner.

Pizarro sends for Huascar

"Directly the captain heard the order of Atahualpa he complied with it. He killed Huascar, cut the body up and threw it into the river Yana-mayu. He also killed the rest of the brothers, relations, and captains who were with him as prisoners, in the year 1533."[15]

Fate of Huascar

A noted contemporary of Sarmiento, the Licenciado Polo de Ondegardo, also became

(15) *History of the Incas*, chap. LXIX.

Polo de Ondegardo

interested in the history of Peru and the ancient institutions of the country, and, at the suggestion of the viceroy, wrote two accounts, or "relaciones," on the revenues and tributes, or, in general, the financial administration of the Inca kingdom.

The time and place of Ondegardo's birth are not known. It has been ascertained, however, that he was in Peru during the period of the civil wars. By Gasca he was appointed governor of Charcas, and he held for a number of years a similar office at Cuzco, to which he was appointed by the Marqués de Cañete as viceroy. Under Francisco de Toledo, Ondegardo was a confidential adviser of the viceroy, and assisted him in drawing up the ordinances for completing the organization of the viceroyalty.

Prescott, who had copies of Ondegardo's narratives, affirms that while he gives his conclusions with an air of modesty, it is evident that he feels conscious of having derived his information through the most authentic channels. He rejects the fabulous with disdain; decides on the probability of such facts as he relates, and candidly

Prescott on Ondegardo

exposes deficiency of evidence. Far from displaying the simple enthusiasm of the well-meaning but credulous missionary, he proceeds with the cool and cautious step of a lawyer, accustomed to the conflict of testimony and the uncertainty of oral tradition. This circumspect manner of proceeding and the temperate character of his judgments entitle Ondegardo to much higher consideration as an authority than most of his countrymen who have treated of Indian antiquities. But his part in the intellectual life of Peru was not limited to his inquiries into Indian antiquities; his considerable contribution to Toledo's extensive legislation entitles him to a place among the writers on law and government, although no formal political treatise by him has appeared in print.

These papers remained long in manuscript, but a translation of one of them was printed in the Hakluyt Society's volume of narratives of the rites and laws of the Incas. The following brief extract is from Ondegardo's account of the origin of the Inca kingdom:

Onde-gardo quoted

"It is enough to understand that these Yncas at first extended their conquests by violence and war. There was no general opposition to their advance, for each province merely defended its land without aid from any other, so that the only difficulty encountered by the Yncas was in the annexation of the districts forming Cuzco. Afterwards the conquered people joined them, so that they always had a vastly superior force as well as more cunning in the art of war." [16]

A little farther on in his report, Ondegardo describes the organization of the districts within the limits of the Inca's jurisdiction:

"As soon as the Yncas had made themselves lords of a province, they caused the natives, who had previously been widely scattered, to live in communities, with an officer over ten, another over every hundred, another over every thousand, another over every ten thousand, and an Ynca governor over all, who reported upon the administra-

(16) Markham, *Narratives of the Rites and Laws of the Yncas*, p. 152, Hakluyt Society, London, 1873.

tion every year, recording the births and the deaths that had occurred among men and flocks, the yield of the crops, and all other details, with great minuteness. They left Cuzco every year, and returned in February to make their report, before the festival of Kaymi began, bringing with them the tribute of the whole empire. This system was advantageous and good, and it was most important in maintaining the authority of the Yncas. Every governor, how great lord soever he might be, entered Cuzco with a burden on his back. This was a ceremony that was never dispensed with, as it gave great authority to the Yncas." [17]

IV

Romero's *Colección*

In the first volume of the *Colección de libros y documentos referentes a la historia del Perú*, Carlos A. Romero has caused to be published the *Relación de las fabulas y ritos de los incas* by Cristóbal de Molina, one of the two writers of that name who flourished in the sixteenth century. The author

(17) *Ibid.* p. 155.

of this *Relación* is known as Cristóbal de Molina of Cuzco; the other as Cristóbal de Molina, the almagrist, or Molina of Santiago. Their similar professions and similar intellectual interests and the little knowledge of them that had come to light made discrimination between them difficult, and caused the writings of both to be thought of as the work of one person. The first suggestion that this name applied to two persons, contemporaries in the south-western part of South America, was made by the Chilean bibliographer Tomás Thayer Ojeda in 1913 in the *Revista chilena de historia y geografía.* The distinct individuality of the two persons has been clearly set forth by Carlos A. Romero in an essay prefixed to the *Relación* already referred to. Little light has been thrown on the origin of Cristóbal de Molina of Cuzco. Romero has, however ventured the opinion that he was a mestizo born in Cuzco, where he spent the greater part of his life, and that his father was Francisco de Molina, who, having made extensive journeys about the country, finally settled in Lima and there took

The Molina muddle

ecclesiastical orders between 1545 and 1550. His thorough knowledge of the Quichna language is referred to as supporting the suggestion that this was the language of his mother. He became a priest of the parish of Nuestra Señora de los Remedios del Hospital de los Naturales in Cuzco, and for his preaching to the Indians he received an annual salary of one hundred and fifty pesos, under a grant by Viceroy Toledo.[18]

Indian ways

By a decree issued at Badajoz, September 23, 1580, the king ordered the viceroy to collect information concerning the usage and customs of the Indians before the Spanish conquest. Under this order a considerable body of data was gathered, and on the basis of this Molina wrote his *Relación*, but the date of the composition cannot be established; it must, however, have been late in 1572 or subsequent to that year, since certain events of 1572 are mentioned in the document itself.

It was first published by the Hakluyt Society in 1873, translated from the manu-

(18) See the viceroy's decree in *Colección de libros y documentes referentes a la historia del Perú*, vol. 1, 193–195.

Rites and Laws of the Incas

script into English by Sir Clements R. Markham, under the title of *The Fables and Laws of the Yncas*. It was printed for the first time in Spanish in 1913, in the fifth volume of the *Revista chilena de historia y geografía* preceded by a biography, not of the author, but of Cristóbal de Molina of Santiago. The edition of 1916, by Romero, was printed from a copy in the National Library at Lima, which was made from the manuscript in the National Library at Madrid (E. 13, 135). The other works mentioned as written by Cristóbal de Molina of Cuzco have disappeared.[19]

Molina's rather slight publication presents certain traditions and customs that prevailed among the Indians of the Inca kingdom. The following is one of several versions of the tradition of a deluge:

Molina on the flood

"They say that a month before the flood came their sheep displayed much sadness, eating no food in the day-time, and watching the stars at night. At last the shepherd, who had charge of them, asked what troubled them, and they said that the con-

(19) *Ibid.* chap. XXIII.

junction of the stars showed that the world would be destroyed by water. When he heard this, the shepherd consulted with his six children, and they agreed to collect all the food and sheep they could, and go to the top of a very high mountain, called Ancasmarca. They say that as the water rose, the high hill grew higher, so that it was never covered by the flood, and when the waters subsided, the hill grew smaller. Thus the six children of that shepherd returned to people the province."[20]

A hint of marriage customs is contained in this paragraph from the same source:

Molina on marriage

"When the Ynca gave women as wives, they were received because it was the command of the Ynca. The man went to the house of the girl's father not to say that the Ynca had given her, but that he desired to serve for her, and so the relations of the girl were assembled, and their consent was obtained. The youth remained in the house of his father and mother-in-law for a space of four or five days, and carried the

(20) See Markham's translation in the Hakluyt Society's volume called *Narratives of the Rites and Laws of the Yncas.*

fuel and straw for them. Thus the agreement was made, and he took the girl for his wife; and because the Ynca had given her, it was considered that she was taken until death, and she was received on this understanding, and never deserted."

Cabello de Balboa

Under the title of *Histoire du Pérou* M. Ternaux-Compans published at Paris in 1840 a translation of a part of the writings of Cabello de Balboa. The author had been a soldier before he became an ecclesiastic. He went from Spain to America in 1566. For a certain period he lived in Bogotá, but later went to Quito, where in 1576, under the protection of Pedro de la Peña, the bishop, he began the composition of his *Miscelánea austral*, which, according to a statement at the end of the work, he completed on July the ninth, 1586. Balboa, like many other chroniclers of his time, thought it desirable to begin his narrative with the creation of the world, and in the first two of the three parts into which it is divided he makes no mention of America whatsoever. In the third part he deals with the history of Peru, but at the same time makes fre-

Francisco de Toledo, 5th Viceroy of Peru

1569–1581

quent reference to events that have no relation to the history of America.

V

The development in the southern part of the continent was slower than in Peru. In Chile at the beginning of the half-century in question, a number of garrisoned posts had been established on the southern frontier, where the inhabitants lived in the presence of the hostile Araucanians. Some of these posts grew into towns, but the residents, whether soldiers or civilians, had always before them the spectre of an Indian War; and it was this war that furnished the epic theme of their earliest literature. After the establishment of Valdivia and his colonists in Chile, that country formed a new province, a new centre of local government, within the viceroyalty that had Lima as its capital. The European advance towards the south encountered the stout resistance of the Araucanians, and the experience gained in this conflict appears to have furnished a motive for writing, and awakened a desire to transmit to pos-

Frontier of Chile

terity accounts of the events they had observed and of enterprises in which they had participated.

Portrait of Valdivia

Pedro de Valdivia is not thought of as a writer, yet his letters deserve recognition, whether regarded as stories of great adventure or as sources of the early history of Chile. Warriors are less often given to writing than priests, but when they undertake the task their productions sometimes have a quality not attained by the literary efforts of ecclesiastics. Valdivia wrote as a warrior might be expected to write: he discussed his tasks of military organization, the extreme want he had to face in effecting his settlement and domination in Chile, his labours in the service of the king, and the exasperating conduct of his enemies. His superior spirit as a man appears in the clearness of his language, in his lack of pretension, in his energy, and in an unwearying consciousness of his own high purpose.

Valdivia as a writer

In writing he evidently set down the word that came first to his mind, that seemed to him to be the word for the idea, and made little or no effort to polish his phrases after

Pedro de Valdivia

the manner of the schools. His *Cartas*, therefore, constitute a work that, of its kind, as Medina has observed, has not been surpassed in Chile.[21]

VI

Two other writers of this southern province were Marmolejo and Lovera. They had little literary training, and were apparently not moved by ambition for literary distinction, but simply by the thought that they ought to communicate to their countrymen their first-hand knowledge of strange natural phenomena and unfamiliar social movements, as well as their experience as soldiers.

Góngora Marmolejo

Alonso de Góngora Marmolejo's *Historia del reino de Chile* is an important early narrative of Chilean warfare and adventure. The author went from Peru in a body of auxiliaries, taken by Pedro de Valdivia for service in his campaign for the conquest of

(21) *Literatura colonial de Chile*, vol. II. Five of these letters are printed in Claudio Gay's *Documentos*, I, and in *Colección de historiadores de Chile*, I. The dates of these are September 4, 1545, June 15, 1548, October 15, 1550, October 26, 1552, September 25, 1561. A letter written to Charles V, July 9, 1549, and another to Fernando Pizarro, September 4, 1545, are printed in Barros Arana, *Proceso de Pedro de Valdivia*.

Mormolejo's *Historia*

Chile, where, for a period of forty years, after 1547, he accumulated honours, but saw his wealth gradually decrease. Then, under the affliction of poverty and disappointment, he undertook to set down and leave to posterity an account of the events, in which he had had part, and of the actors who had been his companions. Halted in the performance of this task by discouragement and the fear of criticism, he nevertheless worked on to the last sentence, which announced the fact that his work was completed in the city of Santiago, in the kingdom of Chile, on the 16th of December, 1575. During the brief period of his life that remained after this date, little is known of him, except that he was charged by Rodrigo de Quiroga, noted for his superstition, fanaticism, and intolerance, to traverse the country occupied by the Indians, and to find out and punish severely those guilty of the crime of witchcraft. But as Quiroga appointed Pedro de Lísperguer to the same office on January 23, 1576, it is inferred that Marmolejo's incumbency was short.

But Marmolejo's fears of the critics were not realized. They have found his narrative animated, without the digressions that appealed to the taste of his time, free from tiresome repetitions and never departing from the course of events to picture imaginary customs of the Indians. In spite of distance and time he makes one turn back and live with a remote generation, causing one to experience the impressions the scenes narrated must have made on the eye-witness. His style partakes somewhat of the rudeness of the primitive conquistadores, but is always fresh and spontaneous.[22]

Among the motives that induced Marmolejo to write, according to his own statement, were his sense of the large number of happenings in Chile that should be recorded and that the only written account of them was found in Ercilla's *Araucana*, " not so full as would be necessary in order to treat properly of all of the affairs of the kingdom." [23]

(22) Medina, *Historia de la literatura colonial de Chile*, II, 15; Barros Arana, *Hist. de Chile*, II, 437; *Biblioteca de escritores de Chile*, I, 14.

(23) Medina, *Lit. col. de Chile* II, 14.

Barros Arana on Marmolejo

Without denying the directness and vividness of Marmolejo's narrative Barros Arana points out the technical defects of the composition, the absence of literary art in the presentation of facts, and the lack of due emphasis on the most notable incidents. Marmolejo wrote almost exclusively of events of which he had personal knowledge, whence his chronicle is confined almost entirely to military affairs. He gave little information of any other class of events and left his chronology defective. Writing a personal narrative, he was not careful to fix adequately his dates, thus obliging future historians to have recourse to other sources of knowledge, if they would make a complete history of the period covered by the author's experience.[24]

Historiadores de Chile

Marmolejo's narrative, in printed form, occupies two hundred and twelve pages of the *Colección de historiadores de Chile,* and deals with the events of Chilean history during the forty years prior to 1575. No single extract is likely to reveal much of the author's quality, particularly when the

(24) Barros Arana, *Hist. de Chile,* vol. II, 436, note.

Jerónimo de Alderete

paragraph quoted is translated into a language as far removed as English is from the original Spanish; yet some features of the author's simple and familiar manner may be discovered even in a translation. The following paragraph on Alderete's appointment as Valdivia's successor may serve as an illustration:

Marmolejo on Alderete

"Jerónimo de Alderete having arrived in Spain to negotiate with his Majesty in the name of Pedro de Valdivia, it became necessary for him to go to England, since the emperor, Charles V, had renounced his authority in all his kingdoms in favour of his Serene Highness, Prince Philip, his son, and retired into a monastery of monks; he was not concerning himself with affairs under any circumstances; whence Alderete had to go to England to see the king, who on account of having married the queen of England was in that country. Having arrived there, and the king, having been informed of his coming, after a few days conferred the government of Chile upon Valdivia for life, and furthermore provided that the person whom he might nominate should succeed him. With this order Alderete left England; on entering France he was overtaken by a messenger, sent by Eraso, secretary to the king, who informed him that by letters the king had learned that Valdivia was dead, and it appeared to Alderete that he ought to return and take up his negotiations. . . Having received this news, Alderete returned to London, where the king was; on account of the good mediators whom he had, and by the good opinion which the king held of him, the king showed him the favour of giving him the government of Chile, as Valdivia had had it, and also conferred upon him the order of Santiago and the title of adelantado. Having received these favours, he left Spain for Chile. After he reached Panama, which is, and has been, the cemetery of Christians, he fell very seriously ill with a fever, and died." [25]

VII

Pedro Mariño Lovera

Another Chilean soldier who turned to literary work after a stormy life in the army

(25) Marmolejo, *Historia del reino de Chile*, cap. XXIII.

was Pedro Mariño de Lovera. His *Crónica del reino de Chile* was the product of his later years. He was born in Pontevedra, in Galicia, where his father, Herrán Rodríguez de Lovera, was a life member of the municipal council. Having served for a period in the army, he yielded to the desire for a voyage to the Indies, which he undertook in 1545. From Nombre de Dios he determined to return to Spain, but at Havana he met Pedro de la Gasca, then on his outward voyage to assume the presidency of Peru. The result of this interview was the sending of Lovera with an important charge to Antonio de Mendoza, the viceroy of Mexico. This service was performed so satisfactorily that when Mendoza was transferred to the viceroyalty of Peru, in 1551, Lovera accompanied him to Lima. Here he appears to have intended to establish himself, but his restless spirit urged him on to Chile, then presenting, in the Araucanian wars, abundant opportunities for adventure. After his sojourn in Chile, he returned to Lima. He was in Lima in 1594, and it was in this later period that he

Lovera and Escobar

gathered up his notes and wrote his chronicle of Chile.

In the Jesuit Bartolomé de Escobar Lovera found a person who was able to supplement his work where his literary deficiencies were most evident. In some places Escobar wrote in his own name, or in the first person. While smoothing the rough places in the soldier's composition, he added as adornments of style references to Biblical history and to the history of the Greeks and the Romans. The simple credulity of Lovera, moreover, led him to accept as miracles many events presented in tales by imposters or by persons of exaggerated faith. Santiago mounted on a white horse and fighting for the Spaniards on the plains of Chile, as one of the stock visions, had naturally to be introduced; perhaps also the view of the Virgin taking up a handful of dust from the ground and throwing it into the faces of the Indians to blind them during the combat. But there were certain rare inventions that also found place in Lovera's pages, as when to the members of the war council of the Indians there ap-

Lovera's credulity

Francisco de Villagra

peared 'una gran señora' placed in mid-air, who reprimanded them for their crimes, infidelity, and blindness. The view of this figure caused them to hang their heads in silence for half an hour, and then "to depart each for his own house." [26] These and other miraculous episodes of the book are ascribed in large measure to the influence of the pious Escobar. The latest personal note in the *Crónica* relating to Lovera is found in his vivid account of the earthquake of December 16, 1575, which follows:

On the earthquake of 1575

"At the end of the year 1575, while the city of Valdivia was enjoying the greatest prosperity it had ever known, and the inhabitants were living in peace and happiness, our Lord did not wish that this state of comfort should remain to them, adding new misfortunes to those of the past. It happened then on Friday, the sixteenth of December, at four o'clock in the afternoon, entirely without warning of such a disaster, that the earth began to tremble, with a great rumbling noise, the earthquake continuing and always increasing, without in-

(26) Medina, *Lit. col. de Chile*, vol. II, 22.

terruption causing great damage, demolishing roofs and walls, with such fright of the people, that they were terrified and beside themselves at seeing an event so extraordinary. It is not possible to paint or describe the manner of the furious tempest, which seemed to be the end of the world. Its onrush was such that it gave no opportunity to many persons to leave their houses, and, therefore, they perished buried alive, the wreckage of the buildings falling upon them. It was an event to make one's hair stand on end, and make men grow pale to see the earth in such convulsions and moving with such fury that not only edifices fell, but persons also were unable to stand, and some lay down in order to clutch the ground. After this, while the earth continued to quake for the space of a quarter of an hour, there was seen in the great river, where ships were accustomed to ride in safety, a very remarkable happening, which was that in a certain place in the river the water was divided, one part of it running towards the sea, and the other part up the river, revealing the bottom at that

The tidal wave

place in such a way that the stones might be seen as Don Pedro de Lovera saw them, from whom I got this account, and who affirms that he saw it with his own eyes. After this the sea left its limits and bounds, running with as great velocity upon the land as the swiftest river in the world. And so great was the fury and force of the water that it extended three leagues inland, where it left a great quantity of fishes dead, among which there were kinds never before seen in this kingdom." [27]

(27) *Colección de historiadores de Chile*, vol. VI.

CHAPTER V

LA ARAUCANA

Change of scene, Peru to Chile

In *La Araucana* by Ercilla the theme is no longer the ancient Peruvian state, described by Cieza de León, Garcilaso de la Vega, and Sarmiento, with its autocratic rulers and submissive subjects, but the plains and forests of Chile and the Spaniards in conflict with a people who boasted they had never had a king and had never been subdued, a people sustained by primitive agriculture and proud of their rigid individualism. The time represented by the poem is the period following the death of Valdivia, who had taken possession of that region after the fruitless expedition of Almagro. Provision had been made that in case of Valdivia's sudden death his authority should pass to Jerónimo de Alderete, but if Alderete had already died, Francisco

LA ARAVCA NA DE DON ALON- SO DE ERZILLA Y CV-

ñiga, Gentil Hombre de ſu Mageſtad, y de la boca de los Sereniſsimos Principes de Vngria. Dirigida a la S.C.R.M. del Rey don Phelippe nue- ſtro Señor.

Con priuilegio.

Impreſſa en Madrid, en caſa de Pier- res Coſsin. Año. 1569.

Esta taſſado a tres marauedis el pliego.

de Aguirre and Francisco de Villagra in this order might claim the succession. At the time of Valdivia's death Alderete was in Europe, Aguirre in Tucumán, where he had been the governor of the province for a year and a half, and Villagra was in Chile. In the absence of Alderete both Aguirre and Villagra were urged by their respective friends to assume the duties of the vacant office. The death of Alderete at Panama left Aguirre as the legitimate claimant, but Villagra's presence in Chile gave him a practical advantage in the contest. This dispute and a natural desire to promote the interests of his family induced Andrés Hurtado de Mendoza, the viceroy of Peru, to set aside the pretensions of both Aguirre and Villagra, and to appoint his son, García Hurtado de Mendoza, to be the governor of Chile.

Contest for governor of Chile

Alonso de Ercilla y Zúñiga was a member of the expedition sent by the viceroy to establish García de Mendoza in his office, and to carry on the war against the Araucanian Indians. He was born in Madrid on August 7, 1533. He was the youngest of

Ercilla's family

the children of Dr. Fortún García de Ercilla and his wife Leonor de Zúñiga. His father was a famous jurisconsult, whose writings were read and commented upon in all the schools of Europe.[1]

He became regent of Navarre and a member of the Council of Castille, and tutor of Prince Philip, who was later Philip II. He died at the age of forty in 1534, the year after the birth of the poet. It was a current tradition of the sixteenth century that the mother of Alonso de Ercilla was descended from the kings of Navarre. If this tradition represented a fact, there might be claimed for Don Alonso an aristocratic as well as an intellectual heritage. The seigniory of Bobadilla, which had belonged to his mother, was reunited to the crown, and the seignior became attached to the court of Charles V, where her young son was educated, subjected, doubtless, to

(1) Ducamin, Jean, *L'Araucane*, Paris, 1909, XII. See, however, particularly the volume containing a life of Ercilla in the magnificent edition of the poem published by José Toribio Medina:—*La Araucana . . . Edición del centenario ilustrada con grabados, documentos, notas históricas y bibliográficas y una biografía del autor*, 5 vols. Santiago de Chile, 1910-1918.

the same system of instruction as that under which Prince Philip had grown up. it is probable that Alonso de Ercilla knew the Latin of Virgil and Lucian, but that his knowledge of Dante, Petrarch, and Ariosto was derived through translations. He entered the service of Philip in 1548, and accompanied that prince to Flanders on the occasion of Philip's taking possession of the duchy of Brabant. The route of this journey was through Saragossa, Barcelona, Genoa, and Luxembourg, and the return was by the same way. A little later he went to Bohemia with his mother, who was in the suite of the Infanta María and her husband, the Archduke Maximilian. The young Ercilla undertook a third journey in 1554, accompanying Philip when that prince went to wed Mary Tudor, the Queen of England.

Ercilla's journeys

While in England Ercilla learned that the Araucanians were in revolt, and that Hernández Girón was leading a rebellion against the legitimate government in Peru. The state into which affairs in Peru had fallen during the rebellion rendered the post

Alderete and Mendoza

of viceroy especially unattractive. Two persons to whom the king had offered it declined the honour. It was, however, accepted by Andrés Hurtado de Mendoza, Marqués de Cañete. Alderete, who had been in America, was in England with Philip's escort. From him Ercilla got information that awakened his adventurous spirit, and he left Europe for America with the fleet that carried Alderete and Viceroy Mendoza. He arrived in Peru on July 6, 1556. Here he joined the expedition sent by the viceroy against the insurgent Araucanians. This expedition was commanded by the viceroy's son, García Hurtado de Mendoza, a youth of twenty-one, who had been appointed governor of Chile.

On his arrival in Chile García de Mendoza arrested both Aguirre and Villagra and sent them to Lima. Thus freed from the embarrassing presence of the two rival claimants, he entered upon his campaign against the Araucanians, and on this campaign Ercilla acquired his first experience in warfare with the Indians. To describe the events of the war and his part in it was the primary purpose in writing *La Araucana.*

Ercilla in Chile

In Chile Ercilla found himself under conditions sharply in contrast with those of his life in Spain. A site had been selected for the town of Santiago, and plots had been assigned to soldier-colonists; but fourteen years after the arrival of Valdivia the Spanish occupation was represented only by a number of garrisoned posts confronting a region in possession of vigorous and hostile Indians. Ercilla had exchanged the circumstances of the artificial life of the Spanish court for warfare with a barbarous people in the presence of primitive nature. To a Spaniard of the sixteenth century an excursion beyond the limits of civilization, into the realm of savage life, was a stranger event than a similar experience would appear to a representative of these later generations. In the unfamiliar presence of primitive man and the primeval forest Ercilla was moved to set down his impressions of the life in which he had part, and of the nature that constituted his strange environment.

Ercilla condemned

Ercilla's relation to the commander of the expedition had its unpleasant episodes. On the occasion of a dispute between him and Juan de Pineda, the supporters of each of the two parties drew their swords, when García de Mendoza interpreted the movement as the beginning of a mutiny, and condemned the two opponents to be beheaded. The activity of their friends, however, caused these ill-advised sentences to be commuted to imprisonment.[2] After his liberation from prison Ercilla continued his exploring expeditions and his participation in campaigns against the Araucanians, but he finally returned to Spain in 1562. Shortly after his arrival, having made a report to the king concerning his service in Chile, he went to Austria, where his mother held the position of a maid of honour at the imperial court. Returning from this journey in 1564, he remained a number of years in Madrid and published there the first part of *La Araucana* in 1569. The next year he married Doña María de Bazán, and in 1571

(2) Figueroa's account of this affair, *Hechos de Don García de Mendoza*, p. 103, is translated in Ticknor's footnote, *History of Spanish Literature*, II, 433.

Canto primero.

EL QVAL DECLARA EL ASSIENTO y deſcripcion de la prouincia de Chile, y eſtado de Arauco, con las coſtũbres y modos de guerra que los naturales tienẽ: y aſsi miſmo trata en ſumma la entrada y conquiſta q̃ los Eſpañoles hizieron, haſta q̃ Arauco ſe començo a rebelar.

NO las damas, amor, no gentilezas
De caualleros canto enamorados
Ni las mueſtras, regalos y ternezas
De amoroſos affectos y cuydados
Mas el valor, los hechos, las proezas
De aquellos Eſpañoles esforçados
Que a la ceruiz de Arauco no domada
Puſieron duro yugo por la eſpada.

the king bestowed upon him the order of Santiago.

Ercilla in Italy

Determined to seek further service, he went to Italy in 1574, to join the fleet, commanded by Don John of Austria, designed to proceed to the relief of Tunis, but before he arrived in Naples, Tunis had fallen into the hands of the Turks. At Rome he met one of his relatives, Juan de Zúñiga, then Spanish ambassador near the papal court. On a fourth journey to Austria he was graciously received by Emperor Maximilian and by the empress, María; also by his godfather, Rudolph, who had become king of Hungary. Ercilla returned to Spain in 1577. This was the last of his journeys into foreign countries. In 1578 he published at Madrid the second part of *La Araucana.*

The argument

The argument of the poem is stated in the first two octaves:

> No las damas, amor, no gentilezas
> De caballeros canto enamorados;
> Ni las muestras, regalos, y ternezas
> De amorosos afectos y cuidados:

Mas el valor, los hechos, las proezas
De aquellos españoles esforzados,
Que a la cerviz de Arauco, no domada,
Pusieron duro yugo por la espada.

Cosas diré también harto notables
De gente que a ningún rey obedecen,
Temerarias empresas memorables
Que celebrarse con razón merecen;
Raras industrias, términos loables
Que más los españoles engrandecen;
Pues no es el vencedor más estimado
De aquello en que el vencido es reputado.[3]

Soon after this publication the king sent Ercilla to Saragossa to confer there with the Duke of Brunswick and to persuade him to postpone his visit to Madrid. At the same time the question of the succession to the Portuguese crown seemed to

(3) I sing neither of women, nor love, nor the gallantry of enamoured knights, nor the pledges, the delights, the tenderness of amorous passion and solicitude, but the valour the exploits, the prowess of those intrepid Spaniards who by the sword placed the heavy yoke upon the untamed neck of Arauco.

I shall declare also especially noteworthy acts of a people who never obeyed a king, its daring and memorable enterprises, which with reason merit celebration, its rare stratagems, its praiseworthy resolutions that greatly magnify the Spaniards, since no conqueror is more esteemed than that one where the vanquished is renowned.

portend war, and Ercilla looked forward to playing a conspicuous rôle in the projected campaign, and to celebrating once more in verse the glory of Spanish arms. But the opposition to Spain's pretensions collapsed, and Portugal was annexed to Spain without exploits worthy of heroic song. The poet turned from literary work to religious devotion and prayer, and his tendency to melancholy was intensified in his last years by the loss of his brother, Juan, who was accompanying Philip II. to Portugal, and by the death of his only son, Diego. Somewhat of this attitude of mind finds expression in the last octave of his poem:

Spain against Portugal

Y yo que tan sin rienda al mundo he dado
El tiempo de mi vida más florido,
Y siempre por camino despeñado
Mis vanas esperanzas he seguido;
Visto ya el poco fruto que he sacado,
Y lo mucho que a Dios tengo ofendido,
Conociendo mi error, de aquí adelante
Será razón que llore y que no cante.[4]

(4) And I, who have given to the world without stint the best years of my life, and always by a headlong course have pursued my vain hopes, having seen how little advantage I have derived, how much I have offended God, and,

The poet's mental depression

This mental depression had also a cause in the withdrawal of the king's favour as well as in the loss of relatives and friends and the fact that the poet faced old age without descendants.

In 1589 Ercilla published the third part of *La Araucana*. Some years later a new edition was issued, with two additional cantos, making the whole number thirty-seven.[5] He died in the city of Madrid on the 29th of November, 1594. The statement sometimes made that he died in extreme poverty does not appear to be supported by the fact that at the time of his

recognising my error, give here the reason why I weep and sing no more.

(5) Medina, in his *Edición del centenario* of the poem, gives (*Ilustración x*) a detailed account of all the editions which have appeared, and his work should be consulted by all students or the subject. The dates of the first editions of the three parts of the poem are given above. In 1597 a revised and augmented edition of the whole work appeared in Madrid. It is on this edition, which contains 37 instead of 35 cantos, that all subsequent texts have been based. In his *Ilustración xiii*, Medina prints a complete table of variants and additions. It is significant of the contemporary popularity of the poem that it was actually the sixteenth (of one or more parts) to be printed in Spain or the Netherlands. It should be noted that the seventeenth edition mentioned by Medina, which also appeared in 1597 in Antwerp, does not contain the alterations and additions of the Madrid edition of that year. It may be added that Medina notices forty-eight editions of *La Araucana*, the last having the date 1911.

death he had a household establishment consisting of twelve persons, to whom he bequeathed considerable sums, but with the statement that these sums were moderate, since all of these persons were expected to remain in the service of his widow, and derive advantage from her liberality. Among other bequests were five thousand ducats to his nieces and nephews, and ten thousand ducats as a contribution for the construction of a monastery, where his body and that of his widow might be buried.

The writing of the poem

Some part of *La Araucana* was written amid the scenes, and in connexion with the events, described. In his *Prólogo* Ercilla has stated that he wrote at hours stolen from the occupations of war in Chile, and sometimes on pieces of leather or of hides for want of paper, or on fragments of letters often only large enough to hold six lines; and it often required much effort and trouble to arrange these fragments in their proper order. This method of writing, as the author confesses, gave to his poem in some respects the quality of a journal in verse. This was especially true of those parts that were written during the campaign against the Araucanians, dealing with what he saw or with the events in which he participated; and these parts may be accepted as having the historical authority of a contemporary chronicle. This quality may be more particularly ascribed to the first fifteen cantos, the first published after the author's return to Spain. And these cantos, during the seven years between the author's arrival in Europe and their publication, underwent extensive modification and elaboration. It does not, however, appear probable that much if any of the second part was written in America, but that the author undertook it, "having promised to continue this history." In the preface to the second part he affirms that he has continued it with no little difficulty and ennui, on account of the severity and monotony of the material, "since from the beginning to the end it contains only one and the same subject."

The early cantos

The composition of *La Araucana* was interrupted many times by the author's journeys and his diplomatic services. After

Ercilla's return to Spain the events of the Indian wars and the spirit of the contending parties gradually became indistinct in his mind. He departed from his original purpose "not to sing of love and the gallantry of enamoured knights," and, under the influence of Italian models, introduced invented tales of romantic adventure, leaving the poem, in some sense, a mechanical mixture of historical narrative and romantic episodes.

Ercillo wanted a hero

The Araucanian war presented no leader on either side whose prominence entitled him to be treated as the prominent hero of the conflict. For this reason Ercilla is obliged to allow one figure after another to occupy the centre of the stage. Although his purpose was to glorify Spanish arms, the heroes who have appealed most strongly even to the inhabitants of Chile are the Araucanian chiefs. In the struggle for emancipation from Spain the Chileans were especially incited to action by the heroism of Caupolicán, Lautaro, Tucapel, Colocolo, and Galvarino. Parents named their children after these heroes, and the name of

Lautaro was applied to the patriotic association of the early advocates of Spanish-American independence. Thus the inspiring figures in the narrative of the war are not the Spanish but the Indian leaders. It is quite possible that Ercilla's resentment at the treatment he received at the hands of García de Mendoza prevented the commander's figure from assuming greater importance in the poem.

The magnified chiefs

Lautaro is described as a young man of medium height, solidly formed, with strong limbs and strong shoulders, and endowed with moral qualities not less advantageous than his physical qualities; audacious and unafraid, prompt to act, resourceful and heroic under critical circumstances; when the circumstances allowed him leisure, he knew how to prepare slowly and carefully for a difficult enterprise, to take as his soldiers even the most reckless and villainous of the Araucanians, to subject them to an iron discipline, and to inspire in them love and admiration for a chief who punished implacably with death the slightest infraction of his orders; yet in the story of the

Statue of Caupolicán in Santiago de Chile

love that existed between him and the beautiful Guacolda the poet has revealed the gentler traits of his hero's character.[6]

Caupolicán

In the list of Araucanian heroes an especially prominent place is accorded to Caupolicán, as typifying the strength and pride of his people, their contempt of pain and even of death. Ercilla gives the following description of him in the forty-seventh octave of the second canto:

Era este noble mozo de alto hecho,
Varón de autoridad, grave y severo,
Amigo de guardar todo derecho,
Áspero y riguroso justiciero,
De cuerpo grande y relevado pecho,
Hábil, diestro, fortísimo y ligero,
Sabio, astuto, sagaz, determinado,
Y en casos de repente reportado.[7]

Tucapel

Tucapel is presented as a noisy and fero-

(6) *La Araucana*, Cant. XIII, Oct. 44-57; XIV, Oct. 13.

(7) He was a young and noble warrior, of dignified bearing, a man of authority, grave and severe, a friend and guardian of every right, a rigid and inflexible advocate of justice, of a great stature, massive shoulders and chest, adroit, skilful, powerful and agile, wise, cunning, keen resolute, and cool and calm in unforeseen exigencies.

cious savage, always ready for any adventure, for a fight with the Spaniards or with the chiefs of his own race, unwilling to recognise any authority from any source, opposed to all arguments and to the traditions of his people; endowed with the physical qualities of a Hercules; turbulent, wilful, impious, and boastful of his ability to conquer the world single-handed. Recalling the heroic character of Milton's Satan, the Araucanian heroes are presented by Ercilla in such a form as to excite admiration, although they appear as the determined enemies of Europeans and of European civilization.

Colcolo's speech

But these great chiefs have become less widely known than the less noteworthy Colocolo, whom Voltaire celebrates in his Essay on Epic Poetry, by quoting the speech to the caciques and by comparing Ercilla's Colocolo with Homer's Nestor. Colocolo addresses the chiefs, or caciques, who are contending among themselves for pre-eminence and leadership, and he seeks for a solution of the contest that will preserve the moral equality of the chiefs:

"Caciques, del estado defensores,
Codicia de mandar no me convida
A pesarme de veros pretensores
De cosa que a mi tanto era debida:
Porque, según mi edad, ya véis, señores,
Que estoy al otro mundo de partida;
Mas el amor que siempre os he mostrado
A bien aconsejaros me ha incitado.

"¿Por qué cargos honrosos pretendemos
Y ser en opinión grande tenidos,
Pues que negar al mundo no podemos
Haber sido sujetos y vencidos?
Y en esto averiguarnos no queremos,
Estando aún de españoles oprimidos:
Mejor fuera esa furia ejecutalla
Contra el fiero enemigo en la batalla.

"¿Qué furor es el vuestro ¡oh Araucanos!
Que a perdición os lleva sin sentillo?
Contra vuestras entrañas tenéis manos,
Y no contra el tirano en resistillo?
¿Teniendo tan a golpe a los cristianos
Volvéis contra vosotros el cuchillo?
Si gana de morir os ha movido,
No sea en tan bajo estado y abatido.

"Volved las armas y ánimo furioso
A los pechos de aquellos que os han puesto
En dura sujeción, con afrentoso
Partido, a todo el mundo manifiesto;
Lanzad de vos el yugo vergonzoso;
Mostrad vuestro valor y fuerza en esto:
No derrameis la sangre del Estado
Que para redimirnos ha quedado.

"No me pesa de ver la lozanía
De vuestro corazón, antes me esfuerza;
Mas temo que esta vuestra valentía
Por mal gobierno el buen camino tuerza:
Que, vuelta entre nosotros la porfía,
Degolláis vuestra patria con su fuerza:
Cortad, pues, si ha de ser desa manera
Esta vieja garganta la primera:

"Que esta flaca persona, atormentada
De golpes de fortuna, no procura
Sino el agudo filo de una espada,
Pues no la acaba tanta desventura.
Aquella vida es bien afortunada
Que la temprana muerte la asegura;
Pero, a nuestro bien público atendiendo,
Quiero decir en esto lo que entiendo.

"Pares sois en valor y fortaleza;
El cielo os igualó en el nacimiento;
De linaje, de estado y de riqueza
Hizo a todos igual repartimiento;
Y en singular por ánimo y grandeza
Podéis tener del mundo el regimiento:
Que este gracioso don, no agradecido,
Nos ha al presente término traído.

"En la virtud de vuestro brazo espero
Que puede en breve tiempo remediarse,
Mas ha de haber un capitán primero
Que todos por él quieran gobernarse:
Este será quien más un gran madero
Sustentare en el hombro sin pararse;
Y pues que sois iguales en la suerte,
Procure cada cual de ser más fuerte."

Canto II., Oct. 28, et seq.[8]

(8) "Caciques, defenders of the state, no desire for command persuades me to regret to see you pretenders, to an honour to which I was justly entitled; because, on account of my age, you see, señores, that I am about to depart for the other world; but the love I have always shown you has moved me to give you good counsel.

"Why do we pretend to honourable offices and to be held in high esteem, since we cannot deny to the world that we have been subdued and conquered? And being still oppressed by the Spaniards we do not wish to inquire into this matter. It would be better to turn this vehemence against the proud enemy in battle.

"How great is your fury, O Araucanos, which, without

García de Mendoza

The prominent Spaniards are sketched less clearly than the Indians, appealing apparently less powerfully to the poet's imagination. Yet the sketch of García de Mendoza, the youthful commander of the expedition, appears exaggerated when it is

your knowing it, is carrying you on to perdition? Why are you turning your hands against your fellows and not using them in resistance against the tyrant? The Christians are at your gates, and you are turning the sword against yourselves. If the desire to die moves you, let it not be in a state so low and dejected.

"Turn your arms and enraged minds against the breasts of those who have plunged you into dire servitude, and subjected you to an ignominious condition manifest to all the world. Throw off from your neck the shameful yoke; thus show your courage and your strength. Pour out the blood that remains to you only to redeem us from this state.

"It does not grieve me to observe the ardour of your spirit; rather it invigorates me; but I fear that your courage badly governed may depart from the right path; that, discord having come back among us, you may destroy your country with its force, then, if this must be, cut first this old throat.

"This enfeebled body, tormented by the blows of fortune, awaits only the sharp edge of the sword, since no such misfortune has overtaken it. That life is indeed fortunate which is sealed by an early death. But, considering only our public welfare, I wish here to utter my opinion.

"You are equal in valour and strength; Heaven has accorded to you equality in birth; it has made among you an equal partition of lineage, of station and of riches; and each of you, individually by his courage and greatness of spirit might govern the world. This precious gift, not recognized by you, has brought you to this present situation.

"I hope that the strength of your arm may soon bring a remedy. There must be a supreme chief by whom all may consent to be governed; this shall be the one who shall be able to bear on his shoulder a great log the longest without interruption; and since fate has made you all equal, let each of you seek to triumph by his superior strength."

García Hurtado de Mendoza, 8th Viceroy of Peru
1590–1596

remembered that he was a youth of twenty-one and that some of his actions showed a wisdom not beyond his years. But among the characters that appear in the poem, not the least conspicuous is Ercilla himself. The references to his journeys and explorations throw an important side-light on the early history of Chile. These references, moreover, show him as a champion of the more admirable features of civilization. He opposes the useless cruelty of his compatriots; he is humane towards the vanquished; proud to repel the indignities offered by the commander; religious but not fanatical; a knight of the Middle Ages, animated by a certain pride in enduring the hardships and facing the dangers presented by a barbarous enemy in an unexplored region; a chivalrous hero, but too sober-minded to be drawn into quixotic enterprises.[9]

Ercilla on Ercilla

(9) There was generally a lack of biographical information concerning early writers whether in Spain or in America. One had only an imperfect knowledge of his contemporaries. Cristóbal Mosquera de Figueroa wrote in 1596 that Ercilla was writing a poem on the victories of the Marqués de Santa Cruz, but at that time the poet had been dead two years. For more than a hundred years after Cervantes' death no biography of him had been published. The first one was

Ercilla's limited knowledge of Indians

Ercilla presents the Araucanian heroes speaking to their countrymen as Spaniards might have spoken under similar circumstances. Evidently his knowledge of them was too superficial to enable him to set forth their psychological peculiarities, but he makes their individuality distinct by descriptions of their dress. His lack of intimate knowledge of the Indian mind may be indicated by the fact that apart from geographical terms he uses few words of a local origin or meaning, or that might not have been understood in Spain before the discovery of America. It is not merely descriptions of dress or of persons that certain critics have found admirable, but descriptions of events, of battles, as well. Considering this quality, however, there has existed a wide divergence of judgments, and the extreme unevenness of the poem suggests that some feature of it may be found to justify each view. The course of the narrative is here and there interrupted by

The poet's philosophy

published in London in 1738. Ercilla, however, in a measure provided against such lack of knowledge concerning himself by recording in *La Araucana* many of the incidents and circumstances of his life. See volume containing Ercilla's *Vida* in Medina's *Edición del centenario*.

the introduction of rhetorical speeches, and by reflections that seem to embody a philosophy or views of life, and these views indicate an uncheerful, if not a pessimistic, philosophy. In the fourth octave of the second canto he announces that "the most assured benefit of fortune is not to have ever had it"; and in the first octave of the twenty-sixth canto he finds that "the coming of one good after another is very doubtful, while one evil after another is always certain. The time of prosperity was never lasting, and the time of misery has never ceased." This mournful note recurs frequently throughout the poem until the final lamentation of the last octave.

Barbarian innocence

But in certain passages there are anticipations of the doctrine that prevailed in France two hundred years later, the doctrine of the uncorrupted virtue of uncivilized society This octave, the thirteenth of the thirty-sixth canto, is an indication:

La sincera bondad y la caricia
De la sencilla gente de estas tierras
Daban bien a entender que la codicia

Aún no había penetrado aquellas sierras;
Ni la maldad, el robo y la injusticia
(Alimento ordinario de las guerras)
Entrada en esta parte habían hallado
Ni la ley natural inficionado. [10]

Orlando Furioso

The marked attention given to *Orlando Furioso* in Spain in the sixteenth century made inevitable its influence on Ercilla. This poem was twice translated into Spanish verse in the year 1549–1550, by Jerónimo de Urrea and Hernando de Alcocer, and later a prose translation was made by Vázquez de Contreras.

Seven editions of Urrea's translation were issued before 1564, and Ariosto appears to have been a principal source of Ercilla's inspiration, but the vigorous and positive spirit of the Spaniard was not able to acquire the Italian's gifts of facility, grace, and fancy.[11]

Style of *La Araucana*

A criticism of the style of *La Araucana* is

(10) "The sincere goodness and the expression of affection of the simple folk of these regions, make it understood that covetousness had not penetrated these mountains; neither had wickedness, robbery, and injustice, the ordinary support of wars, there found entrance, nor had the law of nature been corrupted."—This reference is to the island of Chiloé.

(11) Jean Ducamin, *L'Araucane*, LXXXII.

hardly involved in the purpose of the present writing. Concerning this subject reliance must be placed on the judgment of Spanish critics, by whom one will find the excellences and defects of Ercilla's verses sufficiently emphasized. There are stretches of dull and loose narration, but here and there are spirited verses, and octaves as fine as any found elsewhere in the Spanish language; but in this age of rapid movement, in these days of social impatience, three hundred and forty years after its publication, the reading of the poem is likely to be confined to persons who on account of their nationality or for other reasons have a special interest in the romantic history of the Spanish conquest in Chile. It is on its quality as history that stress must be laid. "Ercilla," to quote a French critic, "n'était qu'un historien fourvoyé dans la poésie. . . . Il manquait surtout de sensibilité, de tendresse, pour mieux dire, et c'est selon nous, la grande cause de son infériorité. Il ne parait avoir ressenti vivement que l'ivresse brutale des combats. Il quitte la patrie

A view of Ercilla

sans un soupir, il la retrouve sans un transport. Il n'a fait parler ni l'amour paternel, ni l'amour filial. Les amants et les époux qu'il met en scène sont des raisonneurs froids, sententieux et subtils, et s'il leur échappe par hasard un cri passionné nous y percevons l'écho d'une plainte antique." [12]

In his *Retórica poética*, Barros Arana affirms that Ercilla "describes with ardour" the combats and naturally and correctly the localities, sketches regularly the characters, and puts beautiful speeches into the mouth of his heroes, but his work lacks the plan and the necessary unity of an epic to such a degree that instead of a poem it appears as a poetical history of the war it celebrates. [13]

Popularity of the poem

But in spite of its shortcomings there are few books that have been oftener printed, and, like the other great modern historical poems, it has enjoyed a very noteworthy popularity. Even in recent times new and popular editions have appeared, and in the

(12) Jean Ducamin, *L'Araucane*, LXXXV, LXXXVI.
(13) *Obras completas*, III, 309.

last half of the nineteenth century Alexandre Nicolas translated it into French prose, published at Paris in two volumes in 1869. It had already been translated into German by C. M. Winterling thirty-eight years earlier. An abridged translation into French, by Gilibert de Merlhiac, appeared in 1824. The metrical translation of parts of the poem into English, published in the translation of Molina's *Historia de Chile* (Middletown, Conn., 1808) hardly merits comment. The most striking success of the poem was achieved in Chile, where the people, ignorant of all the favourable and unfavourable contentions of the critics, have regarded it as their Iliad, celebrating the beginning of their national life.

Hechos de Don García

Ercilla's apparent determination to belittle the achievements of the Governor of Chile called forth the *Hechos de Don García Hurtado de Mendoza, el Marqués de Cañete*, by Suárez de Figueroa, who, although not a Chilean, was induced to write on a Chilean topic. His work was an attempt to overtake and smother an advanced damaging report. Don García, when in command of the expedition against the Araucanians, as already suggested, condemned Ercilla to death, a sentence later modified under the protests of persons who comprehended its injustice. After this incident Don García did not find either his leadership or his character glorified in *La Araucana.* This was a source of regret not only to himself but also to his family. He died in obscurity, and after this event his relatives sought to rehabilitate his memory for posterity. They approached Dr. Cristóbal Suárez de Figueroa, proposing that he should undertake the task, should become the eulogist of a person on whom an unfavourable verdict had already been pronounced. He accepted the proposal, and of the seven books into which his work was divided the first three treat of Don García's campaigns in Chile; the others deal with his government as viceroy of Peru, Mendaña's expedition to the Solomon Islands, and the inglorious years of disgrace. In view of the judgments of history, Figueroa's extravagant panegyric appears absurd. It may be said in favour of the book that it presents papers or docu-

Character of Figueroa's book

ments given to the author by the Mendoza family, which furnish details of the viceroy's life not otherwise known. But, on the other hand, it deals with a country which Figueroa had not visited, and with conditions of which he was almost entirely ignorant, thus making inevitable an abnormal perspective and false emphasis. The book is, however, written in "flowing and elegant language that is only rarely found in the historians of America; and in order to add interest to the work the author introduced rhetorical descriptions of a country he had not seen and of battles that were scarcely referred to in the documents."[14]

(14) Figueroa's book was published in 1613, and was republished in the *Colección de historiadores de Chile*, Santiago de Chile, 1864; see Barros Arana's Introduction to the fifth volume of this collection, also *Obras completas*, VIII, 210.

Life of Figueroa

Figueroa was born in Valladolid in 1578. In his book *El pasajero* he narrates the varied vicissitudes of his early life. His father was a lawyer whose family was from Galicia. Envious of the special attention shown his brother and probably for other reasons, he left his home at the age of seventeen, wishing to go to Italy, and expressing in the presence of his parents his determination not to return to Spain while they lived. He studied at Bologna and was there granted an academic degree. From the governor of Milan he obtained the post of auditor of a body of troops operating in Piedmont against France. After the death of his brother and his parents he returned to Valladolid, where instead of an inheritance he found debts and more debts. In Cuellar, as the result of a quarrel, he "was accused of homicide, and long days of imprisonment followed." He subsequently visited Ubeda, Jaén, and Granada. "Here," to quote from *El Pasajero*, "I became desperately enamoured of a rich and noble lady, an only daughter, much courted by suitors, but in spite of my humble condition I knew how to make myself accepted. Her unexpected death caused in me such a sentiment that again I saw myself at the point of death. . . . From Granada I went to Seville, and at Santa María I began a true friendship with Luis Carrillo. I went then to Madrid, where I took my pen, and wrote a number of *borrones*, which the learned with great courtesy honoured. . . . . Tired of life in Madrid, I embarked a second time for Italy from Barcelona. . . This time I had not the least sentiment in abandoning my native soil, where my childhood had been nourished, my boyhood and youth had received training and education, as the first time, thinking that to the brave any part of the world might serve as a country and a home."—Quoted by Medina, *Lit. col. de Chile*, II, 205–208.

The later years of his life Figueroa spent in the public service, particularly in Naples under the viceroy, as auditor; later he was in the department of justice, where his prompt and severe judgments helped very materially to curb the unruly population. The time of his death does not appear to be surely determined. Opinions range over at least three years, 1616, 1621 and 1624.

The prominent position held by *La Araucana* in the colonial literature of South America has made it the subject of extensive comment. References here may be limited to Jean Ducamin's critical examination of some parts of the poem, published at Paris in 1900; *Colección de los mejores autores españoles*, tomo XXI; Medina, *Historia de la literatura colonial de Chile*, I, 1–117; Barros Arana, *Obras completas*, VIII, 174–184; Ticknor, *History of Spanish Literature*, New York, 1849, II, 426–432; and especially the noteworthy publication by José Toribio Medina embracing in five volumes the life of Ercilla, the text of *La Araucana*, and notes, documents, and illustrations, Santiago de Chile, 1910-1918.

CHAPTER VI

ERCILLA'S IMITATORS

I. *Pedro de Oña.* II. *Juan de Mendoza Monteagudo.* III. *Álvarez de Toledo.* IV. *Diego de Santistevan Osorio.*

I

Oña and Ercilla

The model set by Ercilla in *La Araucana* was followed by later writers. Pedro de Oña acknowledged that he was an imitator of Ercilla, and in *Arauco domado* he wrote of essentially the same series of events, events of the Araucanian war; but the two writers emphasized different phases of their subject. Ercilla celebrated the heroism of the Indians, and devoted little attention to the Spanish governor, who was at the same time the commander of the expedition against the Araucanians; Oña's hero, on the other hand, was García Hurtado de Mendoza, the governor of Chile, who had become viceroy of Peru. García de Mendoza's administration of Chile had fallen in the most critical period of the province. In the beginning of 1560 he was recalled from Chile by Philip II, and returned to Spain, where he apparently outlived the disfavour of the crown; for in 1590 he was sent back to America as viceroy of Peru. He was accompanied by his brilliant wife, Doña Teresa de Castro, who took fifty women with her to the capital. This year Oña took up his residence at the University of San Marcos,[1] and his youthful and inexperienced mind was profoundly impressed by the glories of the viceregal court. He was greatly moved by the contrast it pre-

University of San Marcos

(1) The university of San Marcos was founded in 1553, and was at first carried on in the Dominican monastery. Its creation was confirmed by Pius V, July 25, 1571. It received students from without the order, and the presence of these students in the monastery became, in the course of time, a source of serious disturbance, and the university found temporary quarters elsewhere. In 1574 it received the name of San Marcos, and three years later, in 1577, it was established at its present site. In 1580 the rector acquired jurisdiction over the members of the institution, whether students or officers, in all causes, offences, and crimes relating to the University, and thus became competent to bring the academic community under discipline. But before the university had attained its full development, the colonial mind became paralysed by the terrorizing activity of the Inquisition, which had been established in Peru by the decree of January 25, 1569.

LIT. PEDRO CADOT, HUÉRFANOS, 26.

PEDRO DE OÑA

sented to the circumstances of his boyhood on the Chilean frontier, where the Indians were not counted as heroes but as savages against whom one had constantly to be defended. At Lima, the centre of Spanish life in South America, recalling the unpleasant circumstances of his early youth, it was natural that the dominant note of his poem should be a glorification of the Spanish leader, then occupying the exalted position of viceroy.

Oña in Chile and in Lima

Pedro de Oña was the first native Chilean to achieve distinction in the literature of his country. He was born in the town of Valdivia, when it was merely a frontier post, garrisoned by about forty soldiers. He was the eldest son of Captain Gregorio de Oña, who was a member of the garrison. The exact date of his birth is not known, but it belongs to the decade between 1560 and 1570. There appears to be no record stating the place where his childhood and youth were passed, or what were the circumstances of his early education. But on August 8, 1590, he was matriculated in the university of San Marcos in Lima. He must

Oña's education

have had elsewhere preparatory instruction, for the entry in the university books is that he was matriculated for the "Primer de Artes," took the oath of obedience to the rector, and presented certificates of examination. The next year he matriculated for the second course, and in 1592 for the third course. In the absence of any later matriculation in the arts it is presumed that he left the university with the degree of bachelor. He then appears among the troops sent to put down an insurrection that had broken out in Quito. After his return from this expedition he was matriculated in 1593 for the first course in theology, but it is not known how far he pursued his theological studies. Three years later, in 1596, he published in Lima the *Primera parte del Arauco domado*, and on the title page he sets himself down as "Licenciado." This was two years after Ercilla's death.

Arauco domado

The writer of *Arauco domado*, like Ercilla, not only narrated real events in the history of the conquest, but also introduced episodes that were the products of his imagination, and all were presented with a noteworthy facility of versification. But the real events of which Oña was able to treat did not in his time justify the term "domado" in his title. The historian Olivares affirms that Arauco may be said to be *domado* only in desire, since neither in Oña's time, nor for two hundred years later had all the power of Spain been able to effect the subjugation.[2] And Oña's treatment of the events in the process of this war of subjugation was cut short at the close of the first part of his poem, for the announced second part never appeared.[3]

Mental attitude of Oña

Oña shared the religious views of the bulk of his countrymen; in fact, the only persons who showed a disposition to break with the Church were the encomenderos, when they found the priests intervening to modify their treatment of the Indians. But Oña's devoutness was only such as conformed to the current sentiments of the more or less cultivated colonists. It was a phase of Spanish patriotism and presumed hostility

(2) *Hist. de la Compañia de Jesús en Chile*, cap. viii, § 1.
(3) An elaborate analysis and criticism of *Arauco domado*, by Vicente Chaparro, is printed in Eyzaguirre's *Historia de Chile*, I, 472–480.

to the English heretics. It presumed also that those who fell in conflict with the English, whatever may have been the real origin of the combat, fell in a holy cause. Another item in the mental furniture of Oña and those like him was "the dogma of royal majesty," which involved attachment and devotion to the king of Spain, and ascribed to him all the virtues, and especially love for his subjects, in spite of his mental and moral incapacity and his subjection to corrupt favourites. It involved devotion, service, and sacrifice to an ideal that became farther and farther removed from the reality as one Spanish monarch succeeded another throughout the last half of the sixteenth and the whole of the seventeenth century. Proceeding from an author in this attitude of mind, the poem naturally became a very serious production, not defiled by any breath of humour.

A later work of Pedro de Oña which has come to light appeared in connexion with the celebration of the designation of the Blessed Francisco Solano as patron of the city of Santiago. It is entitled *Río Lima al río Tibre.* This poem was printed in the beginning of Alonso Mendieta's edition of Diego de Córdoba's *Vida, virtudes y milagros del Apóstol del Perú, el V. P. Fray Francisco Solano,* which was published in Madrid in 1643. It is based on the account of Francisco Solano set forth in Córdoba's *Vida,* and other material drawn from the early history of the western coast of South America. Medina indicated his appreciation of it by printing it in the text of his *Historia de la literatura colonial de Chile,* and designating it as the most interesting of the author's poems. And the poet himself he characterized as "without doubt the greatest Chilean poet of the colonial period." At the end of his elaborate account he pronounces a general judgment of the man and his work: "As a man, the remembrance of his kindness, his simple and honourable character, his love of his country and family cannot but awaken profound sympathy; and as a poet the verses of *Arauco domado* are destined to be remembered under their double aspect of history and of literature."[4]

Río Lima al río Tibre

El Ignacio de Cantabra

After a long period, during which the name of Oña had passed from public notice, there appeared in Seville in 1639 a poem by him entitled *El Ignacio de Cantabra*, celebrating the founder of the Jesuits, and setting forth the supernatural events which the poet's fancy associated with the spiritual life of his hero. At the same time the author gives some account of the miracles that justified Ignacio's designation as a saint, and presents certain theological dissertations. The action of the poem is clogged by the numerous descriptions of Ignacio's spiritual views and torments, and the poem itself is overloaded with the narration of events that involve supernatural beings. This later work indicates that with advancing years religious ideas became gradually the prepossession of Oña's mind. It shows, moreover, that he had effected a radical change in his system of versification. The verses of his first work ran without difficulty and without apparent effort, but in the last the writer weighed every phrase,

(4) *Historia de la literatura colonial de Chile*, I, 238; see also Jorge Huneeus Gana, *Producción intelectual de Chile* I, 24. (Bibl. de escritores de Chile), Santiago de Chile, 1910,

Quality of *El Ignacio*

sought for transpositions however violent they might be, parodied the poetic style, and polished his stanzas for fifteen years.[5] The poem appears not to have had a second edition, but it is said to have contributed much to enhance and confirm the poet's reputation in Europe.

II

In the course of his investigations in the National Library in Madrid Barros Arana brought to light a poem in manuscript, belonging to the class of historical narrative poems already considered. There is in the manuscript no indication of the name of the writer, but it has been ascribed to Juan de Mendoza Monteagudo. The poem is divided into eleven cantos, containing a total of about eight thousand lines. It deals with the events and the period treated by Ercilla, the wars between the Spaniards and the Araucanians; it is written in the form of verse used in *La Araucana*.

Here is the author's announcement of his subject :

(5) Medina, *Historia de la literatura colonial de Chile*, I, 215.

Mendoza's subject

La guerra envejecida y larga canto,
Tan grave, tan prolija y tan pesada
Que a un reino poderoso y rico tanto
Le tiene la cerviz ya quebrantada.
Y en el discurso de ella támbién cuanto
Han hecho memorable por la espada
Aquellos que a despecho del estado
El gran valor de Arauco han sustentado.

Los casos contaré más señalados
En el discurso desto acontecidos
Entre los españoles no cansados
Y los rebeldes indios invencidos.[6]

III

The expedition from Spain to America, commanded by General Diego Flores de Valdés, left San Lucar on September 25, 1580. It was organized to conduct Gover-

(6) " I sing the long and enfeebling war, so grave, so prolix and so tedious, that it has already broken the force of a rich and powerful kingdom; and also whatever memorable deeds those have performed by the sword who, in spite of the state, have resisted the great valour of Arauco.

" I here shall sing the most noted events that have happened between the unwearied Spaniards and the unconquered Indian rebels."

The poem was published with an introduction and notes by José Toribio Medina at Santiago de Chile, 1888, under the title *Las Guerras de Chile, poema histórico por el sargento mayor Juan de Mendoza Monteagudo.*

nor Alonso de Sotomayor to Chile. It consisted of twenty-three vessels, which carried about six hundred soldiers and a large number of prospective settlers. Among the passengers was Álvarez de Toledo, who was destined to hold a conspicuous place among the colonists, and to add *El Purén indómito* to the literature of the Araucanian wars. Toledo was born in Andalucía. Before he joined this expedition he had visited Norway and had been a soldier in Flanders, and his experience had in a measure hardened him against the barbarities of Indian warfare.

Toledo with Sotomayor's expedition

In spite of a threatening storm the fleet put to sea at the time announced. When the storm had passed three vessels had disappeared, and nearly all of their crews and passengers were lost. The damage suffered by the remaining vessels caused them to return to Cadiz for repairs. Of these only seventeen were found fit to continue the voyage. These finally left Cadiz on November 30. By desertion and disease the number of soldiers was reduced to five hundred and twenty. Among these were officers

The voyage

who had won distinction in the campaigns in Flanders: Luis de Sotomayor, brother of the Governor, Francisco del Campo, and Alonso García Ramón. After they had suffered storms and equally exasperating calms for many long months, the surviving vessels reached the island of Santa Catalina where they halted for recuperation. These were only eleven; six had paid the toll of the ocean. With eight vessels Diego Flores de Valdés determined to carry out the plan of reaching Chile by way of the straits. Sotomayor determined, however, with the three other vessels to take his soldiers to the Río de la Plata, and thence to cross the plains and go over the Andes to Chile. He lost one of his vessels in the Río de la Plata, together with a quantity of clothing and other stores, but all persons on board were saved.

Buenos Aires, at the time of Sotomayor's landing, had the appearance of a temporary camp. A settlement had been made at that point in 1535, but lack of food and the hostility of the Indians caused it to be abandoned in 1538, for the site of the present city of Asunción. Forty-two years later, in 1580, the abandoned site was reoccupied under the leadership of Juan de Garay, and this new town had entered upon the third year of its existence when Sotomayor and his troops arrived. The horses that had been abandoned there nearly fifty years earlier had multiplied rapidly, and now furnished the animals needed for the trip across the continent. Wishing to assume the government of Chile as early as possible, Sotomayor, accompanied by eight persons, set out in advance of his troops, who were left to follow under the command of his brother Luis. He arrived at San Juan, in the province of Cuyo, on April 12, 1583, and on the 29th of the same month he reached the city of Mendoza. In this province, then within the jurisdiction of Chile, he was received as governor. The mountain pass was already closed with snow, and Sotomayor was obliged to remain in Cuyo until September. In the meantime, the troops, those who had not been induced to desert, about four hundred, were en route across the pampas, where they suffered great privation from lack of food and

Buenos Aires in 1583

Overland journey to Chile

through ignorance of the way. They arrived in Mendoza on August 15. "They came without shoes and so nearly naked," as Sotomayor wrote to the king, "that it broke my heart to see them." [7]

From Mendoza Sotomayor sent two messengers over the Andes in July, the midwinter of the South, with confidential communications for the cabildo of Santiago. The mission was designed to set aside the internal confusion and conflicts that had arisen concerning the encomendero's right to the labour of the Indians. It carried to Chile the governor's appointment of five persons to take over the government of the province and conduct it until Sotomayor's arrival at Santiago. Then, without waiting for the snow to disappear from the pass, he crossed the mountains in the last days of September, and immediately on arriving at Santiago he sent Pedro de Lisperguer to Lima with an order from the king, requiring the audiencia, in the absence of the viceroy, to send assistance to the impoverished and distressed colony.

(7) Quoted by Barros Arana, *Hist. de Chile*, III, 27.

Toledo in Chile

After his arrival in Chile Toledo's time was so distributed that war, agriculture, and poetry each claimed a share. He became an alcalde of Chillán, acquired extensive lands stocked with sheep and cattle, and at least on one occasion he suffered the not uncommon experience of having his estate plundered, his cattle driven off, and his herdsmen and shepherds captured. This loss naturally inflamed his desire to see the campaigns against the Indians carried on with energy, and added zeal to his own participation. In one attack he was felled by a blow on the head that caused him to be unconscious for an hour, and to remain for a period without any recollection of the events of the conflict. Later he was engaged in the battle of Yumbel, a detailed account of which he has given in his writings.

Holding the rank of captain, Álvarez de Toledo had part in numerous encounters with the Indians. He appeared also in the conflict between Cavendish's men and the Spaniards on the coast of Chile. In passing through the strait of Magellan Cavendish

Cavendish rescues Fernando

discovered the moribund remnant of the colony Sarmiento had left in that inhospitable region, and took on board one of the colonists named Fernando in order that he might serve as a guide. Fernando finally betrayed the English, in spite of "all his deepe and damnable othes which he had made continually to our general and all his company never to forsake him, to die on his side before he would be false;"[8] for when Cavendish landed fifty or sixty men on the coast of Chile, at the bay of Quintero, in search of wood, Fernando led them into a position where they were surprised and attacked by two hundred Spaniards. Before Cavendish's men were able to regain their ships, twelve of them were killed by the Spaniards. That Fernando was held as a prisoner by heretics has been advanced as a justification of his deception, in spite of the fact that his removal from the settlement by the strait saved his life. Toledo, who was one of the two hundred members of the attack-

Cavendish's men betrayed by Fernando

(8) Richard Hakluyt, *The principall navigations, voiages and discoveries of the English Nation, etc.*, London, 1589, III, 808.

ing party, has celebrated the event in his *Araucana*.[9]

Toledo and the Indians

Governor Alonso de Sotomayor appointed Toledo high constable in 1590. In this period the tranquility of the Spanish settlers was greatly disturbed by renewed hostilities on the part of the Araucanians, whose raids were extended into regions that had been occupied by towns and villages of Europeans. Toledo was alcalde of Chillán when that city was plundered and destroyed by the cacique Quilacán in 1599. On this occasion Toledo was absent, and to this fact is probably due the preservation of his life.

After he had recovered from the shock caused by the news of this disaster, he hastened to Chillán and joined a force that went in pursuit of the Indians, under the command of Tomás de Olaverría, and was later engaged in other campaigns. In 1600 Álvarez de Toledo married Jerónima de Lemos. At that time he was living as an encomendero, or the proprietor, of an estate in the country near San Juan de la Fron-

(9) *Ibid.* 809; Medina, *Historia de la literatura colonial de Chile*, I, 264–258.

tera, where he died on August 3, 1633, leaving his estancia stocked with goats, sheep, and cattle. Other items of his property were three slaves and a vineyard inherited from his ancestors.

Toledo's *Araucana*

Of Toledo's poem *Araucana* only small fragments have been preserved, and the writer's reputation rests chiefly on the twenty-four cantos of *El Purén indómito*, written at least in part during the author's military service. It lacks most of the essential qualities of a poem but is important as an historical document.[10]

Medina characterizes Álvarez de Toledo as simply a soldier who wrote verses with great facility, and who, without any pretension to divine inspiration, sets forth in an agreeable manner the conflict of arms in which he himself had figured, or of which he had received minute information from the accounts of his companions, narrated at

(10) *El Purén indómito*, edited by Diego Barros Arana, was published in Paris in 1862. Some references to the writer and his work are the following: G. V. Amunátegui, *Fernando Alvarez de Toledo*, in *Anales de la Universidad*, 1866, 204; Medina, *Literatura colonial de Chile*, I, 164; and Domingo Amunátegui Solar, *Don Fernando Alvarez de Toledo*, 1898.

El Purén indómito

night around camp fires. He did not propose to present poetic inventions, episodes of the imagination, but to recount only real and accredited facts.[11] His purpose was to write a chronicle in verse, and the product of his labour lacks the chief characteristics of an epic. In his fifteen thousand lines the scene changes from Chile to Peru, from Santiago to Concepción, from the banks of rivers to the sombre depths of the forests of Arauco, and from the strand of the open sea to the narrow valleys of the mountains; and throughout the narrative there is abundant evidence of the writer's memory of details, of the names of persons, of the exact time of events, and even of the colour of horses. Some of his octaves are composed almost entirely of names, and are therefore, practically unreadable, particularly when these names are of Araucanian persons or objects.[12]

The *Araucana* of Álvarez de Toledo is accepted as a credible historical narrative, and equal credibility is attributed to its con-

(11) *Historia de la literatura colonial de Chile,* 1, 277.
(12) *Ibid.* 1, 279.

tinuation under the title of *Purén indómito.*

IV

Ercilla continued by Osorio

It was Ercilla's fate to be imitated not only by writers of talent, but also by a stupid writer who essayed to continue or to complete his epic. This was Diego de Santistevan Osorio, who undertook a work that was designed to be written in the style of Ercilla's poem and to continue the story of the Indian war and Ercilla's part in it. It was called the fourth and fifth parts of *La Araucana.*[13] But in every respect it falls far below its forerunner. Medina characterizes it as the production of a juvenile brain rendered enthusiastic by reading a masterpiece written by one intensely interested in his subject.[14]

Biographical knowledge of Santistevan Osorio is limited to a few facts: that he was born in León in Spain; that he published his principal work in 1597 ; and that he

(13) The complete title is *La Araucana, quarta y quinta parte, en que se prosigue, y acaba, la historia de D. Alonso de Ercilla hasta la reducción del valle de Arauco, en el reino de Chile.* The first edition was published at Salamanca in 1597.

(14) *Historia de la literatura colonial de Chile,* 1, 122.

published another work on the wars of the knights of Malta and the capture of Rhodes.

Character of Osorio's work

The continuation of *La Araucana* is composed of two parts, the first part embracing thirteen cantos, and the second part twenty. One of the noteworthy features of Santistevan's work is the reckless mingling of the Virgin Mary and the characters of pagan mythology. Then out of the depths of his imagination the author calls forth a being whom he designates Caupolicán the Second; and in the course of the narrative one encounters Zoroaster, Dido, Semiramis and Zenobia, not to mention less conspicuous ornaments of ancient history and mythology; and these are all jumbled together in obscure confusion. The independence, the stoicism and bravery that Ercilla found in the enemy do not appear in the Indians as presented by Santistevan Osorio. Here they are timid, shrinking, and brought into battle only by the employment of various incentives. The moral reflections with which the author introduces the several cantos are vapid dissertations on the instability of fortune. The strength and the passion which move heroes to action seem to appear to our author as mistakes of creation.

These early "historical poems" continued to impress their style upon later writers both in Spain and America, and to call American affairs to the attention of the people of Europe. Gabriel Lasso de la Vega wrote *La Mexicana*, published first in 1588 under the title of *Cortés valeroso*. The theme of the poem on Chilean affairs was taken up by the stage in Spain. *Algunas hazañas de las muchas de Don García Hurtado de Mendoza* was a mediocrè work by a number of authors. *Arauco domado*, by Lope de Vega, had Ercilla as one of its characters; he appeared on the stage beating a drum. Other dramas dealing with the same general subject were *Gobernador Prudente*, by Gaspar de Ávila, and *Españoles en Chile*, by Francisco González de Bustos. In the drama by Bustos the baptism of a prominent Indian chief, the empalement of Caupolicán, and the greatness of the family of Mendoza are presented as three of Spain's claims to distinction.

Juan de Castellanos

CHAPTER VII

JUAN DE CASTELLANOS

Castellanos in New Granada

Besides Ercilla and his imitators, already mentioned, a number of other writers in verse appeared amoug the early chroniclers of South American affairs. The most noteworthy of these were Juan de Castellanos, of Tierra Firme, Martín del Barco Centenera, of Tucumán and Paraguay, and Pedro Peralta Barnuevo, of Peru. The position of Castellanos in relation to the literary history of New Granada, or Colombia, may be compared with that of Ercilla with respect to Chile; but the name of Castellanos in the New Granadan catalogue is preceded by that of Jiménez de Quesada, the discoverer of the territory of the Chibchas and the founder of Bogotá. Quesada was born in Córdoba,but his boyhood was spent in Granada, where his father, Luis Jiménez de Que-

Jiménez de Quesada

sada, was a judge. He studied law, and was graduated with the title of licenciado. Under Governor Lugo he was the chief judicial officer of the colony of Santa Marta, and from this post he was advanced to the leadership of the expedition sent to explore the interior of the country. Having established a settlement on the plateau, August 6, 1538, he returned to Europe in 1539. His account of this expedition was called *Compendio historial.* Lucas Fernández de Piedrahita (1624–1688) affirms, in the *Prólogo* of his *Historia general de las conquistas del nuevo reino de Granada*, that the manuscript of the *Compendio historial* was sent to Spain, where he saw it in one of the libraries of Madrid. It is also reported that for many years it was in the possession of the national library at Bogotá, and that the historian Antonio Plaza took it from the library about 1848, and used it in writing his history of New Granada; moreover, that it was lost among Plaza's papers after that writer's death, which occurred in 1854. Parts of it are preserved in the quotations made from

Quesada's manuscript

it by Plaza and Zamora. A few of these extracts have been reprinted by Vergara y Vergara in his *Historia de la literatura en Nueva Granada.* The *Epitome de la conquista del Nuevo Reino*, by Quesada, recently published by M. Jiménez de la Espada, is found to be different, at least in part, from the original *Compendio historial.*

The events of Quesada's march from the sea to the table-land, the coming of Benalcázar from the south, the appearance of Federmann making his way through the wilderness from Venezuela, the meeting of the three captains, and the ceremonies attending the announcement and confirmation of Spain's claim to the land furnished themes fit for romances framed after the model of the *Cid.* The most noteworthy writer who made use of this material and presented it in verse was Juan de Castellanos; but his work, written in his old age, is rather a history than a romance; it is a metrical chronicle of the early history of New Granada.[1]

(1) While Quesada's account has been lost, that of Federmann has been preserved. It appeared under the following title: *Indianische Historia. Ein schöne kurtzweilige Historia Niclaus Federmanns des Jüngern von Ulm erster raise so er*

Juan de Castellanos

Castellanos was born in the little town of Alanis in the province of Seville March 9, 1523. His father was Cristóbal Sánchez Castellanos. He left Spain as a soldier, began his military career in Porto Rico, and was later at Paria and in the islands of Trinidad and Cubagua. He was transferred to the island of Margarita after the earthquake which caused all of the colonists of Cubagua to remove to Margarita. In 1550 he was living at Cabo de la Vela, and a little later he is known to have been at Santa Marta, where he remained until 1552. He was at Cartagena when that town was taken by pirates in 1559. While there, after his long experience as a soldier, he became a priest, at thirty-nine or forty years of age, and was appointed to be the treasurer of the cathedral, but he refused to accept this office, and removed from the diocese. Finally, in 1561, he was established at Tunja as the parish priest. This posi-

von Hispania unn Andalosia auss in Indias, des Oceanischen Mörs gethan hat 'und was ihm allda ist begegnet biss auff zein widerkunfft in Hispaniam auffs kurtzest beschriben ganz lustig zu lesen, Hagenaw, 1557. A Spanish translation was published by P. M. Arcaya, Caracas, 1916. See also C. Klunzinger: *Antheil der Deutschen au der Entdeckung von Südamerika.*

Parish priest at Tunja

tion he held for forty-five years, and during this period at least a part of his means of support was drawn from well-stocked grazing lands. At Tunja he wrote his *Elegías de varones ilustres de las Indias*, his swan-song, as he described it at the beginning of his first canto:

A cantos elegíacos levanto
Con débiles acentos voz anciana,
Bien como blanco cisne que con canto
Su muerte solemniza ya cercana.

The time of his death is not known, but he was living in 1588, since in his writings he refers to events which occurred in that year, and his holographic will bears the date of 1606, when the author was eighty-four years old.[2]

(2) The following bibliographical note refers to some of the critics who have recently advanced our knowledge of Castellanos and his writings:

Acosta, Colonel José Joaquín, article in the third number of the *Antología española*, Madrid, 1848.

Vergara, *Historia de la literatura en Nueva Granada*, Bogotá, 1905, Cap. II.

Fernández Espino, *Curso histórico-crítico de literatura española*, Seville, 1871.

Caro, Antonio, three articles in the *Repertorio colombiano*, 1879 and 1880. Caro discovered the will of Castellanos, which is preserved in Tunja.

The manuscript of the *Historia del nuevo reino de Granada* by Castellanos, published for the first time by Antonio Paz y Melia in Madrid in 1886, was held by the monastery of Poblet for a considerable part of the seventeenth century. Piedrahita used it as well as Quesada's *Compendio historial de las conquistas del nuevo reino de Granada*;[3] in fact, some part of Piedrahita's work appears as the verse of Castellanos reduced to prose. Castellanos' effective literary activity covers the twenty-two years between 1570 and 1592. During this period at the end of which he was seventy years old, he composed the four parts of his chronicle, containing more than 150,000 lines, and another poem on the life, death, and miracles of San Diego de Alcalá

Compendio historial de Granada

Castellano's *Historia*

Paz y Melia, Antonio, *Historia del nuevo reino de Granada por Castellanos*, Madrid, 1886. Introducción.

Jiménez de la Espada, Marcos, *Juan de Castellanos y su historia del nuevo reino de Granada*, Madrid, 1889.

Schumacher, *Lebensbild*, in *Hamburgische Festschrift zur Erinnerung an die Entdeckung Amerikas*, Hamburg, 1892, II, 145–296.

Menéndez y Pelayo, Marcelino, *Historia de la poesía hispano-americana*, Madrid, 1911–1913, in *Obras completas* Vols. II–III.

(3) Melia calls attention to the fact that the manuscript from which his edition was printed is somewhat more extensive than that used by Piedrahita.—*Introdución*, x.

now apparently lost. Although Castellanos announced, in the preface of his *Historia*, his intention to write a fifth part, this design appears not to have been carried out.

Elegias de varones illustres de India

The parts in print until recently were three parts of the *Elegías de varones ilustres de Indias* and the *Historia*. The first part treats of the discovery of the New World, together with the conquest of certain islands and a part of Tierra Firme. The second part has for its subject events connected with the exploration of Venezuela and the settlement of Cabo de la Vela and Santa Marta; while the third part narrates the happenings in the provinces of Popayán and Cartagena from their discovery to the time of the author's writing. The fourth part is the history of New Granada from the time when the Spaniards first set foot on the soil. In determining the form, in so far as the verses are arranged into rhymed octaves, there appears to be no doubt that the poem of Ercilla exerted a powerful influence; for in the preface to the *Historia* Castellanos refers to the persons who, " enamoured of the sweetness of the verse with which Don Alonso de Ercilla celebrated the Chilean wars, wished those of the north might be sung in the same measure." Castellanos' determination to act in accordance with these wishes was unfortunate. The verses are, indeed, in some cases felicitous, but the author was clearly competent to write well in prose, and, if this form of expression had been employed, he would have given a more satisfactory contribution to historical knowledge: it is affirmed, in fact, that he first composed his work in prose, and spent ten years in turning it into verse. If the purpose in this undertaking was to rival successfully Ercilla's literary effort, this also was unfortunate, for neither the excellence nor the fame of the *Elegías* ever attained the standard of *La Araucana*.

On Castellanos' verses

Views of critics

The opinion of the enthusiastic Colombian historian, Vergara y Vergara, does not coincide with this view; he was disposed to think of Castellanos as "a great poet," and to regard him as superior to Ercilla. This is, however, the view of an indulgent and patriotic critic. Moreover, Acosta, also a

Acosta and Menéndez y Pelayo

Colombian, found that no other chronicler exceeded him "in descriptions of the country, or of skirmishes and encounters with the Indians, and particularly in picturing the impressions which traversing the land and going among the people they had to subdue made on the hardy and courageous conquistadores." [4]

Menéndez y Pelayo, referring to the plan of Castellanos' work, affirmed that "it is not really a poem, not even a chronicle, but a vast collection of rhymed chronicles, in which one may distinguish as many poems as there are personages; but whoever has the time and the courage to enter into this forest, will not count his severe labour a loss when he comes upon episodes such as the shipwreck of Licenciado Zuazo, or the dreadful story of Lope de Aguirre (*Elegía xiv*) or the charming description of the island of Margarita." [5] The poetic quality of the several parts of the work differs greatly, the first part being superior to the

(4) *Compendio histórico del descubrimiento y colonización de la Nueva Granada*, 377.
(5) *Historia de la poesía hispano-americana*, II, 18.

rest. The poetic fire of the author burned lower with his advancing years.

Discurso del Capitán Francisco Draque

The last part of Castellanos' writings to appear in print is the so-called *Discurso del Capitán Francisco Draque*, cut out of the third part of *Elegías de varones ilustres de Indias*, and now, in 1921, published at Madrid by the Instituto Valencia de Don Juan. This third part of the *Elegías* deals with the history of Cartagena, and the pages extracted from the original manuscript contain a narrative of the events associated with Drake's capture of the city in 1586. They present as an introduction to the main theme some account of Drake's earlier adventures, particularly of his voyage around the world, 1577–1580. The motive for extracting these pages and making of them a separate document, and the complete history of its vicissitudes are unknown. Perhaps the censor was solicitous to keep from the public an attractive account of an enemy who had wrought such disaster in the Spanish Colonies. But whatever may have been the cause of its long obscurity, its final public appearance in two hundred and twenty-seven clean pages is a source of great satisfaction to persons interested in the early literature of Spanish America.

CHAPTER VIII

LA ARGENTINA

Barco Centenera

Centenera's "historical poem" called *La Argentina* deals with the events relating to Spanish colonization in the south-eastern part of the continent. The first edition was published in Lisbon in 1602. Martín del Barco Centenera was born at Logrosán in Estremadura in 1535. It is reported, or it is a tradition, that he studied at Salamanca, but no positive record of the fact has been found at the university. When Juan Ortiz de Zárate was preparing his American venture, Centenera joined the expedition, and obtained through the Council of the Indies the title of archdeacon of the Church in Paraguay. The five vessels of Zárate's expedition sailed from Spain in October, 1572, and on the 7th of the following January from the Cape Verde Islands.

Voyage to America

ARGENTINA

Y CONQVISTA DEL RIO DE LA PLATA, CON OTROS ACAECIMIENTOS de los Reynos del Peru, Tucuman, y estado del Brasil, por el Arcediano don Martin del Barco Centenera.

Dirigida a don Cristoual de Mora, Marques de Castel Rodrigo, Virrey, Gouernador, y Capitan general de Portugal, por el Rey Philipo III. nuestro Señor.

Con licencia, En Lisboa, Por Pedro Crasbeeck, 1602.

By a storm one of the vessels was driven into the bay of Río Janeiro, and at a conference of the captains of the other vessels with some of the leaders of the expedition it was decided to halt at Santa Catalina. On leaving Santa Catalina near the end of October 1573 it was discovered that the expedition had lost one hundred and twenty of its members by desertion and disease. Having entered the Río de la Plata, the colonists remained for some months on the island of Martín García and afterwards established a settlement called Zaratina de San Salvador. From this place Centenera passed to Asunción, where he arrived on the 8th of February, 1575. He began his ecclesiastical work at once, hearing confessions and preaching to the Spaniards; his labour with the Guaranis had to be postponed on account of his inability to use their language. The language of the Indians was more generally adopted by the Spaniards in Paraguay than in other colonies.

Centenera with Garay

Centenera joined the expedition against the Indians undertaken in 1579 by Juan de Garay, who at this time was exercising the functions of lieutenant-governor and captain-general, with authority delegated by Juan Torres de Vera y Aragón, the legitimate successor of Zárate. The twentieth canto of *La Argentina* contains an account of this expedition. Early in 1580 Garay returned to Asunción and prepared for the execution of his plan to re-establish Buenos Aires, and before his departure from Asunción he appointed Centenera protector of the Indians. At the same time he petitioned the king to provide an appropriate salary for the office. The province of Río de la Plata during these years gave evidence of the turbulent spirit that characterized it later. Opposition to Garay appeared both in Asuncion and in Santa Fe, based on the fact that the viceroy of Peru had not recognized Garay's authority.

Centenera in Peru

A little later Centenera obtained permission to go to Peru for two years. After his arrival at Chuquisaca the audiencia appointed him its chaplain. He held this post, however, for only a few months, and the next year he appeared occupying the position of vicar at Porco. In August, 1581,

Archbishop Toribio de Mogrovejo called his suffragan bishops to a council to be held in Lima, and appointed Centenera one of the secretaries. The clergy of Cuzco had brought charges against their bishop, Sebastián de Lartain, who wished to have the case considered by the council, but the archbishop decided to send it to Rome. Centenera took the side of Lartain, and by this act incurred the displeasure of Mogrovejo, with the consequent loss of his means of support. While under this embarrassment the Bishop of Charcas appointed him his vicar, and the Inquisition constituted him its commissary for the district of Cochabamba.

While in possession of this office Juan Ruiz del Prado, the inspector of the Inquisition, appointed by Philip II, arrived at Lima, and in August, 1590, Centenera, in consequence of Prado's investigation, was removed from office and subjected to a fine of two hundred pesos. In this year Alonso Guerra, who had arrived in Asunción as Bishop of Paraguay in 1585, was arrested and despatched to Buenos Aires as a pris- Bishop of Paraguay arrested oner. The bishop's offence appears to have been a too rigorous pursuit of funds for the Church and threatening to excommunicate the inhabitants of Asunción for delay in paying the tithes. From Buenos Aires Bishop Guerra went to Charcas, where the audiencia rehabilitated him. Later the king appointed him Bishop of Michoacán, where he died in 1594.

Centenera governor of bishopric

The sentence removing Centenera from his position as commissary of the Inquisition made his further residence in Peru undesirable, and thus, after an absence of nine years he returned to Asunción, where he arrived shortly after the popular uprising against Bishop Guerra. As the bishop had been expelled and the dean was dead, Archdeacon Centenera found himself the highest ecclesiastical dignitary in the province, and he became governor of the bishopric, the see being vacant. The date of his departure from Paraguay has not become known and investigation has as yet thrown little light on the last years of his life. Ricardo Palma accepts as a fact that he died in Portugal in 1605, having returned to

Andrés Hurtado de Mendoza, 3rd Viceroy of Peru
1556–1561

Europe after twenty-four years spent in America.

Attainments of Centenera

Not much is known concerning the literary attainments of Centenera. As a priest he must have known the Latin of the Breviary, but there seems to be no evidence of an extensive knowledge of that language, "since in all of his poem there is no indication of the least influence of the classical Latin poets, either in the conception, in the figures, or in the expressions. Even the locution of the poem, wanting in nobility and elegance, proves that the author was not familiar either with the good society or the good poets of his nation, although in one of the passages of his poem he manifests (Canto XXIV) the highest respect for the author of *La Araucana*." [1] He had, however, a certain knowledge of Tasso and Petrarch.[2]

In the archives of the Indies there is a letter, without signature or date, ascribed by Trelles to Centenera, in which the writer, addressing the king, says, "I have a com-

(1) Supplement to *La Nación*, Buenos Aires, Jan 1, 1907.
(2) J. M. Gutiérrez in edition of poem published in the *Biblioteca de la Junta de Historia y Numismática*, v, 260.

The editions of *La Argentina*

plete history which, with the favour of your Majesty, will be published; in it there is given an account of Río de la Plata and of Peru." This reference is set down as the first mention of *La Argentina*. The writer affirms that this letter was written fifteen years after he left Spain; if, therefore, Centenera was the author of the letter it was written in 1587. Fifteen years later the first edition of *La Argentina* appeared in Lisbon (1602). The second edition was published in 1749 by González de Barcia in his *Historiadores primitivos*, Vol. III ; the third is contained in Angelis' *Colección de obras y documentos, etc.*, Madrid, 1836 ; a fourth appeared in the third volume of the reprint of Díaz de Guzmán's *Historia argentina*, Buenos Aires, 1854 ; the fifth is in the reprint of 1900 of Angelis' *Colección*. In 1912 two separate facsimile reprints of the Lisbon Edition of 1602 were published in Buenos Aires, one in the *Biblioteca de la Junta de Historia y Numismática Americana*, the other in the series *Fuentes de la historia argentina*; the former has bio-bibliographical notes by Enrique Peña and a critical study of the poem by J. M. Gutiérrez, the latter notes by Carlos Navarro y Lamarca.

Centenera's spirit

Centenera presented no great characters, like those immortalized by Ercilla. But Ercilla was not an ecclesiastic. Centenera had entered the New World to contribute whatever power he possessed to the destruction of paganism, and any especially strong characters presenting themselves among the Indians naturally appeared to him as exaggerated manifestations of the evil he was commissioned to combat. His mission was to transform pagan heroic qualities into Christian virtues, and not to make them live in the admiration of later generations. What appealed to Ercilla, the knight, as noble and worthy of honour, appeared to the archdeacon as something to be eliminated and forgotten.

The expedition of Ortiz de Zárate or the voyage from San Lúcar to Santa Catalina is described in the eighth canto. It was carried in two small and three larger vessels. In receiving his appointment as governor of Paraguay Zárate had agreed to

Story of the voyage

introduce into the colony a number of labourers as colonists, a quantity of arms, and also a large number of horses, cows, sheep and goats within a period of three years. The greater part of the animals were to be brought from the ranges near Charcas and Tarija. The little fleet halted at Gomera, the Cape Verde Islands, and Santa Catalina; and on this passage from Santa Lucar and during the stay at Santa Catalina the expedition lost three hundred persons. Among the survivors was the Franciscan missionary, Luis Bolanos, who was the first to apply grammatical rules to the Guaraní language, and the first dictionary of the language is attributed to him.

In spite of storms,the voyage was fortunate until the vessels passed into the calm and heat of the tropics, where all suffered to such a degree that they would gladly have returned to Spain. But their sufferings were greatly intensified after they reached the island of Santa Catalina, where scores of Spaniards died of starvation. The ninth canto sets forth the horrors of this episode, and it is dedicated to "las damas."

El canto vuestro es, pues que contiene
De damas y galanes la caída:

Famine at Santa Catalina

Centenera exposes the details of the famine, pointing out that every animal and reptile, however repugnant at first, was at last found to be as savoury as the flesh of a kid, for

La gran hambre prestaba salmorejo.

The extremes to which men were driven by hunger are narrated at length, the crimes committed to obtain food, and the unusual punishments meted out to the criminals who were detected. But many escaped detection. Some persons encountered a dog alone. They killed him immediately, and without waiting to have him well cooked or roasted, devoured him, in order to avoid being recognized as the offenders by the arrival of the owner. Another person, having stealthily entered an inn kept by two women, was apprehended by them; then without pity they cut off his ears, and nailed them up on the house, either for decoration or as a warning to other thieves.

Recognizing that they had acted without justice, and that they ran a risk of being punished, they returned the ears to their owner accompanied by a quantity of food sent "to shut up his mouth."

Last stage of the voyage

Zárate, having determined to proceed to Río de la Plata, sought from every source food to serve for the voyage, and in this search the Indians were deprived of whatever they possessed. By this their goodwill was completely alienated. The incidents of the voyage and the landing constitute the theme of the tenth canto. The company had apparently not learned by their experience to view with calmness the varying phases of the sea, and when the sparkling waves rose to the stars, the women wept and the men uttered great cries, all assured that they were to be buried in the ocean. And after the storm had subsided, and they had approached the port of San Gabriel, a furious south wind arose, wrought havoc in the rigging of the vessels, and drove one of them upon the shore. Thus after a day of joy the passengers were overwhelmed in grief and agony (Canto x, Oct. 14):

Pilotos y maestres, marineros,
Grumetes, pajes, frailes y soldados,
Mujeres y muchachos, pasajeros,
Andaban dando voces muy turbados.

Among the Charrúas

Having landed, after the storm, they found themselves among the Charrúas, who seemed to Centenera to possess qualities that entitled them to be ranked with the Araucanians (Canto x, Oct. 27).

La gente que aquí habita en esta parte
Charruahas se diçen, de gran brío,
A quien ha repartido el fiero Marte
Su fuerza, su valor y poderío. . . .

Es gente muy crecida y animosa,
Empero sin labranza y sementera:
En guerras y batallas, belicosa,
Osada y atrevida en gran manera.

The Charrúas occupied the region between Maldonado and the Uruguay. They had met with hostility the earlier explorers of the Río de la Plata, and they continued in hostile relations with the Europeans until they were finally exterminated in 1831.

Fight with the Indians

In an encounter between the forces of the chief Zapicán and Zárate's soldiers, all but a few of the Spaniards were either killed or captured by the Indians. Centenera presents an abundance of details concerning this encounter, and refers to the action of Zapicán's forces in the following spirited lines (Canto XI, Oct. 18):

El zapicano ejército venía
Con trompas y bocinas resonando ;
Al sol la polvareda obscurecía,
La tierra del tropel está temblando:
De sangre el suelo todo se cubría,
Y el zapicano ejército gritando,
Cantaba la victoria lastimosa
Contra la gente triste y dolorosa.[3]

Character of *La Argentina*

La Argentina must be viewed in its two aspects, as poetry and history, and the passages illustrating these two phases are widely different in spirit, even when the unlike passages are both founded on a basis

(3) The army of Zapicán came with trumpets and resounding bugles ; the dust obscured the sun, the earth trembled under the tramping of many feet; all the soil was covered with blood, and Zapicán's warriors shouted the songs of the lamentable victory over the sad and sorrowing people.

of facts. But in the poetic figures there are fewer references to the fancies of pagan literature and mythology than may be found in the other poems with which Centenera's work may be compared. Now and then the writer's lamentations, raised to heaven because of the want and misery of the company, reveal the ecclesiastic and suggest passages of the Psalms.

Volved con piedad, Señor, la mano,
Doleos de los tristes afligidos,
Doleos de los niños inocentes,
Que gritan con sus ojos hechos fuentes,
Doleos de las tristes afligidas
Que quedan sin abrigo y compañía:
También de las doncellas doloridas
Que pierden a sus padres y alegría.[4]

From battles with the Indians in the region of Río de la Plata, the founding of Buenos Aires by Juan de Garay, and the insurrection of the mestizos at Santa Fe, Centenera,

(4) Stretch out thy hand, O Lord, with mercy; pity those who are sad and afflicted; pity the innocent children, who cry with their eyes made fountains. Pity the women who are sad and afflicted, who are without protection and fellowship; also the sorrowing maidens who have lost their fathers and joy. Canto xi, Oct. 30.

Topics of later cantos

in his later cantos, turned to happenings of his time on the western coast, to the exploits of Francis Drake, the earthquake of Arequipa, and the council at Lima called by Archbishop Mogrovejo. This change of subject appears to have been due to the writer's removal from the south-eastern province to Peru. Drake had appeared about five years before this event, whence it may be presumed the very favourable opinion of him expressed in *La Argentina* was that entertained by at least a part of contemporary Peruvian society. Centenera found "this English and noble cavalier, given to the art of the sea, a skilful pilot and sailor, a good soldier, astute, sagacious, discrete, courteous, well-bred, brave, magnanimous, and a good friend, but wanting in the greater and more necessary quality, *que es el amor a Jesucristo.*" Centeñera, as an ecclesiastic, was obliged by the spirit of the Spanish Church in the sixteenth century to make this limitation on the character of a Protestant. It is noteworthy, however, that he was able to discover so much excellence in a subject of the

"Babylonian woman"; still this is partially accounted for when it is recalled that the Spaniards in America regarded their calamities, whether brought about by an English corsair or an earthquake, as a divinely directed punishment for their shortcomings, and in this view the piratical agent of God might appear to stand nearer the throne of heaven than those who suffered the infliction. But they feared the invader not merely for his direct influence, but as well for the influence he might have in awakening the spirit of revolt among the Indians.

Spaniards' views of their calamities

In the beginning of the twenty-third canto Centenera expresses his wish to write of what he saw in Peru during the meetings of the council called by Archbishop Mogrovejo. This was the council that met on August 13, 1582, and held its last session on October 18, 1583. Its purpose was to reform the discipline of the Church and to correct the manners and customs of this part of the continent, but it was brought near to disruption through the introduction of a question in dispute between the Bishop and Canons of Cuzco.

Dress reform in Lima

But the council acquired a difficult task when it undertook to reform the dress of the women of Lima. It was the fashion for the women to appear in the streets, in the churches, and in other public places with their faces completely concealed by the rebozo. While protected by this veil it was impossible for their identity to be observed or detected, whence arose numerous abuses and scandals. Centenera refers to their conduct: "In the streets and the square, they place themselves at the windows, where it is a pleasure to see them, with their rich and very gay dresses, and whoever wishes may speak with them; they do not appear shy or severe, and listen to whomsoever wishes to flirt with them, and under their rebozos they utter their little nothings, with which they sometimes fool little boobies." A proposition in relation to the conduct of the women and their manner of dressing was brought before the council, which threatened with excommunication those who persisted in wearing the rebozo to conceal the face. Women should remain in their houses, or, if they appeared in

El Marqués de Guadalcázar, 13th Viceroy of Peru
1622–1629

Decree of church council

public places, it should be with their faces uncovered. For the time being the majority of the women preferred to remain in their houses, but a few of the rich, not objecting to the regulation, appeared in public unveiled, for it gave them an opportunity to display their jewels. The resolution of the council was, however, ineffective; the use of the rebozo as a veil was continued. But about forty years later the Marqués de Guadalcázar as viceroy (1622-1629) issued a royal ordinance, providing that "no woman of whatever state, quality, or condition she may be, may be veiled with a manto or in any other manner while going on the streets of this city, or the alameda or other public places, whether on foot or in a carriage or a sedan chair, or in balconies or windows, but that all shall be obliged to go with their faces uncovered, to the end that they may be seen and known, and the identity of each be recognized."[5]

The real character of *La Argentina* is that of a contemporary chronicle, and considering the breadth of his experience, the

(5) Mendiburu, *Apuntes históricos del Perú*, p. 78.

writer's serious mistake was that he adopted the form of verse instead of prose for communicating his experience and his observations. But in his dedication to the governor of Portugal, then united with Spain, Centenera affirms that he has written in verse, although "poco polido y menos limado," in order that the Marqués de Castel Rodrigo, burdened with the grave affairs of the government, might read it with greater facility than the long and prolix histories he was accustomed to receive. The fact that it is written in verse is perhaps the principal reason for including it in a list with *La Araucana;* moreover, like *La Araucana,* it deals with a colonial undertaking, the privations incident to a voyage from Spain, and conflicts with the Indians. Juan María Gutiérrez finds its indisputable merit in the frank sincerity with which the author communicates what he saw and what he felt, and in this manner presented important data for the early history of Río de la Plata.

Centenera's motive in writing in verse

Nature of poetry

If one conceives of poetry not as the written metrical lines merely, but as these lines uttered orally, he will have no difficulty in answering the question critics have raised regarding the nature of the foregoing metrical compositions. In this view, the words written in measured lines may be compared with printed musical notes. These notes are not music, but only directions for the production of vocal or instrumental sounds, or combinations of sounds, which constitute music. In like manner, the verses that stand on the printed page are indications of tone, accent, and rhythm, and poetry is the utterance of these verses in accordance with their proper indications. Endowed with a certain form and degree of cultivation, one may derive sensations akin to those enjoyed in listening to music, by reading the printed musical notes; and in the same way by passing the eye silently over the printed verses one may experience some of the emotions poetry is designed to awaken; but in neither case are the emotions experienced more than a faint shadow of those aroused by the voice of the skilful reader or by the violinist or the orchestra. Poetry thus conceived is not the utterance of any

Poetry and music

distinct and exclusive body of ideas, or of ideas that cannot be expressed except in metrical language. There are no ideas set forth in the *Iliad* or in *Childe Harold* that cannot be expressed in prose, and the same may be said of *La Araucana* or *Arauco domado*, treating not of the Trojan war, but of the war against the Araucanians.

What of *La Araucana*?

Exalted ideas, or striking images, or mere commonplace thoughts may be presented in prose, and verse possesses the same capacity; the main difference between them would, therefore, seem to be that in verse alone the words are selected so as to conform in their utterance to a prescribed measure. Inevitably in different verses there is a more or a less complete compliance with this rule; and this is characteristic of the verses in question, as well as of many other verses; but when the perfect verses of *La Araucana* or *Arauco domado* are pronounced in their sonorous Spanish tones there is no doubt that we have before us examples of poetry.

CHAPTER IX

WRITERS ON CHILEAN HISTORY

1600–1650.

I. *Alonso González de Nájera.* II. *Francisco Núñez de Pineda Bascuñán.* III. *Caro de Torres.* IV. *Melchor Xufré del Águila.* V. *Alonso de Ovalle.* VI. *Miguel de Aguirre.* VII. *Francisco Ponce de León.* VIII. *Diego de Rosales.* IX. *Santiago de Tesillo.*

I

At the beginning of the seventeenth century, sixty or seventy years after the occupation of Peru, New Granada and the region of the Río de la Plata and its tributaries, the Spanish colonies of South America had acquired their early form of organization. Peru was under the government of a viceroy, whose jurisdiction was nominally co- Spanish South America organised

Heads of the governments

extensive with Spain's possessions in South America; but in New Granada, Chile and the south-eastern provinces other centralized governments had been established, subordinated to the viceroy in certain particulars and directly dependent on the king in other respects. The head of each of these subordinate governments was known as governor, captain-general, or president as one or another of his principal functions was considered.

As governor he was head of the civil administration, as captain-general he was chief of the army or the militia, and his title of president indicated his relation to the audiencia, a body that performed both administrative and judicial functions and in case of a vacancy in the governor's office exercised the chief executive power in the dependency. At that time, moreover, a number of towns had acquired sufficient importance to have local governments consisting of a cabildo, or council, composed of regidores and two alcaldes, the alcaldes serving as justices of the peace and local executives. The occupation of the several districts by the Spaniards was at first a military occupation, a large number of the settlers were primarily soldiers, and their settlements were largely garrisoned posts. In this respect the beginning of the Spanish colonies in America presents a strong contrast with the British colonies, in which the colonists were almost all civilians.

Common ideas of the colonies

The political relations that existed among the Spanish colonies and the common dependence of the colonies on Spain presumed their possession of common ideas and purposes; and the writers who appeared in the different provinces generally observed affairs from a common point of view. The question of the time of their appearance deserves rather to be considered than the place of their residence. This is, of course, pre-eminently true of writers who were ecclesiastics. The Jesuits of Peru, New Granada, or Chile, for instance, wrote rather as Jesuits than as citizens of one province or another. The case of the soldier in this respect was not greatly different from that of the ecclesiastic, and in the first and middle period of the colonial history the larger part of the writers who were not ecclesiastics were soldiers.

Isolation of the colonies

The long intervals between the sailings of vessels from Spain to America, or from America to Spain, made it extremely difficult for the king and the Council of the Indies to have correct information concerning the affairs of the Spanish dependencies. If the colonists wished an unworthy official removed or legislation reformed, it was necessary to send an agent to Madrid to enlighten the king and to persuade him to order the desired change. The difficulties of securing reforms by this method were very great; the long waiting for the departure of a ship, the weary weeks of the voyage from Chile around Cape Horn or over the Andes, across the Argentine plains, and by ship from Buenos Aires, or by way of Peru and the Isthmus, the interminable delays in obtaining an audience with the king or the Council of the Indies, the years sometimes spent by the authorities in reaching a decision regarding the proposition, and then the similar waiting and delays in securing the transmission of the decrees to

America, in case the question was found to be of sufficient importance to warrant action by the supreme government. Priests were often found available for missions of this kind, for various reasons: they were presumed to be educated persons competent to present a case before the high authorities; they were supposed to have the confidence of the king; and it was assumed, in keeping with the rules of their profession, that they were not encumbered with families, and thus freer from bonds holding them to any given place than most secular persons. In the early part of the seventeenth century the Chileans departed from this practice, and selected a soldier, Alonso González de Nájera, to represent them before the king.

Missions to Spain

González de Nájera arrived in Chile in 1601, and passed almost immediately into service on the frontier, to a fort constructed on the Bio-Bio. He remained five years in this service, and during this period acquired extensive information concerning the most vital affairs of the province. In Madrid he rendered to the authorities an account of

Nájera's *El desengaño y reparo de la guerra del reino de Chile*

his observations and experience, and in this manner set forth the conditions of society and the government in Chile. From Spain he was sent to Italy where he completed his work called *El desengaño y reparo de la guerra del reino de Chile*. Regarding this work he affirms that he has not written a history as a consecutive narrative, but reasoned opinions and discourses on the points most essential for the support of the conquest in the kingdom of Chile.[1]

The title given by Nájera to his writing indicates his opinion that the directors of Chilean affairs had been deceived, and that he would undertake to show them their error. He presents a review of the state of the war, and proposes the means that appear to him most suitable for terminating it. In inquiring into these means he finds it especially important that the decree providing for the enslavement of the Araucanians should be maintained in force. Nájera's work was finally published in Madrid, in 1866, in the Volume XLVIII of the *Colec-*

(1) Medina, *Lit. col. de Chile*, II, 319.

ción de documentos inéditos para la historia de España.[2]

II

Pineda y Bascuñán

Among the soldiers of the early part of the seventeenth century who became writers, Francisco Núñez de Pineda y Bascuñán, a native of Chile, acquired a position of distinction. He was born in 1607. His father was a soldier, who for more than forty years was engaged in military campaigns on the frontier. Francisco's school years prior to the age of sixteen were passed in the house of the Jesuits at Arauco. During these years he received instruction in Latin and such elements of philosophy as were then given in the schools. At the age of sixteen he left the school and was given a place in a company of Spanish infantry. In a battle with the Indians he was severely wounded and captured. During the seven months of his captivity his amiability and his friendly intercourse with the Indians immediately in charge of him saved him from the machinations of those who wished

(2) Medina, *Literatura colonial de Chile*, II, 318-21.

to take his life. He returned to the troops and was later promoted to the rank of maestre de campo. After his long military service he found himself in extreme poverty in the last years of his life. Finally he received from the viceroy an appointment as corregidor in Peru, where he died in 1682, before he had derived any advantage from the office that had been conferred upon him.

Cautiverio feliz

The anxieties of his old age in poverty appear to have been relieved by his recollection of the kindness he had received at the hands of his captors, and in this period he wrote of the adventures of his youth, and of his reflexions on the Spanish military system as applied in Chile. These were the general topics of his book called *Cautiverio feliz y razón de las guerras dilatadas de Chile.* This book was "one of the works most extensively read in Chile and even in Peru during the colonial period."[3] It contains a

(3) Medina, II, 354. In a critical note Barros Arana characterizes Bascuñán's work as diffuse, commonplace, and heavy, when he enters upon his eternal digressions and moral philosophy, but his style takes on an air of simple animation, when he recalls certain details of domestic life or describes certain localities; and in the critic's opinion it "ought to occupy an important place in the modest history of our

record of the honourable service of a valiant and faithful soldier, and was rendered especially attractive by the story of the author's captivity. But, in keeping with the spirit of his time, he departed from the plan of a simple narrative and undertook to impart moral and religious instruction and to make a display of erudition. This defect is recognized by Medina, who affirms that if the author had limited himself simply to relating in his admirably simple and true style the story of his adventures among the Indians of Arauco, his work would have merited a place in the literature of any of the most cultivated nations of any time.[4] Still he has been able to give a dramatic interest to his narrative by keeping alive in the reader's mind the inquiry whether Maulicán who promised to secure his escape, or the caciques who proposed to kill him, will be successful. One of the objects of the author in writing this book was to set forth the manner in which the war was conducted in Chile and the fate of those who became

Quality of Bascuñán's book

colonial literature." Introduction to *Cautiverio feliz* in *Colección de historiadores de Chile*, III.

(4) Medina, *Literatura colonial de Chile*, II, 334.

victims of the injustice committed in this war, and at the same time to show the causes that made the Araucanian war interminable. In this part of the work he made use of his own experience, revealing by his narrative the repeated abuses and instances of neglect that contributed to keep the Indians on a war footing. This feature of the narrative throws an especially important side light on the Spanish administration of Chilean affairs.

The verse in *Cautiverio feliz*

Throughout the *Cautiverio feliz* there are various passages in verse, some of which are translations from the poetical books of the Bible, or from Virgil, Horace, Ovid, or other poets, or are original verses written by Bascuñán. Eyzaguirre calls attention to the fact that while in some of these original verses there are "elevated ideas and a sublime conception," in "almost none of them does the author sustain the elevation of thought to the end," and cites as an instance the sonnet to the Virgin on his release from captivity. "At the first glance," he writes, "one recognizes the notable difference between the last part, ordinary and common place in its conceptions as well as disagreeable in its rhythm and the rest of the composition which is certainly beautiful and majestic."[5] The following is the sonnet in question (Discurso V, cap. xiv):

Illustrative sonnet

¿Quién hay, Señora, que valerse quiera
De vuestro santo nombre, que no alcance
Con lágrimas orando al primer lance
Lo que imposible al tiempo pareciera?

¿Quién hay que en vuestras manos se pusiera,
Virgen sagrada, en peligroso trance,
Que en el mayor trabajo no descanse,
Y su esperanza fin dichoso adquiera?

Bien manifiesto está en mi larga suerte,
Pues que entre tantos bárbaros contrastes
Quisistéis libertarme de la muerte.

Gracias os doy ya fuera de debates,
Estimando el favor, y si se advierte,
Jamás imaginado entre rescates.

LAUS DEO.

(5) *Historia de Chile*, I, 491.

III

Torres on Sotomayor

When Caro de Torres undertook to write his *Relación de los servicios de Don Alonso de Sotomayor*, he had the advantage of a full knowledge of his subject. He had long stood in intimate friendly relations with the governor, and their similarity of inclinations and tastes had established between them bonds of respect and sympathy. Torres was born in Seville about the middle of the sixteenth century. His early studies were made in his native city, whence he passed to the University of Salamanca. From the university, which he left prematurely owing to a quarrel with other students, he entered the army, served in Italy under the Marqués de Santa Cruz, and in 1583 under the same leader played a gallant part in the campaign of the Azores. Two years later he was in Seville, where Viceroy Torres was preparing to depart to assume the duties of his office in Peru. Caro de Torres' adventurous spirit induced him to join the expedition. He arrived at Lima on the 30th of November,

Torres' career

1586. During the period of his military service he found time to acquire knowledge of Spain's colonial enterprise in the Indies. The next year Thomas Cavendish appeared in the Pacific, and Caro de Torres was a member of the expedition that was sent against him. A few months later commissioners from Alonso de Sotomayor, the governor of Chile, arrived in Lima, requesting reinforcements for the defence of the Chilean coast and for proposed campaigns against the Araucanians. Responding to this request, the viceroy sent two companies of five hundred soldiers each, under Luis de Carvajal and Fernando de Córdova. Caro de Torres, with the rank of captain, was the second in command of one of these companies, and during this campaign began the long continued friendship between him and the governor Sotomayor. But shortly after this the soldier of many adventures entered the order of St. Augustine. The success of Sotomayor's military enterprises secured his appointment to the post of governor, captain-general, and president of the royal audiencia of Panama,

Soldiers from Lima to Chile

where he was associated with Caro de Torres, and this association was maintained after Sotomayor returned to Spain. When Sotomayor was about to die he charged his friend with the duty of watching over the interests of his family. Holding in memory this long and faithful friendship, and in possession of the documents relating to Sotomayor's political career, Caro de Torres wrote his *Relación de los servicios de Don Alonso de Sotomayor.*[6]

Torres' *Relación*

The significance of this work is solely in the importance of the subject, in the fact that it involves in its narrative a large number of events relating to one of Chile's more distinguished governors. It deals with three phases of Sotomayor's life; his career before he became governor, his administration in Chile, and his activity as governor-general of Panama, together with his retirement in Spain, but all with a minimum of

(6) The following is the complete title: *Relación de los servicios que hizó a su majestad del rey don Felipe segundo y tercero, don Alonso de Sotomayor del Abito de Santiago, y Comendador de Villamayor del Consejo de Guerra de Castilla, en los estados de Flandes y en las provincias de Chile, y Tierra Firme, donde fué capitán general, etc., dirigida al rey don Felipe III nuestro señor, por el licenciado Francisco Caro de Torres*; Madrid, 1620, 4to.

literary skill and method. About half of the bulk of the book consists of documents introduced into the text. These documents, while they interrupt the narrative, give a certain importance to the work. In 1629, nine years after the appearance of the *Relación*, Caro de Torres published in Madrid an imposing folio on the *Historia de las órdenes militares de Santiago, Calatrava y Alcántara, desde su fundación hasta el rey don Felipe segundo, administrador perpétuo de ellas*. In spite of the fact that this book would not seem to appeal to many persons, it met a noteworthy approval in its day, and added to the reputation of its author.[7]

Torres on military orders

IV

In Chile the Araucanian Indians continued yet many decades to menace the security of Spanish settlers, and the campaigns against them continued to furnish a theme for writers. A product of this state of affairs was Melchor Xufré del Águila's *Com-*

(7) Caro de Torres' *Relación de los servicios de Don Alonso de Sotomayor* is available in the *Colección de historiadores de Chile*, v. It occupies about eighty large octavo pages of that volume.

Águila's *Compendio historial*

pendio historial del descubrimiento, conquista y guerra del reino de Chile. Águila accompanied at his own expense the expedition to Peru led by García Hurtado de Mendoza, after that officer had been appointed to the post of viceroy. On their arrival in America the members of the expedition were discouraged by the bad news received concerning the attitude assumed by the Indians. Águila joined the troops that were sent to Chile. He entered upon the campaign under an agreement with the viceroy that he would pay his own expenses, and that he might withdraw and return to Peru whenever he desired. Later, however, he sought from the king a certain remuneration for his services, preferably in the shape of a governmental office or the position of a corregidor. He had not only rendered military services but, at his own expense, had caused supplies to be introduced into Concepción to avert impending famine.

Águila joins the troops for Chile

At the time of his withdrawal from the campaign against the rebellious Indians he had been wounded several times, and had

had one of his legs broken. In his retirement he began to write of the events in which he had had part and those that had happened under his observation.

In 1612 he was elected an alcalde in the municipal council of Santiago, and later, enjoying the confidence of Governor Ribera, he was entrusted with various public commissions. In March of the same year, 1612 a new policy respecting the Indians was proclaimed. It provided that the government should adopt a plan of defence, instead of continuing campaigns for invading Araucanian territory, and the river Biobio should be the boundary line between the territory of the Spaniards and that of the Indians. The Spaniards were to maintain their forces armed and equipped, but they were to be used only for defensive operations. Águila, now an encomendero at Santiago, was the most vigorous opponent of this policy; and the Jesuit Valdivia, the most prominent advocate of it, complained of Águila's opposition in his memorial to the king.

Chilean defensive policy

In the years subsequent to his military

activity there is little known of the events of Águila's life, but, after forty years in Chile, he published in 1630 at Lima his *Compendio historial del descubrimiento, conquista y guerra del reino de Chile.*

V

Alonso de Ovalle

Alonso de Ovalle became more widely known than most of the early colonial historians, partly from the fact that his *Histórica relación del reino de Chile* was one of the first Chilean books of which translations were published in Europe. The author was a son of Francisco Rodríguez del Manzano de Ovalle, who was the holder of an entailed estate in Salamanca, and who went to Chile in command of certain troops that had been equipped at Lisbon. On this expedition he was accompanied by his cousin, Diego Valdez de la Vanda, who had been appointed governor of Buenos Aires. In Santiago Rodríguez del Manzano de Ovalle married María Pastene, a daughter of Juan Bautista Pastene, recognized for his services under Valdivia. Two sons of this marriage, Alonso and Jerónimo, born in the beginning of the seventeenth century, received instruction in the Jesuits' school. By reason of their wealth as compared with the majority of Santiago's primitive society they were conspicuous figures in the town. They were noteworthy for their fine horses with rich trappings, their ostentatious dress and the richness of their jewelry. The gentleness and docility of Alonso, his inclination to religious reflection and his wealth naturally suggested to his Jesuit instructors the desirability of attracting him to enter the order. Their zeal in this matter was stimulated by the knowledge that Alonso's father was making arrangements to send him to Spain to take possession of the estate in Salamanca. The necessary steps for his initiation were hastily taken, and without the knowledge of his parents he took the vows and assumed the obligations of the Jesuits.

Ovalle becomes a Jesuit

When the father learned of the son's act, he used every means to induce Alonso to withdraw from the order, and to persuade the provincial, Pedro de Oñate, to surrender him, but all without any result that was satisfactory to the family. The Jesuit authorities, moreover, in order to avoid any attempt that might be made to rescue the novice, determined to send him to Córdoba, in the province of Tucumán. This project came to the knowledge of Alonso's relatives, who proposed to kidnap him on the journey over the Andes. But the Jesuits and their charges completely eluded the armed men sent to the mountain pass to intercept them. At Córdoba Alonso continued his studies, and at the end of his novitiate he was ordered to return to Santiago. Soon after his arrival in Chile he was ordained priest, and entered with zeal upon the work of his ministry. He undertook the moral and religious instruction of the negroes, and on Sundays preached in the public square of the town. He also went as a missionary to the Indians in various parts of Chile, and had unrealized projects of more extensive work, when the authorities of his order directed him to take up the duties of a professor of philosophy. A little later he was appointed rector of the Seminario at Santiago.

Ovalle as missionary and professor

His reputation for learning and religious devotion increased, and when a few years later it became necessary to treat with the general of the Society concerning questions relating to the vice-province of Chile, the members of the order in Chile resolved unanimously to send Alonso de Ovalle to Rome. He undertook the journey by way of Lima and Panama. At Lima he found that his reputation as a preacher and an orator had preceded him, and the people pressed with gratification to hear him. His presence later in Rome awakened a desire, even in the higher classes, to see him and to listen to his preaching. Towards the propositions of the Chilean Jesuits the general assumed a favourable attitude, and the business of the mission was accomplished without opposition. From Italy Ovalle went to Madrid, where he was received by the monarch. While in Spain he published two minor productions. One of these was called *Relación de las paces*, which was later embodied in his history of Chile. Another was *Memorial y carta*, designed to attract priests to the missionary

Ovalle in Rome

Relación de las paces

field of Chile. A serious difficulty encountered in this enterprise was the profound ignorance that prevailed in all classes in Spain concerning Chile. At this time, eighty or ninety years after the settlement of the colony, Chile occupied an insignificant place in Spanish affairs; there were great patches of the population where even the name of Chile was unknown. It may, perhaps, be assumed that the *Histórica relación* was written to abate this ignorance. The manuscript was submitted for publication on the occasion of Ovalle's second visit to Rome.

Histórica relación

The author writes as if addressing readers who were entirely ignorant of his subject. He treats extensively of the natural features of the country, the soil, the rivers, the lakes, and the mountains. He presents statistics of agricultural products, of the output of the mines, of the plants, fishes, and birds.

A striking characteristic of the *Histórica relación* is the indication it furnishes of the author's superstition, his credulity concerning the reported miracles wrought by

Ovalle's credulity

the image of the Virgin, and by divine interference and predestination, where later generations have seen merely a physical or worldly cause. The extreme to which he is led in this direction, and the large number of miracles he discovers in the course of events detract greatly from the historical character of his work. This quality persuaded the English translator to conclude his translation with the death of Caupolicán; "for in the course of the narrative so many superstitious notions are inculcated, so many improbable miracles are set forth as the basis of great undertakings, and the entire work is so thoroughly permeated by a monkish spirit, that it would rather condemn than recommend a project for its publication."[8]

Contents of the *Histórica relación*

In spite of these defects the translator finds the work 'so admirably performed, that it may be a model for most relations of that kind'. The author's plan of his work is set forth in his preface, where he announces the principal topics of the several books: "the first and second books will

(8) Churchill, *Voyages and Travels*, III, 154.

show the natural state of the kingdom of Chile, both as to its climate and products; the third will describe the qualities of its first inhabitants; the fourth and fifth will describe the first entrance of the Spaniards into it, and the conquest of it by them; the sixth will contain the various events of the war; the seventh will show the first means of peace attempted by Father Lewis de Valdivia; the last, the first means of planting the Christian faith and its propagation among the Indians."

Ovalle's mysticism

But Ovalle's experience in the mountains that look down upon the agreeable valley of Central Chile called him back from his visions of a fictitious spiritual world, and inspired him to present views of nature in its most imposing forms. Passing along narrow trails, on the edge of horrible precipices, descending into the shadows of deep wooded canyons, in the presence of roaring mountain torrents throwing clouds of mist into the clear air, his mysticism was for the moment clarified into a soberer conception of the universal Creator. But ordinarily he was so profoundly impressed by the wonderful and incomprehensible in nature and the course of events that he found it apparently impossible to carry on his narrative without interrupting it here and there to tell the story of some miraculous manifestation. Montalvo affirms that "he did not know how to treat of the earth without introducing into his narrative the events of heaven."[9]

The excellence of Ovalle's style doubtless suggested the fitness of his work for translation; it also persuaded the Royal Spanish Academy to place it in the list of works quoted for illustration in the Academy's *Diccionario de la lengua castellana*.

Ovalle's last years

In 1646 Ovalle was in Rome, attending the sixth general congregation of the Jesuits, in his capacity as procurador of the vice-province of Chile. This year he published his *Histórica relación*, which the same year appeared in an Italian translation. The English translation was first printed in 1703.

From Rome Ovalle returned to Spain, where he assembled the sixteen priests who

(9) *Sol del nuevo mundo*, 88.

were to accompany him to America. Four years after the publication of his *Histórica relación*, in 1650, he embarked for Chile by way of Panama. At Paita, not meeting there the ship he expected to take him to Callao, he set out overland for Lima, over an almost trackless region and across the sandy wastes of the desert-like coast lands, with little preparation for meeting his need of food and water. He arrived in Lima suffering under a violent fever, from which he died a few days later.

Fantastic views of the Scriptures

Ovalle's fantastic interpretations of the Scriptures, as witnessed, among many instances, by his notion that the gold of Ophir was brought from Peru and Chile by Solomon's fleet, did not prevent him from writing clearly and rationally about the events of Chilean history. In the following paragraph he describes the destruction of Concepción by Lautaro and his Araucanians:

Ruin of Concepción

"Misfortunes seldom come alone; and so it happened to this afflicted city, which, instead of receiving comfort from the approaching day, no sooner did it appear, when the noise of drums and trumpets gave a warm alarm of the enemy being at hand. Here the confusion increased; for now the concern was not for the loss of others, but for every one's own safety, the danger threatening them so immediately. There was nothing but disorder, no counsel nor resolution being to be found in the wisest. They could not defend themselves, because they were overpowered in numbers by the enemy; and the retreat, though necessary, was difficult, because of the approach of the Indians. In this hard conflict at last the resolution that prevailed was to abandon the city without pretending to save any thing but their lives. They leave the city then, and all the gold they had got together in such quantities; they go out in long files, the mothers helping their little children along; the way that they undertook was to the city of St. Iago, a long one, in which many rivers were to be crossed, and hard passes to be gone through: this labour was accompanied with the perpetual fright of the enemy's pursuing them. Who can relate the hardships of hunger and other

Concepción abandoned

sufferings through so long a tract of mountains, deserts, and uninhabited countries? How the women, the children, the old men could bear the fatigue, we must leave to imagination to represent the true idea of these misfortunes! Let us, therefore, return to the Indians. The Spaniards had hardly made an end of abandoning the city when the Indians entered it; and not being able to execute their rage upon the inhabitants, they did it upon the houses, to which they set fire, and consumed them to the very foundation, killing even the very animals which the Spaniards left behind them. Thus was lost the city most abounding in gold and situated in the most populous part of the Indian country; for it is said there were not less than a hundred thousand Indians with their families, who were all employed in gathering gold for the Spaniards, whom they enriched to that degree that Pedro de Valdivia, if he had lived, would have had fifty thousand crowns of gold a year, and others twenty and thirty thousand." [10]

The city burned

(10) Translation in Churchill, *Voyages and Travels*, III, Book V, Chap. XX.

VI

About the middle of the seventeenth century a friar of the Augustinian order, Miguel de Aguirre, became conspicuous at Lima not only as the author of the *Población de Valdivia*, but also as a devotee of the Virgin of Copacabana. He was born at Chuquisaca, and took his religious vows very early. In 1641 he appeared at Lima, and entered the monastery of his order in that city, and became there professor of arts and theology. The distinction achieved by his lectures caused him to be appointed to a professorship in the University of San Marcos. He became also censor of the Inquisition. Pedro de Toledo y Leiva, Marqués de Mancera (1639–1648) was then the viceroy of Peru. In order to provide defence against the threatened invasion of the Dutch, he imposed various taxes and called upon certain institutions to make contributions. Aguirre was present at a meeting of the University of San Marcos on October 10, 1641, called to reply to the viceroy's letter. Mancera's plans comprehended the

Población de Valdivia

Aguirre

building of a wall about Lima, and equipping a number of warships to be sent to the coast of Chile. The defence appeared to be especially necessary in view of the fact that the Dutch had taken possession of Valdivia and intended to establish themselves within the limits of Chilean territory. The viceroy fitted out a squadron of twelve vessels, carrying eighteen hundred men and one hundred and eighty-eight guns. These vessels set sail on December 31, 1644, and arrived at their destination on the 6th of February, 1645, but before their arrival the enemy had departed. The minute knowledge of the enterprise displayed by Aguirre in his *Población de Valdivia* (Lima, 1647), has suggested that, with other ecclesiastics, he was a member of the expedition; in fact his known advisory relation to the viceroy has given a certain support to the opinion that he occupied an official position.

Expedition against the Dutch

For three years longer, until the end of Mancera's term in 1648, Aguirre continued to perform his professorial duties at the university, and when he resigned in that year, it was probably in anticipation of his

The Virgin of Copacabana

accompanying the viceroy to Spain; for in 1650 Mancera left Lima for Madrid, taking Aguirre with him as his confessor. Aguirre for his religious consolation and in order to be fortified against possible ill fortune on the voyage, took with him an image of Nuestra Señora de Copacabana. He proposed, moreover, to establish in Europe the cult of Our Lady of Copacabana, in which the Indians about Lake Titicaca had appeared to find a large measure of religious satisfaction.[11]

Aguirre in Spain and Italy

Soon after Aguirre arrived in Madrid Monseñor Gaetano, the apostolical nuncio in Spain, appointed him his confessor, and the Supreme Tribunal of the Inquisition nominated him to be one of its members. From Madrid Aguirre went to Rome in 1655 as general procurador of the province of Peru, and in spite of all of his other cares and occupations he kept in mind his purpose to propagate devotion to the Virgin of Copacabana, and the "American Virgin" was set up with an elaborate ceremony in

(11) For the history of the cult of Nuestra Señora de Copacabana see Andrés de San Nicolás, *Imagen de N.S. de Copacabana.*

the Augustinian hospicio of San Ildefonso; one part of this ceremony was an inaugural mass. Before he left Rome the image of the "American Virgin" and her cult had been established at several places in the city. Aguirre remained in Rome about a year and died in Madrid in 1664.

Although an advocate of devotion to the Virgin of Copacabana, he was in reality more than this, he was a writer to whom his contemporaries attributed great erudition. It is said, however, that his extensive reading in the classics and the Latin ecclesiastical writings had caused him to dislike the Spanish language, and even limited his power to use it in its most approved form.

Purpose of *Población de Valdivia*

His work called *Población de Valdivia* was far removed from subjects that engrossed his attention during the greater part of his active years. It sets forth the dangers to which the southern coast of Chile was exposed from foreign invasion; narrates the history of the various Dutch and English expeditions during the preceding century; gives an account of the preparations for defence made by the different governors; and tells the story of the town of Valdivia, its conflicts with the Indians, and the negotiations had with them. But the method of treatment and the entire lack of literary skill displayed in the composition have rendered an attractive subject devoid of all interest.

VII

Ponce de León

Another friar who wrote on Chile and Chilean affairs in the middle of the seventeenth century was Francisco Ponce de León. His descent from the noble houses of Arcos and Medina Sidonia gave him special consideration, and in the official service of his order (the Order of Mercy), he had an opportunity to visit various parts of South America. The most noteworthy of his expeditions was his missionary journey into the valley of the Marañón, where without stipend of any sort he spent three years preaching to various tribes of Indians. He performed important official functions as a member of his order and as a commissary of the Inquisition. Later by the favour of the viceroy, Diego Fernández de Córdoba,

Descripción del reino de Chile

Marqués de Guadalcázar (1623–1629), he was appointed general chaplain of the military and naval forces, and served for five years in this capacity in Chile. His principal literary production was *Descripción del reino de Chile, de sus puertos, caletas, y sitio de Valdivia*, which was published in Madrid in 1644. He wrote also *Conquistas y poblaciones del Marañón,* but he was not able to secure its publication.

Mapa de Chile

Another descriptive work on Chile was called *Mapa de Chile,* and was attributed to a Franciscan friar named Gregorio de León. It is said to have been printed, but no verification of this statement is at hand. In the same class as the foregoing are the anonymous *Descripción y cosas notables del reino de Chile* and Miguel de Olavarría's *Informe sobre el reino de Chile, sus indios y sus guerras.*[12] This last mentioned paper covers three topics, presenting a description of the cities, the characteristics and condition of the Indians, and finally a brief account of the history of Chile and its governors. Two other historical docu-

(12) Printed in Claudio Gay's *Documentos.*

ments belonging to this period may be noted, a *Relación,* written circa 1607 and still in MS., by Tomás de Olaverría, and *Discursos sobre la centinela del reino de Chile,* by Andrés Méndez; the latter was published in Lima in 1641.

Olavaría and Méndez

The policy of the European inhabitants of Chile respecting the Indians, before the end of the sixteenth century, was simply to subdue them. With the beginning of the seventeenth century it became necessary to review this policy. The Indians had not been conquered; in fact, many of the towns and military posts established by the Spaniards had been swept away; the settlers had either fled or been destroyed; and whatever property they had accumulated had been lost. Two main questions had to be considered: should the Spaniards persist in the war for conquest? and what should be the treatment of the Indians captured or under Spanish domination? The encomenderos were in favour of holding them as slaves, but another party advocated a more humane policy and the adoption of an attitude of military defence. Opin-

Indian policy

ions and discussions on these questions determined the political atmosphere of Chile in the first half of the seventeenth century. There were formed certain definite propositions: that the Indians should be released from personal servitude, or slavery, but that the existing relation should be maintained for two years, a period to be used in collecting voluntary labourers; that during this period all work in the mines should be suspended, and there should be paid to the Indians elsewhere engaged a daily wage, fixed beforehand, for their labour; that a new rule respecting tribute should be published; that the Indian prisoners held as slaves should be liberated, but that the three hundred held in Lima should remain there until the end of the war; and that negotiations should be undertaken with the view of introducing negroes to replace the Indians.[13]

Defence or Conquest

Programme

Although these recommendations received the enthusiastic approval of the viceroy, it was found to be impossible to carry them out in Chile. Many of the

(13) Amunátegui Solar, *Las encomiendas*, I, 317.

Indians, if left free, were averse to labour of any kind under any conditions; the encomenderos resisted every attempt to liberate them; still the audiencia of Chile, when it was established in 1609, was instructed to abolish the personal service of the Indians. This order, however, brought a reaction against the movement for emancipation, and this reaction found a vigorous supporter in Francisco Lazo de la Vega, when he became governor of Chile in 1629. He was an old soldier, who saw a remedy for the unfortunate condition of affairs only in the exercise of a sufficient amount of force to bring the Indians into subjection, and consequently repudiated the plan of a defensive war.[14]

Opposing views

(14) Many of the minor Chilean writers of the seventeenth and the early part of the eighteenth century dealt with this question: Pedro Cortés, *Información de la guerra de Chile*; Jorge de Eguía y Lumbe, *Ultimo desengaño de la guerra de Chile*; Domingo de Eraso, *Relación y advertencias*, and later a *Memorial* in support of active war on the Indians; Fr. Pedro de Sosa, *Memorial del peligroso estado espiritual y temporal del reino de Chile*; Fr. Agustín Carrillo, *Relación de las paces ofrecidas por los indios rebeldes del reino de Chile;* Juan José de Santa y Silva, *El mayor regocijo en Chile para sus naturales y españoles poseedores de él;* Jerónimo Pietas, *Informe al rey sobre las diversas razas de indios que pueblan el territorio araucano;* Martín de Recabarren, *Informe al rey sobre los medios de reducir a los indios y conservar la quietud del reino;* José Ortega, *Método para auxiliar y fomentar a los indios de los reinos del Perú y Chile.*

The practical discussion of the relation of the Spaniards to the Indians awakened an interest in the Indian languages, and promoted a study of their grammar. The principal investigators in this field were the Jesuit priests. Among these, Luis de Valdivia was the most prominent in the affairs of Chile. He was a member of the commission that framed the regulations providing for the abolition of personal service. He had, moreover, advocated the reduction of military operations to a war of defence, in which troops should be maintained, armed and equipped, in such force as might be necessary; and the Jesuits were charged to carry instruction in Christian doctrine to the Indians. The Jesuit, Luis de Valdivia, as visitador-general of the province of Chile, was commissioned to act with the governor in an effort to carry out the new policy.

Proposed state of troops

Luis de Valdivia

Luis de Valdivia arrived in Chile in 1593 with Gabriel de Vega, Fernando Aguilera, Baltasar de Piñas and others, who constituted the first group of Jesuits to visit that province. In 1622 he returned to Spain. During the period of his retirement he wrote, in addition to other things, a *Historia de la provincia castellana de la Sociedad de Jesús*, and *Varones ilustres de la Sociedad*; later, a grammar and a dictionary of the *lengua Allentiac*, and composed a treatise in that language on Christian doctrine.[15]

VIII

Diego de Rosales

The Marqués de Baides (1639–1646) sought to establish peaceful relations with the Indians by friendly conferences and treaties. In these conferences (*parlamentos*) Padre Diego de Rosales rendered the governor noteworthy assistance. This priest of the Society of Jesus won marked distinction not merely for his untiring missionary labours among the Indians of the frontier, but also for the excellence of his *Historia general del reino de Chile*. Considering the absorbing character of his practical activity, whether as missionary or in contributing to the execution of the gov-

Historia de Chile

(15) His *Arte y gramática general que correen todo el reino de Chile con un vocabulario y confesonario* was published in Lima in 1606; a second edition appeared in Seville in 1684. For other works on the Indian languages of Chile, see Medina, *Historia de la literatura colonial de Chile*, II, 371–388, special reference being made to the notes.

Contents of Rosales' *Historia*

ernment's Indian policy, one has ground for surprise that the author found time for the production of a work that indicates an extensive use of documents, particularly in the first of its two volumes. This volume treats of the civil or secular events, and is divided into ten books, of which the first is devoted to the primitive inhabitants of Chile and to the early period of Spanish settlement. The second book presents in greater detail the history of the different expeditions to the coast of Chile made by Spanish seamen and by foreign adventurers, giving an account also of the natural products of the territory whether of value in industry or serviceable in medicine. The attention given to the geography of the country was apparently encouraged by the decree issued in Madrid on December 30, 1633, requiring the governors to make maps of the several provinces, showing their temples, fruits, mines, herds and fortifications, and indicating clearly and briefly the Indians and Spaniards in each. From the third to the tenth book inclusive Rosales presents an account of the political events of Chile down to the administration of Governor Antonio de Acuña y Cabrera (1648–1656). In treating of events prior to his own time, he says, "he escrito muchas cosas por noticias de papeles y relaciones" but "en adelante escribiré lo que he visto y tocado con las manos."[16] Near the end of this part the manuscript shows lack of a careful final revision and closes as abruptly as if pages had been torn off.

Conquista espiritual de Chile

The second volume is entitled *Conquista espiritual de Chile.* Its subject is not the general history of Chile, not even a general account of the spread of Christian doctrine, but a collection of biographical sketches of the Jesuits who had flourished in Chile prior to the date of the author's writing, "a theme in itself much less interesting, and infinitely poorer in execution than the general history of the kingdom," and it is rendered obscure "by the interminable narration of extraordinary and unheard-of marvels attributed by the Jesuit padre to his associates in the mission or in the cloister, and clothed in language without distinction,

(16) Quoted by Medina, *Lit. col. de Chile,* II, 281.

often low, almost always trivial." [17] And this volume, like the first, is incomplete; but, in spite of its general views respecting Chilean affairs, it illustrates to a certain extent the native manners and customs by its account of the circumstances of the missionaries on their peregrinations among the Indians.

Rosales' life

The events of Rosales' life were not greatly unlike the events in the lives of other persons subject to the régime of the Jesuits in America. He was born in the beginning of the seventeenth century, entered the Society in 1620, was sent to Peru, and subsequently to Chile. He became rector of the college at Concepción; as procurador of the vice-province of Chile he was sent to Rome and Madrid. After his return to Chile he was charged with the affairs of the vice-province from 1662 to 1665. He became vice-provincial in 1670.[18]

(17) Medina, *Literatura colonial de Chile*, II, 286.

(18) The title of Rosales' principal work as issued by Vicuña Mackenna is *Historia general del reino de Chile desde la época aborigen hasta la gran rebelión del siglo xvii.* Valparaiso, 1877.

IX

Santiago de Tesillo

There is only a limited known record of facts concerning the life of Santiago de Tesillo. In 1624 he appeared in Peru as a soldier, a member of the garrison of Callao, and it devolved upon the company to which he belonged to repel the Dutch, who that year proposed to land on the coast. Four years later he was promoted to be a sergeant and sent to Chile. After his arrival in Chile he attained the rank of captain, and for somewhat more than two years he was associated with his chief in the capacity of secretary. Later Governor Francisco de Meneses entrusted him with the confidential task of writing his defence in reply to charges against him that had been presented to the government at Lima. This appeared under the title *Restauración del estado de Arauco, y otros progresos militares conseguidos por las armas de S. M.* (Lima, 1665). But the friendly relation between the governor and Tesillo was ultimately changed to one of hostility, and Tesillo was banished to a frontier fort. In 1670 he

Restauración del estado de Arauco

was living at Concepción, and he is supposed to have died three or four years later at the age of about seventy.

Guerra de Chile

His principal work, *Guerra de Chile, causas de su duración, medios para su fin,* was completed in 1641, and published in Madrid in 1647. Its title suggests that the author proposed to treat his theme philosophically, and thus initiate a departure from the chronicle-like writings of his predecessors. Medina finds in the book certain observations that reveal an elevated spirit, a judicial character, judgments on men and affairs, and views more or less developed concerning military operations, described from year to year from the beginning of Lazo de la Vega's administration to the arrival of his successor.[19]

Character of Tesillo's work

In spite of its title, the characteristics of a chronicle are thus seen to be distinctive features of some part of the work, and, like most of the chronicles of the colonies, it fails to maintain a just perspective of the subject, extensive accounts being sometimes given of unimportant events,

(19) Medina, *Literatura colonial de Chile,* II, 228.

while events of greater importance suffer comparative neglect. Still Tesillo is not merely a writer of chronicles; he set forth the causes of movements, reasons for the continuation of the war, the interests of the two belligerents, their conflicts, their methods of warfare, the marching of the troops, the astuteness of the Indians, and all this is done with striking impartiality.[20]

(20) *Ibid.* II, 229. In his introduction to *Guerra de Chile* printed in the fifth volume of the *Historiadores de Chile* Barros Arana writes that Tesillo "composed a book of pretentious form, heavy and difficult to read; nevertheless, those who wish to have a profound knowledge of the history of Chile must not hesitate to make a thorough study of Tesillo's book. In it they will find not only events referred to with sufficient minuteness, but also the observations of a man of intelligence and experience." But, as Tesillo enjoyed the special protection of Governor Lazo de la Vega, the reader must expect to find the events of La Vega's administration especially emphasized. The bulk of the narrative treats of the decade from 1629 to 1639.

CHAPTER X

WRITERS OF PERU AND NEW GRANADA, 1600–1650.

I. *Juan Bautista Aguilar.* II. *Francisco Vásquez and Toribio de Ortiguera.* III. *Cristóbal de Acuña.* IV. *Diego de Torres Bollo.* V. *Antonio de la Calancha.* VI. *Bernabé Cobo.* VII. *Alonso Mesía Venegas.* VIII. *Pedro Simón.* IX. *Rodríguez Fresle and Alonso Garzón de Tahuste.* X. *Pedro Fernández de Quiros, Gobeo de Victoria, and Fernando Montesinos.*

I

Peruvian topics

Writers of Peru and New Granada in the first half of the seventeenth century had no single absorbing topic, such as the Araucanian war provided for the Chileans. Their attention was attracted by the abuses which the Indians suffered under hard masters, the exploration of the Amazon, the development of the religious orders, and the various phases of progress in the colonies. Juan Bautista Aguilar was one of those who appeared as defenders of the Indians. Their need of defence grew partly out of the fact that in Peru the Indians were less warlike than the Araucanians of Chile; they had been cowed by the rule of the Incas, the encomenderos, and the corregidores; and, in many cases, even the clergy and their concubines, taking advantage of a gentle-spirited people, imposed grievous burdens upon them. Aguilar was archdeacon of the cathedral of Arequipa, and in 1615 published, in folio, the *Restauración y reparo del Perú*. In this work and in a report which he sent to the king eight years later, he set forth the unfortunate state of the Indians, their needs, and the scandalous treatment of them by the corregidores, who enriched themselves by defrauding the Indians of their property, and by employing them as labourers with little or no compensation. This report was later sent from Spain to Peru, and Aguilar caused it to be printed together with communications from many prelates commending it. But the Spanish

Aguilar defender of the Indians

Restauración y reparo del Perú

government in America, maintaining a certain esprit de corps, tolerated the notorious extortions of the corregidores, and remained generally unmoved by appeals for a more humane treatment of the natives.

II

Exploration of the Amazon

The most notorious events associated with the discovery and exploration of the Amazon were those connected with the expedition of Ursúa in 1560, embracing the conspiracy and revolt of Lope de Aguirre, the projected creation of an independent state under the nominal headship of Fernando de Guzmán, the tyrannical domination of the expedition by Aguirre after the murder of Ursúa and other members of the company, and the riotous pillaging of Venezuelan towns

Vásquez's *Relación*

A reliable narration of these events is the *Relación verdadera de todo lo que sucedió en la jornada de Omagua y Dorado*, written by El Bachiller Francisco Vásquez, who was a soldier of the expedition, but who refused to take the oath of allegiance to Fernando de Guzmán, or alienate himself from the kingdom of Castile, or renounce his loyalty to the king. Having served in this company until his escape from it at Margarita, Vásquez wrote with personal knowledge of the events he describes. His title of bachiller and the form of his narrative indicate that, although a private soldier, he possessed a degree of cultivation superior to that acquired by the majority of his comrades His account was still in manuscript when Bollaert translated Simón's *Sixta noticia historial,* which contained the history of Ursúa's expedition. From it Simon derived the principal part of his information on the subject in question, and he did not hesitate to copy considerable parts of it and present them as his own in his *Conquistas de Tierra Firme.*[1]

Position of Vásquez

Another account of Ursúa's expedition is found in Toribio de Ortiguera's *Jornada del*

(1) Vásquez's *Relación* is printed by M. Serrano y Sanz in *Nueva biblioteca de autores españoles,* XV (*Historiadores de las Indias,* II), 423–484.

The full title is *Relación verdadera de todo que sucedió en la jornada de Omaguay y Dorado, que el Gobernador Pedro de Orsúa fué a descubrir por poderes y comisiones que le dió el virrey Marqués de Cañete, desde el Perú, por un río que llaman de las Amazonas, que por otro nombre se dice el río del Marañón, el cual tiene sus nascimientos en el Perú, y entra en el mar cerca del Brasil. Trátase ansimismo del alzamiento de don Fernando de Guzmán, y Lope de Aguirre y de las crueldades destos perversos tiranos.*

Ortiguera's *Jornada*

rio Marañón. This is more extensive than Vásquez's narrative, and two of its chapters deal with the expedition of Gonzalo Pizarro and Orellana. Like the narrative by Vásquez, it remained many years in manuscript, but is now readily accessible in the *Nueva biblioteca de autores españoles.*[2] Other narratives of Ursúa's expedition are found in Castellanos' *Elegías de varones ilustres de las Indias* (Part I, Elegía XIV), and in Piedrahita's *Historia general del nuevo reino de Granada.*

The following paragraph is Francisco Vásquez's description of Lope de Aguirre:

Vásquez on Lope de Aguirre

"The tyrant Lope de Aguirre was a man about fifty years old, small of stature and of an insignificant presence: ugly, with a small and emaciated face; eyes, which, if he looked fixedly, were restless in their sockets especially when he was offended. He had a keen and active mind for an unlettered person. He was a Biscayan, and, according to his statement, was born at Oñate in

(2) Vol. XV (*Historiadores de Indias*, II) 305–422. The title is :—*Jornada del rio Marañón con todo lo acaecido en ella, y otras cosas notables dignas de ser sabidas, acaecidas en las Indias occidentales.*

the province of Guipuzcoa. He was, however, unable to find out who his parents were, more definitely than what he communicated in a letter which he wrote to king Philip, in which he affirmed that he was an hidalgo; but judging him by his acts, he appears so cruel and perverse that there was not found or could be observed in him any goodness or virtue. He was turbulent and determined, particularly with his followers. He was a great sufferer from certain difficulties, especially as to sleeping, so that during all the time of his tyrannical rule he was seldom seen to sleep; except during a brief period in the day, he was always found awake. He walked much, and always burdened with considerable weight; he carried continually many arms on his back; went about often wearing two heavy coats of mail, with a sword, a dagger, and steel helmet, and carrying an arquebuse or a lance in his hand. At other times he wore a breastplate. He was naturally an enemy of the good and virtuous, and thus all virtuous and saintly acts appeared to him as bad. He was a friend and com-

Character of Aguirre

panion of low and vile men, and if one was a thief, or had a bad character, or was cruel, he was all the more Aguirre's friend. He was always cautious, inconstant, false, and a deceiver; he was seldom known to tell the truth, and never, or very seldom, kept his word. He was vicious, lustful, gluttonous with all and often overcome with wine. He was a bad Christian, a Lutheran heretic or worse, for he did and said the things we have told in this narrative, the killing of priests, friars, women, and innocent persons for no fault, and without giving them an opportunity to confess, although they requested it, and preparations had been made. He had as a common vice commending his soul and body to the devil, mentioning his head, his legs, his arms, and all members. He never spoke a word without blasphemy and cursing God and His saints. He neither knew how to speak well nor spoke well of anybody, not even of his friends; he was a defamer of everything; and, finally there was no vice that was not represented in his person."[3]

A Lutheran

(3) *Nueva biblioteca de autores españoles*, XV (*Historiadores de Indias*, II), 483.

III

Cristóbal de Acuña

Eighty years after Ursúa's expedition Padre Cristóbal de Acuña made the journey of the Amazon, and recorded the results of his observations and inquiries. Immediately before undertaking this voyage Padre Acuña was the rector of the Jesuits' college at Cuenca. The occasion of this journey was offered by the appearance in Quito of the officers of the expedition organized by Governor Noronha, of Pará. The commander of the expedition was Pedro de Texeira, who arrived in Quito in 1638. He remained in that city eleven months, while the bulk of the personnel of the expedition continued in camp near Ávila. The viceroy finally offered the needed supplies, and ordered Texeira and his followers to go back to Pará by the way they came. He also ordered two Jesuits, on their way to Spain, to accompany the expedition as far as Pará. These were Cristóbal de Acuña and Andrés Artieda. *El nuevo descubrimiento del gran río de las Amazonas* was written by Acuña under orders he had re-

Acuña on the Amazon

ceived to make careful observations, to set down the names of the Indian tribes, to give an account of their manners and customs, to note the rivers flowing into the Amazon, and to describe the natural products of the country bordering on the river. The information gathered he was required to report to the Council of the Indies, and it was contained in a volume published in Madrid in 1641. When this voyage was undertaken, Portugal was still united to Spain, but before the book was issued this connexion had been dissolved. Referring to this subject Sir Clements R. Markham, following the French translator, says, "The wretched government of Philip IV, terrified lest the Portuguese should take advantage of any information contained in Acuña's book, and forgetting that Texeira and all his officers knew quite as much about the Amazons as the Spanish priest, ordered every copy of the work to be immediately and effectually destroyed. It has consequently become exceedingly scarce."[4]

(4) *Expeditions into the Valley of the Amazons*, 1539, 1540, 1639. Translated and edited by Clements R. Markham; London, Hakluyt Society, 1859, XXIV. The French trans-

Acuña was born at Burgos in 1597. In 1612, at the age of fifteen, he entered the order of the Jesuits, and later was sent to America. Shortly after his arrival in South America he became rector of the Jesuits' college at Cuenca de Quito. He was called from this position for the journey from Quito to Pará, which lasted about eleven months, from January 16, 1639, to December 12 following. While waiting at Pará for a ship to take him to Spain, he wrote his *Nuevo descubrimiento*, and after its publication in Madrid in 1641 we find him at Rome as provincial of the Jesuits. Later he returned to America, where he was appointed calificador, or censor, for the Inquisition. He was living in Lima in 1675, and died there in that year.

Service of Acuña

In writing this account of the great river of the Amazons Acuña recognized that he was not the first to make this journey. He was aware that Orellana and Lope de Aguirre had preceded him. He referred also to various other attempts that had

lation was published in Paris, 1682. In 1698 an English translation from the French was published in London, which has been superceded by Markham's translation.

Earlier Amazon explorers

failed. In making clear and apparently well grounded statements of physical conditions as they doubtless appeared to him, the author at the same time shows an inclination to accept as true the marvellous tales that were told him. His mind received calmly the story of "a nation of dwarfs as small as little children," and another story of a "people who all have their feet turned the wrong way, so that a person who did not know them, in following their footsteps, would always walk away from them."[5]

Dwarfs and Amazons

He finds, moreover, "the proofs of the existence of the province of the Amazons on this river are so numerous, and so strong, that it would be a want of common faith not to give them credit."[6]

"There is no saying more common than that these women inhabit a province on the river, and it is not credible that a lie could have been spread throughout so many languages, and so many nations, with such an appearance of truth.[7] The Amazon

(5) Markham's translation, Section 70.
(6) *Ibid.* Section 71.
(7) *Ibid.* Section 71.

women are of great valour, and they have always preserved themselves without the ordinary intercourse with men; and even when these, by agreement, come every year to their land, they receive them with arms in their hands, such as bows and arrows, which they brandish about for some time, until they are satisfied that the Indians come with peaceful intentions. They then drop their arms and go down to the canoes of their guests, where each one chooses the hammock that is nearest at hand (these being the beds in which they sleep); they then take them to their houses, and, hanging them in a place where their owners know them, they receive the Indians as guests for a few days. After this the Indians return to their own country, repeating these visits every year at the same season. The daughters who are born from this intercourse are preserved and brought up by the Amazons themselves, as they are destined to inherit their valour, and the customs of the nation, but it is not so certain what they do with the sons." [8]

Perpetuation of the race

(8) *Ibid.* Section 72. Acuña's narrative appears in a con-

IV

Torres Bollo

Torres Bollo and Calancha were two important writers who dealt extensively with the progress of the religious orders.

Diego de Torres Bollo's known achievement in reorganizing and administering Jesuit affairs in America contributed to the popularity of his *Historia del Perú*. The most striking feature of his practical activity was the creation of three Jesuit provinces out of the hitherto existing single province of Peru. The last third of the sixteenth century and the first third of the seventeenth century were his effective years. He was born in 1550, at Villalpando, in old Castile. He studied at Salamanca, and was later sent to Madrid to enter upon a mercantile career, for which he seemed to find himself unfitted. He therefore withdrew from this undertaking, and was admitted to the order of the Jesuits in 1573. In 1581 he went to Peru. At that time he had already become a priest; and the next

venient form as the second volume of the *Colección de libros, raros o curiosos, que tratan de América*, Madrid, 1891.

year he was appointed superior of the Jesuit establishment at Juli. Earlier that institution had been held to be only a mission, but Torres caused it to be transformed into a permanent residence of the order. He remained in Juli about three years, and was afterwards appointed rector of the college at Quito. On his arrival at Quito he found the inhabitants in revolt as a protest against taxes imposed by Viceroy García Hurtado de Mendoza. Torres' service in allaying the disturbance was recognized by the king in a decree dated August 18, 1593. His residence in Quito was, however, short, for he was called to the college of Potosí, and held there the post of rector until 1599. In that year he was appointed to accompany the visitador, or inspector, of the province on his tour of inspection. The next year he was elected by the provincial congregation at Lima to the office of procurador, and proceeded to Rome and Madrid. At Madrid he received the favour of the king and of the Duque de Lerma. Taking advantage of this favourable reception, he used his influence to secure certain reforms in Ameri-

Torres Bollo's offices

can affairs: the abolition of the decree which forbade the planting of vines in America and ordered the destruction of those that had already been planted; the establishment of a college for the sons of caciques in each bishopric of the Indies; the foundation of a college at Salamanca for the education of sons of American nobles; and also the creation of the Jesuit provinces of Nueva Granada and Paraguay.

Torres Bollo in New Granada and Paraguay

Returning from Spain, he arrived at Lima on the 22nd of November, 1604, accompanied by fifty Jesuits, to be distributed among the three provinces. The inspector Páez, with whom Torres had been associated, had been appointed provincial, and Torres was now sent to New Granada to organize the newly created province. On this journey he visited the religious house at Cartagena, which he had founded in returning from Europe, and at Bogotá he created the establishment called Santa Clara. After three years spent in New Granada, visiting various parts of the country, he returned to Lima in 1607, and then went to the region of the south-east to organize the province of Paraguay. This province was made to embrace Chile besides Tucumán and the region about the great rivers that flow into the Río de la Plata, but Chile soon acquired a measure of independence as a vice-province. He continued his labours as provincial until 1618, when he retired to Buenos Aires. Later he was called to Chuquisaca, and died there August 8, 1638.

Torres Bollo's principal works

Torres' practical achievements established his reputation during his lifetime, and his writings appear to have contributed to maintain the memory of his distinction in later generations. He wrote *Historia del Perú y de los acontecimientos notables acaecidos en los últimos años* and *Comentarios del Perú: breve relación del fruto que se recoge en las Indias*. Translations of these works into several languages appeared in the first decade of the seventeenth century. Torres' other writings, although less widely known, are important as historical sources concerning the events to which the author's life was related.

V

Antonio de la Calancha

Among the historians of the first part of the seventeenth century, who wrote on the affairs of Peru, Antonio de la Calancha occupies a place of special prominence. He was born in 1584 in Chuquisaca. His father was Captain Francisco de la Calancha, a Spaniard; his mother was a creole. At the age of fourteen he became a member of the Augustinian order in his native city. About the same time Miguel de Aguirre, the author of *Población de Valdivia*, was born in Chuquisaca, and also adopted the habit of the Augustinians. From the monastery Calancha went to the Augustinian college of San Ildefonso in Lima. Throughout his life the monastery, either in Lima or elsewhere, remained the principal centre of his activity, from which he went out almost daily to preach and to confess nuns. He was prior in Trujillo when that city was ruined by the earthquake of February 14, 1619. Later he held a similar office in Lima.

Calancha's principal and most widely

known work is the first volume of the *Crónica moralizada del orden de S. Agustín en el Perú.* It was published in Barcelona in 1639. A second volume was completed about 1653, and the next year the author died suddenly at the age of seventy.[9] Under the title of *Histoire du Pérou,* a French translation of the first volume appeared in Toulouse in 1653.[10]

Crónica moralizada

Calancha's first volume embraces the history of the Augustinian order in South America during nearly a hundred years following 1551; the founding of monasteries of the order in Peru, Ecuador, New Granada, and Chile; the succession of priors, and the monks and nuns who were distinguished by

Topics of Calancha's *Crónica*

(9) This second volume is sometimes said to have been written by Padre Torres, and Peralta Barnuevo joins the names of the two writers in the following lines:

Calancha y Torres del Perú esplendores,
Que con purezas escribiendo estrellas,
Harán que sea para cada ejemplo
Cada letra un altar, cada hoja un templo.

Lima fundada, Canto VII, Octave 144.

(10) A work entitled *Historiae Peruanae ordinis Eremitarum Sancti Augustini libri octodecim, auctore Joachimo Brulio,* is said to be merely a translation of Calancha's *Crónica.* Among other works ascribed to Calancha are *De los varones ilustres de la orden de S. Agustín; De Immaculatae Virginis Mariae Conceptione* (*Limae Indorum,* 1629, 4to), an account of the founding of the sanctuaries of Copacabana and of the Prado, and an *Informe al virrey del Perú, sobre los castores que se cazan desde Callao a Chile.*

their labours or their virtues. It deals, moreover, with the topography and natural products of the country; with the antiquities and traditions of the Inca empire; with the events of the conquest and the internal conflicts of the invaders. The history of the Augustinians in Peru begins with the landing of twelve friars at Callao near the end of May, 1551. A month later these friars were installed in a house purchased with funds from the royal treasury.

Study of astrology

Besides his inquiries in ecclesiastical history Calancha was attracted to the study of astrology, from which he presumed to indicate the forces determining the general character of different aggregations of inhabitants within his horizon. Here is the diagnosis of the inhabitants of Potosí:

"In Potosí the signs of Libra and Venus predominate, and thus most of those who live there incline to be covetous, friends of music and festivities, zealous in the pursuit of riches, and somewhat given to lust; their planets are Jupiter and Mercury; the latter inclines them to be wise, prudent and intelligent in their trade and exchanges, and by

Jupiter to be magnanimous and of liberal minds."[11]

The delusions of his age were naturally shared by Calancha. His faith, his superstitions, and his disposition to see the law of nature set aside in a miracle at any moment seem to men of this more critical century incompatible with his evident learning and intellectual ability. Yet with all these qualities that seem to indicate a certain mental simplicity, he wrote a great narrative. The nine hundred and twenty-two double-column folio pages of the first volume, barring the record of the delusions and superstitions of his times, do not suggest weakness, but remain as a monument of intellectual vigor.[12]

Quality of the *Crónica*

VI

The natural history of America is especially emphasized by Bernabé Cobo in his *Historia del nuevo mundo.* This work consists of three parts, each part divided into a num-

Bernabé Cobo

(11) *Crónica*, p. 747. This reference is to the edition of 1639.

(12) An essay on "Fray Antonio de la Calancha" is found in René Moreno's *Bolivia y Perú, Notas históricas y bibliográficas*, 2nd ed., Santiago de Chile, 1905.

ber of books. The fourteen books of the first part deal with the universe in general, the geography of Peru, the animal kingdom, plants, fishes, birds, insects, reptiles, and quadrupeds; the animals and plants introduced by the Spaniards and their increase; the nature, condition, and customs of the Indians, particularly the Indians of Peru. The second part, in fifteen books, contains an account of the discovery and occupation of the provinces of Peru; the governors, the viceroys, the rule of the Spaniards, and the conduct of the government with respect to the Indians; a description of Peru and a description of America outside of Peru. The third part deals chiefly with Mexico; the conquest and the general character of the country; the governors; the foundation of the city of Mexico; and the dependent islands as far as the Philippines.

Historia del nuevo mundo

The *Historia del nuevo mundo,* edited by Marcos Jiménez de la Espada, was published in four volumes (1890–1895) at Seville. Extracts from it had already been printed in Madrid and in Lima. These were a *De-*

scripción del Perú, edited by Antonio José Cavanilles in the *Anales de historia natural* that was issued at Madrid between 1799 and 1804, and *Historia de Lima*, edited by Manuel González de la Rosa, in the first volume of the *Colección de historiadores del Perú*.

Cobo's Career

Cobo had prepared himself for his somewhat ambitious undertaking by his studies at the Jesuit college at Lima, by keeping in mind his plan for many years, and by persistent and systematic observations and inquiries during his many and extensive journeys. He was born in Lopero, a town of Jaén in Spain, in 1582. He left Spain for America in 1596. He was carried away on the current of emigration, moved by the desire for adventure and wealth that set strongly towards Peru in the last half of the sixteenth century. He visited the Antilles and Venezuela, and arrived at Lima in the beginning of 1599. Through the influence of a Jesuit whom he met on the voyage from Panama to Callao, he obtained a scholarship, and entered the college of San Martín. Fifteen years later, in 1615, having been admitted to the Society, he was

Cobo in Peru & Mexico

sent to Juli, and for three years was engaged in missionary work at Potosí, Cochabamba and La Paz. From 1618 to 1621 he was rector of the college at Arequipa, and afterwards, for five years, resided at the house of the Jesuits in Pisco. From 1627 to 1630 he was the rector of the college at Callao; but at the end of this service he was sent to Mexico, where he remained for twenty years. At a date not known with certainty he returned to Lima, and died there on the 9th of October, 1657, at the age of seventy-five. During the sixty-one years of his residence in America he gathered the detailed information that was embodied in his *Historia*, which, with the exception of the fragments already mentioned, remained in manuscript two hundred and fifty years.[13]

In the seventh chapter of the *Historia de Lima* Cobo gives a glimpse of the valley of the Rimac as it appeared to him about a hundred years after the conquest:

"The river of Lima is the larger, the other is called Caraguayllo, and rises in the pro-

(13) For the *Historia de Lima* see also *La revista peruana*, II, 368, 423, 499, 602; III, 65, 112 215, 306, 368, 442, 518; IV, 13, 230, 381, 445.

vince of Canta, in the general cordillera, about twenty leagues from the sea, into which it empties two leagues from the mouth of the river of Lima. The irrigating ditches that lead out from these two rivers are innumerable; they are distributed throughout the valley; some are so big at their beginnings that they appear to be rivers of considerable volume, which draw their water from the river of Lima; we call them ditches of Surco, because they lead to a town of that name, the lands of which they irrigate, as well as those of three other towns, and altogether more than forty estates, or ranches, of Spaniards, residents of this city, and there is among them an estate comprising two leagues of land.

Valley of the Rimac

"Through the efficiency of these canals, or ditches, which develop and fertilize the country, it is at all times green, pleasant, and delightful, offering to the view a fresh and serene spring; and all the country estates have houses whither the residents of Lima were accustomed to go for recreation (without misgivings lest rain might disturb their fiestas and pleasures, for it never

The fair prospect of the Rimac valley

rains); they add greatly to the beauty of the valley; especially are very marked the freshness and verdure, which the olive trees, the plantains, and the cane fields give to it. The innumerable gardens of fruit trees, such as orange, quince, pomegranate and fig; vineyards and orchards with all kinds of the fruits of the country and of Spain; the palms from afar seem to dominate the other trees; and the alfalfa fields with their perpetual and luxuriant freshness beautify all the environs of the city. They are so extensive that they occupy a good part of this level region, for the alfalfa is the common fodder of the horses and other work animals of the city and country, so that this city has very agreeable surroundings on all sides."

VII

Classes of Jesuit writings

The most numerous of the Jesuit writings were the *Cartas anuas*, or reports from the several districts concerning the work of the Jesuits and the most important general events of the period covered; the *Vidas de varones ilustres*, or the lives of distinguished Jesuits; and *Cartas de edificación*. Padre

Alonso Mesía Venegas' *Historia de los varones insignes de la provincia del Perú de la Compañia de Jesús* is a conspicuous instance of the writings of the second class. The author was born in Seville in 1557; went to Peru with the family of Count Villar, the viceroy, in 1585; was educated under Jesuit influence and entered the order; became the procurador of Peru; and subsequently was appointed the rector of the college in Cuzco. In the execution of his duties as procurador he went to Rome and Madrid and on his return to America served as rector of the college at Potosí. It was Venegas who carried to Europe samples of quina, which had already been administered with beneficial results to the Condesa de Chinchón, wife of the viceroy.

Cartas anuas; varones ilustres

For a period of three years, from 1637 to 1640, Venegas was established at the college of San Pablo. Viceroy Mancera suspected him of being the author of certain reports sent to Spain, describing acts of the viceroy as arbitrary and unjust, and expelled him from Peru. A year later, the really guilty person having been discovered, the order of

Venegas suspected and banished

expulsion was revoked. Venegas then returned to the college of San Pablo, where he died October 17, 1649.

Juan de Urquiza

Another teacher and writer of Lima, whose death occurred at Porto Bello twenty years later than that of Venegas, was Juan de Urquiza. He had been engaged for twenty-four years in the college of Lima, and during this period he wrote *Tractatus de profundissima sciencia* and *Relación de la fundación de la real audiencia del Cuzco*. The second of these documents was published in Madrid in 1795.[14]

VIII

Pedro Simón's *Noticias*

An instance of long-delayed publication is offered by that part of Pedro Simón's work which now forms the second, third, fourth and fifth volumes of his *Noticias historiales de las conquistas de Tierra Firme en las Indias occidentales*, written in the first half of the seventeenth century and printed in the last decade of the nineteenth century. Simón was born at Parrilla, near Cuenca, in

(14) Some notion of the extent of the minor writings of the Jesuits in Peru may be obtained from Torres Saldamando's *Antiguos Jesuitas del Perú*, Lima, 1882.

Spain, in 1574, and began writing in 1623. at the age of forty-nine. He was educated in the monastery of San Francisco de Cartagena in Spain, and was sent to South America in 1604 to teach theology and the arts. The early part of Simón's career in New Granada thus fell in the long incumbency of President Juan de Borja (1605--1626), whom he accompanied in the campaign against the Pijaos Indians. The first part of his *Noticias historiales* dealt with the history of the early explorations of the territory now claimed by Venezuela, and is based largely on information gathered on a journey through that region. Embarking at Coro, he visited the Antilles, and returned to Bogotá. Among other places reached in his travels were Antioquía, Cartagena, and Santa Marta. During these journeys he collected much of the material for his narrative directly from persons who participated in the events in question, or who had lived near enough to them to hear and remember the current tales about them. Other sources were the writings of Castellanos and a manuscript of Bachiller Fran-

Life of Simon: his journeys

Simón on Lope de Aguirre

cisco Vásquez. "Indeed page after page of Simón is transcribed word for word from the manuscript of Vásquez." [15] Still another source of information from which Simón may have drawn was Ortiguera's manuscript account of the "Expedition down the Marañón" which does not differ essentially from that of Vásquez. The narration of the events of this expedition constitutes the most noteworthy section of the first part of Simón's work. The four volumes more recently published treat of the discoveries made through the valley of the Magdalena, together with the discoveries, explorations, and early history of the regions about Cartagena, Popayán, Antioquia, and Chocó.[16]

Simón's account of the death of the

(15) Markham's Introduction to Bollaert's translation of a part of Simon's work, under the title, *The Expedition of Pedro de Ursúa and Lope de Aguirre in search of El Dorado and Omagua in 1561*, London, Hakluyt Society, 1881, xxx. Vásquez was a soldier under Lope de Aguirre, and according to the notice on the last page of his manuscript, "credit may be given to his account, and to all he writes, because he was an honest and upright man.'"—Markham's Introduction, xxxi.

(16) The first part of the *Noticias historiales* was issued as a printed volume at Cuenca in 1627. This was reprinted in Bogotá in 1882, and the other four volumes appeared in the latter city in 1891 and 1892.

Death of Lope de Aguirre

bloodthirsty Lope de Aguirre furnishes an indication of the general characteristics of our author's style and a suggestion of the voluminous details of his narratives:[17]

"The maestre del campo, seeing that he had the victory in his own hands, despatched a mounted messenger to inform the governor and others as to the satisfactory state of affairs, and then marched straight on Aguirre's quarters.

"The traitor, on seeing that he had been abandoned by all except Llamoso, asked him why he had not gone with the rest, and taken advantage of the king's pardon? Llamoso replied that he and Aguirre had been friends in life, and that he would live or die with him. Aguirre made no reply; he was crestfallen and lost; he went into an apartment where his daughter was (who was now a woman) in company with another female, named Tarralva, of Molina de Aragón in Castile, who had come from Peru in company with the traitors. She

(17) *Noticias historiales de las conquistas de Tierra Firme, primera parte, sexta noticia*, cap. li. A translation of this *Noticia*, by Clements R. Markham, is printed in Hakluyt Society Publications, London, 1861.

Aguirre murders his daughter

cannot have been of great age, for in 1612 I saw her (she was then very young) in the city of Barquisimeto. The devil instigated Aguirre to kill his daughter, so as to crown all his cruel acts with this most bloody and unnatural one, that of the destruction of his own flesh and blood. He said to her, 'Commend thyself to God, my daughter, for I am about to kill thee,that thou mayest not be pointed at with scorn, nor be in the power of anyone who may call thee the daughter of a traitor.' Torralva tried to save the girl, and even managed to take the loaded arquebuse from the hands or the father, which he was about to fire at his victim; but Aguirre had a poniard, and with it he took her life. Having done this, he rushed to the door of the apartment; but when he perceived that the king's forces were upon him, his very hands lost the power of firing off his arquebuse at them, so as to sell his life dearly; and, in the most dejected manner, he threw all his arms on the ground, and went and leant upon a miserable barbacoa or bed place, that was in the room (opposite that in which he had killed

Ledesme scorned by the traitor

his daughter). One of the first to enter (before the maestre del campo), was one Ledesme, a sword-cutler and inhabitant of Tucuyo, who when he saw García de Paredes enter, thinking to make himself of importance, said, 'Here I have Aguirre as my prisoner.' The traitor replied, 'I do not give myself up to such a villain as you,' and perceiving Paredes, said, 'Señor maestre del campo, I beg that you, who are a caballero, will respect my rank, and listen, for I have many important things to say, for the good of the king's service.'

"García de Paredes replied that he should be respected; but some of Aguirre's former soldiers, fearing if he were allowed to live it might go hard with them—for he might reveal what they had done during the expedition—persuaded the maestre del campo that the best, safest, and most honourable course was to cut off his head at once, and before the governor's arrival. This view of the case was not displeasing to the meastre del campo, and so he told Aguirre to prepare himself for death, and commanded two of his own Marañones to shoot him down with their arquebuses. This they did at once and the traitor fell dead at their feet. . . . . A soldier named Custodio Hernández now fell upon the dead body, and, by order of the maestre del campo, cut the head off and taking hold of the hair, which was very long, he brought it out to show it to the governor, who was just arriving thinking to do him honour."

IX

Rodríguez Fresle

A striking little book of this period, but published later, is *Conquista y descubrimiento del nuevo reino de Granada* by Rodríguez Fresle, sometimes referred to as *El Carnero.* It was written in the first half of the seventeenth century between April, 1636 ,and June, 1638, but it was not printed until 1859. The author was born in Bogotá April 25, 1566. His father was one of the conquistadores of the country. For a time he was in the service of Alonso Pérez de Salazar, a judge of the audiencia of his native city, and he accompanied him to Spain when he was promoted to be fiscal of the Council of the Indies. His patron died, however, six months after his appointment, and Rodríguez Fresle was left, as he said, "como hijo de oidor muerto." He was left in poverty, and remained six years in Spain. After his return to New Granada he was engaged in agriculture, but there appears to be little information extant concerning the success of his undertakings in this field, or, in fact, concerning the later years of his life, and the date of his death is unknown. For a brief period of his later life, beginning the day he completed his seventieth year, he was occupied in writing his chronicle. Vergara refers to the author's style as "natural y correcto, animadísimo a las veces"; no writer of his time excelled him in the *local flavour which he knew how to give* to his lively narrative.[18]

Fresle's book

Two works by Alonso Garzón de Tahuste, belonging properly to this period, were lost

Garzón de Tahuste

(18) *Historia de la literatura en Nueva Granada*, Bogotá, 1905, 86; Rodríguez de Ocampo's *Descripción del reino de Quito* was issued by Marcos Jiménez de la Espada (Madrid, 1897) as an appendix to the third volume of the *Relaciones geográficas de las Indias*, having remained in manuscript since 1650. The Council of the Indies had pronounced it unworthy of publication.

as manuscripts. They were *Sucesión de prelados y jueces seculares del nuevo reino de Granada* and *Historia antigua de los Chibchas*. The first of these existed in two copies, one in Madrid, used by Piedrahita, and the other in Bogotá, used by Zamora. Tahuste was born at Timaná about 1558, studied in Bogotá, and was for fifty years Cura Rector of the Cathedral of Bogotá, from 1585. The loss of these and other manuscripts, many of which would have had very little influence on the progress of literature, was to a certain extent due to the lack of facilities for printing in New Granada, and in a measure also to the neglect suffered by collections of books and papers in periods of social disturbance. One of the poems of the last half of the seventeenth century rescued from complete oblivion was the *Poema heroico de San Ignacio* by Hernando Domínguez Camargo. It was published in Madrid in 1666, although not complete. It was written in octave stanzas, but does not rise above the lower levels of mediocrity.[19]

Poema heroico de San Ignacio

(19) Vergara, *Literatura en Nueva Granada*, 93-108.

X

Quiros' Voyages

Interesting narratives of adventure are contained in the third volume of Pedro Fernández de Quiros' *Historia del descubrimiento de las regiones austriales*, edited by Justo Zaragoza (Madrid, 1876). Parts of the contents of these volumes were published by the Hakluyt Society (London, 1904) in an English translation by Sir Clements Markham, entitled, *The Voyages of Pedro Fernández de Quiros* 1595 *to* 1606. One of the most striking episodes of this work is the story of the dreadful voyage from the Santa Cruz islands to Manila, setting forth the almost complete destruction of the ship, the death of Adelantado Mendaña, the accession of his widow to the chief command, the starvation and death that exhausted and depleted the crew, and the hungry survivors' final arrival in the Philippines. Here they were at first uncertain whether they had reached a friendly country or that of an enemy, for it had been reported in Peru, "that Japan was preparing an attack with a great fleet." [20]

(20) *Voyages of Quiros*, Markham's translation, I, 121.

Half-starved crew in the Philippines

But they found the natives to be "peaceful Christians who brought fowls and pigs at two or three reals a piece together with palm wine, by drinking which some of us talked various languages; also many cocoa nuts, plantains, sweet canes, papayas, roots, water in bamboo joints, and fuel. They took in exchange reals, knives, and glass beads, which they value more than silver. During these days and nights the galley fire was never put out, nor was there any cessation of kneading and cooking, or of eating the boiled of one and the roast of another, so that they were eating day and night. . . The sick, being so little accustomed to abundance of food, and eating without moderation, did themselves serious harm; three or four even died of it."[21] In fact, fifty died on the voyage from Santa Cruz to Manila, where the vessel arrived on the 11th of February, 1596.

Quiros was by birth a Portuguese and was born in Evora in 1565. He was brought up in Lisbon, and at the age of twenty-four, in 1589, he married Ana Chacón, of Madrid.

(21) *Ibid.* I, 121, 122.

Antonio de Mendoza, 2nd Viceroy of Peru

1551–1552

Six years later he accepted the post of chief pilot in the ship destined by Alvaro de Mendaña to take a colony to the Solomon Islands. The prospects for a peaceful voyage were not favourable. Mendaña's wife and her two brothers and a quarrelsome old soldier as camp master offered adequate material for misunderstandings and hostility. The death of Mendaña and his brother-in-law Lorenzo Barreto, seemed to diminish somewhat the elements of conflict, but the arbitrary and unreasonable conduct of the widow in command, and the lack of discipline kept the ship's company in turmoil and sometimes carried it to the verge of mutiny.

Quiros and his great vision

Out of the experience of this voyage there came to Quiros the vision of a great antarctic continent stretching across the southern part of the earth from America to Asia. By proving to the world the existence of this continent he hoped to obtain for himself a place with Columbus and Da Gama in the list of the great discoverers. To acquire the means that would enable him to carry out his proposed undertaking he visited the viceroy in Lima, presented his project to the pope at Rome, and from Clement VIII and the duke Sesa he received letters recommending him to the Spanish government. In spite of the demoralization of the the court and the rapid decline of the government towards bankruptcy there remained still the hope of adding to the glory that Columbus had conferred upon the nation; and through the council of State the king issued an order to the viceroy of Peru instructing him to fit out two ships at Callao to enable Quiros to undertake a voyage for the discovery of the antarctic continent. The inevitable delays followed. Finally two ships were prepared, and in December, 1605, Quiros was ready to set sail to realize the object of his vision. A narrative of this voyage is found in the *Historia* edited by Zaragoza.[22]

Quiros furnished ships by the king

Quiros' return, his disappointment, the poverty of his later years, and his many vain

(22) *Biblioteca hispano-ultramarina*, Madrid, 1876, I, 200, and in Markham's *Voyages of Quiros*, I, 161–320. The second volume of this latter work contains a number of documents relating to Quiros and his voyages. Markham's Introduction and Zaragoza's *Prólogo* contain critical notes on the narratives and their authors.

appeals to the king for further assistance are incidents in the melancholy ending of a great visionary.

Pedro Gobeo de Victoria

The *Naufragio y viaje en las costas del Perú*, by Padre Pedro Gobeo de Victoria, was one of the more widely circulated narratives of personal adventure. The author, whose experience furnished abundant material for his story, was born in Seville in 1560. He went to America at the age of thirteen and during his journeys was at various times engaged in combats with pirates, suffered shipwreck, and encountered about all the other perils known to land or sea. After many years of a troubled existence, he entered the order of the Jesuits at Lima in 1597. For thirteen years he enjoyed a comparatively peaceful existence. He returned to Spain in 1610. He died at Seville at the age of seventy. His book has been translated into various languages. A Latin translation was published in 1647, of which a new edition was issued in 1688. The first edition in Spanish appeared in 1610.[23]

(23) The full title is *Relación del naufragio y peregrinaciones de Pedro Gobeo de Victoria en las costas del Perú; viajes y riesgos que tuvo en él con sus compañeros.*

About the middle of the seventeenth century attention was again directed to the history and institutions of the Inca Kingdom, this time by Fernando Montesinos, who wrote *Memorias antiguas históricas y políticas del Perú.* This treatise shows a large use of the imagination, and in this respect differs from the writings of Cieza de León and Sarmiento. The author passes in review some of the earlier writers on Peruvian history. He laments the confidence given to Garcilaso de la Vega; reproaches Xerez for his brevity; praises the accuracy of Zárate; finds Cieza de León's descriptions true; and regards Las Casas as merely a declaimer. He sets down a long list of kings not discovered by other historians. His imagination is inflamed by the idea of much gold, and is given full play in his description of El Dorado, which he believes to exist in the interior of the continent. His fancy, moreover, determines the character of his work called *Ofir de España o memorias antiguas y nuevas del Perú.* He finds Peru to have been the Ophir of the Old Testament, and describes the route by which Solomon's fleet reached that country. But Montesinos descends to the dreadful reality in his description of the auto de la fe held in Lima January 23, 1639. On this occasion eighty persons were sentenced, of whom twelve were burned. Certain practical treatises on metals were the result of his diligent literary activity; the titles of two of these are the following: *Directorio de beneficiadores de metales y arte de ellos* and *Conservación del azogue que se pierde sobreaguado entre lamas y relaves.* The description of the auto de la fe was published in Madrid in 1640. A translation of the *Memorias* into French was published by Ternaux-Compans in 1840, entitled *Mémoires historiques sur l'ancien Pérou.* In 1920 an English translation was issued in London by the Hakluyt Society.

CHAPTER XI

THE LAST HALF OF THE SEVENTEENTH CENTURY

I. *Juan de Barrenechea y Albis; Luis de Oviedo y Hererra; Juan del Valle y Caviedes.* II. *Ignacio de Arbieto; Jacinto Barrasa; José de Buendía.* III. *Jerónimo de Quiroga; Anello Oliva; Diego Ojeda Gallinato; Martín Velasco.* IV. *Lucas Fernández de Piedrahita.* V. *Pedro Claver; Juan Flórez de Ocáriz.* VI. *Anales del Cuzco.* VII. *Manuel Rodríguez; Samuel Fritz.*

I

The colonial writers of the second half of the seventeenth century and the early decades of the eighteenth century continued to find their principal subjects in the military and civil affairs of the colonies. In Chile the chief topic was the interminable

Indian wars. The *Cautiverio feliz*, by Núñez de Pineda y Bascuñán, was so far successful that it served in some sense as a model for writers who wished to depart from a strictly statistical treatment of their subjects; for, while treating of the common theme, Pineda y Bascuñán gave indications of a certain degree of imagination, and his work appealed to a permanent human interest by presenting the elements of a good story, by its discussion and criticism of public affairs, and by its exposition of abuses and demands for correction.

Cautiverio feliz

The manuscript entitled *Restauración de la Imperial y conversión de almas infieles*, by Juan de Barrenechea y Albis, sometimes rises to a plane of a general interest. The author evidently set out to write an heroic novel, in which should figure elevated sentiments and an intense patriotism, the whole to be drawn on a background of Chilean history; the part of the history that was especially presented was an account of the campaigns of Governor Alonso de Sotomayor. But from this general theme Barrenchea sometimes turned aside to discuss

Juan de Barrenechea y Albis

Restauración de la Imperial

the war, its objects, and the manner in which it had been carried on in Chile. In spite of the more or less dramatic action of the characters, the author shows that he is still dealing with realities by citing governmental decrees, by treating of the customs of the Indians and by raising inquiries as to the most efficacious method of restoring the churches in the destroyed towns. But the author, as a pious friar, could not be expected to leave his work merely as a story with a number of reflections on worldly affairs, and thus throughout the writing runs the conventional babble of his class, that here on earth all is misery, and that only beyond this life there will be no tears and no sorrow. There are introduced into each of these books more or less extensive passages in verse, on account of which the authors are regarded not only as prose writers but also as poets.

Juan Barrenechea was born in Concepción in 1669; was sent to Lima to study theology in the University of San Marcos, and after his return to Santiago became a lecturer on philosophy and theology in the

From the first edition of Oviedo Herrera's *Vida de Sta Rosa de Sta María*

Order of Mercy, to which he belonged. Later he was promoted to be the provincial of his order, and, having returned to Lima, wrote there the work already referred to.

The metrical form of certain writings, as already indicated, does not necessarily exclude them from the realm of historical literature. Thus the "poema heroico" by Luis Antonio de Oviedo y Herrera, Conde de la Granja, on *La vida de Santa Rosa de Santa María* is a bit of history, although in verse. The young woman who is celebrated in Oviedo's verses was born in Lima in 1586 and died there in 1617. Her father, Gaspar Flores, was a member of the viceregal guard under the viceroy, the Marqués de Cañete. Her mother, a native of Lima, was a daughter of Francisco de Oliva, who was also born in Peru. She was baptized as Isabel, but her mother was accustomed to call her Rosa on account of her beauty. She was generally known by this name during her life, and when she was canonized she became Santa Rosa de Santa María. Her devotion to the Church and her religious zeal, manifesting itself sometimes in a

Oviedo's *Santa Rosa*

state of nervous exaltation akin to hysteria, made a deep impression on persons who knew of her, and induced the ecclesiastical authorities to proceed to her beatification and canonization. Evidence of the depth of this impression is seen in the fact that Oviedo, Conde de la Granja, an officer of the army, and governor of Potosí, made her the subject of one of his principal poems, in the first octave of which he states his theme:

The theme of the poem

No canto las hazañas, las victorias
De varón inmortal, campeón guerrero,
Ni de la fama, célebres memorias,
Que en bronce y mármol, esculpió el acero;
De sagrada heroina canto glorias,
Que nació Rosa para ser lucero,
Y con humildo corazón profundo,
Triunfó de Lucifer, de sí, del mundo.

Oviedo's poem on Santa Rosa consists of twelve cantos, and was published in Madrid in 1711. The form is sufficiently indicated by the foregoing stanza. The author describes the city of Lima and the grandeur of its position in the valley of the Rumac; he presents many events in the conquests of Peru: the idolatry of the Indians; the birth and youth of Santa Rosa; and enumerates her virtues with an extravagance of expression supposed to be consistent with the poetic form. In other cantos the author writes of the city of Quito, the kingdom of the Incas, the expeditions of Drake, Hawkins, and Spilberg, and the means of defence organized by the Peruvians. Among Oviedo's other writings reference is made to a long poem on the passion of Christ (Lima, 1717) which sets forth various evil passions in society, such as envy, ingratitude, and the spirit of adulation.[1]

Juan del Valle y Caviedes

In the middle of the nineteenth century Odriozola published a collection of verses written by Juan del Valle y Caviedes in the last part of the seventeenth century. The author was born in Lima, and was the son of a rich Spanish merchant. At the age of twenty he went to Spain, where he remain-

(1) Noteworthy among the accounts of the Peruvian saint is Antonic González Acuña's *Vida de Santa Rosa*, published in Rome in 1665.

ed three years, and at the expiration of this period the death of his father obliged him to return to Lima. Finding himself in possession of a considerable fortune, he entered upon a career of vicious and extravagant expenditure, wasting a large part of his inheritance and greatly impairing his health. After a severe illness he determined to reform his mode of life, married, and, in order to preserve the remainder of his property, he opened a shop for the sale of a thousand and one common and cheap articles. The death of his wife made him feel the need of consolation, and he sought it in alcoholic drink, by which he found oblivion of his sorrow in death in 1692, before he had completed his fortieth year.

Valley Caviedes' poems

His poems, extensively circulated in manuscript during his life, made him widely known, but in the course of the century and a half following his death he passed very largely out of the public memory. The two collections of these poems published by Odriozola were called *Diente del Parnaso* and *Poesías serias y jocosas*. In an introduction to these poems as published, Ricardo Palma wrote: "Caviedes was a most unfortunate poet. Many times I have encountered his verses in periodicals of Peru or of foreign countries, either anonymous or signed by some vagabond, but never have I found under them the signature of the true author. In life Caviedes was the victim of quacks; and in death the victim of literary pirates."

On medical science in Peru

The low state of medical science in Peru in the last half of the seventeenth century called forth from Caviedes numerous critical and satirical references to the ignorance and lamentable practice of Peruvian physicians. Viceroy Liñán y Cisneros (1679–1681), in his account of the state of the viceroyalty, made for his successor, the duke of Palata, refers to the miserable state of medical science and practice in Peru, the lack of revenue and the consequent abandonment of instruction in medicine, and the exposure of the health of the population to the mercy of pretentious ignorance. Gutiérrez wrote of Caviedes that he "had no convictions acquired by study hostile to the uncertainties of the science of medicine.

He knew by observation that the disciples of Hippocrates kill when they make mistakes, and the instinct of preservation and love of life put terrible arms into his hands, against those who, in his view, had once brought him to the brink of the grave. His vengeance was cruel. Ill-will served him as a muse, and it cannot be denied that in many of his compositions there was manifest true inspiration."[2]

II

Sons of nobles sent to Peru

In spite of the wealth which the New World had poured into Spain many of the noble families were poor in the seventeenth century, and some of these found it difficult to give their sons such an education as their talents and station demanded. Frequently young persons of this class secured positions as pages in the viceroy's household, and were educated under his supervision, sometimes remaining in Peru and acquiring distinction in the affairs of the state or the

(2) Odriozola, *Documentos literarios del Perú*, v. The quotation is from Juan Maria Gutiérrez's critical essay on Caviedes and his writings appears, and also (pp. 23–281) the two collections of poems already mentioned.

Church. Some of them with the viceroy's approval joined religious orders. Ignacio de Arbieto is an instance of one who became a Jesuit.

Arbieto's life and writings

He was born in Madrid in 1585. At Lima he studied in the college of San Pablo, later taught Latin in the same institution, became professor of philosophy at Quito, was transferred to the college in Arequipa, where he became rector of the institution, returned to the college of San Pablo in Lima as professor of theology, was appointed rector of the college at Chuquisaca, and subsequently took up his duties as rector of the college of San Martín in Lima. After long service as professor and rector of various colleges of the Society, he died in Lima on August 7, 1676. During his last years he served as counsellor of the provincial, and at the same time was occupied in writing his *Historia del Perú y de las fundaciones que ha hecho en él la Compañía de Jesús*. A *Suma de las obras teológicas del P. Francisco Suárez* is attributed to Padre Arbieto.

The failure of Arbieto's work to receive

Arbieto's successor

Barrasa's *Historia de las fundaciones*

the approval of the General of the Society led to the demand that another person should be charged with writing the history of the Jesuit foundations. By vote of the provincial congregation of 1674 Padre Jacinto Barrasa was appointed to undertake the task, which he completed in a manuscript volume of 1350 pages to the satisfaction of the authorities; but this appears not to have been published. The book was more exclusively devoted to the affairs of the Jesuits than were most of the writings of the Jesuit historians. He treated neither of the political history of the country nor of its geography, affirming that these phases of the subject had been sufficiently presented by Calancha in his *Crónica moralizada.* His course with respect to the second subject was altogether unusual, for from the beginning even to the present geographical description has been a conspicuous feature of South American writings. The real theme of Barrasa's book is sufficiently set forth in its title: *Historia de las fundaciones de los colegios y casas de la provincia del Perú de la Compañía de*

Jesús, con la noticia de las vidas y virtudes religiosas de algunos varones ilustres que en ella trabajaron.

The fame acquired by Barrasa during his life rested chiefly on his work as a professor and as a preacher. Two volumes of his sermons were published in Madrid in 1678, and another volume in Lima in 1678.

Padre Barrasa died at the college of San Pablo in Lima on November 22, 1704.

José de Buendía, the distinguished Jesuit of Lima

Padre José de Buendía, as historian, sacred orator, and philosopher, is called "one of the literary glories of Peru in the seventeenth century." His especially noteworthy *Vida del venerable padre Francisco del Castillo de la Compañía de Jesús, natural de Lima, 1615–1673,* (Madrid, 1693), became more widely known than his other works. Its value consists not merely in its account of the life of Castillo but also in its references to the history of Peru, and to the lives of many other Jesuits of the province. It contains, moreover, an account of the earthquake of 1787. This part was published by Odriozola at Lima in 1863.

La estrella de Lima was issued under the

La estrella de Lima

name of Francisco de Echave y Assu, but it is affirmed by Saldamando that its author was Buendía.[3] But whatever may be the decision on this point, the book itself has a recognized value for the history of Peru. It contains an account of the ceremonies attending the beatification of Archbishop Toribio Alfonso Mogrobejo, later Santo Toribio; biographies of Mogrobejo and of succeeding archbishops; important references to bishops, inquisitors, councillors, judges, viceroys, and other persons whose illustrious lives contributed to the glory of Lima. It describes, moreover, the metropolitan church and cites an abundance of facts of historic interest. Buendía acquired distinction also by his sermons and "funeral orations."

Padre José de Buendía was born in Lima in 1644, left the college of San Martín in 1665, taught philosophy in the college of San Pablo and at Cuzco, and died May 4, 1727. His life, apart from his writings has left no conspicuous record.

(3) *Jesuitas del Perú*, 130. Mendiburu says, "Dicese que el padre Buendía cooperó a la redacción de la obra. *Estrella de Lima.*" (*Dic. hist. biog.* II, 91.)

III

In 1643 rumours ran through the western colonies that the Dutch were preparing to invade Chile. The prospect of this invasion induced the viceroy of Peru to send a body of three hundred soldiers to strengthen the military forces already in the southern colony. Jerónimo de Quiroga, then a youth of eighteen, was a member of this company, and arrived in Chile near the end of the year. He apparently remained there in the service, for a few years later, at the age of thirty-three, he married a young woman of a prominent family of Santiago, and not long afterwards he was advanced to the rank of captain of cavalry. During the next thirty-five or forty years he rendered important services to the state in both military and civil undertakings. One of his military commissions was the taking of three thousand arms from Mendoza over the Andes to Concepción. He was a life member of the ayuntamiento of Santiago by royal confirmation. He had general charge of the construction of the cathedral

Jerónimo de Quiroga

for a period, and contributed largely towards the work from his own funds. He directed the fortification of Valparaiso and Concepción, and repaired the more or less ruined fortifications of the southern frontier.[4] He held various military commands, particularly that of chief of the militia of Chile for a period of seventeen years, and the governor turned to him for a method of reducing the Indians of the frontier to civilization. At the close of his military career, during which, especially in the later years, he encountered opposition and intrigue, at the age of seventy he turned to the task of writing the history of his country down to the events of his own time. His life in Chile had covered a considerable part of this period, and for this reason his book was properly called *Memoria de las cosas de Chile*. Medina reports that only an extract of the first part has been preserved, and that this was published in the twenty-third volume of the *Semanario erudito* of Madrid in 1788. This extract was called *Compendio histórico de los más principales sucesos*

Memoria de las cosas de Chile

(4) Medina, *Lit. col. de Chile*, II, 130.

de la conquista y guerras del reino de Chile hasta el año de 1656. The critical judgment respecting Quiroga's style—his rapidity of narration, conciseness of expression, and the harmony and facility of his phrases—indicates the degree of loss suffered in the disappearance of the complete work.[5]

Quiroga's *Compendio histórico*

Of Padre Anello Oliva little appears to be known aside from the fact that he was born in Naples and became a member of the Society of Jesus. His principal work is entitled *Vidas de varones ilustres de la Compañia de Jesús de la provincia del Perú.* The sub-title describes the contents more fully, announcing that the first of the four books treats of the kingdom and provinces of Peru, the Incas, the discovery and conquest by the Spaniards; and that the three other books describe the lives of the Jesuits written, as one critic informs us, solely with the object of preserving the memory of the Jesuits the most distinguished in the virtues and in the observation of the rules of the Society, in order that they might serve as examples to their successors; but offering no

Anello Oliva's *Varones ilustres*

(5) Medina, *Lit. col. de Chile,* II, 137.

interest to the historian, since they are limited, for the most part, to referring to the manner in which these distinguished Jesuits succeeded in reaching a high degree of perfection, and to eulogizing the merit which they attained.[6]

Histoire du Pérou

In 1857 M. Ternaux Compans published the first book of Oliva's *Vidas* in a French translation made from the unpublished manuscript, under the title, *Histoire du Pérou.* This book of Oliva's work forms in some sense an introduction to the lives of illustrious men. The persons whose biographies made up the body of the work were Ruiz Portillo, José Acosta, Baltazar Pinas, Juan Sebastián, Rodrigo de Cabrevo, Juan de Alienza, Estevan Páez, Juan de Frías Herrán, Gonzalo de Lyra, and Juan Romero. The first book was printed in Lima from the original Spanish manuscript in 1895.

Long and dull years of isolation in the dependencies and ignorance of the conditions of the older countries led the colonists

(6) Torres Saldamando, *Los antiguos Jesuitas del Perú*, 109. Oliva's manuscript is in the British Museum.

to exaggerate or overestimate what they saw in the cities of South America. If they celebrated the accession of a king of Spain, it seemed to them that nowhere else had there been seen such magnificence. In writing, therefore, of the capital of Peru, Diego Ojeda Gallinato very naturally entitled his book *Grandezas de Lima*. This book, Mendiburu says, is extremely rare even in Spain, and that he had not been able to obtain a copy of it. But other writers who had used it give some notions of Ojeda's opinions, particularly of the inhabitants of Peru, who appeared to him, especially those descended from Spanish ancestors, discreet, liberal, energetic, and possessed of most active minds; and what most excited admiration was to see how early intelligence dawned in the children.[7]

Grandezas de Lima

Ojeda's opinions

The grandiloquent style that prevailed in Spanish literature and in Spanish preaching incited the Franciscan friar Martín Velasco, to write his treatise on Rhetoric under the title, *Arte de sermones*, printed in Cadiz in 1675. Little is known of Velasco's life be-

(7) *Dic. hist. biog. del Perú*, VI, 120.

Velasco's *Arte de sermones*

yond the fact that he was born in Bogotá, and lived in the Franciscan monastery of that city. The key to his doctrine appears to be contained in these two sentences: "Words are smoke and noise which do not go beyond their sense; and in serving for what they are, it is not they but the truth they utter that produces the effect. One should try, therefore, to utter much truth in few words after the manner of the Laconians, and not many words and little substance."[8] If the teaching of the inconspicuous friar had had its merited influence much good might have come to Spanish speech even out of America.

IV

Fernández Piedrahita

In the last half of the seventeenth century an historian of considerable merit appeared in the person of Bishop Lucas Fernández Piedrahita, who was born in Bogotá on March 6, 1624. Through his mother, Catalina Collantes, he held by birth a more or less distant relationship to a member of the family of the Incas in Peru. He

(8) Quoted by Vergara, *Literatura en Nueva Granada*, 132.

studied in the Jesuit college of San Bartolomé, and received the degree of doctor from the University of Santo Tomás. The literary ambition of his youth manifested itself in the writing of a number of dramas that are not known to exist. He was appointed treasurer of the cathedral of Popayán, but before he entered upon the duties of that office he was made a prebendary of the metropolitan church in 1654. He was subsequently promoted to various offices in that church and after the death of Archbishop Torres he was elected vicar general and governor of the archbishopric; and he continued to hold the office of vicar general after the arrival of Arguinao, in 1661, the successor of Archbishop Torres. Piedrahita became the favourite preacher of the city, and through his influence and friendly relation with the president Dionisio Pérez Manrique, harmony was established between the ecclesiastical and civil officials. But the arrival of Cornejo as visitador introduced an element of discord into the community. Soon after the accession of Arguinao, Piedrahita was called to Spain to

Piedrahita vicar general

defend himself before the Council of the Indies against charges preferred by the visitador. His defence was so complete that the Council not only absolved him from fault, but also offered him the office of bishop of Santa Marta, and this appointment was immediately confirmed by the Pope. He remained six years in Spain, from 1663 to 1669, and during this period he wrote his *Historia general del nuevo reino de Granada.*

Historia de Granada

In 1669 Piedrahita returned to America, and after his consecration entered upon the exercise of his functions as bishop of Santa Marta. Here he displayed many of the virtues of the primitive Christian teacher, visited and taught the Indians, distributed his income among the poor and lived in poverty. His charitable gifts left him hardly means for decent clothing. In 1676 he was promoted to the see of Panama, but before he left Santa Marta the town was taken by pirates, who, seeing the meanness of the bishop's dress, concluded that by his apparently miserly habits he must have large accumulations concealed. The pir-

Bishop of Santa Marta and of Panama

ates, therefore, took the bishop and tortured him in order to make him reveal the hiding-place of his treasures; unsuccessful in this, they carried him off and brought him before the distinguished and courteous pirate Morgan, who received him with marked consideration, gave him a pontifical robe stolen at Panama, and caused him to be conducted to his new diocese. Here Bishop Piedrahita continued for twelve years the devoted life he had led in Santa Marta, and died at the age of sixty-four. The first part of his *Historia* was published in Amsterdam the year of his death, 1688. According to Vergara, the second part was lost after the death of the author, since there was no one to care for its publication.[9]

Piedrahita's style

With respect to his style, Piedrahita represents a considerable advance over the prose writers of South America who preceded him. He wrote clearly in what might not improperly be called modern Spanish. He had not, however, freed himself from the custom of his time, or the practice of writing long and irrelevant in-

(9) *Literatura en la Nueva Granada*, 118.

troductions to chapters or sections, the custom that induced the chronicler to begin his narrative with the creation of the world.

V

Padre Pedro Claver

A striking subject for a biography was furnished by the life of Padre Pedro Claver, who was born in Cataluña in 1585 and died at Cartagena in 1654. He became a member of the Society of Jesus, entering upon his novitiate in 1602. For his work among the slaves at Cartagena he became known as the "Apostle to the Negroes." Cartagena in the seventeenth century had a much larger population than at present, and, in relation to South America, was a much more important port; it was the port at which were landed most of the ships engaged in the African slave-trade. The ships arrived overcrowded, with their human freight in an indescribable condition. The victims of the slave-trader's greed and inhumanity, in the long voyage in the tropics, had suffered untold misery from an insufficient supply of food, air and water, and at the end of the voyage the living, the

Slave-trade at Cartagena

moribund, and the dead were found packed in a mass of filth more foul than anything which the fancy can picture.

Padre Claver[10] spent forty years of a devoted life in efforts to relieve this misery,[11] and the story of this devotion was written by Alonso de Andrade.[12] A more exten sive account of Claver's life by José Fernández appeared in 1666. Another book relating to Cartagena is Luis Jodar's *Vida de la Venerable Madre Catalina María de la Concepción, fundadora del Convento de Santa Clara de Cartagena.*

Flórez de Ocáriz's *Genealogías*

The *Genealogías del nuevo reino de Granada,* by Juan Flórez de Ocáriz, is a curious monument of patient labour and mediaeval ignorance, produced rather by manual labour than by intellectual effort. It fairly exemplifies the tradition and vices of early, and perhaps of some later, writings on genealogy, in pretending to establish a

(10) Borda, José Joaquín, *Historia de la Compañía de Jesús en la Nueva Granada*, Poissy, 1872.

(11) Fleuriau, *La vie du vénérable père Claver, de la Compagnie de Jésus*, Clermont-Ferrand, 1834, 62.

(12) Vergara says this book was printed under the false name of Licenciado Jerónimo Suárez Sornoza.—*Literatura en la Nueva Granada*, 126.

family connexion between persons of similar names, who lived in widely separated ages and in different parts of the world. But the introduction which takes up about half of the first volume contains important information on the local history of New Granada. An incentive to genealogical inquiry was furnished by the ambition of many creoles to magnify the social importance of their families. Two volumes of this work were published in Madrid in 1674–76; a third remains unpublished.

León y Bezerra

A contemporary account of the events at Panama at the time of Morgan's invasion (1670) was written by Bishop Antonio de León y Bezerra, who, having refused the office of Bishop of Panama three times, finally accepted it in 1672. The following year, after the death of the conde de Lemos the audiencia of Lima appointed Bishop León governor and captain-general of Tierra Firme, and in January, 1674, he assumed the duties of that office. In 1676, he was promoted to the post of Bishop of Trujillo, and a little later was transferred to the bishopric of Arequipa. He died in 1708.

VI

An important source of detailed information concerning Peruvian history, particularly the history of Cuzco, is the anonymous chronicle entitled *Anales del Cuzco* constituting four hundred and thirty-four pages of a volume edited by Ricardo Palma, and published in Lima in 1901. It covers a period of one hundred and fifty years, from 1600 to 1750. Although lacking the attractive style of Calancha and some of the other early writers, it nevertheless throws much light on many obscure points of local history. Ricardo Palma attributes to the writer "a certain independence of character and a standard of criticism not usual at that time," and cites as an illustration the author's condemnation of the extraordinary means employed by the preachers to terrify the Indians, such as frightful pictures of the devil and graphic representations of the sufferings of the damned in hell.[13]

Anales del Cuzco

Palma's criticism

The numerous paragraphs relating to ecclesiastical affairs point to the conspicuous

(13) See *Anales del Cuzco, Renglones preliminares*, p. VII; also the text 295–297.

place held by the events connected with the Church. The following quotation illustrates the style, in so far as the chronicle may be said to have any style, and also the avaricious disposition of certain colonial priests in administering the services of the Church.

Priest Maturana's exactions

"Gaspar de Lagos, of the hospital parish, having died, the priest of the parish demanded five hundred dollars for the funeral service, and finally agreed to receive one hundred and eighty dollars. The widow of the deceased went, on the 30th of December (1743), at eight o'clock in the evening to Bishop Morcello, and showed him that it was impossible for her to pay this amount. The bishop decided that the interment in accordance with the widow's wishes to be just, and, fixing the payment at sixty-one dollars, handed to the widow a paper stating this decision. Then, the widow went to the priest, Julián Maturana, and gave him the paper. The priest threw the paper on the floor and stamped on it, and said that the cross would not go out if she did not bring the one hundred and eighty dollars.

The widow returned to the bishop, now after nine o'clock at night, and he ordered that they should bring the priest. The fiscal and the officer sought for him in the house of the bishop of Panama, where he was living, but they did not find him. The bishop then issued an order that the Franciscan fathers should conduct the burial properly as the widow required, and also ordered that the sixty-one dollars should be applied to the work of the cathedral." [14]

VII

Rodríguez' *El Marañón y Amazonas*

The book by Padre Manuel Rodríguez entitled *El Marañón y Amazonas* and published in 1684 is a history of the discovery and reduction of the tribes that lived in the region of the great rivers. It undertook to set forth the praiseworthy as well as the unfortunate conduct of the conquistadores respecting temporal and spiritual matters, and in six books to present the data that had been acquired and the narratives that had been written concerning the discovery of the Amazon; the services the Jesuits

(14) Ricardo Palma: *Anales del Cuzco*, 326.

had rendered and the missions they had founded; the progress made in the government of Mainas from its establishment by Diego Vaca de Vega; the journey of Captain Texeira to Quito and his return to Pará; the sources of the rivers and their union with the Amazon; the labours of missionaries and the tragic end of many of them; and an account of Acuña's report. This work may still be considered as an historical document of value, and, barring its prolixity, a common failing of the age, is not without literary merit.[15]

Padre Samuel Fritz

Another traveller and missionary labourer in the region of the Amazon was Padre Samuel Fritz, a Bohemian Jesuit who entered the missions of Mainas in 1686. Besides founding a large number of new missions, he made important contributions to what was then known about the geography and languages of the lands adjacent

(15) The sub-title is: *Historia de los descubrimientos, entradas, y reducción de naciones. Trabajos malogrados de algunos conquistadores, y dichosos de otros, así temporales, como espirituales, en las dilatadas montañas y mayores ríos de América. Escrita por el Padre Manuel Rodríguez, de la Compañía de Jesús, Procurador general de las Provincias de Indias en la Corte de Madrid. Con Licencia. En Madrid, Año de 1684.*

to the Amazon and its principal tributaries. He made a map of the region, which was engraved and published in Quito in 1707.[16] He compiled grammars and dictionaries of several native languages and made a map entitled *El gran rio Marañón o Amazonas con la misión de la Compañia de Jesús geográficamente delineado.*

Ponce de León on *El Marañón*

Among the unpublished contributions to the literature of the Amazon one may note the *Conquistas y problaciones del Marañón*, by Francisco Ponce de León, who was a member of the order of Mercy, sometime provincial in Chile, and missionary among the Indians. The manuscript was at one time reported to be in Barcia's library.

(16) "Alors parut pour la première fois en France . . . une copie de la carte gravée à Quito en 1707, et dressée dès l'année 1690 par le Père Samuel Fritz, Jésuite allemand, Missionaire sur les bords du Maragnon, qu'il avait parcouru dans toute sa longueur. Par cette carte, on apprit etc. . . . Du reste le Père Fritz, sans pendule et sans lunette, n'a pu déterminer aucun point en longitude. Il n'avait qu'un petit demi-circle de bois, de trois pouces de rayon pour les latitudes; enfin il etait malade quand il descendit le fleuve jusqu'au Para. Il ne faut que lire son journal manuscrit, dont j'ai une copie, pour voir que plusieurs obstacles, alors et à son retour à la mission, ne lui permirent pas de faire les observations nécessaires pour rendre sa carte exacte, surtout vers la partie inférieure du fleuve." —M. de La Condamine, *Relation abrégée d'un voyage fait dans l'intérieur de l'Amérique Méridionale* (Paris, 1745), pp. 13 et seq.

CHAPTER XII

THE EARLY YEARS OF THE EIGHTEENTH CENTURY.

I. *Jorge Juan y Santacilla and Antonio de Ulloa.* II. *Alonso de Zamora and José de Oviedo y Baños.* III. *Joseph Luis Cisneros and Francisca Josefa de Castillo y Guevara.* IV. *Pedro de Peralta Barnuevo and Juan de Mira.* V. *Juan Rivero, José Cassani and Pedro Gumilla.* VI. *Some minor ecclesiastical writers.*

I

French in South America

The dependence of Philip V on Louis XIV opened to the French an opportunity for commerce and scientific investigation in Spanish South America. In the first fifteen years of the eighteenth century French merchants took advantage of their opportunity and sent an unprecedented amount of exports in a large number of ships from French ports to the ports of Chile and Peru. In these early decades of the century the French undertook also scientific investigations in South America. Feuillée and Frezier led the way, and they were followed by La Condamine's expedition to Ecuador, in which Spanish co-operation was represented by Jorge Juan and Antonio de Ulloa. After the completion of the measurements near Quito Juan and Ulloa made elaborate inquiries into the political and social condition of the colonies. The results of these observations and researches were set forth in two important documents: *Noticias secretas de América* and their *Relación histórica del viaje a la América*.

Feuillée and Frezier

Juan and Ulloa

The former is an extensive report designed for the instruction of the king. It was not generally known until it was published in London by David Barry in 1826. It is the most frank and searching examination of the affairs of the colonies that has come down from the colonial period. It presents the abuses of the courts, the civil employees, the corregidores, and the clergy. It treats, moreover, of the contraband

Noticias secretas

trade, the frauds that appeared in the various branches of the administration, the scandalous acts of the officials, and the oppression and cruelty of the Spaniards in their dealing with the Indians. It describes the state of the ports and the lack of arms and of other means for defending the coast against invaders, and sets forth the increasing hostility betwen the Spaniards and the creoles. It makes exceedingly damaging specifications as to the treatment which the Indians received at the hands of the corregidores, the manufacturers, and the priests. The following passages from the *Noticias secretas* illustrate this subject:

"It was ordered that the corregidores might introduce a quantity of such articles as were suited to the needs of the Indians and distribute these articles among them at moderate prices, in order that, having implements for labour, they might shake off the apathy which is innate in their constitution, and make the exertion requisite for paying their tribute and supporting themselves.

Distribution by Corregidores

"The articles of distribution are chiefly mules, foreign and domestic goods, and produce. The corregidores who are attached to the viceroyalty of Lima must necessarily go to that city to take out a licence and to receive their despatch from the viceroy in order to be inducted into office; and as Lima is the principal depôt of the trade of Peru, it is in that city that an assortment of articles for distribution is to be made, and for this purpose they take the goods required from the shop of some merchant or trader on credit, at an exorbitant price; for, as the traders are aware of the enormous profits the corregidores make in the sale, they raise the prices of the goods in order to have a share in the speculation. The corregidores have no money before they come into office, and, being unable to purchase for cash, they are obliged to submit to any terms which the creditor may prescribe, since they are under great obligatoins, on account of the money which the merchant is to lend them for the purchase of the mules required for transportation

"As soon as the corregidor comes within

Corregidor's wares

his jurisdiction, the first act of his administration is to take a census of the Indians according to their towns and villages. Proceeding to this duty in person, and taking with him the articles of merchandise to be distributed, he goes on, apportioning the quantity and kind he selects for every Indian, and affixing to each article its price, just as suits his caprice, the poor Indians being wholly ignorant of what is to fall to their lot, or how much it is to cost them. As soon as he has finished distributing in one village, he transfers the whole assortment to the cacique, with an exact inventory of the articles belonging to each individual, from the cacique himself to the most humble of all those who are to pay tribute; and the corregidor proceeds to another village in order to continue the distribution. It is a time of anguish both for the cacique and the Indians, when they look at the quantity, quality, and prices of these goods. In vain does the cacique remonstrate, and to no purpose do the Indians raise their clamours; on the one hand, they maintain that their means are not ade-

Despair of the Indians

quate to such a quantity of merchandise as is assigned to them, being absolutely unable to pay for it; again, they urge that goods of such a description are utterly useless to them, and that the price is so exorbitant as to exceed anything they had ever paid before. The corregidor remains inexorable and the Indians are obliged to take whatever has been allotted to them, however repugnant it may be to their wishes, and however straitened they are for want of means to make the payments; for these payments become due simultaneously with the tribute money, and the same penalty is imposed for failure to meet one as the other. All the payments of the first distribution must be made within two years and a half, to make way for the second, which usually does not contain so many wares as the first" (p. 240).

The statement concerning the textile works is equally positive:

"In former years woollen manufacture was confined to the province of Quito; but it has been recently introduced into other districts, although the articles manufactured in the provinces south of Quito are nothing

Indians in the obrajes

but coarse cloths of very ordinary texture. In Cajamarca there are looms for the manufacture of cotton goods. . . .

"The labour of the obraje, or manufactory, begins before the day dawns, at which time every Indian takes his place at the piece which is in process of weaving and the tasks of the day are distributed as may be expedient; and when this process is concluded, the owner of the house closes the door, and leaves them immured as in a prison. At midday the door is opened for the women to go in with their scanty allowance of food, which is soon partaken, and they are again locked in. When the darkness of the night no longer permits them to work, the owner goes round to gather up the stints; those who have not been able to finish, in spite of apologies or reasonings, are punished with indescribable cruelty: and those unfeeling men, as if transformed into merciless savages, inflict upon the wretched Indians lashes by the hundred, for they use no other method of counting; and to complete the punishment, they remand them again to the workshop: and

Punishment of the Indians

although the whole building is a prison-house, a portion of it is reserved for fetters and instruments of torture, where they are punished with greater indignity than could be practised towards the most delinquent slaves. . . .

"We frequently met the Indians on the highway, tied by the hair to the tail of a horse, on which a mestizo is mounted, who is conveying them to the workshops, and perhaps for the trivial offence of having evaded the tyranny of the overseer, from fear of punishment. Let what will be said of the cruelty practised by the patrons (encomenderos) towards the Indians at the commencement of the conquest, we cannot persuade ourselves, after what we have witnessed, that it could ever have been carried to the extent it now is by the Spaniards and mestizos." (pp. 276, 279.)

Some paragraphs of the *Noticias secretas* refer to the immorality of the clergy:

Corruption of the clergy

"The persons who compose the two orders of the clergy are guilty of such licentionsness, that making due allowance for the frailties to which human nature is liable and the weakness to which men of every class are subject, it would appear that those ecclesiastics regard it as theirpeculiar privilege to go before all others in the career of vice; for while they are under the most sacred obligations not only to practise virtue, but to correct the errors incident to frail nature, it is they who, by their pernicious example, sanction the practice of iniquity, and in a measure divest it of its heinous nature.'

"The parish priests are extemely vicious in their habits; but, whether it happens that an error or crime in them attracts less notice, or whether they are more careful to conceal it, or for both reasons, which is the more probable, disgraceful as the consequences are known to be, they never reach such a degree of scandal as do those of the monks; for the latter, from the first step they take, and even without leaving the monasteries, pursue a course of conduct so notorious and shameful that it becomes offensive in the extreme, and fills the mind with horror.

"The fandangoes or balls are usually devised by the members of the religious orders, or more properly by those who call themselves religious, although, in fact, they are far from being so; for it is they who pay the expense, who attend in company with their concubines, and who get up the fray in their own houses. Simultaneously with the dance, the immoderate use of ardent spirits begins, and the entertainment is gradually converted into acts of impropriety so unseemly and lewd, that it would be presumption even to speak of them, and a want of delicacy to stain the narrative with such a record of obscenities; and, letting them lie hid in the region of silence, we shall only remark that, whatever the spirit of malice could invent in respect to this subject, great as it might be, it could never fathom that abyss into which those corrupt minds are plunged, nor give any adequate idea of the degree of excess to which debauchery and crime are carried." (pp. 490, 497.)

Fandangoes of the religious

The *Relación histórica*, by Juan and Ulloa the result of extensive journeys of investigation made by order of the king, was orig-

Relación histórica

inally published in Madrid in 1748. It has been reprinted many times, and translations of it have appeared in various languages. An English translation was issued in London in 1758, entitled *A Voyage to South America*. A small volume by Ulloa called *Entretenimientos* (1772) treats of the geography and productions of Peru and Ecuador, the antiquities of these countries, the customs, language, and religion of the Indians, with suggestions as to the means of increasing the population of America.

Ulloa's public career

In the course of his public career Ulloa rose to the rank of lieutenant-general. He was born in Seville in 1716. His studies prepared him for the position of an officer in the navy, and when Philip V granted the request of Louis XV to be permitted to send a body of scientists to measure an arc of the meridian under the equator in Ecuador, Antonio de Ulloa and Jorge Juan were appointed to join the commission. Ulloa gained distinction by his scientific investigations, and became a member of the scientific societies of London, Paris, Berlin, and Stockholm. From time to time he was

Antonio de Ulloa

charged with various official duties by the government of Spain, and in 1763, when Louisiana was ceded to Spain, Ulloa was appointed to take possession of the country and organize its administration, thus becoming its first Spanish governor.

The *Relación histórica* is an excellent account of Spanish South America as it was near the middle of the eighteenth century, by two men who, although special commissioners appointed by the king, were apparently more disposed to tell the truth than to please their royal master. Designed for the general public, this work is less severe in tone than the *Noticias secretas*, which was written for the instruction of the king and his ministers. Here is a description of the fair at Porto Bello from the *Relación histórica*.

Relación and *Noticias*

"The town of Porto Bello, so thinly inhabited, by reason of its noxious air, the scarcity of provisions, and the barrenness of the soil, becomes, at the time of the galleons, one of the most populous places in all South America. Its situation on the isthmus, betwixt the south and the north sea,

The fair of Porto Bello

the goodness of its harbour, and its small distance from Panama have given it the preference for the rendezvous of the joint commerce of Spain and Peru, at its fair.

"On advice being received at Carthagena, that the Peru fleet had unloaded at Panama, the galleons made the best of their way to Porto Bello, in order to avoid the distempers which have their source from idleness. The concourse of people, on this occasion, is such, as to raise the rent of lodging to an excessive degree; a middling chamber, with a closet, lets, during the fair, for a thousand crowns, and some large houses, for four, five or six thousand.

"The ships are no sooner moored in the harbour than the first work is to erect, in the square, a tent made of the ship's sails, for receiving the cargo; at which the proprietors of the goods are present, in order to find their bales, by the marks which distinguish them. These bales are drawn on sledges to their respective places, by the crews of every ship, and the money given them is proportionally divided.

"Whilst the seamen and European

traders are thus employed, the land is covered with droves of mules from Panama, each drove consisting of above an hundred, loaded with chests of gold and silver, on account of the merchants of Peru. Some unload them at the exchange, others in the middle of the square; yet amidst the hurry and confusion of such crowds, no theft, loss, or disturbance is ever known. He who has seen this place during the tiempo muerto, or dead time, solitary, poor, and a perpetual silence reigning everywhere, the harbour quite empty, and every place wearing a melancholy aspect, must be filled with astonishment at the sudden change, to see the bustling multitudes, every house crowded, the square and the streets encumbered with bales and chests of gold, and silver of all kinds; the harbour full of ships and vessels, some bringing by way of Rio de Chape, the goods of Peru, as cacao, quinquina, or Jesuit's bark, vicuña wool, and bezoar stones; others coming from Carthagena, loaded with provisions; and thus a spot, at all other times detested for its deleterious qualities becomes the staple of the riches of

Arrival of gold from Perú

the old and new world, and the scene of one of the most considerable branches of commerce in the whole earth.

Organization of the trading

"The ships being unloaded, and the merchants of Peru, together with the president of Panama, arrived, the fair comes under deliberation. And for this purpose the deputies of the several parties, repair on board the commodore of the galleons, where, in presence of the commodore, and the president of Panama, the former as patron of the Europeans, and the latter, of the Peruvians, the prices of the several kinds of merchandise are settled; and all preliminaries being adjusted in three or four meetings, the contracts are signed, and made public, that everyone may conform himself to them in the sale of his effects. Thus all fraud is precluded. The purchases and sales, as likewise the exchanges of money, are transacted by brokers, embarking their chests of money, and those of Peru, sending away the goods they have purchased in vessels called chatas and bongos, up the river, Chagre; and thus the fair of Porto Bello ends." (Eng. tr. I, 101.)

II

Alonso de Zamora

Alonso de Zamora is conspicuous among the historians who wrote in the early part of the eighteenth century. His *Historia de la provincia de San Antonino del nuevo reino de Granada del orden de Predicadores* (Barcelona, 1701) is called a first volume, but there is no adequate evidence that a second volume was ever written. The author was born in Bogotá in 1660. He entered the Dominican order in his native city, studied at the University of St. Thomas, and subsequently undertook the work of a missionary. His fame as a theologian and as a writer and preacher doubtless contributed to his appointment, in 1690, as chronicler of his order. He was especially commissioned to write a general history of the ecclesiastical province, then under the direction of the provincial Antonio Choche. At this time Quesada's *Compendio historial* was still in existence, and Zamora used it as a source of information. In 1696 he completed his manuscript and sent it to Spain for publication. In view of the

Character of Zamora's book

circumstances under which Zamora wrote and the nature of his subject, one might very well expect that his book would be a panegyric on the history and character of his order; and the book justifies such an expectation. The author magnified the influences and services of ecclesiastics in promoting civilization in America, which secular opinion had tended to belittle. In his style and the arrangement of his material he falls short of the excellence attained by Piedrahita.[1]

Oviedo y Baños

A higher standard was reached by José de Oviedo y Baños in his *Historia de la conquista y población de la provincia de Venezuela.* This author was born in Bogotá in 1674, but spent the greater part of his life in Venezuela, and died at Caracas, where his *Historia* was written. The first volume was printed in Madrid in 1723. The complete work was issued in the *Biblioteca de los americanistas* (Madrid, 1885), in two volumes, preceded by an introduction by Cesáreo Fernández Duro, in which he says that this narration was made

(1) Vergara, *Hist. de la lit. en N. Granada*, 163–167.

with the impartiality and the high critical spirit of the true historian and forms a source from which those who study the history of Caracas are compelled to draw. Diego, a brother of José de Oviedo, was an oidor in Guatemala, then promoted to the audiencia of Mexico, and later was a member of the Council of the Indies. He wrote a commentary in two volumes on the *Recopilación castellana*.

Conquista de Venezuela

Diego de Baños y Sotomayor, an uncle of the historian, became bishop of Caracas. Educated in Bogotá, he was instrumental in bringing some rays of intellectual light into Caracas after decades of obscurity. He founded the Colegio Seminario de Santa Rosa, and left as evidence of his literary activity the *Constituciones sinodales del obispado de Venezuela*, published at Madrid in 1698. Another writer bearing the name Oviedo, but of a family distinct from the foregoing, has left a long list of volumes on ecclesiastical subjects. This was Vicente de Oviedo. He studied at the college of San Bartolomé in Bogotá, and for more than forty years was parish priest in various

The bishop of Caracas

Vicente de Oviedo

towns of the viceroyalty of New Granada. Efforts to secure the publication of his encyclopedic work in eleven volumes met with the insurmountable opposition of the Spanish government, the grounds of this opposition being utterances unfavourable to the dignity of the monarchy.[2]

Medrano's *Granada*

To the period embracing the end of the seventeenth century and the beginning of the eighteenth century belongs the *Historia del nuevo reino de Granada*, by Francisco de Medrano, of the Franciscan order. But these were unfruitful years in the literary history of New Granada. The principal literary products were chiefly such as were especially demanded by readers in the colonies, sermons and lives of saints.[3]

(2) See 'Un escritor colombiano del tiempo de la Colonia,' by Federico González Suárez, in the *Revista de Quito*, 1890.

(3) Some of the writers were Joseph Ossorio de Paz (*Sermones*), Joseph Ortiz de Morales (*Coronas de oro del patriarca San José*), Felipe Romana y Herrera (*Tractatus de poenitentia*), Juan de Olmos (*La Vida de la Madre Jerónima del Espíritu Santo*) Pablo de Villamor (*La Vida de la Madre Francisca del Niño Jesús*), and Pedro de Tobar y Buendía (*Verdadera histórica relación del origen, manifestación y prodigiosa renovación por sí misma, y milagros de la Imagen de Chiquinquira.*)

III

The publisher of the "collection of rare and curious books treating of America" issued in 1912, as the twenty-first volume of the collection, Joseph Luis Cisneros' *Descripción exacta de la provincia de Venezuela.* The editor of this reprint sets forth his conclusions concerning the author, which he holds were justified by the text of the work itself. These are that Cisneros was born in Venezuela some time between 1710 and 1715; that he was a trader and, as an agent of the Royal Guipuzcoa Company, for a period of twenty-five years traversed and retraversed the province of Venezuela, buying and selling a great variety of commodities; that he made a number of visits to the island of Curaçao, the province of Maracaybo and Santa Marta in New Granada; that he made three trips on the Orinoco to the Dutch towns of Essequibo and Surinam; and that his book was published at Valencia in Venezuela, in spite of the opinion of Aristides Rojas that the Valencia announced on the title-page as the place of publica-

Cisneros of Venezuela

tion was the Valencia of Spain, not the Venezuelan city.

The author displays, as he might be expected to do considering his occupation, extensive and detailed information concerning the state and the products of the country, the markets, and the prices, and this feature of his little book constitutes it a contemporary contribution to the economic history of the province of Venezuela under Spanish rule. Moreover, the simplicity of of the style and the presence of terms especially in use among traders would seem to offer further evidence of the writer's practical experience in commercial affairs.

Trade of Venezuela

The following reference to the foreign trade of the province, taken in connection with his remarks on the internal commerce, indicate a practical familiarity with Venezuela's economic conditions.

" The city of Caracas has a population of somewhat more than twenty-six thousand, in which there are many illustrious families known in Europe; it carries on commerce with the Royal Guipuzcoa Company, which takes the products of the province in exchange for clothing and food-stuffs, which it brings from Spain; it has also trade with Mexico, comprising a large amount of cacao carried from the port of La Guayra to Vera Cruz, bringing back the greater part of its compensation in silver bullion, and the rest in copper, flour, and various products of that country. At present there are fourteen ships engaged in this trade.

Caracas and the Islands

"The city or province has also commerce with the Canary Islands, which, in the same manner, receive cacao, loading their ships with it for the return voyage; they are also desirous of getting silver pesos, of which they carry away large quantities given to them in exchange for the products of their country, which are fine wines, grapes and certain liquors, with all kinds of dried fruit. They also introduce great quantities of taffeta, stockings, and all kinds of silk, a ship arriving once a year. Caracas has, moreover, trade with the Windward Islands, Havana, Santo Domingo, Puerto Rico, Margarita, and Cumaná. The Venezuelans carry on this commerce by sending out certain amounts of cacao, hides, tallow, and various other products of the province not desired by the Royal company, and bringing back in return silver bullion and products of those islands." (p. 59.)

Francisca Josefa de Castillo

The large majority of the men who have hitherto figured in the literary history of New Granada have either been members of the religious orders or functionaries of the Church in some other relation. In the person of Francisca Josefa de Castillo y Guevara a nun appears, who, according to Menéndez y Palayo, "wrote in prose worthy of Santa Teresa." She was born in Bogotá on October 8, 1671, entered the convent of Santa Clara at Tunja in 1689, and died there in 1742. She was afflicted with rickets, and was an invalid from her childhood. In the convent she was encouraged by her confessor to write her sentiments and reflections on her life. Her papers sent to her confessor in obedience to his suggestion gradually accumulated, and were later published in two more or less independent works. These were *Vida de la venerable madre Francisca Josefa de le Concepción, escrita por ella,* and *Sentimientos espiri-*

Jorge Juan y Santacilla

tuales de la V. M. Francisca Josefa. Francisca's early reading is said to have been largely plays, but in the convent she read the writings of Santa Teresa. Confined by her parents and by those persons who controlled her activity to the limited education that was thought to be becoming a woman in the Spanish colonies, her native intelligence enabled her to obtain a profound insight into certain phases of life, and to acquire a style of writing that persuaded the Colombian critic, Vergara, to declare that "Madre Castillo is the most notable writer whom we possess; her style and her language place her by the side of Santa Teresa."[4]

IV

Lima fundada

In the "poema heroico" called *Lima fundada o conquista del Perú,* we have an echo of the earlier historical narratives in verse. The author, Pedro José de Peralta Barnuevo Rocha y Benavides, was born in Lima in 1663, and during a great part of a long life he was a member of the University of San Marcos, at first as professor of ma-

(4) *Historia de la literatura en N. Granada,* 194.

thematics. He was rector of the university for the years 1715, 1716 and 1717. He served as cosmographer from 1708 to 1748. He was a lawyer, directed an academy which he had founded, was for many years engineer-in-chief of Peru, and in this capacity planned and directed important works at the port of Callao. For his great and varied learning Peralta's contemporaries appear to have held him in high esteem, and later opinion has confirmed their view. The statement in Mendiburu's *Diccionario histórico-biográfico del Perú* is that Peralta "was a master of six languages, and in the most of them he wrote poetry correctly and in good taste; he was well versed in sacred and profane history, was a profound mathematician, chemist, botanist, and student in medicine; and his studies in jurisprudence and canonical and theological matters he carried as far as the first professors of his time." (VI, 265.) The long list of his work, moreover, suggests unusual capacity and attainments.[5]

Peralta's writings

(5) These are the titles of some of Peralta's writings: *Desvíos de la naturaleza u origen de los monstruos; Tratado físico-médico-teológico; Lima triunfante; Imagen política, o gobierno*

Quality of *Lima fundada*

Lima fundada, in ten cantos embracing somewhat more than ten thousand lines, treats of the conquest of Peru from Pizarro's invasion to the overthrow of Almagro. In order that the thought may seem to move on an exalted plane, and the stanzas differentiate themselves from ordinary prose, the statements of fact are often made vague and roundabout, and the narration is abundantly sprinkled with intensifying adjectives. The hero is always "the great Pizarro" or "the great marquis," and the soldiers are the "illustrious troops." Large numbers of Grecian mythological characters are drawn into the service; the names of Ulysses, Alcibiades, Trajan and Socrates are woven familiarly into the lines; and the impression is made that the author knew too much to be a successful poet. Persons who seek for

del virrey-obispo de Quito; Causa académica; Jupiter Olimpico; Observaciones astronómicas: Panegírico del Cardenal Alberoni; Templo de la fama: Diálogo de la justicia y de la verdad; Historia de España vindicada; Alegaciones jurídicas; La gloria de Luis el Grande and *El Triunfo de Astrea* (in French); *Lima fundada, o conquista del Perú; Gobierno del Conde de la Monclova; Tratado físico-matemático; Defensa política y militar de Lima; Gobierno del Virrey Castel-Fuerte; Tratado músico-matemático; Nuevo sistema astrológico demostrativo; Geometría especulativa, y aritmética; Pasión y triunfo de Cristo; Obras poéticas, líricas y cómicas* (in two volumes).

an elevated and inspiring form of genuine poetry in these three hundred and eighty pages of verses will hardly find it.

Armas antárticas

The twenty cantos of *Armas antárticas* constitute a document that is properly classed with *Lima fundada.* It was written by Juan de Mira. Unless printed since my latest information concerning it, it is still in manuscript in the National Library of Madrid. It was probably written in Lima between 1612 and 1615, and the writer's aim appears to have been to prevent the deeds of the Spaniards in conquering, pacifying and defending Peru from "remaining hidden in the darkness of forgetfulness."[6]

The opening octave makes a general announcement of the author's theme:

Las armas y proezas militares
De españoles católicos valientes,
Que por ignotos y soberbios mares
Fueron a dominar remotas gentes,
Poniendo al verbo eterno en los altares
De oráculos gentílicos, espanto
Eran del indio, ahora mudos, canto.[7]

(6) An analysis of *Armas autárticas*, by Dr. Felix C. C. Zegarra, is printed in *La Revista peruana*, III, 292, 340, 414, 506.

And the following lines describe the gathering of the gold for Atahualpa's ransom:

Gathering the ransom

. . . . al instante
Chasquis despacha el inca a diferentes
Partes, para quel oro rutilante
Traigan con brevedad todas sus gentes;
No hay noble, no hay cacique, no hay infante,
No hay niños, no hay mujeres, no hay sirvientes
Que así como las próvidas hormigas
No traigan a la sala sus espigas.[8]

V

Among the Indians of the Llanos the Jesuits undertook to carry out a plan of missionary effort similar to that carried

(7) "I sing of arms and the military prowess of valiant Catholic Spaniards, who, over unknown and raging seas, went to dominate distant peoples, placing the Eternal Word on altars which formerly, with the insolent voices of the heathen oracles (now silent) were the terror of the Indian."

(8) "Immediately the Inca dispatched messengers to different parts of the kingdom, in order that all people might bring quickly the shining gold; and there was no noble, no chief, no son of a chief, no child, no woman, no servants, who thus, like the provident ant, did not carry his grain to the storehouse."

Missions of the Llanos

out in Paraguay. The region was divided into a number of districts, or partidos, the partido of Casanare, that of the Orinoco, and that of the Meta. These were under the general government of a procurador, who was under the superior direction of the provincial appointed at Rome to govern the province of Bogotá. During his term of three years the provincial was required to visit the missions at least once, or to send an inspector bearing the title of vice-provincial, who was commissioned to inquire into the state of the missions and to examine their records and accounts. In the last decades of the seventeenth century and later the government supported at each mission a small number of soldiers to assist the missionaries and to ward off hostile attacks. The success of these missions depended upon the establishment of such conditions that they would be economically independent, and for this purpose the missions became proprietors of extensive herds.

Rivero's *Historia de las misiones*

Juan Rivero's *Historia de las misiones de los llanos de Casanare y los ríos Orinoco y Meta,* written in 1736, is an important source of information concerning the history of these missions. It was printed in Bogotá in 1883, after it had remained in manuscript about one hundred and fifty years. The author was born in Miraflores de la Sierra, in Spain, August 15, 1681. He entered the Society of Jesus as a youth, and was sent to Bogotá in 1704. He began his missionary work at Tunja, but, on account of illness caused by the low temperature of the plateau, he was transferred to the college at Honda and later to that at Mompox. He was still moved by a desire for missionary work among the Indians, and, therefore, petitioned his superiors to send him to the Llanos. His petition was granted, and in 1720 he set out for the plains of Casanare. He became exceptionally proficient in a knowledge of the Indian languages, which he was able to make use of in the confessional and in preaching. He held vigorously to the opinion that the Indians could be readily induced to adopt the faith of the Church, and that this act would transform them into civilized men and women. Like many of his countrymen and later workers

Rivero as a missionary

for social betterment, he was a single-force reformer.

Cassani and Gumilla

Other writers took up the subject that had engaged the attention of Rivero and wrote of the region of the Orinoco. Padre José Cassani, writing of the missions, used Rivero's manuscript extensively, making it the basis of his work. Cassani's *Historia de la Provincia de la Compañía de Jesús del Nuevo Reino de Granada* is uncritical and disfigured by marvellous credulity. It was published in 1741. Gumilla's *El Orinoco ilustrado* was also published in 1741, and a second edition was issued in 1745. On the title-page of his book Gumilla describes himself as a "member of the Society of Jesus, missionary, superior of the missions of the Orinoco, Meta, and Casanare, calificador and consultor of the Holy Tribunal of the Inquisition of Cartagena of the Indies, synodal examiner of the bishopric of Cartagena, some time provincial of the province of New Granada, and actual procurador of the missions and the provinces." The title-page furnishes, moreover, a sufficient account of the contents of the book:

"Natural, civil, and geographical history of this great river, and of its abundant tributaries; government, uses, and customs of the Indians, with new and useful accounts of animals, trees, fruits, oils, resins, herbs, and medical roots."

VI

Each of the religious orders had its chronicler, whose writings necessarily involved more or less extensive accounts of the secular events of the societies in which they were established. Bernardo Torres, an Augustinian, secretary of the province of Lima, prior of the monastery of Chuquisaca, and some time professor in the University of San Marcos, wrote the *Crónica de la provincia peruana*, in eight books, which was published in Lima in 1657. A continuation of this work in two volumes, extending to the year 1721, was written by Padre Juan Teodoro Vásquez. The Dominican Antonio de Aguiar wrote the history of the Dominicans. Domingo Marín, in his *Estado de los misiones en Chile*, undertook to defend the Jesuits against their detractors. The Dominican, Meléndez, set forth the achieve-

Torres' *Crónica de la provincia peruana*

Tesoros de las Indias

ments of his order in *Tesoros verdaderos de las Indias*. The Franciscan, Francisco Javier Ramírez, following a suggestion from Aguiar, magnified the services of the Franciscans in the *Cronicón sacro-imperial de Chile*. The *Floresta de la santa iglesia Catedral de Santa Marta*, by Ensign José Nicolás de la Rosa, derives its historical data from the writings of Piedrahita, Simón, and Zamora and certain documents from the cathedral. In addition to the topics suggested by the title, it contains items of information concerning the Indians inhabiting the region about Santa Marta. In spite of its indifferent literary quality and "pésimo gusto literario," it has been twice printed, once in 1756 and again in 1833. After 1767 ecclesiastical writers in the colonies lacked both the breadth of vision and the literary attainments of their predecessors.[10]

Nicolás de la Rosa

Antonio Julián is hardly less widely known than Cassani and Gumilla. He lived for many years in New Granada, chiefly at Santa Marta. He travelled extensively in the province, but left America

(10) Vergara, *Hist. lit. en N. Granada*, 109; Medina, *Bibl. hisp. amer.* IV.

before the expulsion of his order. Neither the place nor the date of his birth is known. In his enforced retirement from his missionary labours he wrote a number of works concerning the part of the Indies with which he had become especially familiar. Of these the most frequently referred to is *La Perla de América, Provincia de Santamarta reconocida, observada y expuesta en discursos históricos.* It was published at Madrid in 1787. Of the others, not printed, perhaps the most noteworthy is *Historia geográfica del rio Magdalena, y de todas las provincias que le tributan de una banda y otra sus rios.*

Antonio Julián

La Perla de América

Few Jesuits who had entered the American field were withdrawn before 1767. Juan Bautista Sánchez shared in the enforced migration under the decree of expulsion. He was born in Peru, and entered the Society in 1729 at the age of fifteen. In Peru he acquired distinction, serving as rector of the Jesuit colleges of Cuzco and Lima. He died in 1774 after a residence of seven years in Europe. The list of his writings seems to indicate that his official

Juan Bautista Sánchez

duties did not encroach largely upon his time for writing.[11]

(11) These are some of the titles of his works: *Historia eclesiástica; Curso de filosofía antigua y moderna; De matrimonio; De la voluntad divina; La obra de los seis días; Historia de la renovación del templo de Jerusalén; Lecciones parafrásticas sobre el maestro de las sentencias; Oraciones latinas; Panegíricos y sermones morales.*

CHAPTER XIII
ON PARAGUAY

I. *Alvar Núñez Cabeza de Vaca; Ulrich Schmidel.* II. *Early sources of information about Paraguay; Nicolás de Techo.* III. *Pedro Lozano.* IV. *José Guevara.* V. *Dobrizhoffer; Pauke; Falkner; Orosz; Cardiel; Quiroga; Jolís; Peramás; Muriel; Juárez; Sánchez Labrador.* VI. *Juan Patricio Fernández; Matías de Anglés.*

I

Núñez Cabeza de Vaca

The earliest important book on the south eastern part of Spanish South America, known as Paraguay, is *La relación y comentarios* of Alvar Núñez Cabeza de Vaca. It was published at Valladolid in 1555. It treats of the appointment of Alvar Núñez de Cabeza de Vaca to be the governor of the colony planted by Mendoza in that region; of the fitting out of the vessels, the voyage, and the landing at Santa Catalina; of the departure of the main body of the men overland; the sending of the women and children to the Río de la Plata by sea and the arrival at Asunción; of the events at Asunción, the return of Irala from an exploring expedition, the revolt of Irala and his followers, and the imprisonment and expulsion of the governor. Nicolás de Techo, in his *Historia Provinciæ Paraquariæ Societatis Jesu,* gives the following account of Alvar Núñez and his promotion to the governorship of Paraguay:

Nicolás de Techo

"Emperor Charles the Fifth, having received the news of the death of James Mendoza, and the ill success of affairs at the river of Plate, and being of a spirit that ever struggled against adversity, he resolved to send thither another governor, with a supply of planters. Several aspiring to the command, Alvar Nunez Cabeca de Vaca carried it, on account of the great merits of his ancestors. For his grandfather, Peter de Vera, had subdued the Canary islands for King Ferdinand, and governed them; in which employment he behaved himself with such integrity, that having spent his own estate, he was reduced to such distress, that he gave his two sons in pawn to a Moor, for a sum of money to support his dignity and maintain his government, and the king afterwards redeemed them. One of these was father to Alvar we now speak of; who being in his youth educated in his father's and grandfather's virtues, going over into Florida under Pamphilo de Narvaez, to be the king's treasurer there, was shipwrecked on the coast of America, and fell into the hands of the Indians; and authors of the first rank tell us, he was so virtuous, that during his ten years captivity among the people, he wrought several miracles, invoking the blessed trinity. This man being appointed governor, embarked seven hundred men besides women and children upon five ships, and sailing from Cadiz with a fair wind, when he came to twenty-eight degrees of south latitude, landed in that part of America with five hundred men, and sending the women and children with the rest by sea, travelled himself by land, almost the same way Alexius Garcia had gone be-

Techo on Núñez Cabeza de Vaca

fore, for three hundred leagues, discovering the country and, in the year 1541, happily arrived at the city of Asunción, and what is most remarkable, he lost not one soul in all that voyage and journey by sea and land."[1]

Views of the common man

It is noteworthy that some of the most striking accounts of exploration in Spanish America were written by common soldiers. Bernal Díaz del Castillo, Cieza de León, and Ulrich Schmidel are instances. They interpreted the thoughts and sentiments of the subordinate class, and help one to see how the private soldier or the common man viewed the enterprises in which he was engaged. The position of men of this class made a sharp contrast between their writings and the writings of leaders. Schmidel's narrative of his twenty years in America was written in German, but in its Spanish translation it has been naturalized in the region of which he wrote, and in which he spent the effective years of his life.[2]

1 Churchill, *Voyages and Travels*, IV, 645.

(2) Schmidel's account of his journey has the curious title: *Warhafftige und liebliche Beschreibung etlicher fürnemen Indianischen Landtschafften und Insulen, die vormals in keiner Chronicken gedacht, und erstlich in der Schiffart Ulrici*

The family of Schmidel has been known in Bavaria since 1364, and is said to have been ennobled. The author's father, Wolfgang Schmidel, was held in high esteem by his townsmen, and was three times burgermeister of Straubing. He died in 1511, leaving three sons, of whom the youngest, Ulrich, was born in the first decade of the sixteenth century. Little or nothing is

Ulrich Schmidel

Schmidts von Straubingen mit grosser Gefahr erkündigt, und von ihm selber auffs fleissigst beschrieben und dargethan. It was first printed in 1567 at Frankfurt am Main at the end of a book of travels issued by Schmidel with the title *Neuwe Welt: Das ist wahrhafftige Beschreibunge, etc., etc.* This book with a new title page but otherwise unchanged was issued in the same year as the second part of a book of travels published by Sebastian Franck (*Erst Theil dieses Weltbuchs von neuwen erfundenen Landschaften. Warhafftige Beschreibunge, etc.*) The second Edition appeared in 1597 in Theodor de Bry's Collection of voyages (*America*, VII, Theil) and a Latin translation by Gothard Artus was issued in 1599 in the Latin version of de Bry's Collection (*Americae Pars VII*). In this year Levinus Hulsius in his collection of voyages issued a revised and somewhat abridged version of Schmidel's narrative under the title *Warhafftige Historien einer wunderbaren Schiffart welche Ulrich Schmidel . . . in Americam . . . gethan*, and, also in 1599, a Latin version of the same revised text (*Vera historia, etc.*). The first Spanish translation is said to have been made and published in 1731 by Gabriel Cárdenas (Z. Cano) (probably a pseudonym of Andrés González de Barcia: note the anagram involved); one was certainly issued by Barcia in 1749 in his *Historiadores primitivos de las Indias occidentales.* The text used is that of Hulsius. This version was reprinted with some corrections by Pedro de Angelis in his *Colección de obras y documentos relativos a la historia antigua y moderna de las Provincias del Río de la Plata* in 1836. The first edition in French was that published by Ternaux-Compans.

known of his boyhood or youth. His narrative indicates only a moderate degree of education. In 1534 he was at Antwerp, probably sent thither as a commercial agent or dependant, and in that year he enlisted as a soldier for service in the New World. At that time he was probably about twenty-five years of age. The same year he arrived at Cadiz, and departed for America with Mendoza's expedition, destined for the Río de la Plata, that had been discovered by Solís and explored by Cabot. Mendoza's fleet consisted of fourteen ships, having on board about two thousand five hundred persons; of these one hundred and fifty were soldiers. Two years after landing at the site of Buenos Aires a review of the colony showed five hundred and sixty survivors; the greater part had died of hunger. Schmidel witnessed the ravages of famine, the abandonment of the settlement at Buenos Aires, the founding of Asunción; was with Irala in the expedition towards Peru; served under Cabeza de Vaca, whom he characterized as an adventurer and unfit for the enterprise in which they were en-

Mendoza's Expedition

Vera hiſtoria,

ADMIRANDÆ CVIVS-
dam nauigationis, quam Hul-
dericus Schmidel, Straubingenſis, ab Anno 1534.
uſque ad annum 1554. in Americam vel nouum
Mundum, iuxta Braſiliam & Rio della Plata, confecit. Quid
per hoſce annos 19. ſuſtinuerit, quam varias & quam mirandas
regiones ac homines viderit. Ab ipſo Schmidelio Germanice,
deſcripta: Nunc vero, emendatis & correctis Vrbium, Regionum & Fluminum nominibus, Adiecta etiam tabula
Geographica, figuris & alijs notationi-
bus quibuſdam in hanc for-
mam reducta.

NORIBERGÆ,
Impenſis Levini Hulſij. 1599.

Title page of the revised edition of Schmidel's "Warhufftige Historien," Latin translation

gaged; and took part in the rebellion of 1549. A letter from his brother Thomas; who had held the inheritance from his father, requested his return to Germany. His petition for a discharge was at first refused, but was finally granted with favourable commendation for the service he had rendered.[3]

Schmidel and affairs of Paraguay

It has been denied that Schmidel was a soldier, but that view appears hardly tenable in the face of his clear designation of himself as a soldier. He was loyal to Irala, and took part in the revolt against the governor. His relation to this undertaking sufficiently explains his opinion of Núñez, and prepares one to find in his book a partisan account of events in Paraguay during these troubled years. The following is Schmidel's reference to Álvar Núñez Cabeza de Vaca's arrival in Asunción after the overland journey from the Atlantic coast:

"This commander was eight whole

(3) Mondschein, J., *Schmidels Reise nach Süd-America in den Jahren 1534–1554*, Straubing, 1893; also Bartolomé Mitre in *Anales del Museo de la Plata*, Buenos Aires, 1890, vol. 1; *The Conquest of the River Plate*, London, 1891, Hakluyt Society, English translation.

Arrival of Núñez Cabeza de Vaca

months on his way, for the distance is reckoned to be five hundred miles from Asunción to the place or harbour of Santa Catalina.

"He also brought with him from Spain his commission from H.I. Majesty, and required that Domingo Martínez de Irala should yield up the whole government to him, and that all the men should be obedient to him in every respect. The commander, Martínez de Irala, and all the people declared they were ready to obey, but with this understanding, that he, Cabeza de Vaca, should before show and lay before them documents to prove that he had received from His Imperial Majesty such powers and authority.

"But this the whole assembly could not obtain from him; only the priests and two or three of the captains affirmed it, that Alvar Núñez Cabeza de Vaca ruled and commanded; but we shall see hereafter how things went with him.

"Now, this said Alvar Núñez Cabeza de Vaca passed all the people in review, and found that there were eight hundred men.

At the same time he made friendship with Martínez de Irala, and they became sworn brothers, so that he, Martínez de Irala, was no less than before commander of the people."[4]

In another place Schmidel gives an account of the arrest and expulsion of Governor Núñez Cabeza de Vaca:

Governor's arrest and expulsion

"Thereupon it was resolved by all, nobleman and commoner, to meet in council, with a view to take prisoner the chief commander, Álvar Núñez Cabeza de Vaca, and to send him to H. I. Majesty, and to report to His Majesty about his nice virtue, and how he had behaved towards us, and how, according to his reason, he had governed; and other things besides.

"According to the resolution come to, these three gentlemen, namely, the treasurer, or judge, the clerk, or master of the toll or custom, and the secretary ordered by H. I. Majesty, whose names were Alonso Cabrera, Francisco de Mendoza, García Vanegas, and Felipe Cáceres, taking with them

(4) Luis L. Dominguez's translation Hakluyt Society, London, 1891.

two hundred soldiers, went to his lodging, and arrested our commander-in-chief, Álvar Núñez Cabeza de Vaca, when he least expected it. And this happened on St. Mark's Day, 1543. They held prisoner the said Álvar Núñez Cabeza de Vaca for a whole year, until a ship called a caravel, provided with victuals and a crew had been prepared. And on board this ship the often-mentioned Cabeza de Vaca, with two other officers on behalf of H.I. Majesty were conveyed to Spain.

Irala's election

"After that we had to elect another who should rule and govern the country until H.I. Majesty had time to designate one himself. And we held it for good, as it was the meaning and the will of the community, to nominate as chief Martínez de Irala, not only because he had formerly governed the country, but especially because most of the soldiers were satisfied with him."[5]

II

Knowledge of the early experience of the Jesuits in Paraguay was communicated to

(5) *Ibid.* 52.

Europeans exclusively by the Jesuits themselves; and the history of the beginning of the missions was written by persons who had been actually engaged in them, or on the basis of reports made by the missionaries. It was, therefore, to be expected that historical accounts framed under these conditions would show a strong partisan bias. The very flattering picture which they presented of the redemption of the Indians from the life of savage nomads naturally excited enthusiasm on the part of persons who knew little or nothing of the labours, difficulties, and discouragements of the missionaries in the wilderness. The first information concerning these labours that reached Europeans was derived from the letters of Padre Manuel de Ortega, Padre José de Catoldino, Padre Ruiz de Montoya, and Padre Roque González that were scattered about Europe. The *anuas* were another source of information. These were the product of a regulation that required every Jesuit house or college to make a report on the work of its members for every period of four months. These re-

Knowledge of Jesuits in Paraguay

Letters from the padres

ports, sent to other provinces or centres of missionary activity, were expected to serve as a stimulus for increasing the zeal of other members of the order. They increased in number to such an extent that it was found difficult to circulate them; it became necessary to make summaries of them to be printed. Sometimes individual *anuas* were given special prominence. Those of 1626 and 1627, written by order of Padre Nicolás Durán and signed at Tucumán on the 12th of November 1628, were translated into Latin and printed at Antwerp in 1636. They were issued under the title *Litteræ annuæ Provinciæ Paraquariæ*. From time to time others were given equal distinction; some by Padre Schirmbeck were published at Munich in 1649 as *Messis paraquariensis*.

Anuas

Additional information was derived from books written by missionaries. Padre Diego de Torres Bollo's *Breve relación del fruto que se recoge en las Indias del Perú* was a book of this kind. The author had been sent to the New World as procurador for the province of Peru. At this time little or no missionary work had been done among the Indians

Bollo's *Breve relación*

of Paraguay; the Jesuit province of Paraguay had not then been organized; this region and the pampas were still embraced in the province of Peru. Torres' book was early translated into Italian, French, German, and Polish.

Ruiz de Montoya

A second book and of greater importance was that by Padre Antonio Ruiz de Montoya called *Conquista espiritual hecha por los religiosos de la Compañia de Jesús en las provincias del Paraguay, Paraná, Uruguay y Tape*. It was a volume of two hundred quarto pages, and was published in Madrid in 1639. Montoya, as if defending himself against criticism beforehand, on account of his style and lack of proper arrangement of his material, confesses his rusticity imposed by long residence among savages; and that he wrote from memory and without the documents that ought to have guided his pen, so that the result was a mass of information thrown together without system or order.

The project of writing a complete general history of the province of Paraguay had been variously considered when it was taken up energetically by Padre Juan Pastor, who had long been a missionary in Paraguay. He completed it in two folio volumes in manuscript, but, when he died in 1658, the work had not been published; and after Techo had made large use of the manuscript in his history of the province of Paraguay, the project to publish it was dropped. Nicolás de Techo was a native of France, born in Lille. His name was Nicolas de Toict, and his history bore the title

Techo's *Historia*

Historia Provinciæ Paraquariæ Societatis Jesu. It is divided into fourteen books, and makes a folio volume of four hundred pages, beginning with a geographical de-

Gist of Techo's book

scription of the La Plata region. Entering upon his main subject the author gives an account of the mission of the first Jesuits from Peru and from Brazil in 1586. Then follows an account in chronological order of the events within his field until 1645. Techo probably intended to write another volume, but his plan was apparently not carried out.

An English translation of this book was published in Churchill's *Collection of Voy-*

ages and Travels (IV, 638–749). The author, a Jesuit, was naturally especially interested in the history of his order's missionary activity among the Indians, the foundation and growth of the Paraguayan missions. The translator, referring to the "abundance of miracles and other pious matters" with which the author had overloaded his book, announces that he has taken care to eliminate these things in his effort to make his translation "acceptable to the reader." But in the account of the dreadful famine during the first settlement at Buenos Aires he seems to find no reason to expunge the story of the lioness, which Techo relates in all sobriety:

"The provisions they brought being spent, there followed such a terrible famine, that many fed upon man's flesh, and things not to be mentioned. . . . The cruelty of the barbarous people, the fear of wild beasts, and the severity of the commanders suffered none to go out of the works. Yet there was a woman, who weighing the misery of famine, chose rather to expose herself to the inhumanity of the Indians

Story of the lioness

and wild beasts, than to suffer the torture of hunger; and therefore stealing out, she wandered a long time about the fields, till at night she went into a cave, where finding a lioness ready to whelp, she renewed her ancient experience and had the boldness to play the midwife, much to her own advantage, for the lioness laying aside her fierceness, fairly divided her prey among her young ones and her midwife, till the latter fell into the hands of the barbarians; and being after many accidents redeemed by the Spaniards, was brought again to the fort. Being then condemned for her rashness and disobedience, she was exposed without the works, to be devoured by wild beasts, where she must have perished, had not God in His providence so ordered it, that the lioness she helped to whelp, came up to her first, and defended her innocent midwife against the rest."[1]

Andrés de León

An early sketch of the south-eastern part of the Spanish possessions was written by Andrés de León y Garabito, who was born

(1) Churchill, *Voyages and Travels*, London, 1732, IV, 642.

in Lima, became judge of the audiencia of Panama, and, in 1643, judge of the audencia of Charcas. Subsequently he was appointed governor of Paraguay. This position he held until 1651, when he went to Buenos Aires as inspector of the royal treasury in that province. He wrote of the origin, the defence, the organization, and other particulars of that region.

III

Pedro Lozano

But the most prolific as well as the most trustworthy of the Jesuit historians of Paraguay was the famous Pedro Lozano. It has been possible to fix definite dates to but few events of his life. Very good reasons, however, have been advanced to show that his boyhood was spent in Madrid, and that he carried on his early studies there. As a youth, he became a Jesuit, and arrived in America in the second decade of the eighteenth century. In the New World he resided habitually at Córdoba, in the Colegio Máximo and at the hacienda Santa Catalina; but he visited Buenos Aires, the pampas, and the Andes;

he examined the archives at Santiago del Estero, Tucumán, and Salta; and the amount and quality of his writings indicate that he could not have been much diverted from his literary activity. Neither the date nor the place of his death has been established beyond a question, but the evidence available points somewhat clearly to the year 1752.

Descripción del Gran Chaco

Lozano's interest comprehended not merely the events in the history of his order, of which he was the official historian, but also the marvels of nature among which his life was cast, as well as the languages, the manners, the customs, and the religion of the natives. More than any of his predecessors he appreciated the importance of official documents, in the search for which he displayed remarkable zeal and energy. His disposition to consider the forms and events of nature found expression in his *Descripción corográfica . . . del Gran Chaco.*

Conquista del Paraguay

In his *Historia de la conquista del Paraguay, Río de la Plata y Tucumán* he brought together a vast amount of important material relating to the history of South America, and the documents which he either refers to or prints constitute a sound basis on which historians are able to build. This was edited by Lamas, and published in Buenos Aires in 1873. Lozano's *Historia de la Compañia de Jesús en la Provincia del Paraguay* was published in Madrid in 1754. It consists of two folio volumes, yet it covers only the first twenty-eight years of the province, and ends with 1614.[2] Padre Pablo Pastells refers to the reliability of its information, the justice of its criticism, and the character of demonstration given to its statements, and affirms that for these qualities Lozano stands above all others who have written on the history of Paraguay.

Historia de la Compañía

Lozano's *Historia de las revoluciones de la provincia del Paraguay* is the history of the conflict between the supporters and the antagonists of the Jesuits in Paraguay, a conflict in which Antequera was the most conspicuous figure. It appears thus from one point of view as a part of the history of the Jesuits; from another point of view it is

Las Revoluciones

(2) *Historia de la Compañía de Jesús en la provincia del Paraguay*, Madrid, 1912, I, xxi.

the history of the rebellion of the Comuneros against the viceregal authority. Lozano's relation to one of the parties made it practically impossible for him to be entirely impartial in his account of it; still the large number of official documents introduced into the text of the narrative helps the reader to avoid the possibility of sharing the author's prejudice.

The following is the list of Lozano's works, printed and in manuscript, according to Andrés Lamás, José T. Medina and others:

Lozano's works

Descripción corográfica del terreno, árboles y animales de las dilatadísimas provincias del Chaco Gualamba. 1733. In Córdoba (Spain), 4to, pp. 9 & 485, with map.

Copy of a letter written by a Jesuit missionary to Padre Juan J. Rico, 1740, 4to, pp. 59.

Vida del P. Julián de Lizardi. Printed in Salamanca in 1741; reprinted, Madrid, 1832; new edition, Buenos Aires, 1901.

Letter to Padre Bruno Morales, dated Córdoba, November 1, 1746.

Letter to Padre Bruno Morales, dated Córdoba, March 1, 1747, containing an account of the earthquake at Lima in 1746.

Carta al Padre Juan de Alzola sobre los Césares.

Meditaciones sobre la vida de nuestro señor Jesucristo, written in Italian by Padre Fabio Ambrosio Espindola, translated by Lozano. Madrid, 1747, two volumes, pp. 569 & 531.

Historia de la compañía de Jesús en la Provincia del Paraguay. Madrid, 1754 & 1755. Two volumes, pp. 760 & 832.

Historia de la conquista del Paraguay, Río de la Plata y Tucumán. Buenos Aires, 1873 to 1875, five volumes, pp. 468, 396, 370, 489, 364.

Máximas eternas puestas en lecciones, written in Italian by Padre Carlos Ambrosio Cataneo, translated by Lozano, Madrid, 1754; Madrid, 1776 & 1788; Valencia, 1884.

IV

Padre José Guevara

Padre José Guevara succeeded Lozano as the official historian of the province of Paraguay. He was a native of Spain, born at Recas in the archbishopric of Toledo on March 19, 1719. On December 31, 1732, he became a novice in the Society of Jesus. and two years later, April 25, 1734, he arrived at Buenos Aires. Almost immediately thereafter he entered upon his studies at

Exercicios espirituales de San Ignacio, written in Italian by Padre Carlos Ambrosio Cataneo, translated by Lozano. Madrid, 1764, pp. 406; reprinted 1776 & 1788.

Diario de un viaje a la Costa de la mar Magallánica en 1745. Buenos Aires, 1836. Also published (in Latin) in Charlevoix, *Histoire du Paraguay* and in Prévost, *Histoire des voyages.*

Various documents communicated to Charlevoix; see Padre Muriel, *Fasti novi Orbis.*

Diccionario histórico-índico, six volumes.

Traslado de una carta dirigida al P. Luis Tavares, Córdoba, June 12, 1739.

Letter on tithes, 1741.

Observaciones sobre el manifiesto publicado por el P. Vargas Machuca.

Representación hecha por la Provincia jesuítica del Paraguay al señor Virrey del Perú a propósito del tratado con Portugal sobre los siete Pueblos de las Misiones del Uruguay, Córdoba, March 12, 1751 (MS. in the library at Lima).

Representación que hace al Rey N.S. en su Real Consejo de Indias el Provincial de la Compañía de Jesús en la Provincia del Paraguay, on the same subject as the preceding, Buenos Aires, April 29, 1752.

Letter to the Procurador General on events in the province of Paraguay, 1752; in the library of Valladolid.

Historia de las revoluciones de la Provincia del Paraguay, (1721–1735). Buenos Aires, 1905.

Córdoba, and for many years this city continued to be the principal seat of his activity. In 1743 he was a teacher of Latin, and the next year he became a lecturer on theology. Eight years later he was appointed to the position that had been held by Lozano as historian of the province. After a residence of thirty-three years in America he was removed to Italy under the decree of 1767, by which the Jesuits were expelled from Spain and the Spanish dependencies. At first he established himself at Faenza, but subsequently he obtained the post of canon at Spello, near Perugia. Guevara died at Spello on February 23, 1806.

Criticism in *Anales de la Biblioteca*

The fifth volume of *Anales de la Biblioteca* (Buenos Aires, 1908) contains a new and complete edition of Guevara's *Historia del Paraguay, Río de la Plata y Tucumán*, superseding the incomplete copies issued by Angelis and by Lamas. In the preliminary essay of this publication Paul Groussac has subjected Guevara's work to a severe critical examination, in which he makes clear Guevara's dependence on Lo-

Fr. GASPAR DE VILLARROEL.

zano's writings, not merely the ordinary dependence of one writer on the results attained by other investigators in the same field, but the dependence of the plagiarist. The principal historical accounts of this southeastern part of America in existence before Guevara wrote were those of Techo, Charlevoix, Lozano, and Centenera's *Argentina*. Guevara's dependence goes so far that the whole substance of his book is found in Lozano, except the final matter of the twelfth decade, which is drawn from Techo. "The ordinary character of Guevara's imitation consists in reproducing more or less servilely the corresponding passage of Lozano. Especially in the parts referring to the flora and fauna, the transcription, either entire or fragmentary, is usually literal, without change of verb or adjective. On the other hand, there are numerous suppressed passages, arbitrary, brutal, really chopped out of the parts mutilated." The critic finds the copying not the chief offence, since it was a practice generally observed in the Society, but the deceit of the preamble and the author's injurious silence respecting the

Guevara's plagiarism

historian to whom he owed everything. But admitting that this severe judgment is well founded, emphasis may be laid on the the fact that Guevara's style represents a considerable advance over that of his predecessors in the same field. If it may be regarded as consciously laboured, it certainly has the great merit of clearness. The author does not give any indication of great learning, or as in possession of an extensive variety of knowledge, but, as Groussac suggests, he had nevertheless "sufficient attainments for the satisfactory accomplishment of his task."[3]

V

Effect of Jesuit expulsion

One of the consequences of the removal of the Jesuits from Río de la Plata was to deprive the world of much information concerning the early events of that region. Some manuscripts were lost and others were never written that would have been written if the members of the Society had been permitted to continue their work undisturbed. Still a small number of the exiles maintain-

(3) *Anales de la Biblioteca*, v, Introduction. Buenos Aires.

ed an interest in subjects connected with the country of their earlier labours. Among these there were four noteworthy foreigners, men not of Spanish stock. Martin Dobrizhoffer, an Austrian, went to Paraguay in 1748, and was a missionary among the Guaranís eleven years, and among the Abipones for seven years. At Vienna he wrote a History of the Abipones, which was published in Latin in 1784. A German translation was published in 1783-4 and in 1822 an abridged translation in English was published in London. Florian Pauke went to Paraguay with Martin Dobrizhoffer in 1748. He was a missionary in the Chaco for fifteen years. An extract from his writings was published in Vienna in 1829, called *Padre Florian Paukes Reise.* In 1870 practically the whole of his manuscript was published with the title of *Padre Florian Pauke, ein Jesuit in Paraguay.*

Dobrizhoffer and Pauke

Although Thomas Falkner was neither creole nor a Spaniard, his long residence of thirty-eight years in South America entitles his *Description of Patagonia and adjoining parts of South America* to a place among the

Thomas Falkner

writings of colonial origin. He was an Englishman, born in Manchester in 1707. He was a surgeon, and embarked for South America on a slave ship belonging to the South Sea Company. At Buenos Aires he fell dangerously ill, and was cared for by Jesuits, who embraced the opportunity to bring about his conversion. He entered the Society of Jesus, and took his place as a missionary among the Indians in the region between the Strait of Magellan and the Río de la Plata. He returned to England in 1768, after the expulsion of the Jesuits.

Description of Patagonia

Six years later, in 1774, his *Description of Patagonia*, edited by William Combe, was published. It does not appear from the book itself what changes Combe made in Falkner's papers, but the style suggests more experience and skill in writing than Falkner may be supposed to have had after nearly forty years among the Indians and other persons, where no opportunity presented itself for the use of the English language.

Gist of Falkner's chapters

The six chapters treat of the soil and products; describe the Indian country and the great river system of the south-east;

Tierra del Fuego and the Falkland Islands; the inhabitants of the country traversed; the religion, the government, the policy, and the customs of the Moluches and the Puelches, with some account of the Moluche language.

Another member of this group was Ladislaus Orosz, an Hungarian. In 1727, at the age of thirty, he went to Río de la Plata, taught philosophy and theology in Córdoba, and after his expulsion from America returned to his native province of Tyrnau, where he died in 1773. Two principal manuscripts are ascribed to him. The first was *Decades quatuor virorum illustrium Paraquariæ*. This was printed in Tyrnau in 1759, and made a folio volume of five hundred and fifty-two pages. The other work was called *Decades quatuor aliæ virorum illustrium Paraquariae*, and was apparently printed but never circulated.

Orosz's writings

There were many others who went into exile from the region of the Río de la Plata and Paraguay. The more conspicuous among them were José Cardiel, José Quiroga, José Jolís. José Manuel Peramás,

Other expelled Jesuits

Domingo Muriel, Gaspar Juárez, and José Sánchez Labrador.[4] Cardiel's literary contributions include *Declaración de la verdad* and *Breve relación de las misiones Guaranies*. Quiroga became known for his attainments in mathematics; was a professor of mathematics in the college of San Ignacio in Buenos Aires; and made a large number of maps of the southern part of South America and, among others, a map of the viceroyalty of Buenos Aires. He left also a treatise called *Observaciones astronómicas para determinar el curso del río Paraguay*. Jolís was a Catalan, born in 1728. He was a missionary in the Gran Chaco for ten years. His most noted literary production was *Saggio sulla storia naturale della provincia del Gran Chaco*. José Manuel Peramás wrote *Vidas de varones ilustres* and *Annus patiens*, the latter consisting of a diary of the journey of the exiles from Córdoba. Domingo Muriel (sometimes in Latin as Cyriacus Morelli)

(4) See Pablo Hernández, *El extrañamiento de los Jesuitas del Río de la Plata*, 306-315, in *Colección de libros y documentos referentes a la historia de America*, vol. VII, Madrid, 1908.

left *Fasti novi orbis* and a continuation of Charlevoix's *Paraguay* under the title of *Historia del Paraguay desde 1747 hasta 1767* Gaspar Juárez was born in Santiago del Estero in 1731, became a Jesuit in 1748, and died at Rome in 1804. His principal works are *Historia ecclesiástica del virreinato de Buenos Aires* and *Historia natural*, treating of the same region.[5]

José Sánchez Labrador

In 1910 there was published at Buenos Aires a part of the writings of Padre José Sánchez Labrador. He was born at Guanda in the diocese of Toledo on September 19, 1717. At the age of fourteen he entered the Society of Jesus, October 5, 1731, and about the middle of the century went to America. Established as a professor of philosophy and theology at Córdoba, he

(5) A few of the works of these men have been printed, but the bulk exists in MS., have been incorporated in the books of other authors, or have been lost. An abbreviated version of Cardiel's *Breve relación* was printed at the end of Muriel's *Historia del Paraguay* under the title *Costumbres de los Guaranies;* Jolís' *Saggio* was printed in Faenza in 1789; the *Annus patiens* of Peramás appeared in a French translation in A. Carayon's *Documents inédits concernant la Compagnie de Jésus*, vol. XVI; for his *Vidas* see *De vita et moribus sex sacerdotum Paraguaycorum*, Faventiae, 1791, and *De vida et moribus tredecim virorum Paraguaycorum*, Faventiae, 1793; Muriel's *Historia* forms vol. XIX of the *Colección de lib. y doc. rel. a la hist. de Amér.*, Madrid, 1919.

won distinction and the high regard of his contemporaries, but the call from the wilds appealed to him, and, abandoning his professorship, he entered upon the life of a missionary to the Indians, with all of its privations and dangers. In the midst of this service he was overtaken by the decree of expulsion (1767). With hundreds of others affected by this act, he was transferred to Italy, where thirty-two years later (1799) he died at Ravenna.

Labrador's literary work

During his travels and residence among the Indians Sánchez Labrador acquired considerable knowledge of their language, translated the catechism into the speech of the Mbayas, and began to compile a dictionary of that language, carrying his work to the letter P in a fair degree of completeness. The rest of his extensive writings treated of either the natural history of Paraguay under the title *Paraguay natural ilustrado*, or the progress of the missions in that region, this part of the work bearing the title *El Paraguay católico*.

The first of these divisions comprehends information on the nature of the country, the soil, the climate, the water, and the most prevalent diseases; the plants, the fields, and the forests with various kinds of trees; the animals, the birds, the fishes, the reptiles, and the insects. The two volumes entitled *El Paraguay católico,* printed in Buenos Aires in 1910, contain a great part of the important work left by Padre Sánchez Labrador concerning the Indians of Paraguay and its provinces, as well as accounts of his extensive journeys, his observations, and his reflections.

VI

Juan Patricio Fernández

The *Relación historial de las misiones de los Indios que llaman Chiquitos,* attributed to Padre Juan Patricio Fernández, was first published in Spanish in Madrid in 1726. It was republished in the *Colección de libros que tratan de América raros o curiosos,* in 1895. It treats briefly of the beginning and progress of missionary work in the province of Chiquitos; the geography of the province and the customs and character of the natives; the invasion and depredations by the Mamelucos; the removal of the settlements; and events in the lives of some of the leading missionaries.

The preface to the Buenos Aires edition of Pedro Lozano's *Historia de las revoluciones de la provincia del Paraguay* affirms that Lozano translated this work from the Italian original, by Padre Bandier, which appears under the name of Padre Patricio Fernández. A mild controversy has arisen about the authorship of this book, into which it is not necessary to enter. The latest utterance observed takes issue with Lozano, and supports the claim of Fernández.

Matías de Anglés

The report made by General Matías de Anglés y Gortari, commissioned by Viceroy Castel-Fuerte to inquire into the causes of the conflict between the Paraguay comuneros and the misiones, is a document of considerable importance for the history of the Jesuit missions in Paraguay and the rebellion led by Antequera. After the rebellion had run a certain course, and Antequera had been imprisoned in Lima, Anglés, who was the corregidor of Potosí, visited Asunción and undertook, in the capacity of judge, by personal investigation to gather information needed to fix the responsibility for the state of war that had existed in the province. He entered upon his inquiry with a mind measurably free from any partisan bias; he had never visited Paraguay before; he had no acquaintances among the inhabitants; and carried only a note of introduction from the viceroy to Bishop José de Palos. This introduction, on account of the Bishop's partisanship, made it difficult for Anglés to maintain his proposed impartiality. But observing the evident partisan character of some of the evidence presented, he sought to correct it by testimony from other sources. Whether he was entirely successful or not in reaching an impartial conclusion, the *Informe* remains a valuable contemporary view of a serious provincial war. It was completed at Potosí, in May, 1731, after the author's return from Paraguay. Thirty-eight years later, in 1769, it was published in Madrid.

Anglés' *Informe*

CHAPTER XIV

SOME ECCLESIASTICS AND THEIR RELIGIOUS BOOKS

I. *Bishop Lizárraga.* II. *Bishop Luis Jerónimo de Oré.* III. *Bishop Gaspar de Villarroel.* IV. *Minor religious writers.*

I

Church as patron of learning

The mediaeval tradition that the Church was the supreme patron of learning was generally recognized in Latin America throughout the greater part of the colonial period. Men of scholarly tastes and aspirations found their greatest opportunities in ecclesiastical office, or as members of a religious order, and many of those who attained the dignity of a bishop became noteworthy also for their writings. One of the early names in this list was that of Bishop Lizárraga, whose family name was

Baltazar de Obando. When he assumed the habit of the order of Santo Domingo in 1560, he became Fray Reginaldo Lizárraga. He went from Spain to Lima with his parents; thence to Quito among the first European settlers; and finally he returned to Lima. He was living in Chuquisaca when Viceroy Francisco de Toledo (1569–1581), committed the crime of taking the life of Tupac Amarú and of furthering the extermination of the other members of the Inca family.

Bishop Lizárraga

From the post of prior he was appointed provincial of the newly-created province in Chile. After Lizárraga's service as provincial, he was for a brief period a missionary in the valley of Jauja, and while there he received notice of his presentation as bishop of Imperial. This office had come to him through Viceroy García Hurtado de Mendoza's (1590–1596) recommendation to Philip II. The king's letter of appointment was written on June 7, 1597, and on June 12 one year later, Lizárraga replied, accepting the offered dignity. His consecration was delayed until October 24, 1599.

State of Chile

This was not an auspicious moment to be looking towards southern Chile as a place of residence. The Araucanian war had assumed an unfavourable aspect; Governor Loyola was dead; the Indians had organized a general insurrection, and had laid siege to the towns in the diocese of Imperial. The destruction wrought in this uprising and various other considerations induced the bishop to hesitate to take up his episcopal duties. In May, 1602, he was still in Lima, but he arrived in Chile in December of that year, or in January, 1603, thus between five and six years after his appointment. The ruined condition of Imperial led to the removal of the see to Concepción; and, in view of the discouraging prospect, the bishop, a few weeks after his arrival, sent his resignation to the king, with the request that it might be forwarded to the Pope. For this act the king wrote to him a severe rebuke, calling upon him to regard his obligations, to remain with his church, to mend the state of his diocese, to preserve it for the Church, and to offer his consolation to his subjects. The number of Euro-

Lizárraga in Chile

peans within the limits of the bishop's jurisdiction was small, and these for the greater part were poor and discouraged. The bishop was about as poor as the others, and was obliged to live in a cell offered him in the Franciscan monastery. Yet he showed zeal and wisdom in the management of the diocesan affairs; more wisdom and zeal, it is said, than one had reason to expect, considering the indifference, hesitation, and timidity he had displayed in Lima. Nevertheless, he was discontented in his office, and, with its annual revenue of only three hundred dollars, he was able to maintain neither his church nor himself. His recommendation, therefore, appears reasonable, that his diocese should be united with that of Santiago, and he be permitted to return to the monastery of his order. This plan was, however, not carried out, and in 1608 he was presented by the king for the bishopric of Paraguay, to succeed Martín Ignacio de Loyola, who was promoted to be archbishop of Charcas. At the end of 1607, or at the beginning of 1608 he took final leave of Chile.

Descripción y población de las Indias

The greater part of his writings deal with religious subjects. There was a volume on the Pentateuch, two volumes on places mentioned in the Scriptures, a volume of sermons, a treatise on the life and eminent services of Jerónimo Loayza, the first archbishop of Lima. These and most, if not all, of his religious productions, have remained unpublished.

Lizárraga's most important work was rather secular than religious. It was called *Descripción y población de las Indias*. Doubt has arisen as to where this book was written, whether, as indicated in the text, in "the valley of Jauja," or in Chile. Medina has discussed the question, and has reached the conclusion that it was written in Chile, during the second sojourn of Lizárraga in that country, and from the number of known copies of it, he infers that it must have enjoyed a certain popularity, if that may be said of a manuscript necessarily confined to a few readers.[1]

Among the topics treated in this book are the geography of Chile and Peru, the vice-

(1) Medina, *Literatura colonial de Chile*, II, 71–73.

roys and the governors, the bishops and the provincials, the territory of Cuyo, and the road over the cordillera. One notes in this part of it the imposing effect of these mountains with their grand panoramas and their majestic summits of eternal ice. Lizárraga, like many other writers, was moved by the grandeur of nature here displayed. At the same time some of his views suggest the crude faith of his generation. For instance the appearance of the comet of 1577 he interpreted as an announcement that God was about to punish the people for their sins, and that Drake the same year was sent to inflict the punishment.

Contents of Lizárraga's book

As bishop of Paraguay, like the great majority of the priests who attained episcopal rank in America, Lizárraga led a life of virtue and devotion. He died at the age of eighty, and the time of his death accorded with his own prophetic announcement: "a las seis de la tarde iré a dar cuenta a Dios."

Bishop of Paraguay

In the last half of the sixteenth century, while the New World was displaying to Europeans its magnificent scenery and its untold wealth, there were persons, particularly among the clergy, who, in the midst of the general hopefulness, assumed to be disillusioned respecting earthly affairs. Julián Martel's reflections of this character were set down in a book entitled *Desengaño del mundo.* He was born in Granada, and went from Spain to Peru as a member of the secular clergy, but he became an Augustinian friar, and later rector of the college of his order and prior at Lima. He was esteemed for his austere life and for his learning, particularly for his knowledge of Latin and of the writings of the Fathers of the Church.[2]

Desengaño del mundo

II

Two especially prominent writers among

(2) Lizárraga's *Descripción y población de las Indias* is said to have been extensively used by Padre Juan Meléndez in writing *Tesoros verdaderos de las Indias* (Rome, 1681). Meléndez was a Dominican born in Lima. After holding various offices in his order he was sent on a mission to Spain and left Callao September 2, 1673. He wrote also a chronicle of his order in Peru, and *Descripción de las fiestas hechas por la beatificación de Santa Rosa.* He was the first member of his order, born in Lima, to attain the office of bishop. The *Descripción breve de toda la tierra del Perú, Tucumán, Río de la Plata y Chile* is printed in *Nueva biblioteca de autores españoles*, xv (*Historiadores de Indias*, II), 485–661. See also Eyzaguirre, *Historia de Chile*, Valparaiso, 1850, I, 454–559.

the ecclesiastics of the first half of the seventeenth century were Luis Jerónimo de Oré and Gaspar de Villarroel. Oré was the successor of bishop Lizárraga in the diocese of Imperial. During the first period of his active life he was a zealous missionary among the Indians; later he was in Spain and Italy, where he appears as a writer; and this activity was followed by a period of devotion to his duties as bishop of Imperial. He was born in Guamanga, Peru, in 1554, and was the third of the four sons of Antonio de Oré, who, besides these sons, was blessed with three daughters. He entered the order of the Franciscans at Lima, and here won distinction through his studies. His work called *Símbolo católico indiano* was published at Lima in 1598. It contains the matter of two distinct books, the first treating of the mysteries of the Catholic faith, "a philosophico-theological treatise on God and his attributes," in a word, "the dogmas of the Catholic church;" the second being a description of the New World and its native inhabitants. Like certain later writers Oré would have the name of the continent

Jerónimo de Oré

Símbolo católico indiano

derived from Columbus instead of from Amerigo Vespucci.

Relación de los martires

Shortly after publishing his *Símbolo católico indiano* Oré went to Spain, and in 1604 published, in quarto, *Relación de los mártires que ha habido en la Florida.*[3] From Spain he passed to Italy, and in Rome published a treatise on Indulgences, written in Latin. Three years later, in Naples, was issued his *Rituale seu manuale peruanum*[4] which contains the prayers and forms of the Roman ritual in Latin and in Spanish, together with translations into Quichua, Aymará, and other Indian languages. It was designed to govern the priests and missionaries to the Indians in the administration of the sacraments, and to guide them in giving instruction in Christian doctrine. On account of its translation of the Roman

(3) Cárdenas, Gabriel de, *Ensayo cronológico para la historia general de la Florida,* Madrid, 1723, 181, see Medina, II, 89, n.

(4) The full title of the book is: *Rituale seu Manuale Peruanum et forma brevis administrandi apud Indos sacrosancta Baptismi, Poenitentiae, Eucharistiae, Matrimonii, et Extremae Unctionis Sacramenta iuxta ordinem Sanctae Romanae Ecclesiae . . . et quae indigent versione vulgaribus idiomatibus Indicis, secundum diversos ritus omnium Provinciarum novi orbis Peru, aut per ipsum translata, aut ejus industria elaborata,* Naples, 1607.

ritual into the Indian languages of South America, this work is of special importance for the study of these languages.

Rituale seu manuale peruanum

In 1612 Oré visited Garcilaso de la Vega in Córdoba, and Garcilaso has given an account of this visit in his *Historia general del Perú* (Madrid, 1722, II, 460): "He told me that in the Franciscan monastery in Lima there were deposited five heads, that of Gonzalo Pizarro, that of Francisco de Carvajal, that of Hernández Girón, and two others which he could not identify; that that religious house had them on deposit, not buried, but in keeping; and that he desired very much to know which of them was that of Francisco de Carvajal, on account of the great renown he had left in that kingdom. I said to him that he might know which of them was Carvajal's by the inscription there was on the iron cage; but he informed me that they were not in iron cages, but free, each one by itself, without any sign by which it could be identified.

Garcilaso to Oré

"This monk, Luis Jerónimo de Oré, was going from Madrid to Cadiz, under orders from his superiors and from the Council of

Oré and the priests for Florida

the Indies to send two dozen monks, or to go with them, to the kingdom of Florida, to preach the gospel to these gentiles. It was not determined whether he would go with the monks, or return, having despatched them. He requested me to give him some part of my history of Florida, which those religious might take with them for their information concerning the provinces and the customs of the inhabitants. I gave him seven books; three were of the *Florida*, and four were of our *Comentarios*, for which he acknowledged himself greatly obliged."[5]

Some mystical books

After his return from Cadiz to Madrid, Oré continued his religious or mystical writings. Two of his books of this character were *Relación de la vida y milagros del P. Fr. Francisco Solano* and *Corona de la sacratísima Virgen María*. The religious character of his writings had doubtless much influence in causing him to be presented for the bishopric of Imperial in Chile in 1620. The appointment by Philip III

(5) Medina has considered the question whether Oré went to Florida or remained in Spain, and reached the conclusion that the Franciscan's commission was fulfilled when his companions had left the port, and that he did not accompany them.—*Lit. col. de Chile,* II, 95, n.

Bishop of Imperial

was confirmed by Paul V, and near the end of 1620, or in the beginning of 1621, the new bishop arrived in Lima. Oré's return to his native country, clothed with literary and ecclesiastical honours, was naturally a source of supreme satisfaction to his relatives and friends, with whom he spent nearly two years; and finally, in 1622, he took possession of his church at Concepción, and entered upon the exercise of his episcopal functions. He continued to discharge the duties of his high office for a period of five years, and spent a year of this time among the untamed inhabitants of Chiloé and the adjacent islands, whom he found less docile than had formerly appeared to him the Indians of Peru. He died in 1627.[6]

III

Fray Gaspar de Villarroel, another writer already referred to, was born in Quito about

(6) Concerning Oré's life and family, reference may be made to *Crónica de la religiosísima provincia de los Doce Apostoles del Perú de la Orden de N.P. San Francisco, compuesta por Fr. Diego de Córdoba Salinas* (Lima, 1651, see page 421, cap. 3, lib. 1), and two manuscripts: *Cronicón sacro imperial de Chile*, by Fr. Francisco Javier Ramírez, and *Relación de la fundación de la santa Provincia de los Doce Apostoles del Perú*, by Fr. Diego de Córdoba.

Gaspar de Villarroel

1587, of parents who were extremely poor, but who are said to have descended from a noble family. His father was a lawyer, and for a certain period was a judge in Cuzco. While his son was still young, he removed from Quito to Lima in order that the lad might have the advantage of instruction. In Lima he lived in extreme poverty, but continued his studies.

The zeal of the father to attain a higher degree of education stimulated the son to pay special attention to his own cultivation. Like many others of his time, who would be scholars, Villarroel entered the Church and assumed the habit of St. Augustine. This was in 1607–1608, and after this event he turned with new energy to studies in letters and theology. Later he received the degree of doctor. After a few years his attainments warranted him in becoming a candidate for a professorship that was vacant in the university at Lima. His rival, Pedro de Ortega Sotomayor, was successful, but Villarroel's candidacy made his merits so well known that he was elected prior at Cuzco. This office he held until his departure for Spain, a journey that he made by way of Buenos-Aires.

Villarroel in Spain

Born and educated in America, Villarroel was unknown in Spain, where there existed a strong prejudice against all creoles, against their intellectual attainments, and their fitness for positions in the public service. To allay this prejudice with reference to himself was one of the purposes of this journey; and he took with him a manuscript for the first volume of a work to be entitled *Semana santa, tratado de los comentarios, dificultades y discursos literales y místicos sobre los Evangelios de la Cuaresma.* This he caused to be published in Lisbon in 1631 with an adulatory dedication to the king. This work was a commentary and an interpretation of passages from the Bible, involving much that appears frivolous, sterile, and commonplace, when considered from the viewpoint reached after these intervening three hundred years. A second volume was published in Madrid in 1632, and a third and last volume in Seville in 1634; in 1626 he published a commentary on the Book of Judges. This was written in Latin, and

Semana Santa

contained an abundance of extracts from the Scriptures and from the Fathers of the Church.

These publications gave evidence of his spirit and his learning; they made an impression on influential persons at the court; and García de Haro, after he had heard him preach, became his enthusiastic champion. Moreover, the court and other persons of distinction conceived an especially favourable opinion of Villarroel; he was frequently called to preach before the king and the Council of the Indies; the fashionable applauded him; and the poetasters wrote verses in his honour. The practical result of all this for Villarroel was his presentation in 1637, after a residence of eight years in Madrid, as the bishop of Santiago. He was consecrated the next year in his monastery in Lima.

Appreciation by the court

In its isolation the limited society of Santiago, like other colonial communities, was afflicted with social antagonisms. There was rivalry between the civil and ecclesiastical officials, and the task that devolved upon Bishop Villarroel was to establish and preserve a just balance between the conflicting parties. This task he appears to have performed with marked success. Herrera, the historian of Ecuadorian literature, affirms that "he made himself not only notable among the bishops of America for his wisdom, but also for his eminent virtues and for his indefatigable zeal in the exercise of his pastoral functions." [7]

Villarroel's pastoral influence

Villarroel's benevolence and charity found ample opportunity for exercise in the afflicted community of Santiago after the earthquake of May 13, 1647, when the earth is said to have trembled and fluctuated like the sea. The shock caused a terrifying noise, threw down the houses and churches, and killed six hundred persons in the ruins.

Gobierno eclesiástico pacífico

Gobierno eclesiástico pacífico, Villarroel's most important work, was written during his incumbency as bishop of Santiago. It was originally published in 1656–7, and in 1737 Padre Francisco Vásquez de Sandoval caused a new edition to be issued. This book treats of the prerogatives and duties of holders of ecclesiastical and civil office.

(7) *Ensayo sobre la historia de la literatura ecuatoriana*, 37.

In it the author makes manifest his desire for harmony and conciliation, and shows that no opposition exists between the legitimate designs of the church and the state. It is not possible to describe this treatise in terms applicable to a modern work on government. It has the character of a voluminous mediæval book, containing much that is relevant to the general subject and much more that from the modern point of view is irrelevant. It is interspersed with numerous and extensive quotations, and is crowded with references to both pagan and Christian authors. According to tradition, these two massive volumes were written within a period of six months, but they were not published until ten years later than the date assigned as that of their completion, and there are various reasons for believing that the work of composition occupied at least some part of these intervening years.[8]

Historias sagradas

Historias sagradas y eclesiásticas morales was also written in the years during which Bishop Villarroel was a resident of San-

(8) Eyzaguirre, *Historia de Chile*, 1, 465.

tiago. It was divided into fifteen *coronas*, each *corona* into seven *consideraciones*, and each of the latter into *historias*. The mystical significance and religious use of these divisions are pointed out by the author, but neither the explanation nor the book itself makes any effective appeal to modern thinking; in fact, only the *Gobierno eclesiástico pacífico* retains a place among books at present useful. Villarroel's other works are important chiefly as illustrating the mental attitude of a distinguished ecclesiastic of South America in the seventeenth century.

Villarroel: "Tengo a Lima en el corazón"

In spite of the esteem in which he was held by the inhabitants of Santiago, Villarroel felt himself an exile in Chile. His thoughts always turned with longing towards Lima, the scene of his youth and early manhood, and of the development of his religious life.' "Tengo a Lima en el corazón" was often the refrain of his conversation. But in spite of absence the Spanish court had kept his memory green in Spain, and in 1651 he was promoted to the bishopric of Arequipa, where he enjoyed a larger

In Arequipa and Las Charcas

income and a more benignant climate, and where, by his control of more extensive means, he was able to expand the field of his charity. Even his library he distributed among various monasteries, and shortly after his transfer to Las Charcas, as archbishop, he died leaving no earthly possessions, and he was buried at the expense of his chaplain.

Bernado Torres, chronicler of the Augustinians, asked him for data concerning his life, and received this answer:

"Nací en Quito en una casa pobre, sin tener mi madre un pañal en qué envolverme; porque se había ido a España mi padre; entreme fraile, y nunca entró en mi la frailía; porteme vano, y aunque estudié mucho, supe menos delo que de mí juzgaban otros."[9]

(9) "I was born in Quito in a humble dwelling, my mother not having swaddling clothes in which to wrap me; as my father had gone to Spain, I became a friar, without having the spirit of a friar; I became vain, and although I studied much, I had less knowledge than was attributed to me by others."

Villaroel's letter containing this statement was dated at Arequipa August 8, 1654, and is printed in *El suelo de Arequipa convertido en cielo*, by Dr. Ventura Trabada. This work is now available in print in Odriozola's *Documentos literarios del Peru*, x, 1-324. It contains an account of the foundation of Arequipa, the cathedral, and the monasteries, and describes the lives of the bishops and other noted

IV

Semana espiritual

Books like the *Semana espiritual con meditaciones del principio y fin del hombre para cada día, y documentos de oración*, by Juan González Gutiérrez (Madrid, 1656) and the numerous religious works of the friar Andrés de San Nicolás have little significance except to illustrate the prolific industry of certain ecclesiastical writers in the realm of mysticism. San Nicolás' *Historia general de los Agustinos Descalzos de la Congregación de España e Indias* (tomo I, Madrid, 1664), is, however, accorded value as an account of the establishments of his order in Europe and Asia, but it treats only briefly of the history of the order in America. In spite of his voluminous writings San Nicolás appears to have been little known in New Granada, and Vergara

San Nicolás and Bautista de Toro

ecclesiastics, who have lived and laboured in the city. Among less important works, there appeared about the middle of the seventeenth century *Epítome de la vida y muerte del ilustrísimo señor doctor don Bernardino de Almansa . . . Arzobispo de Santafé de Bogotá*, by Pedro de Solís y Valenzuela, published in Lima in 1646; *Lengua eucarística del hombre bueno*, by Cristóbal de Torres, issued in Madrid in two folio volumes, containing an exposition of the doctrines of Thomas Aquinas; and various other purely religious works by Torres.

naively remarks that he has considered this forgetfulness as a punishment inflicted by posterity for the author's lack of love for his country.[10]

El secular religioso

Another voluminous ecclesiastical writer of Bogotá was Juan Bautista de Toro. The most important of his works is the big volume called *El secular religioso*, published in Madrid in 1721, and republished there in 1778. A feature of the work which the historian is bound to consider is its denunciation of the injustice and greed of the corregidores and the inhumanity of their treatment of the Indians In an article on *Curiosidades literarias*, Miguel Antonio Caro, in *Repertorio colombiano*, calls attention to the fact that Toro wrote a natural, simple and harmonious style at the time when "Gongorism with the authority of the peninsular writers had passed to the Indies and perverted completely the literary taste."[11] The fact is also noted that in spite of Toro's constant eulogy of the Jesuits, and his energetic condemnation of the conduct of Span-

(10) *Historia de la Literatura en Nueva Granada*, III.
(11) *Ibid.*, 187 n.

ish officials in America, a second edition of this book was issued from the royal press of Charles III.[12]

Juan de Alloza

In the seventeenth century mystical writings encountered fewer obstacles to their publication, and were more extensively read in the Spanish colonies than were books treating of purely secular subjects. The works of Padre Juan de Alloza were chiefly of this kind. His *El breve oficio del nombre de María* was reprinted many times. His *El cielo estrellado de María* and his other books of a similar character found numerous devoted readers. This was assured by the great reputation acquired by the author in his lifetime. In gaining this reputation he had the advantage of membership in an eminent colonial family. One of his brothers, who was a priest at the cathedral, became rector of the University of San Marcos, and died as bishop-elect of Santiago de Chile. Another brother in 1651 and in 1652 was also rector of the University, and an uncle, Gregorio de Loaysa, was vicar-general of the archbishopric.

(12) Vergara, *Hist. de la lit. en N. Granada*, 188 n.

No todos eran Alloza

Juan de Alloza studied at the Jesuit school in Lima, passed to the university, entered the Society of Jesus, and became the most forceful preacher of his time. In a sermon delivered on the occasion of the festival of St. Paul, he commented on the bad example set by the viceroy's speech and acts. For this he was reprimanded by the superior ecclesiastical authorities, and his right to preach was withdrawn. The viceroy, informed of this action, ordered that Alloza should be permitted to continue his preaching. "If Alloza," he said, "does not tell us the truth, who will tell us what especially concerns us? Let him continue in the pulpit, and let the first sermon which he pronounces be preached in my palace." Acting on the suggestion of this episode, a preacher of another order undertook to exercise a similar freedom of criticism, but he was called to account, and the viceroy, on imposing the merited punishment, bade him remember "que no todos eran Alloza." [13]

(13) Early appreciative reference to Alloza are contained in the *Biblioteca de la Compañía de Jesús*; in Antonio José Pastrana, *Jardín ameno de San José*, and *Empeños del poder y amor a Dios*, in Firmín de Irisarri, *Vida de Alloza* and in Mendiburu, Dic. hist. biog. del Perú.

Padre José Silva's life falls principally in the first half of the eighteenth century. He was born in Lima in 1703, became a Jesuit in 1720, and died two years after the edict of expulsion. He served many years as a professor of philosophy, part of the time in the University of Cuzco. Besides a treatise on the civil law in two volumes, he wrote extensively on ecclesiastical subjects; on the evils of Calvinism; on the necessity and the existence of a divine revelation; and on the eucharist.

José Silva

Francisco de la Cruz, a Dominican, was not less prolific than Alloza as a writer on religious questions. He was born in Granada, studied in Lima, made his profession of faith in the monastery of his order in Cuzco in 1616, and became a professor in the University of San Marcos. Entrusted with various important ecclesiastical offices he finally attained the dignity of a bishop, and was charged with relieving the Indians of Potosí from the burdens imposed upon them by the miners. In executing this commission he aroused the hostility of the Spaniards, whose interests were affected.

Francisco de la Cruz

The mystical character of his writings is sufficiently indicated by some of the titles of his books, such as *De la concepción de María* (Lima, 1653), *Historia del rosario a coros* (Alcalá, 1652), and *El jardín de María* (Salamanca, 1655).

Juan Cajica

In the vast mass of unpublished writings by ecclesiastics are comprised the numerous manuscripts by Juan Cajica, an Augustinian who arrived in Peru in 1573. His extensive knowledge of the native languages greatly facilitated his missionary labours, and his diligence and persistence in writing are made abundantly evident by the statement that he produced thirty-two volumes. Twelve of these were designed to be printed in folio, and twenty in quarto, all in Spanish. They were, however, never printed, because, according to Calancha, the publication of them would have cost one hundred thousand pesos, and no fund of that amount was available. They treated extensively of religious instruction and of the doctrines requisite for a knowledge of the Catholic faith.

The manuscripts of Cajica

Few writers of Peru achieved greater distinction while living than Padre Juan Pérez de Menacho, who was born in Lima in the last half of the sixteenth century. He studied in the schools of his native city, and entered the Society of Jesus, He was called to a professorship of philosophy in the University of San Marcos in 1601, and served in that office for twenty years. Many statements were current during his life concerning his marvellous memory and profound knowledge, among others that he knew by heart the works of Thomas Aquinas; and these statements were heard not merely in America, but also in Europe, where, referring to him, it was affirmed that the mind of St. Thomas was in Peru. In later centuries he passed to a certain extent out of public knowledge, largely because the bulk of his works were never published.[14]

Juan Pérez de Menacho

(14) Some of Menacho's works are: *Summa theologiae Sancti Thomae*, six volumes; *Theologiae moralis tractatus*, two volumes; *Tractatus de preceptis ecclesiae*; *Privilegios de la Compañía de Jesús; Privilegios de los Indios; Rentas eclesiásticas; Preeminencias de las iglesias catedrales respecto de sus sufragáneas;* and a considerable number of works dealing with the doctrines and administration of the Church. Among the historical references to Menacho are those found in the *Mercurio peruano*, No. II, by José Rosi y Rubi; in *Vida de Alloza*, by Padre Irisarri; in *De virtute fidei divinæ*,

Menacho's writings

El perfecto confesor

El perfecto confesor y cura de almas was a purely religious book of the middle of the seventeenth century that had a certain vogue in its day. It was written by Juan Machado de Chávez, who was born in Quito, and who was educated in Lima and in his native city. He held various offices in the Church, and was appointed bishop of Popayán in 1651, but died two years later, before assuming the duties of his episcopal office. *El perfecto confesor* was published in Barcelona in two folio volumes about 1641. In 1661 Francisco Apolinar published in Madrid a summary of Dr. Machado's works.

Fernando de Vergara

Fernando de Vergara Azcárate and his brother José de Vergara Azcárate, added materially to the mass of ecclesiastical writings of the first half of the eighteenth century. They were both natives of Bogotá. Fernando de Vergara was born near the end of the seventeenth century, studied at the college of San Bartolomé and

by Padre Leonardo Peñafiel; in *Del amor de Dios*, by Adrián Alesio; in *Vida de Santo Toribio*, by León Pinelo; in *El sol del Nuevo Mundo*, by Montalvo; in the *Estrella de Lima*, by Echave y Assu; in the *Crónica franciscana* by Córdoba Salinas; and in *Varones ilustres*, by Juan Anello Oliva.

entered the order of the Jesuits. He became the rector of the Jesuits' college at Cartagena, and, after his return to Bogotá, he became the rector of the Jesuits' college in that city, where he died on October 12, 1761. José de Vergara was born on January 22, 1684. He inherited from his father the encomienda of Serrezuela, which had been held by his grandfather. In 1703 he left the college of San Bartolomé, and was appointed to the office of corregidor. After the death of his wife and of all of his numerous children but one son, within a period of two months,[15] he became a priest. He received the degree of Doctor of Theology at the University of Santo Tomás, became the cura of Topaga in 1726 and was transferred later to Socorro, where he died in 1746. His surviving son conducted the negotiations at Socorro with the rebellious communeros. The works of these writers are noteworthy now chiefly as indicating what subjects claimed the attention of colonial ecclesiastics of superior education and standing.[16]

José de Vergara

(15) Vergara says, "la muerte de diez y ocho hijos y de su esposa."—*Historia de literatura en N. Granada*, 188.

Domingo Antomas, mystic

Another Jesuit whose name is set down in the list of the mystics was Domingo Antomas. From his birthplace, Carcar in Navarre, he went to Chile, and in 1742 was assigned to the projected missions on the island of Juan Fernández, where he remained a year. After his return to Santiago he was charged with the direction of the monasteries of Carmen and Rosas. While in the island he wrote his little book called *Arte de perseverancia final en gracia.* José Torres wrote on the privileges and prerogatives of the Spouse of the Mother of God. The most striking of the works under consideration is Manuel Lacunza's *La venida del Mesías en gloria y majestad,* which Vicuña Mackenna describes as "an indecipherable myth, of which all speak as if it were one of

(16) The following are some of the works of Fernando de Vergara: *Resoluciones morales, o explicación de los contratos en común y en particular; Cuestiones canónicas; Sermones de la santísima Virgen y de los santos; Breve noticia de la congregación de Nuestra Señora del Socorro; Dictamen de prudencia de nuestro padre San Ignacio de Loyola; Novena de San Agustín, doctor de la Iglesia.* The following are titles of José de Vergara's works: *El sacerdote instruido; Historia de las capellanías fundadas por laicos y religiosos en este arzobispado; Sermones morales y doctrinales; Historia de Gedeón, Ester y la casta Susana; De las reliquias y veneración de los santos; Cuestiones del cabildo de Santafé; Reparos dignos de atención en la erección de parroquias.*

the nation's titles to glory, without having opened the volume."[17] As the title indicates, the book deals with the second coming of the Messiah, the millennium, the Last Judgment, presenting pictures of the imagination that suggest the visions of Milton.

Manuel Lacunza

Lacunza was born in Santiago in 1731; he entered the Society of Jesus at the age of sixteen. After his expatriation, in 1767, he lived at Imola, in Italy, until his voluntary withdrawal from the order, when he retired to the suburbs of the city, and lived there for more than twenty years the life of an anchorite, preparing his own food and permitting no one to enter his habitation. He died there in 1801.

The influences of colonial life generally stimulated practical activity rather than philosophical or religious reflection, but now and then minds appeared so predisposed to mysticism that they could not be awakened out of their dreams even by the uproar of the frontier. Among such persons, Medina mentions Ignacio García, Domingo Antomas, José Torres, Pedro de

(17) *Historia de Santiago*, II, 161 n.

Ignacio García

Tula Bazán and Manuel Lacunza. García was born in Galicia in 1696, studied at Coruña, entered the order of the Jesuits, and completed his academic career at Salamanca. His request for service in America having been granted, he sailed from Cadiz for Buenos Aires, and made the journey of nearly a thousand miles from that town across the plains and over the Andes into Chile. The first field of his mission was Coquimbó. From this place he was transferred to Santiago, but in 1730 he was in Concepción, where he gave instruction in philosophy. This was the year that witnessed the destruction of Concepción by an earthquake, and after that event García returned to Santiago, where he performed the duties of a professor of theology. He died in that city in 1754 as rector of the Colegio Máximo. His work entitled *Desengaño consejero* was published in Lima the year of his death. In this he emphasized especially the need of fervent prayer, confirming this by citations from the Scriptures, and proposing exercises for meditation in retirement. Another work of a similar char-

Desengaño consejero

acter was called *Respiración del alma en afectos pios*, which set forth the exercises needed to keep alive the spirit, as respiration keeps alive the body. In view of approaching death he requested Padre Javier Zevallos to present to bishop Alday the manuscript of a volume entitled *Cultivo de las virtudes en el paraíso del alma* (Barcelona, 1759).

Respiración del alma

CHAPTER XV

GOVERNMENT AND LAW

I. *Melchor Calderón, Francisco Falcón and Francisco Carrasco de Saz.* II. *Nicolás Polanco de Santillana, Juan Matienzo, Juan de Solórzano Pereira, and Gaspar de Escalona y Agüero.* III. *The brothers Antonio, Diego, and Juan de León Pinelo and Juan del Corral Calvo de la Torre.* IV. *Jorge Escobedo y Alarcón and José Rezabal y Ugarte.* V. *Alonso de la Peña Montenegro.*

I

Spanish autocracy

The autocratic government under which the Spanish colonists in America lived exercised a notable influence on the opinions and theories held by colonial writers on politics in the seventeenth and the early part of the eighteenth century; but in the later decades of the eighteenth century the new creole-mestizo society, or party, revolted against the hitherto current political philosophy and accepted doctrines that had found expression particularly in the United States and in France. While the government of the Spanish-American dependencies was in process of development, many persons very naturally became interested in the new laws and the gradual growth of the system. As new phases of the organization appeared, new questions arose that attracted attention. In the British colonies, where provision was made for a large measure of popular local control, interest in governmental affairs found expression in addresses, projects of law, and debates in popular meetings and legislative assemblies, and through the still more popular exponent of opinion furnished by the public press. In the enjoyment of these facilities, there was almost no incentive to write or publish formal treatises on political subjects. The Spanish colonies, on the other hand, presented a very different state of affairs. The people had no voice in the colonial government; the popular orator, except in the pulpit, did not exist; there

British and Spanish colonies compared

Rôle of Council of the Indies

were no legislative assemblies; the viceroys, the governors, the judges of the audiencia, and the corregidores were appointed by the king or by the Council of the Indies acting for the king; only the municipal council, when not dominated by a superior authority, stood as a feeble representative of the people. The laws under which the colonists were governed were framed and issued by the king and the Council, who ruled autocratically through officials rendered practically absolute by their distance from the supreme head of the state and by the difficulties and the infrequency of the communication. Any discussion of current political or governmental questions had, therefore, to take the form of a treatise, a report, or a petition to the king or the Council of the Indies. During the greater part of the colonial period no facilities for publication existed except in Lima, the city of Mexico, and Spain; for no printing presses existed in Spanish America, except in these two capitals and certain Jesuit houses, until the last part of the eighteenth century; and until the last decade of that

Public discussion

century there was no periodical in the South American dependencies through which public questions might be discussed.

Question of Chilean Indians

The question as to what disposition should be made of Chilean Indians captured in war with the Spaniards was raised very early and continued under discussion for many decades. This was the subject of a treatise[1] by Melchor Calderón, who went from Spain to Chile in 1555, and who became a canon and the treasurer of the cathedral of Santiago de Chile, later a commissary of the Inquisition and vicar-general of the bishopric. In 1579 he was appointed a member of the cabildo of Santiago. His book, published late in his life, in 1607, was designed to bring to the attention of the viceroy the views of the more competent colonists concerning the advisability of enslaving the rebellious Araucanians. Calderón's argument was that since the conquerors were able to kill the Indians, it would be carrying out a more humane policy to enslave them.

(1) *Tratado de la importancia y utilidad que hay en dar por esclavos a los indios rebelados de Chile.*

Diversity of opinions

There was a wide diversity of opinions concerning the treatment the Indians ought to receive at the hands of the government. The severe policy, supported by the encomenderos and the bulk of the secular authorities, was generally opposed by the members of the clergy; but now and then a secular writer appeared as the vigorous advocate of a just and righteous treatment of the Indians. Such an advocate was Francisco Falcón, who was a lawyer in Lima during the last part of the sixteenth century. At the ecclesiastical council of Lima, of 1582, Falcón set out with great force and freedom verified instances of injustice, oppression, and robbery by the Spaniards, and urged the council to take remedial measures and to suppress with a firm hand "those detestable excesses." He raised the question of the right of conquest, and denied that the Spaniards had any such right, or any reason to make war on the natives. He declared that the encomiendas had been awarded only for such a period as the emperor might wish to have them continued, and that whatever these kingdoms produce

Francisco Falcón

for the king should be spent for the Indians themselves, since there was no law allowing the removal of the revenues from these kingdoms to supply the needs of other countries, and before all the king should satisfy the needs of those by whom the production is effected. Falcón maintained, moreover, that no more towns of Spaniards should have been founded than were necessary "to support and furnish a backing for the preachers of the gospel." He condemned the establishment of towns in regions already cultivated by the Indians. He opposed the exaction of a tribute from the Indians greater than that which they had paid to the Incas; at the same time he emphasized the fact that the revenues collected by the Incas were expended in the kingdom, and not sent to a foreign country.[2]

Critical view of policy

Another phase of the Indian problem was taken up by Dr. Francisco Carrasco de Saz.[3] He discussed extensively the payment of

(2) Mendiburu, *Dic. hist. biog. del Perú*, III, 81–84.
(3) Two of Carrasco's works are *Interpretatio ad aliquas leges recopilationis regni Castellae* (Seville, 1620), and *De casibus Curiae* (Madrid, 1630).

Francisco Carrasco

tithes by the Indians, and reached the conclusion that they should make this payment. For the legal aspects of this question he was fitted by his broad knowledge of law. In the practice of his profession in Lima he acquired the reputation of being one of the ablest and most distinguished lawyers of his time. He was rector of the University of San Marcos in 1613, and became fiscal of the royal tribunal called the Crusada. Later he went to Panama as oidor, or judge, of the audiencia.

II

The judges, or oidores, of the audiencia were usually men of legal knowledge. Nicolás Polanco de Santillana was a member of the audiencia of Chile about the middle of the seventeenth century. He was in Santiago at the time of the earthquake of 1647,[4] and, prompted by the questions that arose concerning the attitude the government should assume in the presence of such a disaster, he wrote *De las obligaciones de*

(4) On this earthquake see Barros Arana, *Historia de Chile*, II, 415, 426-442; Moses, *Spanish Dependencies in South America*, II, 172-174.

los jueces y gobernadores en los casos fortuitos, beginning and completing his book while the city still lay in ruins about him. Polanco de Santillana is accredited also with *Comentario a las leyes del título primero del libro primero de la recopilación;* but both of these works appear to have been lost. A colleague and contemporary of Polanco de Santillana, Machado de Chavez, wrote *Discurso políticos y reformación del derecho*, and this also has disappeared.

Three especially important works on politics in the colonies are Matienzo's *Gobierno del Perú*, Solórzano's *Política indiana*, and Escalona's *Gazofilacio real del reino del Perú*. These are treatises on government and law, dealing with the institutions and offices through which the administration of the dependencies was carried on, and describing the powers and processes of the civil and military organization. Matienzo's book is the earliest of these; it was written prior to 1573, while the author was a judge of the audiencia of Charcas. The two par s of the manuscript constituting this volume found their way into the British Museum, and re-

Matienzo

Gobierno del Perú

mained unpublished until 1910, when they appeared in print under the auspices of the Faculty of Philosophy and Letters of Buenos Aires. The volume was edited by Dr. José Nicolás Matienzo, a descendant of the author. It forms an important addition to the printed sources of knowledge relating to the early history and organization of the Spanish dependencies in South America. The first part treats almost exclusively of the Indians under the Incas and in their subsequent relation to the Spaniards; while the second part treats of the Spaniards and of the governmental institutions established by them in America.

Matienzo affirms the justice of the Spanish conquest, and some of the grounds of his opinion are, that the Spaniards had rereceived a concession from the pope; that they found America not occupied by any civilized power; that the Indians did not wish to receive the Catholic faith; and that by this act the Indians were relieved from the tyranny of the Incas. This point having been settled to the apparent satisfaction of the author, he passed to the consideration of the various classes of the Indians, classes indicated by the relation they are made to hold to the Spaniards, and by the tribute they are required to pay. In justification of the position of the encomenderos, who became the notorious oppressors of the Indians, it is asserted that when Indians were assigned to encomenderos the principal purpose was that "they might, with greater facility, be taught our holy Catholic faith" (Cap. XIV).

Matienzo's views

After a detailed statement of the status of the Indians under the Laws of the Indies Matienzo devotes the second half of his volume to an extensive examination of the organization and operations of the government established by the Spaniards in Peru, thus giving to the whole treatise the character of a legal and historical exposition, of importance not merely for its analysis of the laws and customs prevailing in the Spanish colonies of South America in the sixteenth century, but also for its presentation of the views entertained by a judge of the audiencia, and, presumably, of other high secular officials.

Audiencias

The audencia was not only a supreme court, but also a high administrative body. In the vacancy of the viceregal office the audiencia conducted the government in the interim. To increase the efficiency of the administration, audiencias were established in certain provincial capitals. In the fully developed colonial organization, there were, in South America, audiencias in Panama, Bogotá, Quito, Lima, Charcas, Caracas, Buenos A res, and Santiago de Chile. Concerning the creation of the audiencia, of which he was a member, Matienzo wrote:

Gobierno del Perú quoted

"There are very important reasons for founding the audiencia of Charcas, in addition to the one that had been established in the city of Lima; for the Indians from the mountainous regions coming to Lima become ill and many die from the effects of the climatic change; and, moreover, for the Spaniards it is a great grievance to be obliged to go three hundred leagues from those mountains to Lima, and five hundred leagues from Tucumán and other places; and crimes ordinarily remain without punishment, because of the

HISPANIA
AMERICA
SVBDIDIT OCEANV SCEPTRIS ET MARGINE COELI
CLAVSIT OPES.
D.PHILIP.IV.HISP.ET IND.REGI OPT.MAX.
IOANNES
DE SOLORZANO PEREIRA I.V.D.
Ex Primarijs olim Academiæ Salmanticensis Antecessoribus. Postea Limensis Prætorij in Peruano Regno Novi Orbis Senator.
Nunc verò in Supremo Indiarum Consilio Regij Fisci Patronus;
DISPVTATIONEM
DE INDIARVM IVRE,
Sive
De iusta Indiarum Occidentalium inquisitione, acquisitione, et retentione
TRIBVS LIBRIS COMPREHENSAM,
D.E.C.
CVM PRIVILEGIO. MATRITI.
Ex Typographia Francisci Martinez ANNO 1629.
FIDES
RELIGIO
Roberto
Cordier

distance from the court; and since the region of Charcas adjoins the Chiriguanos, Indians hostile to the Spaniard in neighbouring places, who have a great desire, if they were able to do so, to return to Peru; and if the leaders were badly treated, they might begin a war, and do a great amount of damage in the country. The audiencia is there to resist them, and it is a great wall and defence."

Solórzano Pereira

The second of the three important works mentioned is entitled *Política indiana*, by Juan de Solórzano Pereira. He was a student, and later an instructor, at Salamanca. In 1609 Philip III sent him to Lima as a member of the audiencia in that city. Subsequently he became governor of Huancavelica and inspector of quicksilver mining. After his return to Spain and service in various offices, he was finally promoted, in 1629, to membership in the Council of the Indies. In the dedication of his work to Philip IV he affirms that he was ordered to write, at his discretion, on the subjects of law and government; moreover, that on his return to Spain he caused to be printed two

Política indiana

volumes in Latin entitled *De Indiarum jure et gubernatione*, and that he was given to understand that the king would be pleased and served if those books were translated into Spanish, in order that they might be used by those persons who did not understand Latin; and many persons by letter had expressed their desire for such a translation. But on account of certain difficulties attending the making and using a literal translation, he decided not to bind himself to the letter of the Latin text, but to improve it by adding to it in many places and by abbreviating it in others. In this way was formed the text of *Política indiana*. In this form it treats of the discovery, acquisition and retention of the Indies; of the natural features of the continent; of the government; of the Indians, their services under the Spaniards, and the tribute paid by them; of the tithes and encomiendas; of the royal patronage; of the Church, the various classes of ecclesiastical orders and their officers; and of the secular magistrates: the viceroys, the presidents, the audiencias, and the various councils and committees.

The work thus appears as a digest of the laws and decrees issued with application to the Indies prior to the last quarter of the seventeenth century. While the bulk of the references are to the *Recopilación de los leyes de las indias*, other writings, such as those of Matienzo, Acosta, and Torquemada, are frequently cited, and, in keeping with the fashion of the times, there is embodied a profusion of citations from classical authors. With all its superfluous display of learning *Política indiana* still holds and will continue to hold a conspicuous place among the books of the first order for students of the laws and government of the Spanish colonies in South America.

Sources of *Política Indiana*

The third member of this group is Gaspar de Escalona y Agüero. It is not positively known where he was born. Three cities have contended for the honour of being recognized as the place of his origin. Alcedo, the author of the geographical and historical dictionary, and the historian Cevallos affirm that he was born in Ecuador, but other evidence points to Lima as his native town. Wherever the honour may rest, it

Gaspar de Escalona

was in the schools of Lima and the University of San Marcos that he was educated. He held a number of public offices: he was corregidor of Jauja, governor of Castrovireyna, procurador-general of the city of Cuzco, and oidor, or judge, of the audiencia of Chile. His principal work, entitled *Gazophilatium regium Perubicum*, was printed in Madrid in 1647; the first part in Latin, and the second part in Spanish. It treats particularly of matters of justice, of questions concerning the civil administration and the treasury, and of the affairs of the army. Its analyses and descriptions present minute details both of the organization and the functions of the public offices.

Gazophilatium regium Perubicum

These writers were not reformers after the manner of persons who aim to supplant the established government by a new form of administration; they were loyal to the system which they served, but this loyalty did not withhold them from criticising the practical execution of the existing laws; they condemned with severity the criminal exactions of the corregidores of Indians,

Juan de Solórzano Pereira

and other abuses due to the dishonesty of officials and their remoteness from the centre of superior authority.

The three works compared

Matienzo's exposition presents the state of public affairs only thirty or forty years after the conquest of Peru, and is the earliest attempt to set forth systematically the immature political organization and the social state of this part of the Spanish dominions. The author's undertaking was comparatively simple, and he carried it out simply; but sixty or seventy years later, when Solórzano wrote, the colonial system had become more fully developed; the volume of laws had been greatly increased; and new institutions had been created. In the presence of this more complex state of society, Solórzano undertook to present the substance of these laws, to describe the institutions, and to make use of earlier writings in forming an organzied body of knowledge relating to the colonies. Escalona Agüero, in his *Gazophilatium regium Perubicum* (*Gazofilacio real del Perú*), supplements both the *Gobierno del Perú* and the *Política indiana*. He describes the colonial

Escalona's book

institutions and deals extensively with the officials, indicating the qualities they are required to possess; gives minute directions for official action; specifies the salaries attached to the various offices; presents an elaborate description of official accounts, the method of keeping them, and of the tribunal of accounts; discusses the mines and the manner of distributing their products; and describes the system of taxation, with special emphasis laid on the *Alcabala*, or tax on the price of articles when sold. This book, printed in Madrid in 1647, consists of three parts; the first part of one hundred and ninety-nine folio, double-column pages is printed in Latin; the second part has three hundred and two pages in Spanish. In this work the author has examined not only the laws and regulations referring to what are ordinarily known as governmental affairs, but also those relating to economic affairs.

III

A more voluminous writer on politics than any of the foregoing appeared in the

Antonio de León Pinelo.

person of Antonio de León Pinelo, who dealt with the legal and governmental affairs of the Spanish dependencies. The circumstances of his early life are still obscure. An article on him in the *Mercurio peruano* throws no light on the date or the place of his birth, and other available sources offer very little definite information; but it is inferred from statements in his life of Santo Toribio that his childhood and youth were passed in Lima, and that, with his younger brothers, Juan and Diego, he studied at the University of San Marcos. Having completed his studies at the university, he went to Spain; there his talents and learning were recognized, and he was appointed *Relator* of the Council of the Indies. In 1624 he published a discourse on the importance, the form, and the arrangement of a collection of the laws of the Indies, and under the authority of the Council of the Indies he compiled two volumes of these laws. In accomplishing this task he encountered the notorious confusion and contradictions prevailing in the body of laws and decrees issued for the government of Spain's possessions in America.

The project to publish these two volumes met apparently insurmountable obstacles, but, in accordance with a previous plan, the compiler formed an abridgement of their contents, which was called *Política de las Indias*. Three other works appear to have been drawn largely from the original compilation. These were *Bulario índico, Tratado de las confirmaciones reales*, and *Historia del supremo concejo de las Indias*. Pinelo's bibliography of authors who had written on the Indies was entitled *Biblioteca oriental y occidental*, and was published in Madrid in 1629. It was reprinted in three folio volumes in 1737 under the direction of the minister Andrés Gonzales de Barcia.[4]

Pinelo's works

Antonio de León Pinelo mentions Gutierre Velásquez Altamirano, who was a pro-

(4) Other works by Pinelo are: Printed: *Aparato a la historia . . . de la Ciudad de los Reyes, Lima, etc.*, Madrid, 1631. *Diálogos de la pintura, etc.*, Madrid, 1633. *Aparato político de las Indias occidentales, etc.*, Madrid, 1653. *Vida del . . . D. Toribio Alfonso Mogrovejo*, Madrid, 1653. *Autos, acuerdos y decretos del . . . real consejo de las Indias*, Madrid, 1658. MSS.: *El paraíso en el Nuevo Mundo, commentario . . . de las Indias occidentales* (1656). *Historia de la villa imperial de Potosí, descubrimiento y grandeza de su rico cerro; El patriarcado: historia eclesiástico-política del Nuevo Mundo; El gran canciller de las Indias; Anales . . . de Madrid, hasta el año 1658.*

fessor of law in the University of San Marcos while Pinelo was a student there. Later Altamirano was appointed oidor of the audiencia of Guatemala, but died in Madrid before assuming the duties of his office. As a native of Lima, and as a student of law, he very naturally became interested in the government of the colonies, and wrote a work entitled *Del oficio y potestad del vicario del principe, y gobierno universal de las Indias*, which was apparently never published.

Del oficio y potestad

Antonio's brother, Diego de León Pinelo, became a professor in the University of San Marcos and rector of that institution for the years 1656 and 1657. He was appointed Protector of the Indians, and later fiscal of the audiencia of Lima. His extensive knowledge of legal and ecclesiastical matters was generally recognized, and many of his writings on juridical subjects were made public. In 1660 the Council of the Indies sent Padilla's letter to the viceroy, the letter treating of the grievances, frauds, and acts of injustice under which the Indians suffered. At the same time

Diego de León Pinelo

the king ordered that a commission should be formed to examine the evils referred to, and seek a remedy. In obedience to a request from the viceroy Diego de León Pinelo set forth the misfortunes and extortions imposed upon the Indians. Pinelo's report and Padilla's letter were printed at Lima. The amount of attention given to this subject by the viceregal government may be inferred from the fact that the decrees, complaints, and claims issued during Alva's term as viceroy, between 1655 and 1661, filled, when written, twenty-five books with 9,660 leaves. The attention bestowed upon this subject gives some indication of the extent of the abuses and excesses perpetrated by the corregidores and parish priests.[5]

Oppression of the Indians

Juan de León Pinelo

The second brother of Antonio, Juan de León Pinelo, who, as already indicated, studied at the University of San Marcos, became a cura at Potosí, and later went to Spain with Antonio. He was subsequently transferred to Puebla de los Angeles, and

(5) Concerning these abuses and excesses Juan and Ulloa in their *Noticias secretas de América* give an extended account.

became a canon in the Cathedral of that city. His writings, published and unpublished, deal chiefly with ecclesiastical questions.[6]

Corral Calvo de la Torre

Juan del Corral Calvo de la Torre, born in the town of La Plata, in Upper Peru, studied in Lima, and was granted the title of advocate by the audiencia. He became a member of the audiencia in Santiago in 1698, and while occupying this position prepared his extensive work, designed to be three volumes in folio, under the title of *Expositio ac explanatio omnium legum Recopilat Indiarum.* But his application for permission to publish it received from the king the following reply:

"El Rey. Don Juan del Corral Calvo de la Torre, oidor de mi Audiencia del reino de Chile. En carta de 1° de marzo del año próximo pasado, dais cuenta del método que habéis observado en la ejecución de los

(6) Some of these are: *Vida de Santa Margarita*, Madrid, 1629; *El predicador de las gentes, San Pablo; Ciencia, preceptos y obligaciones de los predicadores; Panegírico de Felipe IV; El martirio de los que han padecido en las Indias por la fe; Viajes de los galeones de las Indias en 1607 con descripción de los puertos en que entraron; Parecer sobre la pintura*, Madrid, 1633; *El prudente confesor*, Valencia, 1645.

Royal refusal of manuscript

comentos y exposiciones de las leyes de las Indias, teniendo ya acabados dos tomos, y el primero remitido a Lima, y para enviar el segundo; y habiéndose visto en mi consejo de las Indias, con lo expuesto por su fiscal, se ha considerado que la aprobación que pedís de esta obra, como el que sea su impresión de cuenta de mi real hacienda, se debe suspender por ahora hasta tanto que se vea y reconozca, en cuyo caso, y siendo digna de darse a la prensa, se podrá ejecutar en España, para cuyo efecto la podréis ir remitiendo en las ocasiones que se ofrecieren. De Madrid a 25 de mayo de 1726. Yo el Rey."

Estado político del reino del Perú

A subject similar to Escalona's is treated in an anonymous publication of ninety-two folio pages entitled *Estado político del reino del Perú;* but the treatment is of a very different character, and it is written with a very different purpose. Escalona aimed to set forth a comprehensive and impartial view of the political structure, and to describe it as it was defined by law. The *Estado político,* on the other hand, is designedly critical, as may be inferred from certain phrases from the long sub-title, such as "government without laws, officials without industry, treasures without poverty, fertility without cultivation, wisdom without esteem, militia without honour, cities without patriotism, and justice without a temple." After these and other similar phrases, the author ends his title-page with the remark that "these attributes constitute a grave detriment to this kingdom, and as a remedy two expedients are proposed to his Majesty by a loyal vassal who writes them, solely moved by a true love of his prince and natural Lord, and for the greater good of the kingdom of Peru and of his Patria Lima." The first of these expedients was a reform in the militia, or the military affairs of the kingdom: the second was a reform in the commercial affairs.[7]

The *Memorias* by the viceroys

The formal treaties on government and law are supplemented by a number of public documents that have been printed. Important among these are the *Memorias* and

(7) The date of this book as given at the end of the dedication is Madrid, April 30, 1747.

Relaciones delivered by the viceroys to their successors. They present contemporary accounts of public affairs, the actual state of the government, recent changes, and projects for future modifications.[8]

IV

Escobedo y Alarcón

A large number of the colonial writers on law and government were at the same time practical administrators. This has contributed to make their literary productions reliable and worthy of confidence as sources of information concerning the political affairs of the dependencies. In the last half of the eighteenth century Jorge Escobedo y Alarcón appeared in this double capacity. He was appointed a judge of the audiencia of Charcas in 1776; he held an important

(8) Some of the more noteworthy are: *Memorias de los virreyes que han gobernado el Perú durante el tiempo del coloniaje español*, Lima, 1859 (6 vols., ed. by M. A. Fuentes); *Relaciones de los virreyes y audiencias que han gobernado el Perú*, Lima 1867–1872 (3 vols. ed. by Sebastián Lorente); *Memoria del virrey del Perú, Marqués de Avilés*, Lima, 1901 (ed. by Carlos Alberto Romero); *Relaciones de los virreyes del nuevo reino de Granada* (ed. by García), New York, 1869; *Relaciones de mando* (Bibl. de Hist. Nacional, VIII), Bogotá, 1910, a reprint of García's publication with additions; See also Zinny, *Historia de los gobernadores de las provincias argentinas*, Buenos Aires, 1879, I, XLVII-XCVI.

post in the government of Potosí; he was the superintendent of the mint, the mines, the bank, and the royal treasury of that city. He participated in the defence of Potosí against the insurgents of 1780, and thus helped to make that town an asylum for the threatened inhabitants of the neighbouring region during the rebellion of Tupac Amaru. He was promoted to the position of a judge of the audiencia of Lima, and in 1782 Charles III appointed him visitador-general of the courts of justice and of the royal treasury of the viceroyalties of Peru and Río de la Plata. He became political governor and intendant of the province of Lima, and in this capacity he was president of the municipal council for the years 1785 and 1787; and at the same time he presided over the superior council of the treasury, which he created, and his administration of these offices was signalized by important reforms. And during these active years of his life he wrote on the development and exploitation of the mines, on the former repartimientos of the corregidores, and on the means of aiding the In-

Escobedo's official positions

dians without imposing upon them the burdens which that system entailed. These and some of his other writings were published in Lima in 1784. After the conclusion of his work in America, Escobedo retired to Spain, and in 1805 he was president of the second division of the Council of the Indies.

Rezabal y Ugarte

José Rezabal y Ugarte was one of the later writers on legal and political questions. Although a native of Spain, the greater part of his life was spent in America. He studied at Salamanca, and in 1777 he was appointed judge of the audiencia of Chile. In 1780 he was transferred to Lima, and in 1787 he became a member of the audiencia of Cuzco. In 1792 the king appointed him regent of the audiencia of Chile. This career naturally fixed his attention particularly on affairs of administration, and while oidor in Chile he prepared instructions for inferior municipal officials, compiling for this purpose a large number of ordinances bearing on this subject. He compiled also two thousand royal orders designed for the government of America, which had been issued subsequent to the publication of the *Recopilación de las leyes de las Indias*. He discussed, moreover, the king's rights in the matter of secular medias anatas, and the obligations of service under certain Castilian titles. This report was published in 1792.[9] Among other writings were a dissertation on the various forms of money referred to in the Laws of the Indies, a treatise on the introduction of negroes into America, and various subjects relating to their utility and their government; and a work dealing with the status of regents of audiencias in America, their creation in 1776 and their powers and prerogatives. His *Biblioteca* of the writers who had belonged to the four greater colleges of Salamanca was published in 1805. Rezabal died in Chile in 1800.

Rezabal's *Biblioteca*

V

The fact that the Church was embodied in the state in the Spanish dependencies sometimes led ecclesiastics to discuss po-

(9) Rezabal y Ugarte, *Tratado del real derecho de las medias anatas seculares y del servicio de lanzas a que están obligados los títulos de Castilla*, Madrid, 1792.

litical questions, or governmental problems involving the Church. An instance of this is found in Villarroel's *Gobierno eclesiástico pacífico*.

Alonso de la Peña Montenegro

Moreover, it is to Bishop Alonso de la Peña Montenegro that we are indebted for an important treatise of this character, presenting what may properly be called the constitutional position of the Church as a part of the colonial organization, as determined by decrees, rules, and regulations, particularly those affecting the doctrineros de Indios. We have here in great detail the provisions elaborated and approved by superior authority for fixing the duties of priests and missionaries in the exercise of their functions in America, as well as the obligations of all persons within the sphere of their ministerial influence. Although the reciprocal obligations here defined may not in all cases have been observed, still these provisions make clear the theory and expectation of the superior authorities with respect to the ecclesiastical part of the social organism. It is true that the inquiries of Juan and Ulloa regarding this subject,

Doctrineros de Indios

which have been set down in their *Noticias secretas de América,* throw much light on the departure of many priests from the rules and regulations by civil or ecclesiastical authority, nevertheless the law stands although it may be sometimes violated.

Ecclesiastical functionaries

The author describes the parish and the parish priest, discusses the manner of electing the doctrineros de Indios, or missionaries to the Indians, and shows the participation of the civil authority in ecclesiastical affairs by pointing out the fact that "no archbishop, bishop, prebend of any cathedral, doctrinero de Indios, or parish priest in a parish of Spaniards may be appointed without first having been presented by his Majesty, or persons empowered to represent him."

Topics of Peña's treatise

In this treatise other subjects of vital importance were considered, such as the appointment of members of the regular clergy to the position of missionary or parish priest; the mortal sin of accepting a mission without knowing the language of the Indians; instruction in Christian doctrine; questions concerning revenues and alms; preaching to the heathen and their conversion; the functions of the priests respecting the wills, or last testaments, of the Indians; the tribute, idolatry, witchcraft, and drunkenness of the Indians; projects for extending the dominion of the Church; the relation of the Indians to mining and work in manufacturing establishments; provisions regarding discipline and the ritual; and the vast array of problems that had arisen in the process of organizing the church and adapting its ministrations to a people who had no share in the heritage of Christian traditions.[10]

(10)The full title of this book is *Itinerario para párrocos de Indios, en que se tratan las materias más particulares tocantes a ellos, para su buena administración.* It was published in Madrid in 1668, 1771; Lyons, 1678; Antwerp, 1698, 1726, 1737, 1754.

CHAPTER XVI

LATE EIGHTEENTH-CENTURY HISTORIANS

I. *José Eusebio Llano y Zapata.* II. *Miguel de Olivares and Pedro de Córdoba y Figueroa.* III. *José Pérez García and Vicente Carvallo y Goyeneche.* IV. *Geographical description; Molina and Vidaurre.* V. *Dionisio and Antonio Alcedo, Zamacola, Segurola, and Martínez y Vela.* VI. *Concolorcorvo.*

I

Llano y Zapata

A notable figure of Peru in the eighteenth century was José Eusebio Llano y Zapata. He was born in Lima, where his father held the office of alcalde in 1690 and again in 1708. He appeared as the most precocious mind of his time in Peru. At the age of nineteen he had published papers on vari-

Zapata's precocity

ous topics in medicine, physics, and literature; and before he was twenty-five he had added to these, among other writings, a panegyric on Marcellos, bishop of Cuzco, the true method of preserving health, the nature and origin of comets, a discussion on the books of Judith and Isaiah, and the moral philosophy of Seneca. He possessed an extensive knowledge of languages, and, as evidence of his interest in this branch of study, he founded at Lima a public school for instruction in Greek. In pursuit of knowledge of natural history he made extensive journeys throughout South America during a period of five years, and afterwards went to Spain, where he completed his most important book: *Memorias histórico-físicas-críticas-apologéticas de la América meridional*, in four volumes. The first volume (*Reino mineral*) was printed, the MSS. of others have disappeared. In the second, the author is known to have treated of the vegetable kingdom, " from the most magnificent tree to the most humble plant "; in the third, of the animal kingdom, from the highest to the lowest; in the fourth, the author described certain geographical features of South America, particularly the great rivers, and in all parts attention is given to the historical phases of the subject. A little volume published at Cadiz in 1759 contains the preliminary discourse of the first volume of the *Memorias* and a number of Zapata's letters.

The Cadiz volume and letters of Zapata

A more extensive collection of Zapata's letters began to be published at Cadiz in 1764. They present important details of a great variety of subjects in the history of South America during the two centuries of Spanish rule then completed.

Zapata was an ardent champion of the designs and spirit of Spain's government of America. He praised the zeal of the conquistadores, excused in some measure their faults, excesses, and avarice. He denounced the writings of Las Casas as false and exaggerated, and condemned them as utterances unworthy of a Spaniard. At the same time he showed an appreciation of the Indians, maintaining that under a proper system of instruction they would have manifested in the course of time "las fuerzas del espíritu y la eficacia de la razón." [1]

Support of Spanish system

II

Olivares' career

The *Historia militar, civil y sagrada de lo acaecido en la conquista y pacificación del reino de Chile* by the Jesuit Miguel de Olivares is one of the more important works of the eighteenth century on Chilean history. The author was born in Chillán, in Chile, in 1674. It is believed that he went to Spain, and was there ordained priest; but in whatever manner he may have passed the early years of his life, there appears to be conclusive evidence that in 1700 he was in Chile, engaged as a missionary in the region between the Maipo and the Maule. A little later he was a missionary in the valley of Quillota, and still later he was preaching in Valparaiso. Between 1706 and 1720 he was continuing his missionary labours in various fields. In 1722 he was living in Santiago, and in 1730 at Concepción. Through his journeys he acquired much knowledge of Chile, of its geography, of its inhabitants and of the conditions

(1) See *Mercurio peruano*, No. 42, May 26, 1791. Mendiburu, *Dic. hist.-biog. del Perú*, v, 109–114.

under which rude settlements were growing into civilized communities. In 1736 he was in Santiago, gathering and putting into order the sources of information that furnished the basis of his *Breve noticia de la provincia de la Compañia de Jesús de Chile*, a work not designed at that time for publication, but only as material which a future historian might use.[2]

Breve noticia de la Compañia de Jesús

From this task he turned again to his missionary labours at first in the province of Cuyo and later, from 1744 to 1758, in Araucania. During this period he added extensively to his knowledge of the country as well as of the language and customs of the Indians.

Olivares was apparently induced to undertake his *Historia militar, civil y sagrada* by the encouragement of certain other Jesuits who had seen his manuscript on the Jesuits in Chile. This larger work was begun at Chillán in 1758, continued in Santiago, and a clean copy of it made in Concepción in 1767. Thus, after nine years of work, it was completed the year in which

(2) Medina, *Lit. col. de Chile*, II, 407.

Historia militar, civil y sagrada

the author, together with the other members of his order, was expelled from the colonies. Olivares at that time was ninety-two years of age; but his great age did not prevent his inclusion with the others under the decree of expulsion. The first stage of his journey to Europe was from Chile to Peru. He remained two months in Lima. Here, by order of the viceroy, Manuel de Amat y Juniet, his manuscripts were taken from him, but by the intercession of José Perfecto Salas, who had lived in Chile, Olivares recovered the first part of his *Historia*. But on his departure from Callao he was obliged to leave the second part in the hands of Peruvian officials. His companions in exile at Imola wished to spread in Italy a knowledge of the history and social affairs of Chile, and for this purpose they desired to make use of Olivares' manuscript and very naturally raised the question of procuring the second part. In 1788 Olivares caused the first part of his manuscript to be presented to the king of Spain through the Spanish ambassador at Rome, and at the same time communicated to the king

Fate of Olivares' manuscript

Ambrosio O'Higgins, 36th Viceroy of Peru
1796-1801

the fact that the second part was in Peru, and expressed his desire to obtain it in order to complete it and to add to it his final corrections. But this was a wish not to be fulfilled. The second part was, indeed, found and sent to Madrid in 1790, but the author had already fallen under the weight of more than a hundred years.

Olivares' sources

The manuscript sent to the king of Spain in 1788 is the part of Olivares' work which has determined his place in the literature of the colonies. It is not known what was the fate of the second part sent from Chile to Madrid in 1790 by Governor Ambrosio O'Higgins. In writing his *Historia militar, civil y sagrada*, Olivares used the works of Antonio de Herrera, Ovalle, Ercilla, Xufré del Águila, Tesillo, and Bascuñán, as well as the *Voyage* of Frezier, the writings of Juan and Ulloa, the chronicle of Techo, the description of the bishopric of Santiago by José Fernández de Campino, and the manuscript history by Córdoba y Figueroa, which, according to Medina, "served as his principal guide." Documents in the archives were not accessible to him, and this limitation of his sources made certain errors inevitable; but his experience and observations enabled him to present especially valuable descriptions of the country and the customs of the Indians. In his pages, moreover, one may find independent judgments regarding the defensive military operations, and on the extent of success achieved by the missionaries in their efforts to convert the Indians. Compared with his work on the Jesuits in Chile, the history written later shows a more marked maturity of judgment and a greater degree of originality. "But anyone who may wish to examine the book on the Jesuits will find in it not only a mass of facts most useful for a knowledge of the history of the Jesuits in Chile, but also for a complete understanding of the political and civil history."[3]

Character of Olivares' work

Historians of the 18th century

The Chileans of the eighteenth century, who wrote on the history of their country, show a somewhat clearer conception of the proper nature of history than their predecessors. One of the books of this time was *Apuntes de lo acaecido en la conquista de*

(3) Medina, *Lit. col. de Chile*, II, 415; see also pp. 504–420.

Chile, desde sus principios hasta el año de 1672, by José Basilio de Rojas y Fuentes, of whose life too few facts are known to constitute the basis of a biography. Of Pedro Córdoba y Figueroa, the author of a *Historia de Chile*, much more is known. He was a descendant of one of the early conquistadores, and was born in Concepción in 1692. Having passed under the instruction given by the Jesuits in his native town, he embraced the career of a soldier, acquired official rank in 1734, became a member of various expeditions against the Araucanians, participated in at least three parlamentos, or conferences, with the Indians, and was finally established at Concepción, where he held the office of alcalde. The fact that little mention is made of him during the period between 1739 and 1751 suggests that these were tranquil years of his life. During this time he was making his historical studies, using such works on Chilean history as had been printed at that time, and certain manuscripts, some of which, Medina says, are not now known.[4]

Córdoba's *Historia de Chile*

(4) Medina, *op. cit.*, II, 404.

His work, the product of these studies, has been commended as showing patient investigation and judicious criticism. He was, however, afflicted with a common infirmity of this time, the desire to show his erudition respecting subjects quite foreign to the history of Chile, in the field of Latin classics and the writings of the Fathers of the Church.

III

José Pérez García

Two writers on Chilean history during the last years of the colonial period were José Pérez García and Vicente Carvallo y Goyeneche. Pérez García was born in 1721, at Colindres, a little town in Spain near Santander. His parents are described in their letters patent of nobility as "*caballeros nobles, hijodalgos de sangre y naturaleza.*" He acquired only the limited education ordinarily obtained by young persons who intended to devote themselves to commerce. At the age of twenty he left Spain for America in company with an older brother, who made a considerable fortune in Upper Peru, and also conducted a commercial house in

Buenos Aires. For ten years Pérez García remained in that city engaged in mercantile pursuits. Here he laid the basis of the fortune that later insured his independence. About the middle of the century he went to Chile, and continued his activity in mercantile affairs in Santiago. Here his recognized honesty and his wealth acquired for him an honourable position in the community, and his marriage with María del Rosario Salas y Ramírez, the daughter of a rich Spanish merchant, added to his fortune, and fixed his intimate relations with the most conspicuous elements of Chilean society. After his withdrawal from active business he continued to live in Santiago. In his retirement he sought unsuccessfully from the king the rank and title of lieutenant-colonel, not with a view of exercising the functions of command, but for the sake of the social distinction this title would confer. One of the characteristic features of this colonial society is seen in the importance attached to titles and distinctive rank.

García's social position

For six years in the first decade of the nineteenth century Pérez García was engaged in writing his *Historia general, natural y militar, civil y sagrada del reino de Chile,* completed, as he announced on the last sheet of his manuscript, March 19, 1808. The first part of this book is taken up with references to the Virgin as the "discoverer, conqueror, and colonizer of the kingdom of Chile"; with a discussion of the origin of the Americans, with an inquiry as to the probable population of this continent before the Noachian flood, and with the question as to the presence of the Apostle Thomas on this continent. This part has neither interest nor historical value. And, considering the author's lack of literary training, one ought not to be disappointed in finding the writing crude and the language in many instances incorrect. "But the real merit of Pérez García's manuscript," according to Barros Arana's judgment, "resides in the historical narrative which constitutes about three-quarters of the whole work. This writer has prepared himself with a profound study of the chronicles, those in manuscript as well as those in print, and of the documents that came to his hands, and although with

Contents of García's book

Lack of literary skill

complete neglect of literary forms, he was able to make a book which has a true value and which may be consulted with profit now, after many documents have been discovered, and after the history of the conquest and colonization have begun to be re-written with the new light which they furnish. The reason of the superiority of the history of Pérez García over those that preceded it is found in the fact that the author has not always accepted as unquestionable truth what he found written by other authors; that he has attempted to verify the statements for himself and by means of comparing those narratives with the documents; and that finally he has corrected in many points numerous errors, and has set down facts from his own investigations that are not found in the other chronicles."[5]

Ground of García's superiority

The work by Carvallo was entitled *Descripción histórico-geográfica del reino de Chile.* On account of the extensive investigations on which it is based and its independent spirit it may be properly classed with the writings of Pérez García. Both of

Carvallo's work

(5) *Revista chilena*, I.

these authors were, moreover, distinguished from many of their predecessors by their secular status. García was a merchant and Carvallo was a soldier. As a soldier Carvallo was subordinated to Ambrosio O'Higgins while that officer was in general command of the southern frontier, and afterwards when he had become governor and captain-general of Chile. The friendly relation that at first existed between them was later changed to hatred and hostility, by which O'Higgins was moved to use his influence to obstruct the execution of Carvallo's plans. This is seen in the failure of Carvallo to obtain the office of corregidor in Peru for which he had applied, and also in the objections raised by O'Higgins to granting Carvallo leave to go to Santiago to consult authorities for his proposed history of Chile, as well as in his later refusal to grant his request for permission to go to Madrid to secure its publication. When Carvallo proposed to abandon his military career and enter a monastery, he requested that in his ecclesiastical position his military salary might continue to be paid to

Carvallo and O'Higgins

him. This O'Higgins firmly and definitely refused. But by persistence and a subsequent petition he succeeded in obtaining O'Higgins' permission to go to Santiago; and directly from the government in Spain he obtained leave to go to Madrid.

Life of Carvallo

The life of Carvallo was that of a vigorous and restless spirit in revolt against the narrowness and monotony of Chilean social conditions in the last half of the eighteenth century. He was born in Valdivia in 1742, the son of the governor of the district, and the youngest of three brothers. Until his twentieth year he was under the instruction of Jesuits; he then entered the military service, in which he continued for many years in his native city, where he married and became the head of a numerous family. The dull routine of garrison duties in a stagnant colonial town irked him. Hoping to find an open field for his ambition, he sought and secured his transfer to the frontier. At this time the project of President Guill y Gonzaga to establish towns or forts on territory not previously occupied by the Spaniards provoked the opposition and hostility of the Indians. It would be difficult to imagine a more complete contrast to Carvallo's life at Valdivia than that presented by his experience on the frontier; but the freer life of the frontier had its compensations; he found there abundant material for the diary which he kept throughout the whole period of his military career. The writing of this diary is said to have suggested to him the project to write a history of Chile. Moreover, daily contact with the Indians for more than thirty years gave him a secure basis of judgment concerning the long conflict which furnishes the main theme of Chilean history; he acquired sufficiently the Indians' viewpoint to enable him to discern the unjust features of the Spanish policy respecting them, and by his spirit of impartiality he was led to oppose the governors and to point out their abuses and unworthy conduct.

Carvallo's project to write a history

When Carvallo finally obtained permission directly from the government in Spain to visit Madrid, O'Higgins sent to Buenos Aires an order for his arrest, but the order arrived too late to prevent Carvallo's departure, and he was consequently able to pass a number of years in the Spanish capital, where he completed his History of Chile in 1796.

Carvallo at Madrid

At Madrid Carvallo was able to command influence sufficient not only to defeat the efforts of those who wished to excite hostility to him at the court, but also to secure the favour of the king and incorporation in the army at Buenos Aires. It is not definitely known how long he remained at Madrid, long enough, however, as already indicated, to complete his manuscript, the narrative of which extends to 1788, to the end of the *interim* government of Tomás Álvarez de Acevedo. He was not able to secure its publication, but before it was printed it was extensively used as a source by later writers. Two of the volumes of Gay's *Historia física y política de Chile*, as pointed out by Amunátegui, "are a simple transcription of some of the books of Carvallo's work."

Early in the nineteenth century he entered upon his duties as captain in the army at Buenos Aires; the date of this event is sometimes given as 1803. When the famous junta gobernativa was formed, May 25, 1810, Carvallo took up the cause of the revolution with great enthusiasm, but his failing health prevented him from rendering the efficient service he had desired to give.

Carvallo's death and legacy

He died in 1816. Some time after his death Juan Arias, his son-in-law and sole heir, appeared at Buenos Aires to receive his meagre inheritance. The following is Arias' report of his conversation with the officer in charge of Carvallo's affairs:

"My friend, your father-in-law is dead."

"I am already aware of that misfortune."

"He declared that you were his sole heir."

"I have read the will, and I wish you would please to order that the poor articles of his property may be given to me."

"These articles were reduced to his clothing in use and a few silver spoons."

"Where shall I be able to get them?"

"My friend, as you were not here, I gave the clothing to some Chilean immigrants, who were in want."

"But the spoons?"

"I sold them and used the proceeds in

causing masses to be said for the eternal repose of Carvallo."

"Besides the clothing and the spoons, I am especially interested in the manuscript of a History of Chile, which my father-in-law had written. Please let me know where that bundle of papers is."

"I sold it for two hundred pesos on account of masses for the departed Carvallo."[6]

IV

Some geographical descriptions

Throughout the colonial period geographical description held a prominent place among the writings of Spanish Americans. *Descripción de Chile,* by Ponce de León, *Población de Valdivia,* by Miguel de Aguirre and *Explicación de la plaza y puerto,* by Pedro de Moreno, are among early works of this kind. Ponce de León and Aguirre wrote in the seventeenth century, while Moreno's *Explicación* was published in 1731. A little later Pedro Usauro Martínez de

(6) Carvallo's work was published (1875) about sixty years after his death in the *Colección de historiadores y documentos de Chile,* with an introduction on the life of Carvallo by M. L. Amunátegui; see also Barros Arana, *Obras completas.* IX, 222, 264, and Medina *Historia de la literatura colonial de Chile,* II, 489–508.

Bernabé wrote an account of the presidio and city of Valdivia. This author arrived in Chile very young, and at the age of seventeen, in 1749, he was already under military training. For many years later he was in service as a member of the garrison of Valdivia, and through his long service in this region he became familiar with the natural peculiarities and the state of affairs in the southern part of Chile. The extent and accuracy of his observations, and his ability to attain general views based on these observations give his writings a certain superiority over many of the works in this field.

Ciudad encantada de los Césares

Belief in the tradition of the "Ciudad encantada de los Césares" was rife in Martínez's time, and, having had some part in an investigation designed to make clear the grounds of the popular belief, he wrote *Reflexiones críticas político-históricas sobre los nominados Césares.* He had also in mind to free his countrymen from their illusion; for at Valdivia he had knowledge of those who had faith in the tradition, and of the expeditions organized to discover the famous city of the Césares.

This tradition was exploited by Ignacio Pinuer, who conducted an expedition organized to search for the famous city. Pinuer was born in Valdivia, and this tradition interested him from his boyhood. In his mature years he was brought into frequent communication with the Indians, and from them he sought confirmation or explanation of it.[7] His expedition was naturally fruitless, but his *Relación sobre una ciudad grande de españoles situada entre los indios* (1774), has kept alive the memory of his undertaking. A part of this *Relación* is contained in Pedro de Angelis' *Colección de documentos*, reproduced from the *Semanario erudito* of Madrid. Another document relating to this expedition is Benito Delgado's *Diario*. Delgado was the chaplain of the expedition, and his account was addressed to Governor Joaquín de Espinosa. Gay, the historian, printed it in *Historia de Chile* (*Documentos*, I, 431–485). But even when this tradition was gradually losing its hold on the minds of Chileans, the court of Spain was still influenced by it, and commissioned

Pinuer's *Relación*

(7) Vicuña Mackenna, *Relaciones históricas*, 40.

Orejuela's Commission

Manuel José de Orejuela to continue the search. But in spite of his royal patent Orejuela encountered opposition in America. The viceroy of Peru and the governor of Chile recognized the folly and absurdity of the enterprise, and persuaded him to relinquish his projected expedition.

Order for information

Before the delusion concerning a city of the Césares had run its course, the government in Spain ordered the officers of the royal treasury at Santiago and the corregidores to formulate information concerning districts under their direction. As results of this order there appeared a number of reports or statistical accounts covering various parts of Chilean territory. One of these was José Fernández Campino's *Relación del obispado de Santiago de Chile*, a dry statistical description of central Chile. Another similar production was Pedro González de Agüeros' *Descripción historial de Chile*, which was published in Madrid in 1791.

Juan Ignacio Molina

In the preface to the second volume of his history of Chile Molina affirms that when he undertook that work he had in his possession the first volume of Olivares' manu-

Juan Ignacio Molina

script, and that he was in constant expectation of receiving from Peru the second volume, but that this volume, on which he had confidently relied, he had never received, and in consequence he had been compelled to seek from various other sources the information which it would have furnished. Although Molina lived long in Chile, and wrote the geographical, natural, and civil history of that country, his work was originally published in Italian. The first part, treating of natural history, was issued in Bologna in 1782. A Spanish translation appeared in Madrid in 1788. The second part, treating of the civil history, appeared several years later. Like Olivares and the other Jesuits, he was expelled from America in 1767.

Another contemporary writer who suffered the same fate was Felipe Gómez de Vidaurre. As in the case of Molina, Bologna became Vidaurre's residence in exile, and here he wrote his *Historia geográfica, natural y civil del reino de Chile*, the imperfection of which is in a large measure due to the fact that he wrote at a distance from the

Vidaurre's *Historia de Chile*

scenes he described, and without the documentary and other requisite authorities. Vidaurre's work is divided into eleven books, the first relates to geography, the second, third, and fourth to natural history, and the others treat of political events. Critics appear to have found this book not without merit, but not equal in merit to the writings of Olivares and Molina.

V

Dionisio de Alcedo y Herrera

Dionisio de Alcedo, although less widely known than his son, nevertheless played an important rôle in the affairs of the colonies, and made certain contributions to the published information concerning the Indies. He was born in Madrid, and, in 1706, he left Spain for Peru. In 1708, while returning to Europe, he was taken prisoner by the English. Having been liberated and sent to Quito, he arrived there in time to accompany Bishop Diego Ladrón de Guevara to Lima, where provision had been made for Guevara's succession to the viceregal office after Castelldosrius. During the succeeding years Alcedo was charged with important offices and commissions until he was finally appointed, in 1728, president of the province of Quito. This post he held until 1737. He was thus at the head of the government of Quito when the French commissioners with Juan and Ulloa began their observations and measurements under the equator. Subsequently, having returned to Spain, he was appointed president and commanding general of Panama. He served in this capacity from 1743 to 1749. He retired from this office in consequence of charges presented by the judges of the audiencia, which proved, however, to be entirely unfounded. He retired to Spain in 1752, and died there in 1777 at the age of eighty-seven. Two works by Dionisio de Alcedo y Herrera were published in Madrid. The first was *Aviso histórico político geográfico con noticias particulares de la América meridional* (1741); the second, *Compendio histórico de la provincia, partidos, ciudad, astillero, ríos, y puerto de Guayaquil* (1741).

Dionisio de Alcedo's works

Antonio de Alcedo, a son of Dionisio de Alcedo, born in Quito in 1735, availed himself of material presented by his father and

Antonio de Alcedo's *Diccionario*

by various writers on America, and compiled the well-known *Diccionario geográfico de las Indias*, which was published in five volumes at Madrid in the years 1786 to 1789 This was later translated into English, with various additions and corrections, the translation thus becoming more valuable than the original. It was designed to embrace descriptions of the provinces, the cities, and the most striking natural features of the whole of America, but the parts devoted to British America, as might very well be expected, are less important than those treating of Latin America.

Zamacola, priest of Arequipa

The activity of Juan Domingo de Zamacola, a priest of Arequipa, appears to have been divided between building and writing. He made considerable and important additions to church edifices in Arequipa, and his written work deals extensively with the affairs of Peru. In a descriptive itinerary from Buenos Aires to Arequipa he gave an account of the towns and the roads on the way. Another work contained an account of the events of the revolutions in the provinces of Peru between 1780 and 1785.

He also wrote a "narrative of the earthquake at Arequipa of May 14, 1784," also a diary of the visit of Bishop Pedro Chávez de la Rosa to the provinces of Tarapacá, Tacna, and Moquegua, containing an abundance of statistical information. Of a similar character was his work on the history and geography of Arequipa, and that on the foundation of the town of San Fernando in the valley of Socaboya. In a lighter vein were his satirical papers against idleness, against "the women who smoke," against luxury, and against the use of colours on the face.

Segurola's *Diario*

An enlightening account of one phase of the war known as the rebellion of Tupac Amaru is found in the *Diario de los sucesos del cerco de la ciudad de La Paz en 1781*. It was written by Sebastián de Segurola, a brigadier in the royal army, in command of the forces in La Paz during the siege, and was printed in the first volume of the *Archivo boliviano* (Paris, 1872). It recounts in a series of daily entries the flight of the Spaniards to La Paz from the neighbouring towns, the fortification of a certain part of the city, the gathering about the city of great bodies of Indians, the gradual diminution of food within the city, the consumption of the bulk of the horses and mules, and even the utilizing of rawhide trunks as food; until finally, after facing famine for months, the besieged saw loyal troops on the heights around the city and were assured of relief.

Career of Segurola

The author of this diary was a Spaniard born in the province of Guipuzcoa on January 27, 1740. He joined the army at the age of eighteen, and after eighteen years of service left Spain for America in the force commanded by Zeballos, when that officer, as viceroy of the newly created viceroyalty of Río de la Plata, went to defend the Spanish settlements against the encroachments of the Portuguese. Segurola had been decorated with the cross of Calatrava and appointed corregidor of the province of Larecaja; and after the conclusion of Zeballos' campaign he entered upon the duties of his provincial office, taking up his residence at the town of Sorata, later destroyed by the Indians in the rebellion. While at

Sorata he learned of the outbreak of hostilities, and on January 1, 1781, he took command of the forces at La Paz and in the neighbouring provinces, as directed by the president of the audiencia of Charcas. After the rebellion Segurola remained at La Paz in the office of governor and intendant that had been provided for in the reformed organization of the viceroyalty. He was married in 1786, but his wife died two years later at the birth of a second daughter. His death occurred the following year. In recognition of his loyalty and his distinguished services, he was admitted to the order of Santiago, appointed field-marshal, and president of the audiencia of Charcas, but the notification of these honours reached La Paz a few days after his death.

Anales de Potosí

In this first volume of the *Archivo boliviano* appears also an important document relating to the marvellous history of the city of Potosí, a city that had been called into existence by the rich mines of Upper Peru. This document is entitled *Anales de la Villa Imperial de Potosí*, and was written by Bartolomé Martínez y Vela, a resident of Potosí. It is one of the principal historical sources of Vicente G. Quesada's *Crónicas potosinas: costumbres de la edad medioeval hispano-americana*, and of the author's chapter called a *Mining Town in Upper Peru.*[8]

The *Diario* of Segurola

The *Diario* of Segurola contains the story of a critical event in the Indian insurrection of 1780 and 1781, namely, the siege of La Paz. The position of that city at the bottom of a great ravine in the inter-Andean plateau gave a certain theatrical setting to the event. From the rim of the cañon the Indians could look down into the city, and the inhabitants from the fortified part of the town could watch the movement of the enemy from day to day. The diary is an account of the flight of Spaniards from neighbouring towns to La Paz as a place of refuge; of the formation of a line of intrenchments enclosing the densely populated area of the city, and of an exhausting defence continued for many months. Some idea of the character of the narrative may be de-

(8) See *The Spanish Dependencies in South America*, II, chap. I.

rived from the following translations of daily entries:

March 27, 28, and 29, 1781

"March 27, 1781.—This day the Indians attacked with great force all parts of the city, setting fire to the houses that were outside of the trenches, assaulting these and the wall, from which they were repulsed with great vigour. This engagement lasted from 11 o'clock in the morning till 4 in the evening. At this hour the rebels retired with much loss, which was given at more than one hundred and fifty killed, without a loss on our part.

"March 28.—It was recognized to-day that the number of Indians who approached was considerably increased. At 8 o'clock in the morning they attacked all parts of the city, aided by some guns which they fired, and at the same time they went on burning the houses outside of the fortifications, and we resisted them with great valour. The attack lasted until five o'clock in the afternoon, when the enemy retired with more than three hundred and fifty dead, according to our calculation, and on our side we had only two.

"March 29.—The Indians have been coming down from all sides since daybreak, and at ten o'clock assaulted the city with desperation, and this attack, repulsed by us, lasted till half-past five in the afternoon, at which hour they retired with a loss of more than one hundred and fifty men, and we had the misfortune, by the bursting of a cannon in one of the forts, to have three killed and several severely wounded, and among the killed was Captain José de Roxas."

Martínez y Vela on Doña Clara

In the troubled life of Potosí, Martínez y Vela found an abundance of incidents that enabled him to give his *Anales* a piquant flavour not usually discovered in chronicles. The following is his entry for the year 1690.

"This year died in Potosí, that famous Señora, Doña Clara, commonly called Amaltea, or Achacosa, who was at first a great sinner, extremely rich, vain, and proud, and later very poor, humble, and virtuous. At the age of twelve she became very well known not only in Potosí and everywhere in Peru, but her fame extended also to Spain. She was, moreover, beautiful, very discreet,

The elegance of Doña Clara

lively, and agreeable; nature had bestowed upon her all its gifts; she sang sweetly, played and danced gracefully. She exercised a very great influence, since besides her great patrimony as a woman of excellent standing she acquired at the cost of her virtue immense wealth in gold, silver, jewels, precious stones, pearls, and rich ornaments. She controlled everything, even the wills of her associates, and was vain in the extreme; the various rooms and patios in her house were sprinkled every day with scented water. The neatness of her stables was such that one never saw in them even a straw. Continually every day perfumed water was kept boiling in the porch and reception rooms, in apple-shaped receptacles of silver, and there were braseros of the same metal. She had as many chemises of fine linen from Holland and Cambray as there are days in the year, and she put on a fresh one every night. She had four rich bedsteads of wood and bronze with feather-beds and draperies of beautiful cloths, and she changed from one to another every three months. In a word, she was the most affluent woman in Potosí,

Doña Clara in poverty

but these goods were acquired by a violation of the will of God, and in the end pleasures of the world are such that even before they pass their retribution appears; thus it happened to this famous woman; for in a short time, by means it would be long to relate, she saw herself without gold, silver, jewels, pearls, servants, and ornaments and what was more, without even an old dress to hide her nakedness, and even more lamentable still, her poverty was so great that she had not even a crust to eat, and lived by charity, she whose weekly expenses in her house amounted to two thousand pesos in daily banquets and other worldly pleasure. She received from charity a skirt and an old chemise, cast-off finery, which was no longer of use. She washed the clothes of strangers, because they gave her food, she who had been disgusted on seeing a little spot on her dress. She worked for even the humblest for a piece of bread, she who had had white servants and many black female slaves, such an abundance of servants, that two of them were employed solely in wiping up with towels the spittle with which those who came to visit her had soiled the floor. Finally she expiated in this life the disorders of her past, and suffered with admirable patience her labours, giving by her experience a lesson to the proud, the rich, and the avaricious, and thus she died very poor in material goods, but rich in virtues. She was buried by the charity of her noble and pious neighbours. I present this case to undeceive and correct those who believe themselves secure in the possession of their temporal goods."

VI

El lazarillo de ciegos caminantes

El lazarillo de ciegos caminantes is rather an elaborate guide-book than a history. It treats of the route from Buenos Aires to Santiago de Chile, but its principal subject is the south-eastern part of Spanish South America, the region between Buenos Aires and Lima. It indicates the various lines of communication, describes the towns, the roads, the resources, the manners and customs of the country traversed, and the difficulties, privations, and dangers of a journey over this route. The style is plain and direct, the writer's point of view is often humorous, and his references are now and then vulgar; but the clearness of his descriptions and the picturesqueness of the lighter parts make the book eminently readable. As a contemporary account of the Peruvian cities in the last half of the eighteenth century it has no successful rival.

Concolorcorvo

By the title-page of the original edition one is informed that the book was written by Don Calixto Bustamante Inca, alias Concolorcorvo, and that it was printed in Gijón in 1773. But, in spite of this reference to Gijón it is held that it was printed in Lima. A new and excellent edition was issued by the historical and numismatic society of Buenos Aires in 1908.

The author was born in Cuzco. As a youth he visited Lima, and soon afterwards set out for Spain, where he affirmed he had an uncle who was an Indian of the royal Inca family; but learning of the death of this unnamed uncle, he went on this occasion only as far as Buenos Aires. Later he undertook the voyage to the Peninsula and returned from Coruña to Montevideo in the ship "El Tucumán." From Buenos Aires to Lima he accompanied the visitador Alonso Carrión de Lavandera, to whom he frequently makes reference in describing this journey, and who figures in certain passages in a dialogue with the author. Carrión had been commissioned by the king to arrange the affairs of the postal service preparatory to its passing from private hands to the crown. Bustamante, who assisted Carrión, took this occasion to gather at least a part of the information set down in his description of the country traversed, and much of this information refers to the existing postal service and the special need of it at certain points.[9]

Dialogue with Alonso Carrión

The following extract gives some indication of the author's manner.

"I promised to write a description of

(9) Among the notes made by General Mitre in his copy of this book is found the following remark: "Whoever may be the author, the journey is real and contains data and "noticias preciosas" which can be found only in this work. The traveller was in Montevideo and Buenos Aires in 1749, and gives many details of the condition, customs, and inhabitants of these cities. Critical and humorous anecdotes are scattered throughout the work, and on arriving at Cuzco he inserts four discussions in the form of dialogues between the author and the visitador on the condition of the Indians, of whose character he makes a very sad picture."

The merits of Lima and Cuzco

Lima, but the visitador told me that was an undertaking, in which many men of superior talents had not been able to succeed, and that it would be ridiculous for a pigmy to undertake it. But, Señor Inspector, is it possible that I must conclude such a detailed itinerary without saying anything about Lima? Certainly, Señor Inca, for this great city does not concern you, is not your affair, and here ends my commission. Señores Jorge Juan, Antonio Ulloa, he added, and the principal cosmographer of the kingdom, Dr. Cosme Bueno, wrote with a swan's quill of all the most important things in this capital, and you cannot add anything material with yours which is the quill of a goose. Nevertheless, I replied, please tell me what is the difference between this great city and that of my birth. I suppose Señor Inca, he answered me, that you are prejudiced in favour of Cuzco, your native town, and would wish me to say that it is superior in every respect to Lima, but you are greatly mistaken; for, leaving aside the situation and the parks, you ought to observe that in this great capital the king maintains a viceroy with great magnificence and with an allowance equal to the total revenue of all the great estates of Cuzco. It has also three bodies of guards supported by the king, one of cavalry, well mounted and paid, others of infantry and halbardiers, which serve not only for ceremony and ostentation, but also for the protection of the persons and the peace of this great town. There may be added, moreover, the audiencia, the superior tribunals of accounts, the inquisition, the university, the theatre, and the public promenades near the city, which are not found at Cuzco, or at any other city of the kingdom.

Carriages, dress, and aristocracy of Lima

"Lima maintains two hundred and fifty public carriages and more than a thousand calesas, which are distinguished from the carriages by the fact that they have two wheels and are drawn by a mule, and are more readily upset. There is nothing of this kind in your great city. In the matter of dress, one is as crazy as the other, with a difference of tastes, and in the extent of families and commerce Lima greatly exceeds Cuzco. In this city there are many marquises and counts, and a much greater number of persons who have been decorated with the orders of Santiago and Calatrava, who with rare exceptions have sufficient incomes to maintain themselves in splendour, and to whom may be added persons having entailed estates and gentlemen who are supported by their lands and other proper kinds of business, so that they may live in a manner to give brilliancy to the society of the city. There is no doubt that in your native city, as in others of the vast viceroyalty, there are illustrious families, but the number of them is not comparable with those of this city" (Chap. XXVI).

CHAPTER XVII

OUTLOOK TOWARDS EMANCIPATION

I. *The intellectual movement after the expulsion of the Jesuits.* II. *Political reformers.* III. *Poets.* IV. *Literary periodicals: Mercurio Peruano; Gaceta de Lima.* V. *Contributors to Mercurio Peruano.* VI. *El Telégrafo Mercantil.* VII. *Tadeo Haenke.* VIII. *El Volador.*

I

Expulsion of the Jesuits

The expulsion of the Jesuits in 1767 produced an immediate decline of literary activity in the Spanish colonies. It had, moreover, a far-reaching influence on the means of instruction; it closed the most efficient schools, and silenced those persons who might have continued to spread enlightenment through their writings. The most

Signs of new intellectual life

noteworthy salvage from the wreck was the collection of books and manuscripts that were gathered up from the Jesuits' colleges. In Bogotá some of these books and papers, placed in charge of a librarian and made accessible in the building of the ancient Jesuit college, formed what was then known as the Royal Library. It was formally opened to the public January 9, 1777, and at that time contained 13,800 volumes. Another act tending to stimulate the intellectual life of New Granada was the organization of the Botanical Expedition, or bureau of scientific investigation, under the direction of José Celestino Mutis. A little later literary production was encouraged by the formation of literary societies, or "circles," and the founding of periodicals. The new intellectual movement appealed particularly to the rising generation of creoles. A phase of it was seen in the attention given to political questions and the enthusiastic patriotism manifested by Antonio Nariño and his associates. But this movement did not close abruptly the period of mediævalism in the colonies. Writers, like Manuel de Caycedo Ladrón de Guevara (Bogotá, 1718–1781), continued to produce voluminous works which made clear only the author's ecclesiastical erudition. But in view of the approaching revolution in the British colonies and in France, more men began to think in terms of worldly things; instead of exercising their imaginations in creating a heavenly state, they began to look forward to a new earthly state. The new idealism, imposed upon men by the rising spirit of revolution, contained a force competent to transform the world.

The old views and the new

A writer who may be said to have spanned the gulf between the old and the new order of things was Felipe de Vergara y Caycedo, who was born in Bogotá on May 20, 1745. He was educated in the college of Rosario, received there the degree of Doctor, accepted a professorship of theology, and while holding this position gave instruction also in mathematics. He visited Spain, carrying letters from the viceroy, the audiencia, and the archbishop. He returned as contador of Panama, and later he became contador of the Royal Tribunal of Accounts in Bogotá. After the Revolution of 1810 he was a member of the Assembly and of the electoral college of Cundinamarca, and later was secretary and counsellor of state to President Nariño. He died December 18, 1818. The long list of his work is evidence not only of his vast erudition but also of his indefatigable industry.[1]

Bogotá a centre of reform

Bogotá as the centre of the intellectual movement in New Granada was already provided with institutions competent to further this movement. The University of Santa Fe was under the direction of the Dominicans in the Dominican monastery. The college and seminary of San Bartolomé had been for a century and a half under the control of the Jesuits, but after the expulsion of the Society it was placed in charge of the archbishop. The college of Rosario, like that of San Bartolomé, was by royal decree made equal in privileges to the University of Salamanca, the type of the Spanish university. In these institutions the early curriculum, limited to Latin, theology and

(1) A partial list of his writings is printed by Vergara in his *Historia de la literatura en Nueva Granada*, 234, 235.

philosophy, was increased by the addition of courses of instruction in jurisprudence, medicine and mathematics.

Change in the religious orders

Throughout the greater part of the colonial period the religious orders had in many instances been true to their mission as advocates of the Christian faith. Many of the members had led lives of devotion and heroism in their efforts to impart to the Indians a new and higher conception of life. But in the course of time the zeal of their militancy declined. With the contributions of the faithful they built imposing edifices and filled them with books and works of art. A few still became writers, and all, in virtue of the history of their institutions, continued to hold a high place in the esteem of the public, even when many of them had fallen into indolence and were leading more or less useless lives.

The monasteries, however, in the course of time ceased even to be centres of historical study. The Dominicans had produced Zamora, the Franciscans Simón, and the Augustinians San Nicolás, but the orders developed no successors to these writers;

Reaction and Progress

rather, in the presence of the intellectual awakening, they assumed an attitude of protest and denial. They disputed the affirmations of Galileo and the conclusions of other scientific investigators; and thus, with the progress of the inquiries instituted by Mutis and carried on by his pupils and followers, there appeared a widening breach between the monasteries, representing mediævalism, and the investigators of nature, presaging a new day.

It was clear to some minds that in order to make continuous the forces of intellectual progress it was necessary to reorganize the schools of the country and to bring them into harmony with the new views of knowledge. In sympathy with this thought Viceroy Guirior commissioned Francisco Antonio Moreno to form a new plan of instruction, that would provide not only for a new curriculum, but also for the establishment of a school wherever one had been closed by the expulsion of the Jesuits. In the judgment of the persons most eminent in the affairs of New Granada Moreno appeared admirably fitted for this undertak-

Francisco Antonio Moreno

ing. He was born in Mariquita on October 25, 1736, and was educated at Bogotá, his studies taking a somewhat wider range than that provided by the conventional curriculum. He held in succession various high offices in the viceregal government, to which he was promoted with the spontaneous support of the viceroy, the secular cabildo, the university, the archbishop, and the audiencia. Towards the end of his career he was appointed an oidor, or judge, of the audiencia at Lima; a little later he was transferred to Chile as regent, and died at Santiago on February 24, 1792.[2]

Moreno's plan received the enthusiastic support of the viceroy and men of liberal intelligence, like Mutis and Félix Restrepo, and promised to introduce an enlightened revolution in the field of education, but when it was brought to the attention of the crown it was disapproved by the Council of the Indies. The Council held rigorously to the old plan of instruction, but two years were spent in making the application for

(2) Marroquín, J. M., *Biografía de don Francisco Antonio Moreno*, in *El Mosaico*, iv, No. 7.

approval and in receiving the reply, and in this period important steps were taken in the execution of Moreno's proposed reform. And finally, when the order of the council arrived, Viceroy Guirior had been succeeded by Flórez, and Flórez had been shoved into the background by Visitador Piñeres. Then came the revolt of the Comuneros of 1781, and the governmental authorities had a mind for no other phase of internal affairs. In this period, when the government was paralysed, the advocates of the new plan succeeded in carrying out many of its features; other persons were converted to its advocacy, and Zea published in the *Papel periódico* an article entitled *Hebéfilo*, a vigorous argument against the old scheme of studies.[3]

Revolt of the Comuneros

II

Mutis and literary unions

The new intellectual movement expressed itself not only in the researches directed by Mutis but also in the formation and activity of literary unions, or "circles." At the meetings of these circles a great variety

(3) *Papel periódico* de Santafé de Bogota, No. 22.

of scientific subjects were discussed. Two persons especially conspicuous in the decade between 1790 and 1800 were Antonio Nariño and Francisco Antonio Zea. Nariño was born in Bogotá in 1765, studied philosophy and jurisprudence in the college of San Bartolomé, and was appointed treasurer of tithes. Provided with an adequate income and moved by his zeal for instruction, he collected in his house an extensive library of books imported from Europe, and the facilities which they offered for acquiring information attracted about the owner the serious youths of the city. By diligent use of modern European works Nariño not only acquired a knowledge of several modern languages, but was also able to correct the instruction he had received in the college as it was conducted under its mediæval régime; he also acquired the progressive ideas of Europe and the British colonies then putting into operation the independent government of the United States. Inspired by these ideas, he became a vigorous advocate of liberty and independence, but the vicissitudes of ill-fortune prevented

Antonio Nariño

him from attaining the object of his early ambition. For printing a Spanish translation of *Les droits de l'homme* he was arrested and condemned to imprisonment in Africa. At Cadiz he escaped, fled to Madrid, visited France and England, and finally returned to Bogotá. In spite of the good offices of friends, he was again arrested, and kept in confinement until the revolution of 1810 set him free.

Antonio Zea

Antonio Zea was sent to Spain as a prisoner with Nariño and the others who at that time had fallen under the condemnation of the colonial authorities. He was five years younger than Nariño, having been born in Medellín in 1770. He received his early instruction in the seminary of Popayán, and passed from that institution to the college of San Bartolomé, in Bogotá, where he studied theology and civil law. Through his association with Mutis, he was introduced to the study of the inductive sciences. On the withdrawal of Valenzuela from the botanical expedition, Zea was appointed to the position thus made vacant, with a salary of five hundred dollars a year. Zea was then nineteen years old, and for a person so young he had extraordinary attainments. It was after two years in this service that he was arrested, in 1794, for conspiracy and sent to Spain. In the long trial to which he was subjected with the other political offenders, the charges were not sustained. The next three years he spent in Paris on a scientific mission, receiving a stipend of twelve hundred dollars a year, the Spanish government being apparently solicitous that he should not go back to New Granada; for when he sought permission to return to America, his request was refused and he was appointed adjunct, and later director, of the botanical collections in Madrid. In 1805 he was appointed professor of Botany. His residence in Madrid extended over the years from 1804 to 1807, and during this period he was elected to membership in various scientific societies, and wrote a number of memoirs embodying the results of his observations and studies in New Granada. His scientific studies were interrupted in 1807, when he was drawn into the revolution of Aran-

Zea in Spain

juez. He belonged to the "afrancesados", the party in sympathy with French ideas and plans, and believed that the triumph of this party would be followed by the emancipation of his country. During the following years he was in the service of the government, now as director of one of the sections of the Department of the Interior, and subsequently as prefect of Malaga. He was occupying this latter post when the Spanish colonies in America struck for independence.

Zea in Spanish service

The opposition to various provisions of the Spanish government, which found expression in revolts and rebellions in the eighteenth century, occasionally appeared also in writings of that time. The pamphlet called *Concordia en discordia,* by Alonso de la Cueva Ponce de León, was a document of this class. It criticized prevailing doctrines, attacked the royal prerogatives, and argued against many of the recognized rights of the crown. The author was a native of Lima, became an ecclesiastic, was appointed vicar-general of the bishopric of Panama, was attorney for the

Concordia en discordia

Inquisition of Cartagena, and became the historian of the archbishopric of Peru. His criticism of political affairs aroused hostility and, in consequence of this, as one writer has expressed it, he was "pulverizado" by the distinguished jurist Pedro José Bravo de Lagunas y Castilla, who, about the middle of the eighteenth century was a judge of the audiencia of Lima, and in 1761 published in that city a number of pamphlets under the general title of *Colección legal.*[4]

Lagunas' *Colección legal*

III

Besides the group of political reformers associated with Nariño there was a society of young men of letters who formed a literary union called "Eutropélica." At the head of this company stood Manuel S. Rodríguez. Among the other members were José Maria Valdés, Francisco Antonio Rodríguez and José María Gruesso. As a young man Gruesso prepared himself for the practice of law. He had finished his legal studies, when the sudden death of the

José María Gruesso

(4) For some account of Bravo's writings see Lavalle in *Revista de Lima.*

young woman whom he was about to marry caused him to change completely his plan of life. Under the influence of this shock he turned from the legal profession to the Church. He entered the college of San Bartolomé, and began at once his ecclesiastical studies. Two years later he returned to Popayán as a priest, and lived there, it is said, "triste hasta la muerte." During this period, and while in this state of mind, he wrote *Las noches de Geussor* in imitation of Young's *Night Thoughts*. The plan of this work provided for thirty cantos, or nights, but whatever may have been the number written, only three have been preserved. These are entitled *La soledad*, *La noche*, and *El remordimiento*.

Gruesso's *Las ncches de Geussor*

Buen Gusto

Another group of writers formed a society known as " Buen Gusto." These writers were accustomed to meet at the house of Doña Manuela Sanatamaría de Manrique, who was esteemed not only for her attainments in literature, but also for her knowledge of nature. The members of this group were chiefly poets, born in New Granada, and educated in either the college of Rosario or the college of San Bartolomé. They wrote, among other things, certain plays that were presented in the theatre of Bogotá. Two of these were the *Sacrificio de Idomeneo* and *El Zagal de Bogotá*. Perhaps the most widely known of the poets of the Buen Gusto was Dr. José Fernández de Madrid, whose studies had given him the title of Doctor of Laws as well as that of Doctor of Medicine. Whether in prose or verse, the writings of the persons who were thus drawn together in these associations are rather indications of beginnings in literature than of a culmination of literary progress. They are not reminiscent of colonial dependence but premonitory of an emancipated population.

José Fernández de Madrid

The poems of Juan Bautista Aguirre are found chiefly in a manuscript collection called *Versos castellanos, obras juveniles, misceláneas*. The author was born in Guayaquil, and as a youth was sent to Quito by his parents to prepare for his career as a man of letters. The university was then under the control of the Jesuits, and Aguirre accepted membership in the

The poems of Aguirre

Society. It is, moreover, reported that he became a lecturer on philosophy in the university. An elegy on the death of Philip V and an account of the earthquake of 1746 suggest that he was writing before the middle of the century. In 1767 he was involved in the general expulsion of the Jesuits from South America. Later he lived in Rome. His lectures on philosophy, whether in Quito or Rome, apparently did not turn his mind from his inclination to write verses, and some part of his writings indicate that they were produced when religious thoughts and the image of the Bible were uppermost in his mind. In the *Concepción de Nuestra Señora* he is lost in profound mysticism, and in *La rebelión y caída de Luzbel y sus secuaces* he is sezied by the subject which Milton evidently found the most inspiring in his great theme, the pride and ambition of Satan to rule the universe:

La rebelión y caída de Luzbel

Falsear haré con ira fulminante
Del alto cielo en un vaivén ruidoso,
La azul muralla y subiré triunfante
A ser Señor del reino luminoso:

Si son estorbo a mi ímpetu arrogante
Aire, mar, tierra o firmamento hermoso,
Haré que sientan mi furor violento
El mar, la tierra, el aire, el firmamento.

When Aguirre sang of "amores profanos" he may be thought to have gone beyond the limits of his proper field as a priest, but he took the precaution, as Gutiérrez remarks, to indicate in a note that if he wrote erotic verses it was purely for diversion and exercise, and that they should be considered like the innocent love-talk of Don Quijote with the impalpable Dulcinea.[5]

A una tórtola quejosa

An opinion of the quality of Aguirre's lighter poems may be derived from his sonnet *A una tórtola quejosa,* which a distinguished critic affirms embodies the style and sentiment of Petrarch:

Por qué, Tórtola, en cítara doliente
Haces que el aire gima con tu canto?
Si alivios buscas en ajeno llanto
Mi dolor te lo ofrece; aquí detente.

(5) *Estudios biográficos y críitcos*, 247.

Al verte sola de tu amante ausente
Publicas triste en ayes tu quebranto;
Yo también ¡ay dolor! suspiro tanto
Por no poder gozar mi bien presente.

Pero cese ya ¡oh Tórtola! el gemido,
Que aunque es inmenso tu infeliz desvelo
Mayor sin duda mi tormento ha sido:

Pues tú perdiste un terrenal consuelo
En tu consorte; pero yo he perdido
En mi adorado bien la luz del cielo.

Later poets

The Chilean poets of the later decades of the colonial period lacked the inspiration that the writers of the sixteenth century received from the events of the conquest. They had no longer the spirit that moved Ercilla to attempt to weave the circumstances and happenings of the Araucanian war into an epic. The *Cauteverio feliz,* by Francisco Núñez de Pineda y Bascuñán, the *Restauración de la Imperial,* by Juan de Barrenechea y Albis, and *Tucapelina,* by a writer who assumed the name of Pancho Millaleuba, reveal a less exalted vision and purpose than the earlier writers, less seriousness of thought and a less effective use of the Spanish language. They drifted towards the expression of subjective moods, and into giving their verses a distinctly satirical tone. "The muse of Bascuñán, with philosophico-moral tendencies in sentiment, was not long in becoming entirely mystical." [6] The verses of Juan de Barrenechea y Albis are passed over by the Chilean critic as "in reality without animation or sentiment," leaving the writer with no higher rank than that of a rhymer.[7] The writer of *Tucapelina* calls his work an "heroic poem." It consists of ten divisions called *decadas*, and aims, among other objects, to represent the changes that had come over the Araucanian country in the period between the time of Ercilla and the last half of the eighteenth century, when the inhabitants had ceased to be rebellious and the sons of caciques were taking advantage of facilities for education provided by the Spanish government. The critic suggests

Tucapelina

(6) Medina, *Literatura colonial de Chile*, I, 314.
(7) *Ibid.* II, 324.

that the element of burlesque and satire in the poem may have been one of the reasons why the author wished to conceal his identity under an assumed name.

Padre López and his kind

Among other verse-makers who obtained a certain local celebrity Padre López was especially noted. He was a Dominican friar, and was known as a wit and an improvisator, but very naturally, having gained this reputation, many sayings were attributed to him for which he was not answerable; yet an attempt has been made to attach to him the designation of the Chilean Quevedo. Most of his productions that have survived are occasional satirical pieces; in fact, the serious things of life seem not to have come within the field of his vision. He was a pronounced enemy of the Jesuits but a welcome participant in meetings pervaded by a spirit of revelry. Another ecclesiastic, Padre Escudero, a Franciscan, wrote much in the same vein as Padre López, and showed no more inclination than López to abide by the regulations that are supposed to control the conduct of monks.

Minor poets

In the last quarter of the eighteenth century appeared a number of poems narrating events that had made an impression on the public mind. Those narrating in metrical form the tale of thieves asphyxiated in their attempt to carry off the treasures of a mine, the death of Bishop Alday, and the destructive flood of the Mapocho in 1780 are chiefly noteworthy by reason of having been remembered by the people, thus magnifying and immortalizing their subjects. There is also manifest at this time a tendency to invent new forms of verse in which to express commonplace thoughts. To these late years of the century belong also the satirical verses of Fernández Ortelano, issued under the title: *Ensalada poética jocoseria.*[8]

With the spiritual awakening and the extension of education among the creoles it was to be expected that many persons would essay poetic flights; still the most im-

(8) The rest of the title is as follows: *en que se refiere el nacimiento, crianza y principales hechos del célebre don Plácido Arteta, compuesta por un íntimo amigo suyo, tan ignorante de las cosas del Parnaso que jamás ha subido a este monte, y aún apenas llegó alguna vez a sus faldas.*

portant intellectual tendencies were along political, not poetical, lines. Whatever ideas came from other nations, from North America or from France, tended to arouse the people to practical action rather than to stimulate their poetic fancies. The poets were distinctly minor poets: Jerónimo Hurtado de Mendoza, Antonio Campusano.

Ecuadorian poets

José Orozco is probably the most widely known of the Ecuadorian poets. He was born in Riobamba in 1733. His principal literary product was the "epic poem" called *La Conquista de Menorca*. At nearly the same time there was born in Ibarra a writer, Ramón Viescas, who as a lyric poet held a place comparable with that held by Orozco as an epic poet. Two other poets, Ambrosio and Joaquín Larrea, born about the middle of the eighteenth century, became residents of Italy and in their later writings made use of the Italian language. Although Juan de Velasco is especially known for his *Historia del reino de Quito*, he left certain mediocre writings in verse. He was born in Riobamba in 1727. The minor poets are, like the poor, always with us, and among these in Ecuador in the eighteenth century may be classed Juan Ullauri, Manuel Orozco, José Gorrido and Nicolás Crespo.[9]

Juan Manuel Lavarden

The name of Juan Manuel Lavarden had passed almost completely out of memory in Buenos Aires, when it was recalled by the publication of the *Oda al Paraná* in *El Telégrafo mercantil.* Later researches have revealed very little concerning the youth and early education of the author. He was known in Buenos Aires as a licenciado, honorary oidor of the audiencia of La Plata, and auditor de guerra. The title of *auditor de guerra* was created by Philip V (1738), and first held by Florencio Antonio Mereiras. It passed to Juan Manuel Lavarden, a lawyer of distinction, under the approval of the king dated April 30, 1761. Lavarden's title to a place in the literary history of his country rests on a *Sátira*, the drama of *Siripo*, and the *Oda al Paraná*.

It is through various persons that Lavar-

(9) A diffuse discussion of the early Ecuadorian poets is found in Juan León Mera's *Ojeada histórico-crítica sobre la poesía ecuatoriana*, 2nd ed. Barcelona, 1893.

den voices his satire of things colonial. The new nobles are among his victims. Resenting the contemptuous attitude of Lima towards Buenos Aires, the poet was pleased to point to the fact that in spite of the haughtiness and family pride of the nobles they did not hesitate to abase themselves even by mingling Spanish blood with the dark and turbulent blood that flows in the veins of the daughters of Mozambique.[10]

Political radicalism in poetry

In some of the lines a political radicalism appears, which is a youth's anticipation, in 1786, of the revolutionary democracy of three decades later:

> El pueblo que de libre se gloría,
> Produce nobles almas, que a ninguno
> Quisieran conceder la primacía.

Lavarden's *Siripo*

Siripo takes its title from the leading character of the drama, one of two caciques, Mangore and Siripo, of the tribe of Timbu, pacified residents at the fort of Santó Espíritu, who both conceived an ardent passion for Lucía Miranda, the wife of the Spaniard

(10) Gutiérrez, J. M., *Estudios biográficos y críticos*, p. 63, Buenos Aires, 1860.

Sebastián Hurtado. These pacified savages traitorously get possession of the fort in the absence of Hurtado. Lucía remains the captive of Siripo on the taking and burning of the fort, but Hurtado returns and is persuaded that Lucía still lives. He goes in pursuit of her and gives himself over to the caciques, with whom he finds Lucía. The previous appearance on the scene of Miranda, the father of Lucía, with a suggestion that Siripo shall become a Christian on condition of receiving the hand of Lucía, although, aside from the main story, is too grim a proposition to be thought of as furnishing the comedy element of the play. Hurtado and Lucía are unable to conceal their mutual affection, and the savage jealousy of Siripo is aroused. The drama was played at several towns in Argentina, but only a fragment of it has been preserved. The text of a few scenes have been printed by Gutiérrez.[11] The following lines, a part of the twelfth scene of the second act, will give a sufficient idea of Lavarden's verses:

The gist of *Siripo*

(11) *Estudios biográficos y críticos*, 67–89.

Act II, Scene 12

LUCÍA (*apresurada*).

Compasivo es mi Dios con una ingrata?
Respiras todavía, esposo amado?
Aún duran mis delicias, dueño mío?
Mis lágrimas los cielos apiadaron.
Cómo evitaste a Lambaré sangriento?
Te miro y me parece que es milagro.
Sin duda te herirían (*abriéndole la ropilla*) y por eso
En venirme a buscar has sido tardo.

HURTADO (*lloroso*).

Hiciéronme creer mis camaradas
Que murieras la noche del asalto.

LUCÍA.

Qué, tu lloras mi bien? Y qué la dejas
A mi terneza entonces? Los amargos
Fenecidos pesares no dilates
Que se tornaron gozos en tus brazos.
Sí, mi bien. Cuando en dulces soledades
De afanes tan crueles recorramos
El recuerdo, serán del amor nuestro
Testimonios que estrechen nuestros lazos.

HURTADO.

O consuelo infeliz! Consuelo estéril,
El monstruo del furor has abortado!

Más amargo, mi bien, hace este gozo
De nuestra desventura el triste plazo.
Me perdiste y te pierdo. Ya el cacique
Quien soy, sabe.

LUCÍA.

Mi Dios! Mas cuando te hallo
Constante y amoroso, esposo mío,
El morir junto a tí será regalo.

HURTADO.

Ello hemos de morir de alguna suerte,
Y, ya que es fuerza, con honor muramos.
Lucía, mi Lucía, muestra el cielo
Que ha tomado nuestra honra por su cargo.
Me mandó a confortarte. Ten presentes
Tu patria y religión, y cuánto te amo.

LUCÍA.

Qué, ya no me conoces? Tú me animas?
Dudas que alegre moriré a tu lado?

French influence

Whatever influences had been exerted in South America by the ancient classic forms and spirit was subdued by the French literary spirit during and after the reign of Philip V; and the drama of *Siripo,* as Gutiérrez suggests, was cast in the classical mould of the French school, in so far as the subject and the condition of some of the characters permitted it.[12]

Oda al Paraná

The *Oda al Paraná*, offering an opportunity to set forth the riches of unspoiled nature in the New World, was Lavarden's most noteworthy literary achievement. It became the model for later poetic efforts to glorify the country, like Vicente López's *Triunfo argentino.*

IV

Gil de Taboada Lemus

Viceroy Gil de Taboada Lemus (1790–1796) stimulated literary activity in Lima by extending his friendly patronage to men of letters. He gathered about the viceregal court persons of talent, who were interested in the spread of knowledge, and whose special attainments fitted them to become instrumental in the development of cultivation. These persons decided to co-operate in issuing a literary and historical periodical, and their plan was approved by the viceroy. He offered to furnish from the archives and the records of public offices such data or material as might be useful in

(12) Gutiérrez *Estudios biográficos y críticos*, 94.

Francisco Gil de Taboado, 35th Viceroy of Peru
1790–1796

Mercurio peruano

executing the project. In this way the famous *Mercurio peruano* came into existence. The entire lack of freedom of printing in the Spanish dependencies made the established relation to the viceroy indispensable, and thus under his sanction there was organized a private literary association designed, by the co-operation of its members, to provide the articles required for the pages of the proposed periodical. The viceroy was a member of this association, and held the title of Protector, and the association itself assumed the title of "Amantes del pais."

Prior to the founding of the *Mercurio peruano* there had existed a periodical for the presentation of economic and commercial subjects called *Diario erudito*, which ceased publication at the end of its second year. The first number of the *Mercurio* appeared on the first of January, 1791, under the editorial direction of Jacín de Calero y Moreyra. The periodical itself was designed to treat of scientific, political commercial, historical, and statistical subjects, in a manner hitherto quite unknown in the colonies. It was continued until eleven volumes had been completed by the association; and on the failure of funds to meet further expenses of publication, Padre Cisneros, who had succeeded the former secretary of the society caused a twelfth volume to be printed at his own expense. In this year, 1791, there was formed, moreover, a new society called "Tertulia poética," which held frequent meetings for the examination of articles or poems presented, some of which were published in the *Mercurio peruano*.

Tertulia poética

In 1793 the viceroy decided to publish a *Gaceta de Lima*, reviving a title that had been used in the middle of the century. in order that the inhabitants of the viceroyalty might have a properly accredited journal that would inform them regarding the excesses of the French Revolution, of which various rumours were reaching their ears. For this purpose the viceroy concluded that it would be better to have an independent journal rather than to give to the *Mercurio peruano* an official character. The number of the persons associated with

Gaceta de Lima

the *Mercurio* would make it practically impossible to prevent their intervention in the determination of what should be published. These persons, for the greater part, were men of high ideals and not in sympathy with all of the views and practices of the government, and the viceroy had doubtless reason to believe that their interference would furnish a source of embarrassment, for he evidently did not propose, in the gazette, to present the unvarnished truth, but, on the other hand, through its pages, to carry on a propaganda against revolutionary doctrines, free criticism of the Church, and republican attacks on the absolute state. The *Gaceta* was continued until 1821; and it made public only such facts or documents as the government wished to have known, in other words, falsified and garbled information.

Anti-revolutionary propaganda

V

Hipólito Unánue

Some of the ablest writers of the transition period were interested in the *Mercurio peruano* as contributors. Dr. Hipólito Unánue was of this class. He was a native of

Peru, born in Arica in 1755. He completed his studies for an ecclesiastical career, but was persuaded by his uncle, Padre Pedro Pabón, to abandon his plan to enter the Church and to direct his attention to scientific studies. Under this advice he turned to the study of medicine, and at the same time he became known for his attainments in mathematics, physics, and natural history. Between 1783 and 1797 he wrote a political, ecclesiastical and statistical account of the viceroyalty of Peru. He held a professorship of anatomy in Lima, and exerted an affective influence in increasing facilities for anatomical study in that city.

Amantes del país

Under the name of "Aristio" he wrote for the *Mercurio peruano*, and was a member of the society of "Amantes del país," which consisted of thirty members, twenty-one of whom were residents of Lima. In order to acquire membership one had to offer two discourses; these having been found acceptable, the case was presented to the viceroy for his approval. On the occasion of his inauguration the new member was required to deliver an address. A committee of "censors" examined productions presented to decide as to their fitness for publication.

Unánue's *El clima de Lima*

Among Unánue's writings, his *Observaciones sobre el clima de Lima y sus influencias en los seres organizados; en especial el hombre,* attracted much attention; it was published at Lima in 1806 and at Madrid in 1815. It is divided into three sections. The first section treats of the history of the climate of Peru; the second of the influence of climate on organized beings; the third of the influence of climate in relation to health and disease. This section contains an extensive review of the means essential to the preservation of health under different climatic conditions, particularly under the climatic conditions prevailing in Peru.[13]

The bulk of the writings of Hipólito Unánue belong to a period subsequent to that here under consideration.[14]

(13) An available copy is found in the sixth volume of *Documentos literarios del Perú* collected and arranged by Manuel de Odriozola, Lima, 1874.

(14) A biographical essay on Dr. Hipólito Unánue is printed in Odriozola's *Documentos literarios del Perú,* vi, 535-548. That volume contains many of his discourses.

González Laguna

Padre Francisco Gonzâlez Laguna was also a contributor to the *Mercurio*. He wrote under the name of "Thiméo." He had marked attainments as a botanist, and participated in the work of the botanical expedition directed by Ruiz and Pavón and in that of Malaspina's expedition. The plant *Gonzalaguna dependens* was named in his honour by Hipólito Ruiz. Laguna and Juan Tafalla were commissioned to arrange the botanical garden of Lima. Besides articles published in the *Mercurio*, Laguna wrote various papers on natural history and a work called *Celo sacerdotal para con los no-nacidos*, in which one may find data with respect to the number of missionaries who had perished at the hands of the Indians in the wilds of Huanuco, Huamalíes, and Tarma; also an account of the exotic plants that had been introduced into Lima during the previous thirty years.

Celo sacerdotal para con los no-nacidos

Another writer for the *Mercurio* was José Ignacio Lecuanda, who held various offices in Peru between 1782 and 1801; accountant in the tribunal of accounts, treasurer of Guamanga, royal official accountant at

Trujillo, and later accountant of the customs at Lima. His articles dealt with geographical questions, agriculture, industry and commerce. He wrote also on matters of politics and administration. In the *Mercurio* he published an account of the vagrants in Lima and of the means proposed for employing them. He affirmed that in Lima two-thirds of the inhabitants supported the rest, and that this state of vagabondage was due to the freedom with which the inhabitants, the foreigners as well as other classes, acceded to requests for charity, in this way developing in large numbers of persons an unwillingness to work. The sons of artisans, as well as many persons of other classes, refused to take up the careers of their fathers. The women refused to work preferring to attach themselves to families where they might obtain mere subsistence, or to acquire a livelihood in some other way. The existence of distinct classes added to the social confusion: the whites and the mestizos refused to treat as their equals the negroes and the mulattoes, while these in turn refused to undertake domestic

Ignacio Lecuanda

Social confusion in Lima

service or labour in the fields, and attempted to imitate the members of the dominant class.

This peridoical contained also notable articles on quina. These appeared in the eighth and twelfth volumes. Juan López Canizares is said to have been the first European to acquire knowledge of the medicinal properties of this plant, communicated to him by an Indian. In 1630, knowing that the wife of the viceroy, the Condesa de Chinchón, was ill with an exhausting intermittent fever, Lopez sent a quantity of quina to the viceroy, and this was administered to the countess by Dr. Juan de Vega, with eminently satisfactory results. This incident induced Linnæus to give the plant the name of Chinchona. Some of the bark in the form of a powder was taken to Madrid, where it was examined by physicians and rejected as a medicine. It was nevertheless used, and noteworthy cures were effected. Here it was known as "pulvos de la condesa." It was later taken to Rome by Jesuits, and became known in Italy, France, and Germany as Jesuits' powder.

Chinchona

Some light is thrown on the spirit of the seventeenth century by its reception generally in Europe. Persons who observed its effects could not deny its efficacy, but they attributed these effects to a pact which the Peruvians had made with the devil. It was discredited in France and Germany; the English prohibited its use; and the learned men of Salamanca maintained that it was an unpardonable sin for a physician to prescribe it. Late in the eighteenth century, in spite of the fact that Charles III tried to encourage the extraction of chinchona bark, certain physicians in Spain continued to speak of it as a remedy that was worse than the disease; but its properties had already attracted the attention, and called forth the commendation of Dr. José Celestino Mutis, the distinguished botanist of New Granada.[15]

Opposition to use of quina

Dr. Gabriel Moreno, a distinguished physician, who was born in Peru in 1735, occupied a prominent place among the scientific

Gabriel Moreno

(15) A treatise on *quina*, by Sebastián Bado, was published in Genoa in 1663, entitled *Anastasis corticis peruvianae seu chinae defensio*, dealing also with its introduction into Europe.

men of South Amerinca during the last half of the eighteenth century. His special field of research was Botany. The *Mercurio peruano* contains an article on coca by him. He published other papers and a series of biographies of distinguished Peruvians: Francisco Ruiz Lozano, professor of mathematics; Dr. Juan Ramón Koenig, the first cosmographer of Peru; and Dr. Cosme Bueno, a physician of note in Lima. Dombey, who went to Peru with the botanical expedition of 1778, dedicated a plant, which he discovered to Dr. Moreno, calling it *Morena peruana*.

Politics and literature, as well as the sciences of nature, claimed some part of the attention of contributors to the *Mercurio*. Dr. José Ignacio Moreno, a professor in the University of San Marcos, born in Guayaquil, published here certain of his discourses on various subjects: one of these was on freedom of worship; another treated of the supremacy of the pope; a third was a report concerning the creation of the bishopric of Junín. Dr. Moreno lived on beyond the limit of the colonial period, and, as a member of a patriotic society created in 1822, his discourses concerning a form of government for Peru produced great popular dissatisfaction; for he spoke in opposition to the general sentiment of Spanish America, which accepted the principles of democratic rule. He died in 1841.

On one occasion at least the Amantes del país got into embarrassment through the freedom of their criticism. The Franciscan Antonio Olavarrieta, writing in the *Semanario,* undertook to treat of the public amusements, the dress, the balls, promenades, and receptions of Lima. Writers in the *Mercurio* analysed Olavarrieta's article, and made certain satirical allusions to the subjects treated, and their observations displeased many persons, who appear to have had influence with the authorities; for the number of the periodical for June 23, 1791, was suppressed. It was, however, replaced by another number of the same date.

Mercurio suppressed

VI

The noteworthy success achieved by the *Mercurio peruano* was one of the inducements leading to the establishment of *El telégrafo mercantil* at Buenos Aires in 1801. The founder and editor was Francisco Antonio Cabello. His announced purpose in founding this periodical was to advance science and the arts, to create a school of philosophy that would banish the barbarous forms of scholasticism, to extend the knowledge of agriculture, and to inform the readers of the progress and new discoveries in history, archæology, literature and other departments of human learning. The first number was issued on April 1, 1801, and it appeared thereafter during its continuance generally twice a week. The first volume of thirty-five numbers covered the months of April, May, June and July; the second volume, September, October, November, and December; the third volume, January, February, March and April, of 1802; the fourth volume, May, June, July, and August; but the fifth and last volume was

Telégrafo mercantil

The volumes of the *Telégrafo*

never completed. It's fourth number, the last issued, appeared on October 17, 1802; it contained an article which the public found extremely objectionable. In this article the editor wrote that there existed no place under the sun more effective than Río de la Plata for encouraging the idleness of foreigners, on account of the abundance of food and of the superabundance of unmarried women, lovers of society and of luxury. And in order to remedy this evil this article further proposed that towns should be built on the coast of Patagonia; that all Spanish bachelors in the country should be arrested and induced to marry; and afterwards sent to the new Patagonian towns under penalty of a forced return to Spain of all those who would not accept the hand of some poor young woman of Buenos Aires, and who would not be willing to establish themselves either at the bay of San Julián or the bay of San Matías.

The end and character of the *Telégrafo*

This article put an end to the *Telégrafo mercantil*; the viceroy, in justice to those who had been offended, ordered the publication to be suspended. The Argentine critic, José María Gutiérrez, says the editor "proposed to realize in Buenos Aires the design conceived by the editors of *Mercurio peruano* without possessing the judgment, the serenity of character, and the literary qualities that distinguished Unánue, Baquijano, and other writers of that part of America, the founders and supporters of that famous publication." "But one must confess," he continues, "that in spite of the incompetence of the editor and the great defects displayed by the *Telégrafo mercantil*, the appearance of that publication marks an epoch of progress, and that, by awakening a curiosity for reading and the natural ambition to write for the press, it gave a visible impulse to minds and to ideas. In its pages appeared for the first time the ode of Lavarden to the Río Paraná, the fables of Azcuénaga and other contributions, which are not to be underestimated and are an honour to the country, the first essays of the patriotic muse. In it one finds also descriptions of some of the Argentine cities and provinces, and various contributions by Haenke; the first meteorolo-

Influence of the *Telégrafo*

gical observations published in Buenos Aires; important and curious isolated data concerning commercial practice, and the price of objects of production and consumption throughout the whole viceroyalty."[16]

Another periodical publication was established in Buenos Aires in 1802. This was the *Semanario de agricultura, industria, y comercio.* The first number appeared on September 1, 1802, and the last on February 11, 1807. It was edited by Juan Hipólito Vieytes. It greatly surpassed its predecessor with respect to the method shown in the arrangement of its material and in the judgment displayed in selecting this material

The *Semanario de agricultura, industria y comercio* at Buenos Aires

VII

The expedition of Malaspina was also a factor of the movement, in the last third of the eighteenth century, to increase the world's scientific knowledge of South America. This expedition would merit no special remark in this place but for the fact

Malaspina's expedition

(16) See Medina's extended account of *El telégrafo mercantil* in his *Historia y bibliografía de la imprenta en América española : Imprenta en Buenos Aires*, La Plata, 1892.

Tadeo Haenke

that Tadeo Haenke, one of its members, remained to be a permanent resident of Upper Peru, and became a contributor to the intellectual activity of that part of the continent. Haenke was born in Treibitz, Bohemia, near the Saxon frontier, on October 5, 1761. He studied at Prague, and was promoted to the degree of Doctor in 1782. Four years later he removed to Vienna, and continued his studies in mineralogy under Profesor Ignacius Born and botany under Professor Nicolas Jacquin. His relation to these men was also that of a collaborator. Under the initiative of the latter he made a botanical exploration of the Alps. He was also charged with the preparation of the eighth edition of Linnæus' *Genera plantarum.*

At this time, 1788, the Spanish government was preparing the scientific expedition to be commanded by Malaspina, and asked Professors Born and Jacquin to designate a person who might join the expedition in the capacity of naturalist. Without hesitation they nominated Tadeo Haenke, who, although only twenty-seven years old, had already given evidence of remarkable knowledge and ability. Their suggestion was accepted, and Haenke entered upon the journey from Vienna to Cadiz; but by a miscalculation of the time required for it, and by delays in Paris and Madrid, he arrived at the port shortly after the "Descubierta" and the "Atrevida" had sailed. He followed by the first merchant ship available. This was wrecked at the mouth of the Río de la Plata, and through this misfortune Haenke lost most of his books, papers and instruments. He arrived at Montevideo eight days after Malaspina had departed for the Strait and the Pacific. Aided by the government of Buenos Aires, Haenke now undertook the overland journey across the pampas and over the Andes. When he arrived at Santiago, April 10, 1790, Malaspina's ships had already anchored at Valparaiso.

Haenke joins the expedition

The expedition sailed northward along the coast, and the most important halt was in the port of Callao. The ships were left under the necessary guard, and the members of the company established themselves for four months in the valley of the Rimac. The viceroy Francisco de Gil y Lemus received the officers and the scientists, but the festivities of the viceregal court did not prevent somewhat elaborate investigations in Peru. Haenke accompanied by the botanist Tafalla and the draughtsman Pulgar, went over the Andes to Tarma and visited Huanuco and the mines of Cerro del Pasco. Tafalla and Pulgar had been associated with the botanical expedition under Ruíz and Pavón, and after its return to Spain, they remained under orders from the government to continue their botanical investigations in Peru, and to make collections to replace those that had been lost at Macora.

Voyage northward and to the Far East

Towards the end of 1790 Malaspina's expedition continued its northward voyage, halting at Guayaquil, Panama, Acapulço, and advancing to the Strait of Fuca and into the Behring Sea. In the beginning of 1792 it entered upon the voyage across the Pacific, to the Philippine Islands and Australia, and, returning, arrived at Callao July 23, 1793. This long voyage was for Haenke a period of fatiguing and profitless idleness; and when the expedition started on its homeward voyage from Peru it was determined by Malaspina and approved by the viceroy that Haenke should be temporarily separated from the ships and go to Buenos Aires by way of Huancavelica, Cuzco and Potosí, for the purpose of continuing his investigations in botany and zoology. Luis Nee, another member of the scientific staff, was permitted to leave the "Atrevida" at Concepción in Chile, and proceed by land to Buenos Aires and meet the ships at Montevideo. But Haenke, on account of the great extent of his proposed journey, had permission to delay his arrival in Buenos Aires until October or November 1794. Nee complied with the stated requirements, rejoined the expedition at Montevideo, and returned to Spain. Haenke, on the other hand, failed to carry out the conditions under which he was permitted to cross the continent. Letters from him received by his companions at Montevideo announced that on account of the extent of his explorations, reaching to

Haenke leaves the expedition

the territory of the Mojos and Chiquitos, he would be delayed beyond the time specified for his arrival in Buenos Aires, but that he believed he would be in Montevideo and embark for Europe in the early part of the following year.

But this belief was not well founded; he never left America. He was granted a pension by the viceroy, established himself at Cochabamba, and continued his scientific researches. The principal product of his inquiries was his *Historia natural de Cochabamba*. This was written in 1798. To the same period belong his *Memoria sobre los ríos navegables que fluyen al Marañón* and *Descripción del Perú*. Numerous fragments of these works were published in the *Telégrafo mercantil* but without his name.

Haenke's Writings

Groussac on Haenke

Paul Groussac, who caused the Natural History of Cochabamba to be published in the first volume of the *Anales de la biblioteca* characterized its style, in the preliminary essay on the life of Haenke, as "that of descriptive science, simple and positive, and as far from the incorrect creole verbosity as from the elegant precision of the

French travellers. Of Haenke he affirms "We find ourselves in the presence of a savant of high quality, worthy by his own ideas as well as by his vast and varied knowledge to take his place, if destiny had not decreed otherwise, in that illustrious galaxy near the end of the last century, in which Priestly, Scheele, and Lavoisier shine as stars of the first magnitude."[11]

Haenke's late years and death

But his marvellous zeal for exploration and investigation gradually waned; isolation, lack of the results attained by other investigators, the spiritual inertia of frontier conditions, and a relaxing climate wrought, in the course of time, their deadly work, dulling the acuteness of his mind, and destroying his energy. And the end, it is reported, was hastened by the carelessness of a servant, who, in his illness at his hacienda, administered by mistake a dose of poison in place of the beneficent medicine. He died in 1817.

(17) *Anales de la biblioteca*, I, 48, 54. Buenos Aires. Other known manuscripts by Haenke are :—*Descripción del reino de Chile* ; *Observaciones sobre el volcán de Arequipa*; *Estudios de las aguas termales de Yura*; *Descripción de las montañas de indios yuracarées*; *Artículos sobre el molle y sobre un arbusto alcanforado*; *Itinerario de Oruro a Jujui*; *Planos de Chulamani y Omasuyos*.

VIII

Santiago Cárdenas

Perhaps to these indications of an intellectual awakening in Spanish South America one ought to add a reference to a forerunner of modern aviation, who achieved fame to such an extent that he became known as El Volador This was Santiago Cárdenas, who was born in Callao about 1726. Here he lived with his parents, who were extremely poor, until they secured for him, while he was still very young, a position on a vessel trading between Callao and and the coast of Chile. The tidal wave that succeeded the earthquake of 1746 threw the vessel, to which he was attached, upon the shore. This event deprived the seafaring life of some of its attractions for him, and he left his service and went to Lima. Here he devoted himself to work in practical mechanics. Having acquired noteworthy skill in this field, he became ambitious to invent a machine for flying, and petitioned Viceroy Amat for support to enable him to carry out his project. The inhabitants of Lima did not receive

El Volador

with favour his proposal to fly from the hill San Cristóbal to the great square of the city, and on his appearance on the streets they hooted at him and stoned him. The government, however, intervened, and set aside the proposed attempt. Thereafter El Volador's efforts were directed to writing a book on flying, which he called *Nuevo sistema de navegar por les aires.*

In 1860 the manuscript of this book was in the library of the school of medicine; it was afterwards transferred to the national library at Lima, but some pages at the end had been lost, as also some of the rude pen drawings. But in 1878 Ricardo Palma had the manuscript copied and printed at Valparaiso in a little volume of one hundred and thirty pages. In the introduction he set down certain curious facts regarding Cárdenas. The next year Pedro Ruiz published a pamphlet in which he discussed the art of flying. Mendiburu, from whose notice of the Volador these facts are taken, refers to a manuscript in the library of Lima entitled *Viaje al globo de la luna*, giving some account of Santiago El Vola-

On art of flying

dor. In the course of time the populace recovered from its aversion to Cárdenas' project, and it is reported that he had to seek asylum in a church to escape from the crowd that wished to compel him to fulfil his promise to fly.

Intellectual movement in the last decades

Although this general survey of the intellectual activity in Spanish South America in the last decades of the colonial period brings to light no epoch-making achievements, there is revealed, however, an increasing interest in the real world, in the sciences that deal with natural phenomena, in literature that is worldly in its tone and subjects, and in the spread of enlightenment through the press that might lead to the formation of a reasonable public opinion. In many quarters there were signs that the new generation was arousing itself to overcome the dulness of the middle years of the eighteenth century. The creoles and the mestizos had been drawn together, and through their union a new society had come into existence. The young creoles in New Granada gathered about Mutis as his disciples and co-workers in the field of scientific investigation, and, with Nariño as their leader, announced their adherence to the doctrine of political liberty. Everywhere they displayed a spirit of revolt against the institutions through which Spanish absolutism had found expression, and they resented with increasing vigour and determination their exclusion from participation in the direction of public affairs that vitally concerned their welfare.

Mutis and Nariño

THE END

APPENDIX

A Catalogue, under Authors' Names, of the Books mentioned in the Text

Wherever possible the dates and places of publication of first editions have been given; modern working editions are also included, where they exist. If a given edition is to be found in the British Museum, the letter L *is printed, in square brackets, immediately after the date. The English alphabet has been followed. The spelling of the Spanish names and titles has been modernized throughout. The chapter reference at the end of an entry indicates where in the text an account of the author will be found.*

Acosta (Joaquín). *Compendio histórico del descubrimiento y colonización de la Nueva Granada.* Paris, 1848. [L]
— *Elegías de varones ilustres de Indias, compuestas por Juan de Castellanos.* Short Article printed in *Antología española,* Vol. III, *q.v.* Cap. VII.
Acosta (José de). *De natura novi orbis et de promulgatione evangelii apud barbaros, sive de procuranda Indorum salute.* Salamanca, 1589. [L] The *De promulgatione* was published separately. Salamanca, 1594. [L]
— *De vera Scripturae interpretandae ratione, ac de Christo in Scripturis revelatis.* Rome, 1590. [L]
— *Historia natural y moral de las Indias.* Seville, 1590. [L]
— *Histoire naturelle et morale des Indes, etc.* Trans. by R. Regnauld. Paris 1597. [L]
— *Historie naturael ende morael van de Westersche Indien, etc.* Trans. by J. Huyghem van Linschoten. Haarlem, 1598. [L]
— *The naturall and morall historie of the East and West Indies.* Trans. by E. Grimestone, London, 1604. [L] London, 1880. [L]
— — German Trans. from the Dutch in T. de Bry's *Amerika, teil IX,* Frankfurt a. M., 1601. [L]

[Acosta (José de): *cont.*]

— — Latin Trans. from the Dutch in T. de Bry's *America, pars IX*, Frankfurt a. M., 1602. [L]

— *Sumario del concilio provincial, que se celebró en la Ciudad de los Reyes, el año 1567*. Madrid, 1591.

— *Concilium limense celebratum anno 1583*. Ascribed to Acosta. Madrid, 1591. See Medina (J. T.), *Bib. hisp. amer.*, Vol. I.

— *De temporibus novissimis*. Lyons, 1592. Cap. IV, i.

Acuña (Cristóbal de). *El nuevo descubrimiento del gran río de las Amazonas*. Madrid, 1641. [L]

— — Printed in *Colección de libros que tratan de America raros o curiosos*, Vol. II, *q.v.*

— *Relation de la rivière des Amazones*. Transl. by M. de Gomberville. To which is added *Journal du voyage qu'ont ait les pères J. Grillet et F. Bechamel de la Cie. de Jésus, dans la Goyane, l'an 1674*. 4 vols. Paris, 1682. [L]

— *New Discovery of the Great River of the Amazons*. Trans. and ed. by Sir Clements Markham in *Expeditions into the Valley of the Amazons*, *q.v.* Cap. X, iii.

Aguiar (Antonio). *Razón de las noticias de la provincia de San Lorenzo Mártir de Chile, etc.* MS. (1742). Cap. XII, v.

Aguilar del Río (Juan Bautista). *Restauración y reparo del Perú*. 1615.

— [A report, dated 1623, to the King on the misfortunes and needs of the Indians. Later printed. See Mendiburu, *Dic. hist. biog. del Perú*.] Cap. X, i.

Aguirre (Juan Bautista). *Concepción de Nuestra Señora* and *La rebelión y caída de Luzbel y sus sequaces*. Both contained in *Versos castellanos, obras juveniles, misceláneas*. Manuscript in possession of a collector in Guayaquil. See Gutiérrez (Juan María), *Estudios biográficos y críticos*, p. 237. Cap. XVII, iii.

Aguirre (Miguel de). *Población de Valdivia*. Lima, 1647. Cap. IX, vi. Cap. XVI, iv.

Alcedo (Antonio de). *Diccionario geográfico-histórico de las Indias occidentales*. 5 vols., Madrid, 1786–1789. [L]

— *The Geographical and Historical Dictionary of America and the West Indies*. Translation with large additions by G. A. Thompson. 5 vols. London, 1812–15. [L] Cap. XVI, v.

Alcedo y Herrera (Dionisio de). *Aviso histórico-geográfico con noticias particulares de la América meridional*. Madrid, 1741. [L]

[Alcedo y Herrera (Dionisio de): *cont.*]
— *Compendio histórico de la provincia, partidos, ciudad, astillero, ríos, y puerto de Guayaquil.* Madrid, 1741. [L] Cap. XVI, v.
Alcocer (Hernando de). *Orlando furioso . . . nuevamente traducido. . . . por H. de A.* Toledo, 1550. [L] Cap. V.
Alesio (Adrián de). *Vida de Santo Tomás de Aquino en quintillas.* Madrid.
— *El Angélico* (A poem in praise of St. Thomas Aquinas). Murcia, 1645. [L]
— [Said to have written *Del amor de Dios.*]
See Antonio (N.), *Bibliotheca hispana nova,* and Mendiburu. *Dic. hist. biog. del Perú,* article, "Menacho." Cap XIV, iv.
Algunas hazañas de las muchas de Don García Hurtado de Mendoza. Madrid, 1622. A comedy composed by several authors (Mira de Amescua, etc.).
— — Printed in *Colección de aut. esp.*, Vol. XX, *q.v.* Cap. VI, iv.
Alloza (Juan de). *El breve oficio del nombre de María.*
— *El cielo estrellado de María.* Madrid, 1654.
See Mendiburu, *Dic. hist. biog. del Perú.* Cap. XIV, iv.
Alvarez de Toledo (Fernando). *El Purén indómito.* Publ. in *Bibliotheca americana, q.v.*
— *La Araucana.* MS. lost. Several octaves quoted in *Histórica relación del reino de Chile,* by Alonso de Ovalle. *q.v.* Cap. VI, iii.
Amador de los Ríos (José). *Vida y escritos de Gonzalo Fernández de Oviedo y Valdés.* Prefixed to Span. Academy's 1851 ed. of Fernández de Oviedo's *Historia general, q.v.* Cap. II, i.
Amunátegui (Gregorio Victor). *Fernando Álvarez de Toledo.* Article publ. in *Anales de la Universidad de Chile.* Vol. XXVIII. (March, 1866) *q.v.*
Amunátegui Solar (Domingo). *Las encomiendas de indígenas en Chile.* 2 vols. Santiago de Chile, 1909–10. [L]
— *Don Fernando Álvarez de Toledo.* Santiago de Chile, 1898. Cap. VI, iii.
Anales de historia natural. Edited by C. Herrgen, L. J. Proust, D. Fernández and A. J. Cavanilles. Madrid, 1799–1800. [L] Continued as: —
Anales de ciencias naturales. Madrid, 1801–1804. [L]
Anales de la Biblioteca (Biblioteca Nacional de Buenos Aires) Buenos Aires, 1900, etc. [L]

Anales de la Universidad de Chile. Santiago de Chile, 1843–45, Valparaiso, 1846, etc. [L]. In progress. The set in British Museum imperfect, wanting the vols. for 1845–46, –48, –53, –58.

— *Indice general de los Anales . . . compuesto por Ramón Briseño.* Santiago de Chile, 1856. [L]

Anales del Cuzco. See Palma (Ricardo).

Andagoya (Pascual de). *Relación de los sucesos de Pedrarias Dávila en las provincias de Tierra Firme, etc.* Publ. by Fernández de Navarrete (M.) in *Colección de viajes y descubrimientos . . . del siglo XV*, Vol. III, *q.v.*

— *Narrative of the proceedings of Pedrarias Dávila in the provinces of Tierra Firme.* Transl. and edited by Sir Clements Markham. Hakluyt Society, London, 1865. [L] Cap. II, iii.

Andrade (Alonso). *Vida de P. Pedro Claver*, under pseudonym, Jerónimo Suárez Sornoza. Madrid, 1657. Cap. XI, v.

Angelis (Pedro). *Colección de obras y documentos relativos a la historia antigua y moderna de las provincias del Río de la Plata.* 6 vols. 1836–37. [L]

Anglés y Gortari (Matías de). *Los Jesuitas en el Paraguay. Copia del informe . . . sobre los puntos que han sido causa de las discordias sucedidas en la ciudad de la Asunción.* Madrid, 1769. [L] Cap. XIII, vi.

Annales des voyages, de la géographie et de l'histoire ; ou collection des voyages nouveaux . . . traduits de toutes les langues européennes, etc. Publ. by M. Malte-Brun. 24 vols. Paris, 1808–14. [L]

— *Nouvelles annales des voyages.* Publ. by M. Malte-Brun, M. Ternaux-Compans and others. 6 series. Paris, 1819–1870. [L]

Antequera y Castro (José de). *Carta primera que escribió el Señor Doctor Don J. de A. y C. a Fray José de Palos, Obispo del Paraguay.* Lima, 1726. Printed by Jesuit Mission in Pueblo de S. Fr. Xavier, Paraguay, 1727. Cap. I.

Antología española. Ed. by C. Herrgen, L. J. Proust, D. Fernández, and A. J. Cavanilles. Madrid, 1848. [L]

Antomas (Domingo). *Arte de perseverancia final en gracia.* Lima, 1766. Cap. XIV, iv.

Antonio (Nicolás). *Bibliotheca hispana nova.* Madrid, 1783. [L]

— *Bibliotheca hispana vetus.* Madrid, 1788. [L]

Apolinar (Francisco). *Suma moral y resumen brevísimo de todas las obras del Doctor Machado.* Madrid, 1661. Cap. XIV, iv.

Arbieto (Ignacio de). *Historia de la Provincia del Perú.* MS. was in the Archives of Lima, but is lost.

— *Suma de los obras teológicas del P. Fr. Suárez.* See *Bib. de la Cie. de Jésus.* Pt. I. Cap. XI, ii.

Archivo boliviano. See Ballivián y Rojas (V.).

Astete (Miguel de). See Estete (Miguel de).

Ávila (Gaspar de). *Gobernador prudente.* Printed in *Primera parte de comedias escogidas*, Vol. XXI. *q.v.* Cap. VI, iv.

Azcuénaga (Domingo de). [*Fables.* Published in *Telégrafo mercantil*, Buenos Aires, 1801-2]. See Medina (J.T.), *La imprenta en Buenos Aires.* Cap. XVII, vi.

Bado (Sebastian). See Baldi (Sebastiano).

Baldi (Sebastiano). *Anastasis corticis peruvianae seu chinae defensio.* 2 Parts. Genoa, 1663. [L] Cap. XVII, v.

Ballivián (Manuel Vicente) and Kramer (Pedro). *Tadeo Haenke. Escritos, precedidos de algunos apuntes para su biografía y acompañados de varios documentos ilustrativos.* La Paz, 1898. [L]

Ballivián y Rojas (Vicente de). Ed. *Archivo boliviano. Colección de documentos relativos a la historia de Bolivia durante la época colonial, con un catálogo de obras impresas y de manuscritos que tratan de esa parte de la América meridional.* Paris, Leipzig, 1872.

Baños y Sotomayor (Diego). *Constituciones sinodales del obispado de Venezuela.* Madrid, 1698. Reprinted, Caracas, 1848. [L] Cap. XII, ii.

Baquijano y Carrillo (José de). *Elogio del excelentísimo señor don Agustín de Jáuregui y Aldecoa . . . virrey, gobernador, y capitán general de los reinos del Perú, Chile, etc.* Lima, 1781.

— *Relectio extemporanea ad explanationem legis Pamphilo XXXIX. D. de legatis et fidei . . . commissis III . . . 1788.* Lima, 1788. [L]

— *Alegato que en la oposición a la catedra de prima de leyes de la Universidad de San Marcos de Lima dijo el Dr. J. de B. y C. . . . 29 de Abril de 1788* (Lima, 1788). [L] Cap. XVII, vi.

Barcia (A. González de). See González de Barcia Carballido y Zúñiga (A.).

Barco Centenera (Martín del). *La Argentina.* Lisbon, 1602. [L]

— — Printed by González de Barcia in *Historiadores primitivos, etc.* Vol. III, *q.v.*

— — Printed by Angelis (P.) in *Colección de obras y documentos relativos a la historia . . . del Rio de la Plata. q.v.*

— — Printed by Díaz de Guzmán in *Historia argentina.* Vol. III, *q.v.*

— — Facsimile reprint of 1st Lisbon edition, with preface by J. M. Gutiérrez, publ. by Junta de Historia y Numismática Americana. Buenos Aires, 1912. [L] Cap. VIII.

Barrasa (Jacinto). [1st vol. of Sermons. Madrid, 1678. 2nd vol., Madrid, 1678.]

— *Historia de las fundaciones de los colegios y casas de la provincia del Perú de la Compañía de Jesús, etc.* MS. in possession of Monseñor García Sanz.

See Torres Saldamando. *Los antiguos Jesuitas del Perú.* Cap. XI., ii.

Barrenechea y Albis (Juan). *Restauración de la Imperial y conversión de almas infieles.* MS. See Medina, *Bibliotheca americana.* Cap. XI, i.

Barros Arana (Diego). *Historia general de Chile.* 16 vols. Santiago, 1884–1902. [L]

— *Historia general de la independencia de Chile.* 4 vols. Santiago, 1854–58. [Vol. I in L]

— *Proceso de Pedro de Valdivia y otros documentos inéditos concernientes a este conquistador.* Santiago de Chile, 1873. [L]

— *El Inca, Garcilaso de la Vega.* Printed in B. A.'s *Obras completas,* VIII, 151–158.

— *Retórica poética. Obras completas,* III, 309.

— *Obras completas.* 11 vols. Santiago de Chile. 1908–1911.

— See also *Revista chilena* and *Bibliotheca americana.*

Benzoni (Girolamo). *La historia del mondo nuovo.* Venice, 1565. [L] Cap. III, viii.

Bertonio (Ludovico). *Arte y gramática muy copiosa de la lengua aimara.* Rome. 1603. [L]

— *Arte de la lengua aimara con una silva de frases y su declaración en romance.* Chucuito, 1612. [L]

— *Confesionario muy copioso en dos lenguas, aimara y española, con una instrucción acerca de los siete sacramentos de la Santa Iglesia.* Printed by Jesuits in Pueblo de Juli. Chucuito, 1612. [L]

[Bertonio (Ludovico): *cont.*]

— *Vocabulario de la lengua aimara, etc.* 2 pts. Juli (in province of Chucuito), 1612. [L]

— — Republished by J. Platzmann. Leipzig, 1879. [L] Cap. IV, i.

Biblioteca de autores españoles desde la formación del lenguaje hasta nuestros días. 71 vols. Publ. by Rivadeneyra. Madrid, 1849, etc. [L]

Biblioteca de escritores de Chile. Santiago de Chile, 1910.

Biblioteca de historia nacional. Edited by Eduardo Posada and Pedro M. Ibáñez. Bogotá, etc. [L]

Biblioteca de la Compañía de Jesús. See Ribadeneira (Pedro de).

Biblioteca de los americanistas. Madrid, 1828, etc. [L]

Biblioteca hispano-ultramarina. Publ. by Manuel G. Hernández. Madrid, 1876, etc. [L]

Bibliotheca americana. Edited by D. Barros Arana. 3 vols. Leipzig and Paris, 1861–64. [L]

Bibliothèque de la Compagnie de Jésus. Pt. I. Bibliography; by Fathers Augustin and Aloys de Backer. Pt. II, History; by Father Auguste Carayon. New edition by Carlos Sommervogel. 10 vols. and supplement. Brussels, 1890. [L]

Borda (José Joaquín). *Historia de la Compañía de Jesús en la Nueva Granada.* 2 vols. Poissy, 1872. Cap. XI, v.

Bravo de Lagunas y Castilla (Pedro José). *Colección legal de cartas, dictámenes y otros papeles de derecho. Los da a luz P. de Colmenares Fernández de Córdoba.* Lima, 1761. [L] Cap. XVII, ii.

Brulio (Joaquín). *Historiae Peruanae ordinis eremitarum Sancti Augustini libri octodecim.* Louvain (?) 1651–2. [L]. (Extract translated into Latin from Antonio de Calancha's *Crónica moralizada.*) Cap. X, v.

Buendía (José de). *Vida del V. P. Francisco del Castillo.* Madrid, 1693. [L]. Part was published by Odriozola in Lima on pp. 23–33 of *Terremotos*, *q.v.* Compendium of the whole work pub. by Monseñor García Sanz, Rome, 1863. Cap. XI, ii.

Bueno (Cosme). *Disertaciones geográficas y científicas.* Published by Odriozola (M. de) in *Colección de documentos literarios del Perú*, Vol. III, *q.v.*

NOTE.—These dissertations first appeared in issues of *El conocimiento de los tiempos*, from 1757–1798 (*q.v.*). During these years C.B. as royal cosmographer edited this yearly almanac. Cap. XVI, vi

Bustamante Carlos (Calixto) alias Concolorcorvo. *El lazarillo de ciegos caminantes desde Buenos Aires hasta*

[Bustamante Carlos (Calixto) alias Concolorcorvo: *cont.*]
Lima, etc. Lima, 1773.]L] (Title page gives Gijón as place of publication, but it was apparently printed secretly in Lima.)
— — New edition publ. by the Junta de Historia y Numismática Americana. Buenos Aires, 1908. [L] Cap. XVI, vi.

Cabello de Balboa (Miguel). *Miscelánea austral.* MS. Completed in 1586. Part published as *Histoire du Pérou*, by Ternaux-Compans (H.) in his *Voyages, relations, etc.*, Vol. XV, *q.v.* Cap. IV, iv.

Cajica (Juan). [Numerous MSS. not printed.] See Mendiburu, *Dic. hist. biog. del Perú.* Cap. XIV, iv.

Calancha (Antonio de la). *Crónica moralizada del orden de S. Agustín en el Perú.* 1st vol., Barcelona, 1638. [L] 2nd vol., Lima, 1653. [L]

NOTE.—Vol. II was arranged for publication after the death of the author by Fr. Bernardo de Torres, who continued the chronicle. See Torres (Bernardo de); also Medina, *La imprenta en Lima*

— — French trans. (Extract, with additions by translator). Toulouse, 1653.
— — Latin trans. (extract) by J. Brulio. See Brulio.
— *De los varones ilustres de la orden de S. Augustín.*
— *De Immaculatae Virginis Mariae Conceptione.* Lima, 1629.
— *Informe al virrey del Perú sobre los castores que se cazan desde Callao a Chile.* Lima, 1642. Cap. X, v.

Calderón (Melchor). *Tratado de la importancia y utilidad que hay en dar por esclavos a los indios rebelados de Chile.* Madrid, 1607(?). Cap. XV.

Calvete de Estrella (Juan Cristóbal). *De rebus indicis.* MS. in Academia de la Historia, Madrid. Cap. III, v.

Campusano (Antonio). [Ballad dedicated to Fernández de Campino. Quoted by J. T. Medina in *Hist. de la lit. col. de Chile*, pp. 425–6, Vol. I, *q.v.*] Cap. XVII, iii.

Carayon (Auguste). *Documents inédits concernant la Compagnie de Jésus.* 23 vols. Poitiers, 1863–86. [L]

Cárdenas (Santiago)., El Volador. *Nuevo sistema de navegàr por los aires.* Publ. by Ricardo Palma, Valparaiso, 1878. Cap. XVII, viii.

Cárdenas Z. Çano (Gabriel de), pseudonym. See González de Barcia Carballido y Zúñiga (Andrés).

Cardiel (José). *Declaración de la verdad.* Published by Misiones del Paraguay. Reprinted Buenos Aires, 1900.

[Cardiel (José): *cont.*]

— *Breve relación de las misiones guaraníes.* Latin original still in MS.

— — Spanish Trans. abbreviated with title *Costumbres de los guaraníes*, printed at end of D. Muriel's *Historia del Paraguay* in *Colección de lib. y doc. ref. a la historia de América.* Vol. XIX, *q.v.*

— See Lozano (P.). Cap. XIII v.

Caro (Miguel Antonio). [Three articles on Juan de Castellanos in the *Repertorio colombiano.* Bogotá, 1879–80.]

— *Curiosidades literarias*, an article in *Repertorio colombiano*, (*q.v.*), on, inter alia, J. B. de Toro's work. Cap. VII.

Caro de Torres (Francisco). *Relación de los servicios de Don Alonso de Sotomayor.* Madrid, 1620. [L]

— — Reprinted in *Col. de historiadores de Chile.* Vol. V, *q.v.*

— *Historia de las órdenes militares de Santiago, Calatrava y Alcántara, etc.* Madrid, 1629. [L] Cap. IX, iii.

Carrasco del Saz (Francisco). *Interpretatio ad aliquas leges recopilationis regni Castellae.* Seville, 1620.

— *Tractatus de casibus Curiae.* Madrid, 1630. Cap. XV. i.

Carrillo de Ojeda (Agustín). *Relación de las paces ofrecidas por los indios rebeldes del reino de Chile.* MS. (1648). Cap. IX, vii.

Cartas de Indias. A collection of letters written from Mexico, Central and South America, and the Philippines by Christopher Columbus, Amerigo Vespucci, Bartolomé de las Casas, Bernal Díaz del Castillo, Cristóbal Vaca de Castro, Pedro de la Gasca, Viceroys, Prelates and others. It contains biographical notes, facsimiles, signatures, and reproductions of four old maps, one of which was consulted by Sir Walter Raleigh as indicating the position of *El Dorado.* Published by the Ministerio de Fomento. Madrid, 1877. [L]

Carvallo y Goyeneche (Vicente). *Descripción histórico-geográfica del reino de Chile.* Printed in *Colección de historiadores de Chile*, Vols. VIII, IX, X, *q.v.* Cap. XVI, iii.

Casas (Bartolomé de las). *Brevísima relación de la destrucción de las Indias.* Seville, 1552. [L]

— *The Spanish Colonie*, or *Briefe Chronicle of the Acts and Gestes of the Spaniardes in the West Indies, etc.* London, 1583.

— *A briefe narration of the destruction of the Indies*, in *Purchas his Pilgrimes*, Part 4. London, 1625. *q.v.*

— *The Tears of the Indians, etc.* London, 1656. [L]

— *Tyrannies et cruautés des Espagnols aux Indes Occidentales.* Antwerp, 1579. [L]

[Casas (Bartolomé de las): *cont.*]

— *Narratio regionum Indicarum per Hispanos quosdam devastatarum verissima.* De Bry. Frankfurt, 1598. [L]

— *Regionum Indicarum per Hispanos olim devastatarum accuratissima descriptio. . . . Editio nova priori longe correctior.* Heidelberg, 1664. [L]

— *Neue Welt. Wahrhafftige Anzeigung der Spanier greulichen . . . Tyrannen.* 1597. [L]

— *Treinta proposiciones pertenecientes al derecho que la iglesia y los príncipes cristianos tienen contra los infieles, etc.*, Seville, 1552. [L]

— *Una disputa entre el dicho obispo y el doctor Ginés de Sepúlveda.* Seville, 1552. [L]

— — Printed in *Bib. de aut. esp.* Vol. LXV, *q.v.*

— *Disputa o controversia con Ginés de Sepulveda contendiendo acerca la licitud de las conquistas de las Indias.* Reproduction of the Seville edition of 1552, with a bibliographical note by the Marqués de Olivart and an essay on *Fray B. de las Casas, su obra y tiempo,* by Fray Enrique Vacas Galindo. Madrid, 1908. [L]

— *Un tratado que . . . B. de las C. . . . compuso sobre la materia de los indios que se han hecho . . . esclavos, etc.* Seville, 1552. [L]

— — Printed in *Bib. de aut. esp.* Vol. LXV, *q.v.*

— *Remedios que B. de las C. refirió por mandado del emperador al ayuntamiento de prelados . . . por la reformación de los indios.* Seville, 1552. [L]

NOTE.—The *Breve relación* and the four preceding titles were also printed in *Las Obras de B. de las C. v. infra.*

— *Historia general de las indias.* First printed in 1875 in *Colección de doc. inéd. para la hist. de España.*, Vol. LXII–LXVI. *q.v.*

— *Historia apologética de las Indias.* Printed in *Nueva bib. de aut. esp.* Vol. XIII. (*Historiadores de Indias* Vol I), *q.v.*

— *Las obras del obispo . . . B. de las Casas, etc.* Barcelona, 1646. [L]

— *Colección de las obras del. . . . obispo de Chiapa . . . enriquecida . . . con . . . notas . . . y apéndices históricos . . . y su vida por. . . . J. A. Llorente.* 2 vols. Paris, 1822. [L]

— See also Fabié (A.M.) and San Martín (T. de).

GENERAL NOTE.—With one or two exceptions, all the works of B. de las

[Casas (Bartolomé de las) : *cont.*]

Casas have been reprinted in *Colección de documentos inéditos para la historia de España.* Vols. LXII–LXVI and LXXI, *q.v.* Cap. II, i.

Cassani (José). *Historia de la Provincia de la Compañía de Jesús del Nuevo Reino de Granada.* Madrid, 1741. [L] Cap. XII, v.

Castellanos (Juan de). *Elegías de varones ilustres de las Indias. Primera Parte.* Madrid, 1589. [L]

— — Pts. 1, 2, 3 (2 and 3 for first time) printed in *Bib, de aut. esp.* Vol. IV, *q.v.*

— *Discurso del Capitán Francisco Draque* (extracted from *Elegías*, part 3). Madrid, 1921.

— *Historia del Nuevo Reino de Granada* (being Pt. 4 of the *Elegías, etc.*). Published by Antonio Paz y Melia, 2 vols., in *Colección de escritores castellanos, q.v.*

— See also Schumacher (H. A.). Cap. VII.

Castillo y Guevara (Francisca Josefa). *Vida de la V. M. Francisca Josefa de la Concepción, escrita por ella.* First published Philadelphia, 1817.

— *Sentimientos espirituales de la V. M. Francisca Josefa.* First published Bogotá, 1843. Cap. XII, iii.

Castro Tito Cusi Yupangui (Diego de). *Relación de la conquista del Perú y hechos del Inca Manco II.* Printed in *Colección de libros y documentos referentes a la historia del Perú*, Vol. II, *q.v.* Cap. III, v.

Caycedo Ladrón de Guevara (Manuel de). *Doctrinas sobre el credo y artículos de la fe.*

— *Doctrinas sobre la reincidencia en el pecado.*

— *Doctrinas sobre la palabra de Dios.*

Note.—These and three other works without title pages are all in MS. See Vergara y Vergara, *Hist. de la lit. en Nueva Granada.* Cap. XVII i.

Cevallos (Pedro Fermín). *Historia del Ecuador.* Lima, 1870.

— *Geografía de la república del Ecuador.* Lima, 1888. [L]

— *Ecuatorianos ilustres . . . Reproducción hecha, por E. C. Monge para el centenario del autor.* Quito, 1912. [L]

Charlevoix (Pierre François Xavier de). *Histoire du Paraguay.* 3 vols. Paris, 1756. [L]

— — Spanish trans. by Pablo Hernández and embodying the notes and corrections of Domingo Muriel in *Colección de libros y documentos referentes a la historia de América*, Vols. XI–XVII, *q.v.* Cap. XIII, v.

Churchill (Awnsham) and (John). *A collection of voyages and travels, etc.*, 6 vols. London, 1704–32. [L]

Cieza de León (Pedro de). *Primera parte de la crónica del Perú que trata la demarcación de sus provincias; la descripción de ellas; las fundaciones de las nuevas ciudades; los ritos y costumbres de los indios; y otras cosas extrañas y dignas de ser sabidas.* Seville, 1553. [L]

— — Printed in *Bib. de aut. esp.* Vol. XXVI, *q.v.*

— *La prima parte dell' istorie del Peru, dove si tratta l'ordine delle provincie, delle città nuove in quel paese edificate, i riti e costumi degli Indiani, con molte cose notabili, etc.* Venice, 1556. [L]

— *The seventeen years travels of Peter de Cieza through the Kingdom of Peru and the Provinces of Carthagena and Popayan in South America, etc.* Transl. by John Stevens, London, 1709. [L]

— *The Travels of Pedro de Cieza de León,* A.D. 1532–50, contained in the first part of his *Chronicle of Peru.* Trans. by Sir. C. Markham. Hakluyt Society, London, 1864. [L]

— *Segunda parte de la crónica del Perú que trata del señorío de los incas yupanquis y de sus grandes hechos y gobernación.* Published by M. Jiménez de la Espada in *Biblioteca hispano-ultramarina.* Madrid, 1880. [L]

NOTE.—The second part had been previously published in 1873 in Edinburgh by González de la Rosa (M).

— *The Second Part of the Chronicle of Peru.* Trans. by Sir C. Markham. Hakluyt Society, London, 1883. [L]

— *Guerras civiles del Perú.* I, *Guerra de las Salinas, II, Guerra de Chupas.* First published in *Colección de documentos inéditos para la historia de España.* Vols. LXVIII and LXXVI, *q.v.*

— *Tercero libro de las guerras civiles del Perú, el cual se llama la guerra de Quito.* Printed in *Biblioteca hispano-ultramarina.* Madrid, 1877. *q.v.*

— — Printed in *Nueva bib. de aut. esp.* Vol. XV. (*Historiadores de Indias,* Vol. II,) *q.v.*

— — Printed in *Colección de documentos inéditos para la historia de España.* Vol. LXVIII, *q.v.*

— *Civil Wars of Peru . . . the War of Chupas.* Transl. and ed. by Sir Clements Markham. Hakluyt Society, London, 1918. [L]

— *The war of Quito . . . and Inca Documents.* Transl. and ed. by Sir Clements Markham. Hakluyt Society, London, 1913. [L] Cap. III, vii.

Cisneros (Diego), Ed. *Mercurio peruano*. Vol. XII, *q.v.* Cap. XVII, iv.

Cisneros (José Luis). *Descripción exacta de la provincia de Venezuela*. Valencia (Venezuela), 1764. [L]

— — Printed in *Colección de libros que tratan de América raros o curiosos* Vol. XXI, *q.v.* Cap. XII, iii.

Cobo (Bernabé]. *Historia del nuevo mundo*. First complete edition publ. by M. Jiménez de la Espada, 5 vols. Seville, 1890–95. [L]

NOTE.—Two extracts published previously under titles *Descripción del Perú*, ed. by A. José Cavanilles in *Anales de historia natural*, Madrid, Vol. VII, *q.v.*; and in *Historia de la fundación de Lima*, ed. by González de la Rosa, in *Colección de historiadores del Perú*, Vol. I, *q.v.* Cap. X, vi.

Colección de autores clásicos españoles. Vol. I (no more published). Madrid, 1840. [L]

Colección de autores españoles. 48 vols. Leipzig, 1863–87. [L]

Colección de documentos inéditos del Archivo de Indias. Ed. by J. F. Pacheco and L. Torres de Mendoza. 1st series, 42 vols. Madrid, 1864–84. 2nd series, 13 vols. Madrid, 1885–1900. [L] Cap. III, viii.

Colección de documentos inéditos para la historia de Chile. See Medina (J.T.).

Colección de documentos inéditos para la historia de España. Edited by Fernández de Navarrete (M.) and others. Madrid, 1842, etc. [L]

NOTE.—For a continuation of this series see *Nueva coleccion de documentos inéditos para la historia de España, etc.*

Colección de documentos literarios del Perú. See Odriozola (M.)

Colección de escritores castellanos. Madrid, 1880. etc. [L]

Colección de historiadores clásicos del Perú. Edited by Carlos A Romero and others. Lima, 1918, etc. [L]

Colección de historiadores de Chile, y documentos relativos a la historia nacional. Santiago de Chile, 1861, etc. [L]

Colección de historiadores del Perú. Obras inéditas o rarísimas e importantes sobre la historia del Perú. Ed. by M. González de la Rosa. Vol. I. Lima, 1882. [L]

Colección de libros españoles raros o curiosos. Edited by Ramírez de Arellano (Feliciano), Marqués de la Fuensanta del Valle, and Rayón (José Sancho). 24 vols. Madrid, 1871–1896

Colección de libros que tratan de América, raros o curiosos. 20 vols. Madrid, 1891–1902. [L]

Colección de libros y documentos referentes a la historia de América. See Romero (C. A.)

Colección de libros y documentos referentes a la historia del Perú. Lima, 1916, etc. [L]

Colección de los mejores autores españoles. 60 vols. Paris, 1835-72. [L]

Colección de obras y documentos relativos a la historia antigua y moderna de las provincias del Río de la Plata. See Angelis (Pedro).

Colección de obras, documentos y noticias, inéditos o poco conocidos, para servir a la historia física, política y literaria del Río de la Plata, publicada bajo la dirección de Andrés Lamas. Buenos Aires, 1878, etc. [L]

Colección de poemas épicos relativos a Chile o escritos por chilenos durante el período colonial. Santiago de Chile, 1888, etc. [L]

Colección de viajes y descubrimientos . . . del siglo XV. Edited by Fernández de Navarrete (M.) 5 vols. Madrid, 1825–37. [L]

Colección hispano-americana. Madrid, 1913, etc.

Concolorcorvo. See Bustamante Carlos (Calixto).

Confesionario para los curas de indios. Con la instrucción contra sus ritos y exhortación para ayudar a bien morir . . . compuesto y traducido en las lenguas quichua y aimara . . . Lima, 1585.—Reprinted Seville, 1603. This contains *Los errores y supersticiones de los indios*, of Polo de Ondegardo (J.). *q.v.*

Conocimiento (El) de los tiempos. Ephemerides del año de 1738—1796 con calendario de las fiestas etc. Lima, 1738–96. [L]

NOTE.—The British Museum set is imperfect, wanting the following years :—1740–49, –52, –55–61, –63, –64, –66, –68, –78, –82–84, –86, –89, –90, –93, –95, and some leaves for 1738, –50, –62, –70

Córdoba Salinas (Diego de). *Crónica de la religiosísima provincia de los doce apóstoles del Perú, de la Orden de N.P.S. Francisco de la regular observancia.* Lima, 1651.

— *Relación de la fundación de la santa provincia de los doce apóstoles del Perú.* MS.

— *Vida, virtudes y milagros del Apóstol del Perú el V. P. Francisco Solano, etc.* Lima, 1630.

— — Second edition augmented by Alonso Mendieta and containing Pedro de Oña's *Río Lima al Río Tibre.* Madrid, 1643. [L]

— — Third edition without Mendieta's additions. Madrid, 1676. [L]

Cap. XIV, ii.

Córdoba y Figueroa (Pedro). *Historia de Chile.* (Unfinished, reaches 1717). First printed in *Colección de historiadores de Chile.* Vol. II, *q.v.* Cap. XVI, ii.

Corral Calvo de la Torre (Juan del). *Expositio ac explanatio omnium legum. Recop. Ind.* MS. 3 vols. See Medina, *Hist. de la lit. col. de Chile.* Cap. XV, iii.

Cortés (Pedro). *Información de la guerra de Chile, etc.* MS., (1598.) See Medina, *Lit. col. de Chile,* Appendix. Cap. IX., vii.

Cruz (Francisco de la). *De la concepcíon de María.* Lima, 1653.

— *Historia del rosario a coros.* Alcalá, 1652.

— *El jardín de María.* Salamanca, 1655. Cap. XIV, iv.

Crespo (Nicolás). [For account of his poetry, see Mera (L. J.), *Ojeada histórico-crítica sobre la poesía ecuatoriana.*] Cap. XVII, iii.

Cueva Ponce de León (Alonso del). *Concordia de la discordia, sobre un punto grave de inmunidad eclesiástica.* Lima, 1749. For account of it, see Medina (J. T.), *La imprenta en Lima,* Vol. II, p. 450. Cap. XVII, ii.

Delgado (Benito). *Diario del R. P. . . . capellán de la expedición que se hizo para el descubrimiento de los Césares.* Publ. by C. Gay in *Documentos.* Vol. I, *q.v.* XVI, iv.

Descripción y cosas notables del reino de Chile . . . en el año de 1655. MS. Bib. Real. Madrid. Cap. IX, vii.

Diario de Lima, curioso, erudito, económico y comercial. Lima, 1790–1793. Cap. XVII, iv.

Díaz de Guzmán (Ruy). *Historia argentina del descubrimiento, población y conquista de las provincias del Río de la Plata. Escrita en el año de 1612.* 3 vols. Buenos Aires, 1854. [L]. Buenos Aires, 1882. [L]

— — Printed by P. de Angelis in *Colección de obras . . . rel. a la hist . . . del Río de la Plata.* Vol. I, *q.v.*

Díaz del Castillo (Bernal). *Historia verdadera de la conquista de la Nueva España.* Madrid, 1632.

— — Printed in *Bib. de aut. esp.* Vol. XXVI, *q.v.*

— — *Unica edición hecha según el códice autógrafo.* Published by Genaro García. 2 vols. Mexico, 1904. [L]

— *The True History of the Conquest of New Spain by B. D. del C., one of its conquerors.* From the only exact copy of the original MS. ed. . . . by Genaro García. Transl. . . . with Introduction and Notes by A. P. Maudslay. 5 vols. Hakluyt Society, London, 1898–1906. [L] Cap. III, iv.

Dobrizhoffer (Martin). *Historia de Abiponibus, equestri*

[Dobrizhoffer (Martin): *cont.*]
bellicosaque Paraquariae natione, etc. 3 Pts. Vienna, 1784. [L]
— *Geschichte der Abiponer . . . aus dem lateinischen übersetzt.* 3 Pts. Vienna, 1783–84. [L]
— *An account of the Abiponas, etc.* London, 1822. [L]
Cap. XIII, v.

Doctrina cristiana y catecismo para instrucción de los indios . . . con un confesionario, y otras cosas necesarias para los que doctrinan . . . y . . . traducida en los dos lenguas generales de este reino, quichua y aimara. La Ciudad de los Reyes (Lima), 1584. [L]
NOTE.—This was the first book to be printed in South America, but the second publication: the first being a pamphlet, *Pragmática sobre los diez días del año, q.v.* Cap. I.

Domínguez Camargo (Hernando). *Poema heroico de San Ignacio.* Publ. incomplete. Madrid, 1666. [L]
Cap. X, ix.

Ducamin (Jean). *L'Araucane. Morceaux choisis précédés d'une étude biographique et littéraire.* Paris, 1900. [L].
See Ercilla y Zúniga (A. de).

Durán (Nicolás). See Jesuits.

Echave y Assu (Francisco). *La estrella de Lima . . . descripción sagro-política de las grandezas de la ciudad de Lima, y compendio histórico-eclesiástico de su Santa Iglesia Metropolitana.* Antwerp, 1688. [L]
Cap. XI, ii.

Eguía y Lumbe (Jorge de). *Ultimo desengaño de la guerra de Chile.* Madrid, 1664(?). [L] Cap. IX, vii.

Enciso. See Fernández de Enciso (M.).

Enríquez de Guzmán (Alonso). *Libro de la vida de Don Alonso Enríquez de Guzmán.* MS. in Bib. Nac., Madrid.
— *Life and Acts of Don A. E. de G. etc.* Trans. and ed. . . . by Sir Clements Markham, Hakluyt Society. London, 1862. [L]
Cap. III, v.

Eraso (Domingo de). *Relación y advertencias . . . sobre . . . la pacificación del dicho reino (de Chile).* Madrid (?), 1605(?).
— *Memorial, etc.* No date or place.
See Medina *Lit. col. de Chile.* Cap. IX, vii.

Ercilla y Zúñiga (Alonso de). *La Araucana*. Part I. Madrid, 1569. [L]; Pts. 1, 2. Pt. 2, Madrid, 1578; [L] Pts. 1–3. Pt. 3, Madrid, 1590 (89). [L]

— — Revised and augmented edition, Pts. 1–3. Madrid, 1597.

— — Printed in *Biblioteca de autores españoles*. Vol. XVII, *q.v.*

— — Reproduction in facsimile of the first editions of Pts. 1 and 2. The Hispanic Society of America, 1902, 1903. [L]

— — *Edición del centenario ilustrada con grabados, documentos . . . y una vida del autor.* 5 vols. Published by J. T. Medina, Santiago de Chile, 1910–1918. [L]

— *L'Araucane*; *Morceaux choisis, etc.* See Ducamin (Jean).

— *L'Araucana, poème épique espagnol . . . traduit . . . en français . . . par A. Nicolas.* 2 vols. Paris (Corbeil), 1869. [L] Cap. V.

Escalona Agüero (Gaspar de). *Arcae Limensis Gazophilatium regium Perubicum*: (i) *Administrandum*, (ii) *Calculandum*, (iii) *Conservandum*. [*Gazofilacio real del reino del Perú—Ordenanzas generales*], Madrid 1647(?). [L]. Book I pt. 2 and Book II in Spanish).

— — Revised and slightly abridged edition. Madrid, 1775. [L] Cap. XV

Escobedo y Alarcón (Jorge). *Instrucción para aprobación de matrículas y cobranza de tributos, etc.* Lima, 1784.

— *Instrucción de revisitas o matrículas, etc.* Lima, 1784.

— *Proyecto que sobre la extinción de repartos, y modo de verificar los piadosos socorros, que la generosa bondad del rey . . . quiere se franqueen a los indios, etc.* Lima, 1784.

— *Discurso sobre el trabajo de minas, beneficio de metales y medios de fomentarlo.* Mentioned by Mendiburu as publ. in Lima, 1784. See *Dic. hist. biog. del Perú.*

— *Reflexiones políticas sobre el gobierno y comercio del Perú.* Lima, 1786 (?) Cap. XV, iii.

Escudero (El padre). *Poesías sueltas.* One "décima" printed by A. Valderrama in *Bosquejo histórico de la poesía chilena* p. 65, *q.v.*
See also Medina (J. T.) *Lit. col. de Chile*, Vol. I, p.337. Cap. XVII, iii.

Estado político del reino del Perú, Madrid, 1747. [L] Cap. XV, iii.

Estete (Miguel de). *La relación del viaje que hizo el señor capitán Hernando Pizarro . . . desde el pueblo de Caxamalca a Parcama, y de allí a Jauja.* Embodied in *La conquista del Perú*, by Francisco de Jerez, *q.v.* Cap. III, i.

Explorations made in the Valley of the River Madeira from 1749–1868. Published for the National Bolivian Navigation Company, London, 1875. [L]

Eyzaguirre (José Ignacio Victor). *Historia de Chile.* 3 vols. Valparaiso, 1850. [L]

Fabié (Antonio María). *Vida y escritos de don fray Bartolomé de las Casas.* Printed in *Colección de documentos inéditos para la historia de España.* Vols. LXX, LXXI, *q.v.* Cap. II, i.

Falcón (Francisco). *Representación . . . sobre los daños y molestias que se hacen a los indios.* Printed in *Colección de libros y documentos referentes a la historia del Perú.* Vol. XI, *q.v.* Cap. XV, i.

Falkner (Thomas). *Description of Patagonia and adjoining parts of South America.* Edited by William Combe. Hereford, 1774. [L]

— *Descripción de Patagonia, etc.* Translation publ. by P. de Angelis in *Colección de obras y documentos ref. a la hist. . . . del Río de la Plata.* Vol. I, *q.v.* Cap. XIII, v.

Federmann (Nicolaus). *Indianische Historia.* Hagenau, 1557.

— *Belle et agréable narration du premier voyage de N. F. le jeune, d'Ulm, aux Indes de la Mer Océane, etc.* Trans. into French and publ. by H. Ternaux-Compans in *Voyages, relations, etc.* Vol. I, *q.v.*

— *Narración del primer viaje de Federmann a Venezuela.* Translated from the French and annotated by Pedro Manuel Arcaya. Caracas, 1916. [L] Cap. VII.

Fernández (Diego). *Primera y segunda parte de la historia del Perú.* Seville, 1571. [L]

— — Printed by Odriozola in *Colección de doc. lit. del Perú.* Vol. VIII, *q.v.*

— — Printed by Lucas de Torre in *Colección hispano-americana.* 2 vols. Madrid, 1913, 1916. [L] Cap. III, v.

Fernández (José). *Vida del P. Pedro Claver.* Saragossa, 1666. Cap. XI, v.

Fernández (Juan). *Relación cierta y breve de los desasosiegos sucedidos en Perú después de la muerte del Sr. Virrey D. Antonio de Mendoza . . . por el licenciado Juan Fernández.* Printed in *Colección de documentos inéditos del Archivo de Indias,* Vol. III, p. 246, *q.v.* Cap. III, viii.

Fernández (Juan Patricio). *Relación historial de las misiones de los indios que llaman chiquitos.* Madrid, 1726. [L]

[Fernández (Juan Patricio): *cont.*]

— — Printed in *Colección de libros que tratan de América raros o curiosos*, Vol. XII, *q.v.* Cap. XIII, vi.

Fernández Campino (José). *Relación del obispado de Santiago de Chile.* MS. (1744). Cap. XVI, iv.

Fernández de Enciso (Martín). *Suma de geografía.* Seville, 1519. [L]

— *Descripción de las Indias Occidentales . . . Sacada de la "Suma de geografía," por J. T. Medina.* Santiago de Chile, 1897. [L] Cap. II, iii.

Fernández de Madrid (José). *Ensayo analítico sobre la naturaleza, causas y curación, . . . de la calentura amarilla de América, etc.* Habana, 1821. [L]

— *Memoria sobre el comercio del tabaco de esta isla (Cuba).* Habana, 1821. [L]

— *Memoria sobre el influjo del clima de la Habana.* Habana, 1824. [L]

— *Poesías* (2nd edition). London, 1828. [L] Cap. XVII, iii.

Fernández de Navarrete (Martín). See *Colección de documentos inéditos para la historia de España* and *Colección de viajes y descubrimientos . . . del siglo XV.*

Fernández de Oviedo y Valdés (Gonzalo). *De la natural historia de las Indias.* Toledo, 1526. [L]

NOTE.—This work is often referred to by its sub-title, *Sumario de la natural y general historia de las Indias, etc.*

— — Printed in *Bib. de aut. esp.*, Vol. XXII, *q.v.*

— — Printed by González Barcia (A.) in *Historiadores primitivos de las Indias.* Vol. I, *q.v.* Cap. II, ii.

— *The hystorie of the West Indies.* Included in *The Decades of the Newe Worlde, etc.*, by Peter Martyr of Angleria. Translated into English by Richard Eden. London, 1555. [L]

— *Extracts of G. F. de O. his Summarie and Generall Historie of the Indies.* Printed in *Purchas his Pilgrimes*, Pt. 3, *q.v.*

— *La historia general de las Indias.* Pt. I (Books 1–19), and *Libro último de los infortunios y naufragios, etc.* (part of Book 50 from Pt. 3). Seville, 1535. [L]

— *Libro XX de la segunda parte de la historia general, etc.* (*i.e.* Book 1 of Pt. 2.) Valladolid, 1557. [L]

— *Historia general y natural de las Indias.* Edited with introduction, notes, and a life of the author by J. Amador de los Ríos

[Fernandez de Oviedo y Valdés (Gonzalo): *cont.*] and published by the Real Academia de la Historia, 4 vols. (50 books in 3 parts). Madrid, 1851–55. [L]

Fernández de Piedrahita (Lucas). *Historia general de las conquistas del Nuevo Reino de Granada.* 1st part. Antwerp, 1688. [L]. No more published.

— — Reprinted. Bogotá, 1881. [L] Cap. VII Cap. X, ii., Cap. XI, iv.

Fernández de Quirós (Pedro). *Historia del descubrimiento de las regiones austriales.* Published by Justo Zaragoza in *Biblioteca hispano-ultramarina.* 3 vols. Madrid, 1876-82.

— *The voyages of Pedro Fernández de Quiros, 1595–1606.* Transl. by Sir C. R. Markham, Hakluyt Society, 1904. [L]

— [Several short *Memoriales*, by or on P. F. de Q. Published in *Colección de documentos inéditos del Archivo de Indias.* Vol. V, *q.v.*] Cap. X, x.

Fernández Espino (José María). *Curso histórico-crítico de literatura española.* Seville, 1871. [L]

Fernández Ortelano (Manuel). *Ensalada poética jocoseria, etc.* M.S. Full account given by Medina in *Lit. col. de Chile.* Cap. XVII, iii.

Feuillée (Louis). *Journal des observations physiques mathématiques et botaniques, faites . . . sur les côtes orientales de l'Amérique méridionale, et dans les Indes occidentales, depuis l'annee 1707 jusques en 1712.* 2 vols. Paris, 1714. [L]

— See also Frezier (A. F.) Cap. XII, i.

Figueroa (P. Córdoba y). See Córdoba y Figueroa (P.).

Fleuriau (Bertrand Gabriel). *La vie du vénérable père Claver de la Compagnie de Jésus.* Paris, 1751, 1830, Liège, 1851.

— *The life of the Ven. Father Claver.* From the French of B.G.F., contained in Faber (F. W.). *The Saints and Servants of God.* London, 1847, etc. [L] Cap. XI, v.

Flórez de Ocáriz (Juan). *Las genealogías del Nuevo Reino de Granada.* Vols. I and II. Madrid, 1674 and 1676. [L]. Vol. III unpublished. See Vergara y Vergara, *Hist. de la lit. en Nueva Granada.* Cap. XI, v.

Frezier (Amédée François). *Relation du voyage de la Mer du Sud, aux côtes du Chily et du Pérou, fait pendant les années 1712, 1713 and 1714, etc.* Paris, 1716. [L]

— — Another edition containing *Mémoire touchant l'établissement des*

[Frezier (Amédée François) : *cont.*]

Pères Jésuits dans les Indes d'Espagne. 2 vols. Amsterdam, 1717. [L]

— — Another edition with a reply to the critical preface of L. Feuilleé in his book, *Journal des observations, etc.* Paris, 1732. [L]. See Feuillée (Louis).

— *A Voyage to the South Sea and along the coasts of Chili and Peru in . . .1712, 1713 and 1714.* Trans. from the French. With an account of the settlement of the Jesuits in Paraguay, London, 1717. [L]

— *Relación del viaje por el mar del sur a las costas de Chile y el Perú durante los años de 1712, 1713 y 1714.* Trans. from 1st French edition by M. Nicolás Peña. Santiago de Chile, 1902. [L] Cap. XII, i.

Fritz (Samuel). *El gran río Maranón o Amazonas con la misión de la Compañía de Jesús geográficamente delineado etc.* Engraved by P. Juan de Narváez, Quito, 1707. A facsimile of this map is in the British Museum and is also contained in :—

— *Journal of the travels and labours of Father Samuel Fritz in the river of the Amazons between 1686 and 1723.* Translated from the Evora MS. and edited by George Edmundson. Hakluyt Society, London, 1922.

NOTE.—The title of the MS. is *Misión de los Omaguas, Jurimaguas, Aysuares, Ibanomas y otras naciones desde Napo hasta el Río Negro.* The author is unknown. Cap. XI, vii.

Fuentes (Manuel Atanasio) Ed. *Memorias de los virreyes que han gobernado el Perú durante el tiempo del coloniaje español.* 6 vols. Lima, 1859. [L]

— See also *Mercurio peruano.*

Gaceta de Lima. Lima, 1744—1767. See facsimile of first issue and account of others publ. John Carter Brown Library, Brown University, Providence, Rhode Island. [L] See also Medina (J. T.) *La imprenta en Lima,* Vol II.

— New journal issued to counteract the influence of the French revolution. Lima, 1793–95. Cap. XVII, iv

García (Ignacio). *Desengaño consejero.* Lima, 1754.

— *Respiración del alma en afectos píos.* Lima, 1755.

— *Cultivo de las virtudes en el paraíso del alma.* Barcelona, 1759. Cap. XIV, iv.

García Sanz (Monseñor). *Historia eclesiástica.*

— [A compendium of José de Buendía's *Vida del V. P. Francisco del Castillo.*] See Buendía (J. de). See also Medina, *Biblioteca hispanoamericana*

García y García (José Antonio). See *Relaciones de los virreyes del Nuevo Reino de Granada.*

Garcilaso de la Vega, el Inca. *Los comentarios reales.* Pt. 1. Lisbon, 1609. [L]. Pt. 2. Córdoba, 1617. [L]

— — Printed in *Colección de historiadores clásicos del Perú.* Vols. I *et seq.* Lima, 1918 etc. [Vols. I–V in L.]

— — Printed in *Historia de la conquista del Nuevo Mundo, q.v.*

— *The Royal Commentaries of Peru, in two parts, etc.* Rendered into English by Sir P. Rycaut. London, 1688. [L]

— *Observations of Things most remarkable, collected out of the first part of the Commentaries Royall, written by the Inca G. de la Vega, etc. The Supplement of the History of the Incas, briefly collected out of the author's second part.* Publ. in *Purchas his Pilgrimes,* Pt. IV, *q.v.*

— *The Royal Commentaries of the Yncas of Peru.* Part I. Trans. and ed. by Sir C. Markham. Hakluyt Society, 2 vols. London, 1869. [L] Extract from Part II also trans. by Sir C. M. and publ. in *Expeditions into the Valley of the Amazons. q.v.*

— *Le commentaire royal ou l'histoire des Yncas, Roys du Pérou, etc.* Trans. by Jean Baudouin from Pt. I of the *Comentarios reales.* Paris, 1633. [L]

— — A revised and illustrated edition including a translation by J. Baudouin of *La Florida del Inca.* 2 vols. Amsterdam, 1737. [L]

— *Histoire des guerres civiles des Espagnols dans les Indes.* Trans. by Jean Baudouin from Pt. II of the *Comentarios reales.* Paris, 1650.

— — Revised edition published in Amsterdam, 1706. [L]

— *La Florida del Inca; historia del adelantado Hernando de Soto, gobernador y capitán-general del reino de la Florida, y de otros heroicos caballeros españoles e indios.* Lisbon, 1605. [L]

— — Printed in *Historia de la conquista del Nueva Mundo, q.v.*

— — Edited by Gabriel de Cárdenas (*i.e.*Andrés González de Barcia), and containing G. de C.'s *Ensayo cronológico para la historia general de la Florida.* Madrid, 1723. [L]

— *Histoire de la Floride, ou relation de ce qui s'est passé au voyage de F. de Soto, etc.* Translated by P. Richelet. 2 pts. Paris, 1670. [L]

— *Geschichte der Eroberung von Florida.* Trans. from the French version by H. L. Meier, Leipzig, 1753. Cap. IV, ii.

Garzón de Tahuste (Alonso). *Sucesión de prelados y jueces seculares del Nuevo Reino de Granada. MS.*

— *Historia antigua de los Chibchas.* M.S.

Both MSS. said to be lost. See Vergara y Vergara. *Hist. de la lit. en Nueva Granada.* Cap. X, ix.

Gay (Claudio). *Historia física y política de Chile*. 24 vols. *Historia*, 6 vols; *Botánica*, 8 vols; *Zoología*, 8 vols; *Documentos*, 2 vols. Paris, 1844–54. [L]

— — *Atlas*. 2 vols. Paris, 1854. [L] Cap. XVI, iii.

Gayangos (Pascual de). *Memorial histórico-español*. 4 vols. Madrid, 1860–63.

Ginés de Sepúlveda (Juan). See Casas (B. de las). Cap. II, i.

Gobeo de Victoria (Pedro). *Relación del naufragio y peregrinaciones en las costas del Perú; viajes y riesgos que tuvo en él con sus compañeros*. Seville, 1610. Cap. X, x.

Gómez de Vidaurre (Felipe). *Historia geográfica, natural y civil, del reino de Chile*. Published by J. T. Medina. 2 vols. Santiago de Chile, 1889. [L] Cap. XVI, iv.

Góngora Marmolejo (Alonso de). *Historia del reino de Chile . . . hasta el año de 1575*. First printed by Pascual de Gayangos in *Memorial histórico-español*, Vol. IV, *q.v.*

— — Reprinted by Barros Arana in *Colección de historiadores de Chile*. Vol. II, *q.v.* Cap. IV, vi.

González de Acuña (Antonio). *Compendium vitae admirabilis et pretiosae mortis B. Rosae de S. Maria limensis peruanae. . . . Ex prolixiore vita a P. Leonardo Hansen anno superiore edita contractum*. Rome, 1665.

— *La vie de la bienheureuse épouse de Jésus Christ, Soeur Rose de Sainte Marie, etc.* Trans. from the Latin by J. B. Feuillet. Paris, 1668. [L].

— *Rosa mística. Vida y muerte de Santa Rosa de S. María Virgen*. Rome, 1671.

— *Life of St. Rose of Lima*. Trans. from French of J. B. Feuillet. Publ. by F. W. Faber in *The Saints and Servants of God*. London, 1847. [L] Cap. XI, i.

González de Agüeros (Pedro). *Descripción historial de Chile*. Madrid, 1791. [L] Cap. XVI, iv.

González de Barcia Carballido y Zúñiga (Andrés) Ed. *Historiadores primitivos de las Indias occidentales*. 3 vols. Madrid, 1749. [L]

— (Under pseudonym of Gabriel de Cárdenas). *Ensayo cronológico para la historia general de la Florida . . . desde el año 1512 . . . hasta el de 1722*. Printed with G. de B.'s edition of Garcilaso de la Vega's *La Florida del Inca*. Madrid 1723. [L].

— — Printed in *Historia de la conquista del Nuevo Mundo*, *q.v.*

— See also Schmidel. (U.)

González de Bustos (Francisco). *Los españoles en Chile.* Printed in *Primera parte de comedias escogidas.* Vol. XXXVI, *q.v.* Cap. VI, iv.

González de Nájera (Alonso). *El desengaño y reparo de la guerra del reino de Chile.* Published by J. T. Medina. Santiago de Chile, 1889. [L]

— — Printed in *Coleccion de documentos inéditos para la historia de España,* Vol. XLVIII, *q.v.* Cap. IX, i.

González Gutiérrez (Juan). *Semana espiritual con meditaciones del principio y fin del hombre para cada día, y documentos de oración.* Madrid, 1656. Cap. XIV, iv.

González Holguín (Diego). *Gramática y arte nueva de la lengua general de todo el Perú, llamada lengua quichua o lengua del Inca.* Ciudad de los Reyes (Lima), 1607.

— — Repub. in emended edition, Genoa, 1842. [L] Cap. IV, i.

González Laguna (Francisco). *Celo sacerdotal para con los niños no-nacidos.* Lima, 1781.

— *Necesidad de la historia natural científica.* Published in *Mercurio peruano,* 1794. Vol X, *q.v.*

— *Memoria de las plantas extrañas que se cultivan en Lima, etc.* Published in *Mercurio peruano* (1794). Vol. XI, *q.v.*

Note.—Fr. G. L. also contributed to the *Mercurio peruano* under the pseudonym Thimeo. Cap. XVII, v.

González Suárez (Federico). *Un escritor colombiano del tiempo de la colonia.* An article on Basilio Vicente de Oviedo publ. in *La República del Sagrado Corazón de Jesús.* Quito, 1890. Cap. XII, ii.

Gorrido (José). See Mera (Juan León), *Ojeada histórico-crítica sobre la poesía ecuatoriana.* Cap. XVII, iii.

Groussac (Paul). Ed. *Publicación de documentos relativos al Río de la Plata.* Published in *Anales de la biblioteca.* (Buenos Aires) *q.v.*

Gruesso (José María). *Las noches de Geussor.* MS. dated Santafé de Bogotá, 1804. See Vergara y Vergara, *Hist. de la lit. en Nueva Granada.* Cap. XVII, iii.

Guevara (José). *Historia del Paraguay, Río de la Plata y Tucumán.* Printed in *Anales de la Biblioteca* (Buenos Aires), Vols. V and VI, *q.v.*

— — Printed by P. Angelis in *Colección de Obras . . . rel. a la hist. . . . del Río de la Plata.* Vol. II, *q.v.* Cap. XIII, iv.

— — Printed by R. Diaz de Guzmán in *Historia argentina.* Vol. I, *q.v.*

Gumilla (José). *El Orinoco ilustrado*. Madrid, 1741. [L] Cap. XII, v.

Gutiérrez (Juan María). *Estudios biográficos y críticos*. Buenos Aires, 1865. [L]

Haenke (Thaddeus). *Introducción a la historia natural de la provincia de Cochabamba y circunvecinas, etc.* (written in 1798). MS. in Real Acad. de la Hist., Madrid.

— *Memoria sobre los ríos navegables que fluyen al Marañón, etc.* (Written in 1799.)

— *Descripción geográfica, física e histórica de las montañas habitadas de la nación de indios yuracarées, etc.*

NOTE.—The above three works were first published integrally by P. Groussac in *Anales de la biblioteca*, (Buenos Aires). Vol. I, *q.v.*

— *On the navigable rivers which flow into the Marañon etc.* Printed in *Explorations made in the valley of the River Madeira from 1749-1868. q.v.*

— *Descripción del Perú.* First published by the Biblioteca Nacional del Perú. Lima, 1901. [L] MS. in British Museum.

NOTE.—The volume also contains the *Memoria sobre los ríos . . . que fluyen al Marañón.*

— *Descripción del reino de Chile.*

— *Observaciones sobre el volcán de Arequipa.*

— *Estudios de las aguas termales de Yura.*

— *Artículos sobre el molle y sobre un arbusto alcanforado.*

— *Itinerario de Oruro a Jujui.*

— *Planos de Chulamani y Omasuyos.* MS. in British Museum.

— *Reliquiae Haenkeanae seu descriptiones et icones plantarum, quas in America Meridionali et Boreali, in insulis Phillipinis et Marianis collegit T. H.* 5 Fascicules. Prague, 1825–1830. [L]

— — Vol. II. 2 Fascicules. Prague, 1831-35. [L]

— See also Ballivián (M. V.) and Kramer (P.), *Tadeo Haenke, Escritos, etc.* Cap. XVII, vii.

Hakluyt (Richard). *The principall navigations, voiages and discoveries of the English nation, etc.* London, 1589. [L] 3 vols. London, 1598–1600. [L] 12 vols., Glasgow, 1903–5. [L] Cap. VI, iii.

Hansen (Leonardus). *Vita mirabilis et mors pretiosa venerabilis Sororis Rosae de S. Maria limensis, etc.* Rome, 1664. See also González de Acuña (A.)

Harrisse (Henry). *Bibliotheca americana vetustissima.* Description of works relating to America published between 1492 and 1551. Paris, 1866–72. [L]

Herize y Salinas (Martín de). *Felices progresos que las armas de Su Majestad han conseguido en el reino de Chile . . . 1657–1658.* Lima, 1658.

— — Reprinted in *Colección de libros españoles raros o curiosos.* Vol. XIII. *q.v.*

Hernández (Pablo). *El extrañamiento de los Jesuitas del Río de la Plata y de las misiones del Paraguay.* Printed in *Colección de lib. y doc. ref. a la hist. de Amér.* Vol. VII, *q.v.*
Cap. XIII, v.

Hernández Girón (Francisco). See *Rebelión de F. Hernández Girón.*

Herrera (Pablo). *Ensayo sobre la historia de la literatura ecuatoriana.* Quito, 1860. Quoted frequently by Medina in *Hist. de la lit. col. de Chile.*

Herrera Tordesillas (Antonio de). *Historia general de los hechos de los castellanos en las islas y tierra firme del mar océano . . . cuatro decadas* [1492–1531] and *Descripción de las Indias occidentales.* Madrid, 1601. [L]. *Decadas* 5–8 [1532–1554]. Madrid, 1615. [L]

— — Complete work edited by Andrés González de Barcia. 4 vols. Madrid, 1730 (?) [L]

— *Histoire générale des voyages et conquêtes des Castillans dans les îles et terre-ferme des Indes Occidentales.* Trans. by N. de la Costa. 3 vols. Paris, 1660–71. [L]

— *The General History of the Vast Continent and Islands of America, commonly called the West Indies, from the First Discovery thereof, etc.* Trans. by Capt. John Stevens. 6 vols. London, 1725–26. [L]

— *Descripción de las Indias occidentales.* Included in *Historia general, etc. v. supra.*

— *Description des Indes Occidentales, qu'on appelle aujourdhui le Nouveau Monde. Par A. de H.* Amsterdam, 1622. [L]

— *A description of the West Indies.* Printed in *Purchas his Pilgrimes,* Pt. 3. See Purchas (S). See also Churchill (A.) and (J.). *Collection of Voyages and Travels, etc.,* Vol V.

— *Beschreibung dero Insulen und dess festen Landes dess hohen oder grossen Meers, so man nennet West Indien.* Published by T. de Bry, *Amerika, Theil XII, q.v.*

— *Descriptio Indiae Occidentalis.* Published by T. de Bry in *Americae Pars XII, q.v.*

— *The Voyage of Francisco de Orellana down the River*

[Herrera Tordesillas (Antonio de): *cont.*]
of the Amazons A.D. 1540–41. Transl. from the Sixth Decade of A. de H.'s *General History of the Western Indies.* Published by Sir Clements Markham in *Expeditions, etc., q.v.* Cap. XVI, ii.

Historia de la conquista del Nuevo Mundo. 9 vols. Madrid, 1829. [L]
NOTE.—This contains:—Vol I, *Historia de la conquista de Méjico, etc.,* by Antonio de Solís; Vols. II to V, *Los comentarios reales* by Garcilaso de la Vega; Vols. VI, VII, *La Florida del Inca,* by Garcilaso de la Vega; Vols. VIII and IX, *Ensayo cronológico* by Gabriel de Cárdenas.

Historiadores de Indias. See Serrano y Sanz (M.)

Holguín. See González Holguín (Diego de).

Huneeus Gana (Jorge). *Cuadro histórico de la producción intelectual de Chile.* Printed in *Biblioteca de escritores de Chile.* Vol. I, 24. *q.v.* Cap. VI, i.

Hurtado de Mendoza (Jerónimo). [Poems, one of which is quoted by J. T. Medina in *Hist. lit. col. de Chile.* Vol. I, pp. 420–23 and p. 251 note.] Cap. XVII, iii.

Ibáñez (Pedro). See *Biblioteca de historia nacional* and *Relaciones de mando.*

Irisarri (Fermín de). *Vida de Alloza.* Madrid, 1715. Cap. XIV, iv.

Jerez (Francisco de). *Conquista del Perú. Verdadera relación de la conquista del Perú y provincia del Cuzco.* Seville, 1534. [L] Salamanca, 1547. [L]
— — Printed by González de Barcia (A.), in *Historiadores primitivos, etc,* Vol. III, *q.v.*
— — Printed in *Bib. de aut. esp.* Vol. XXVI, p. 319. *q.v.*
— *Libro primo de la conquista del Peru e provincia del Cuzco del le Indie occidentali.* Translated by Domingo de Gaztelu. Venice, 1535. [L]
— — Milan, 1535. [L]
— *Relation véridique de la conquête du Perú et de la Province de Cuzco nommée Nouvelle-Castille, etc.* Published by H. Ternaux-Compans in *Voyages, relations, etc.* Vol. IV, *q.v.*
— *A true account of the province of Cuzco, called New Castille, etc.* Translated by Sir Clements Markham in *Reports on the discovery of Peru, q.v.* Cap. III, i.

Jesuits. *Annuae litterae Societatis Jesu anni 1581 ad patres et fratres ejusdem societatis.* Rome, 1583. Such yearly letters were published in Rome, 1584, –85, –86, –89. Florence, 1600–01; Naples, 1604–07; Lyons, 1607; Antwerp, 1618; Douai, 1618; Magunza, 1618, etc., etc. [L]

[Jesuits : *cont.*]

— *Lettres édifiantes et curieuses, écrites des missions étrangères par quelques missionaires de la Compagnie de Jésus. Recueils 1–34.* Paris, 1707–76. [L]

NOTE.—Rec. 1–8 ed. by Ch. le Gobien ; 9–26 ed. by J. B. du Halde ; 27–28 ed. by L. Patouillet ; 29–30 ed. by Maréchal (?) ; 31–34 ed. by L. Patouillet.

— *Cartas edificantes y curiosas escritas de las misiones extranjeras, por algunos misioneros de la Compañía de Jesús.* Trans. from the French by Diego Davín. 16 vols. Madrid, 1753. (Vol. XVI contains matter not included in the *Lettres édifiantes et curieuses, etc.*)

— *Edifying and curious letters of some missioners of the Society of Jesus from foreign missions.* (A translation of part of the collection *Lettres édifiantes et curieuses.*) 2 vols. London, 1707–09.

— *Travels of the Jesuits into various parts of the world : compiled from their letters.* (Chiefly translated from *Lettres édifiantes et curieuses, etc.*) 2 vols. London, 1743. [L]

— *Litterae annuae provinciae Paraquariae.* Antwerp, 1636. [L]. Latin translation of *Cartas anuas.* written by order of Nicolás Durán in 1626, 1627 and signed in Tucumán on Nov. 12th, 1628.

— *Relation des insignes progrez de la religion chrestienne, faits au Paraguai. . . . 1626 et 1627.* Trans. from Latin into French by J. de Machaud. Paris, 1638. [L]. See *Litterae annuae provinciae Paraquariae,* of which this is a translation.

— See also *Bibliothèque de la Cie. de Jésus,* and Carayon (A.).

Jiménez de la Espada (Marcos). *Juan de Castellanos y su historia del Nuevo Reino de Granada.* Madrid, 1899. [L]

— Ed. *Tres relaciones de antigüedades peruanas.* Publ. by the Ministerio de Fomento. Madrid, 1879. [L]

— Ed. *Relaciones geográficas de Indias.* 4 vols. Madrid, 1881–1897. [L] Cap. VII : Cap. X, ix.

Jiménez de Quesada (Gonzalo). *Compendio historial.* MS. lost.

— *Epítome de la conquista del Nuevo Reino.* (An account using part of the material contained in *Compendio historial,* publ. by M. Jiménez de la Espada and by him attributed to G. J. de Q.) Cap. VII.

Jodar (Luis). *Vida de la V. M. Catalina María de la Concepción, fundadora del Convento de Sta. Clara de Cartagena.*

See Vergara y Vergara, *Hist. de la lit. de Nueva Granada.* Cap. XI, v.

Jolís (José). *Saggio sulla storia naturale della provincia del Gran Chaco.* Vol. I. Faenza, 1789. [L] Cap. XIII, v..

Juan y Santacilla (Jorge) and Ulloa (Antonio de). *Noticias secretas de América.* 2 pts. London, 1758. [L]

— See also Ulloa (A. de), *Relación histórica, etc.* Cap. XII, i

Juárez (Gaspar). *Historia eclesiástica del virreinato de Buenos Aires.* MS.

— *Historia natural de Buenos Aires.* MS. Cap. XIII, v.

Jufré del Aguila (Melchor). *Compendio historial del descubrimiento, conquista y guerra del reino de Chile.* Lima, 1630.

— — Reprinted, with life of author by D. Barros Arana, by the University of Chile. Santiago, 1897. [L] Cap. IX, iv.

Julián (Antonio). *La perla de América, Provincia de Santa Marta, reconocida, observada y expuesta en discursos históricos.* Madrid, 1787. [L]

— *Historia geográfica del río Magdalena, etc.* MS. Cap. XII, vi.

Kelly (James Fitzmaurice-). *A History of Spanish Literature.* Forms Vol. V. of *Short Histories of the Literatures of the World*, ed. by E. W. Gosse. London, 1898. [L]

— *Historia de la literatura española, tercera edición, corregida.* Madrid, 1921. [L]

— *Litterature espagnole . . . 2e édition, refondue et augmentée.* Paris, 1913. [L]

Kelly (Julia Fitzmaurice-). *El Inca, Garcilasso de la Vega.* The Hispanic Society of America, London, 1921. [L] Cap. IV, ii.

Klunzinger (Carl). *Antheil der Deutschen an der Entdeckung von Südamerika.* Stuttgart, 1857. [L]. Founded on Federmann (Nicolaus), *Indianische Historia, q.v.*

La Condamine (Charles Marie de). *Relation abrégee d'un voyage fait dans l'intérieur de l'Amérique Méridionale . . . en descendant la Rivière des Amazones.* Paris, 1745. [L] Cap. XI, vii.

Lacunza (Manuel). *La venida del Mesías en gloria y majestad, por Juan Josafat Ben-Ezra* (pseud.). 3 vols. Mexico, 1825. [L] Cap. XIV, iv.

Laguna (Francisco González). See González Laguna (F.).

Larrea (Joaquín) and (Ambrosio). [Poetry in Italian. See J. L. Mera, *Ojeada histórico-crítica sobre la poesía ecuatoriana*, where several of their poems are printed. Cap. XVII, iii.

Las Casas. See Casas (Bartolomé de las).

Lasso de la Vega (Gabriel). See Lobo Lasso de la Vega (G.)

Lasso de la Vega (García) El Inca. See Garcilaso de la Vega, el Inca.

Lavarden (Juan Manuel de). *Invocación al Paraná*. First printed in the *Telégrafo mercantil*, Num. I. Buenos Aires, 1801, *q.v.*

— *Sátira*. Printed in account of Lavarden's life and writings. See Gutiérrez (J. M.), *Estudios biográficos*.

— *Siripo* (a drama). Acted for the first time in 1789. Second act preserved and printed by J. M. Gutiérrez, in his *Estudios biográficos*, *q.v.* Cap. XVII, iii.

Lecuanda (José Ignacio). *Discurso sobre el destino que debe darse a la gente vaga de Lima*. A series of articles publ. in *Mercurio peruano*, Vol. X, *q.v.* Other articles, many of them topographical, in Vols. VIII–XII. Cap. XVII, v.

León (Gregorio de). *Mapa de Chile*. Said to have been printed, but no copies known to exist. See Medina, *Lit. col. de Chile*, Vol. II, p. 170. Cap. IX, vii.

León Pinelo (Antonio de). *Discurso sobre la importancia, forma y disposición de la recopilación de leyes de las Indias*. Madrid, 1624.

— *Política de las grandezas y gobierno del supremo y real consejo de las Indias*. Madrid, 1625. [L]

— *Epítome de la biblioteca oriental y occidental, náutica y geográfica*. Madrid, 1629. [L]

— — New edition publ. by González de Barcia. Madrid, 1737–38. [L]

— — Facsimile reprint. Buenos Aires, 1919. [L]

— *Tratado de confirmaciones reales de encomiendas, oficios y casos en que se requieren para las Indias*. Madrid, 1630. [L]

— *Diálogos de la pintura, etc.* Madrid, 1633.

— *Vida del ilustrísimo y reverendísimo don Toribio Alfonso Mogrovejo, arzobispo de, etc. Lima*. Madrid 1653. [L]

— *Aparato político de las Indias occidentales, etc.* Madrid, 1653.

— *Autos, acuerdos y decretos del gobierno del supremo y real consejo de las Indias*. Madrid, 1658. [L]

— *Rico cerro de Potosí, historia de su imperial villa*. MS.

— *Bulario índico*. MS.

— *Anales de la insigne y coronada villa de Madrid*. MS.

[León Pinelo (Antonio de): *cont.*]
— *Fundación y grandezas históricas y políticas de la insigne Ciudad de los Reyes.* MS.
— *El paraíso en el nuevo mundo, comentario apologético, historia natural y peregrina de las Indias occidentales, islas, etc.* MS.
— *El Gran Canciller de las Indias.* MS.
— *Patriarcado de las Indias, historia eclesiástico-política del Nuevo Mundo.* MS.

NOTE.—All these MSS. in Biblioteca del Palacio Real, Madrid.
Cap. XIV, iv. Cap. XV, iii.

León Pinelo (Diego de). *Contestación al memorial de Juan de Padilla.* Lima, 1660. [L]
The answer was compiled and printed at the command of the Duke of Alba, Viceroy of Peru, and gives Padilla's document in sections, each separate complaint being met by a suggested remedy. Cap. XV, iii.

León Pinelo (Juan de). *El martirio de los que han padecido en las Indias por la fe.* Madrid, 1639.
— *Viajes de los galeones de las Indias en 1607, con descripción de los puertos en que entraron.* Madrid, 1633.
— *Parecer sobre la pintura.* Madrid, 1633.
— *El prudente confesor.* Valencia, 1645.
— *Vida de Santa Margarita.* Madrid, 1629.
— *El predicador de las gentes, San Pablo.* Madrid, 1638.
— *Ciencia, preceptos y obligaciones de los predicadores.* Madrid, 1638.
— *Panegírico de Felipe IV.* Madrid, 1639.
Cap. XV, iii.

León y Bezerra (Antonio de). [An account of events in Panama during Morgan's invasion in 1670, and later. See Mendiburu, *Dic. hist. biog. del Perú.*] Cap. XI, v.

León y Garabito (Andrés de). [A pamphlet on the origin, organization, defence, etc., of the province of Río de la Plata. See Mendiburu, *Dic. hist. biog. del Perú.*] Cap. XIII, iii.

Lizárraga (Reginaldo). *Descripción y población de las Indias.* First publ. in the *Revista del Instituto Histórico del Perú,* with a prologue by C. A. Romero. Lima, 1908. [L]
— *Descripción breve de toda la tierra del Perú, Tucumán, Río de la Plata y Chile.* Printed in *Historiadores de Indias,* Vol. II, *q.v.* Cap. XIV, i.

Llano y Zapata (José Eusebio de). *Memorias histórico-físicas-críticas-apologéticas de la América Meridional.* MS. in *Bib. Nacional de Madrid,* and a copy in *Bib. Nacional de Lima.* First publ. by the Bib. Nac. de Lima, Santiago de Chile, 1904. [L]. Only 1st vol. extant.

— [A small work containing preliminary discourse to above, and some letters. Cadiz, 1759.]

— *Carta, o diario, que escribe D. J. E. de Ll. y Z. . . . en que le da cuenta de todo lo acaecido en esta capital del Perú desde el 28 de Oct. de 1646 . . . con el grande movimiento de tierra . . . hasta el 16 de Feb. de 1747, etc.* Lima, 1747. Madrid, 1748. [L]

— — Printed by Odriozola in *Terremotos, q.v.*

— *Relación del auto particular de Fe, que el Santo Oficio de la Inquisición celebró . . . el día 19 de Oct. de 1749, y breve noticia de la ruina y estrago, que padecieron la capilla y casas del Sto Tribunal el día 28 de Oct. 1746 con el grande terremoto, etc.* Lima, 1750.

— — Printed by Odriozola in *Doc. lit. del Perú.* Vol. VII, *q.v.*

— For other publications see Medina *La imprenta en Lima,* see also Mendiburu, *Dic. hist. biog. del Perú.* Cap. XVI, i.

Lobo Lasso de la Vega (Gabriel). *Primera parte de Cortés valeroso, y Mejicana.* Madrid, 1588. [L]

— — Revised edition with thirteen additional Cantos. Madrid, 1594. See Mendiburu, *Dic. hist. biog. del Perú.* Cap. VI, iv ; Cap. XVI, i.

López (El Padre). [Satirical verses. Printed in *Bosquejo histórico de la poesía chilena,* by Adolfo Valderrama, Chap. I and Appendix, *q.v.*]

— — See also Medina, *Hist. de la lit. col. de Chile.* Vol. I and appendix. Cap. XVII, iii.

López de Gómara (Francisco). *La historia de las Indias y conquista de Méjico.* 2 Pts. Saragossa, 1552. [L]. Medina del Campo, 1553. [L]. Antwerp, 1554. [L]

— — Printed in *Biblioteca de autores españoles,* Vol. XXII, *q.v.*

— *Histoire général des Indes occidentales, etc.* Translation of Pt. 1 of *La historia de las Indias, etc.,* by M. Fumée, Sieur de Marly le Chastel. Paris, 1568. [L] Cap. IV, ii.

López de Zúñiga (Francisco), Marqués de Baides. See *Relación verdadera de las paces , etc.*

López y Planes (Vicente). *El triunfo argentino.* Buenos Aires, 1808.

— — Printed by Medina in *La imprenta en Buenos Aires.* pp. 298–306, *q.v.*

Lorente (Sebastián). *Historia antigua del Perú.* 4 vols. 1860–1863. [L]

Lozano (Pedro). *Descripción corográfica del terreno, ríos, árboles, y animales de las dilatadísimas provincias del Gran Chaco, etc.* Córdoba, 1733. [L]

— *Vida del P. Julián de Lizardi.* Salamanca, 1741. Madrid, 1832.

— *Relación del terremoto que arruinó a Lima.* Printed by Odriozola in *Terremotos*, q.v.

— *Diario de un viaje a la costa de la mar magallánica desde Buenos Aires hasta el Estrecho, formado sobre observaciones de los P. P. Cardiel y Quiroga, por el P. L. en 1745.* Printed by P. Angelis in *Colección de obras . . . rel. a la hist. . . . del Río de la Plata, Vol. I. q.v.*

— *Historia de la Compañía de Jesús en la Provincia del Paraguay.* 2 vols. Madrid, 1754–1755. [L]. Madrid, 1912.

— *Historia de las revoluciones de la provincia del Paraguay, 1721–1735.* Publ. by the Junta de Historia y Numismática Americana. Buenos Aires, 1905. [L]

— *Carta al P. Juan Rico* (1740).

— *Carta al P. Bruno Morales, etc.* (dated Nov. 1, 1746) 1747 (?) [L]

— *Carta al P. Bruno Morales.* (Córdoba, March 1st, 1747.) Printed in *Cartas edificantes*, Vol. XV, p. 391. and in *Cartes édifiantes, Recueil* 27. See *Jesuits.*

— *Historia de la conquista del Paraguay, Río de la Plata y Tucumán.* Publ. by A. Lamas in *Colección de obras, documentos y noticias . . . del Río de la Plata.* Vols. I–IV, *q.v.*

— *Representación hecha por la provincia jesuítica del Paraguay al señor virrey del Perú a propósito del tratado con Portugal sobre . . . las misiones del Uruguay.* (Córdoba, 1751.) (MS. in Library at Lima.)

— *Carta al P. Juan de Alzola, sobre los Césares.* Printed by P. Angelis in *Colección de obras y documentos, etc.* Vol. I, *q.v.*

— *Diccionario histórico índico.* 6 vols. MS.

— *Representación que hace al Rey . . . el provincial de la compañia de Jesús en . . . Paraguay,* dated Buenos Aires, 1732. MS.

— *Carta al procurador general sobre lo sucedido en la provincia de Tucumán,* dated 1752. MS. Cap. XIII, iii.

Machado de Chávez (Juan). *El perfecto confesor y cura de almas.* 2 vols. Barcelona, 1641.
— See also Apolinar (Fr.). Cap. XIV iv.
Machado de Chávez (Pedro). *Discursos políticos y reformación del derecho.* MS., 1644 (?) Probably lost. Cap. XV, ii.
Manuale ad usum patrum Societatis Jesu. Printed by the Jesuit Mission in Paraguay, 1721. Cap. I.
Marín (Domingo). *Estado de las misiones en Chile.* MS. See Medina, *Lit. Col. de Chile.* Cap. XII, vii.
Mariño de Lovera (Pedro). *Crónica del reino de Chile reducida a nuevo método y estilo por el P. Bartolomé de Escobar.* Printed in *Colección de historiadores de Chile,* Vol. VI, *q.v.* Cap. IV, vii.
Markham (Sir Clements Robert), K.C.B. *Expeditions into the Valley of the Amazons. . . .* Trans. and ed. by Sir C. R. M. Hakluyt Society, London, 1859. [L]
— *Reports on the Discovery of Peru.* Trans. and ed. by Sir C. R. M. Hakluyt Society, London, 1872. [L]
— *Narratives of the Rites and Laws of the Yncas.* Trans. and ed. by Sir C. R. M. Hakluyt Society, 1873. [L]
— *The Conquest of New Granada.* London, 1912. [L]
— *Early Spanish Voyages to the Strait of Magellan.* Trans. and ed. by Sir C. R. M. Hakluyt Society, London, 1911. [L]
— *The Incas of Peru.* London, 1910. [L]
— See also: Acosta (J. de), Andagoya (P. de), Cieza de León (P. de) Enríquez de Guzmán (A.), Garcilaso de la Vega, El Inca, Simón (P.), Fernández de Quirós (P.), Sarmiento de Gamboa (P.).
Marmocchi (Francesco Cost). *Raccolta di viaggi dalla scoperta del nuovo continente fino a di nostri.* 2 vols. Prato, 1840–41. [L]
Marroquín (José Manuel). *Biografía de don Francisco Antonio Moreno.* Quoted at length by Vergara y Vergara in his *Hist. de la lit. en Nueva Granada,* pp. 251–256, *q.v.* See also *El Mosaico.* IV, No. 7. Cap. XVII, i.
Martel (Julián). *Desengaños del mundo.* See Mendiburu *Dic. hist. biog. del Perú.* Cap. XIV, i.
Matienzo (Juan?), *Gobierno del Perú.* First publ. Buenos Aires, 1910. [L]. MS. in British Museum in folio, 2 pts. Cap XV, ii.
Martínez de Bernabé (Pedro Usauro). *Reflexiones críticas político-históricas sobre los nominados Césares* (1782). MS.
— *La verdad en campaña; relación histórica de la plaza,*

[Martínez de Bernabé (Pedro Usauro): *cont.*]

puerto y presidio de Valdivia, etc. MS. (1782) See Medina, *Lit. col. de Chile.* Cap. XVI, iv.

Martínez y Vela (Bartolomé). *Anales de la villa imperial de Potosí.* Printed in *Archivo boliviano,* vol. I, *q.v.,* where the contraction Mnez is wrongly taken to represent Muñez. Cap. XVI, v.

Medina (José Toribio). *Historia de la literatura colonial de Chile.* 3 vols. Santiago de Chile, 1878. [L]

— *Colección de documentos inéditos para la historia de Chile.* Santiago de Chile, 1888–1902. [L]

— *Diccionario biográfico colonial de Chile.* Santiago de Chile, 1906. [L]

— *Historia y bibliografía de la imprenta en América española.* Publ. in *Anales del Museo de la Plata. Sección de historia americana.* La Plata, 1892. [L]

— *Biblioteca hispano-americana.* 7 vols. Santiago de Chile, 1898–1907. [L]

— *Biblioteca hispano-chilena.* 3 vols. Santiago de Chile, 1897–99. [L]

— *La imprenta en Lima.* 4 vols. Santiago de Chile, 1904. [L]

— *Notas bibliográficas sobre la imprenta en Arequipa, El Cuzco, Trujillo, Caracas, Cartagena de las Indias. Mérida de Yucatán, Oaxaca, Quito, Vera Cruz, y la imprenta del ejé:cito realista.* Santiago de Chile, 1904. [L]

— *La imprenta en Buenos Aires.* La Plata, 1892. Contained in *Historia y bibliografía de la imprenta en América española.*

— *La imprenta en Quito.* In *Notas bibliográficas, etc., v.s.*

— *La Araucana, edición del centenario.* See *Ercilla y Zúñiga (A. de)*

— *Descripción de las Indias occidentales, etc.* Extract from *Suma de geografía,* Santiago de Chile, 1897. [L] See Fernández de Enciso (M.).

— See also Mendoza Monteagudo (J. de); Ovalle (A. de); Pérez García (J.); *Pragmática sobre los diez días del año.*

Medrano (Francisco de). *Historia del Nuevo Reino de Granada.* MS. See León Pinelo (A.), *Epítome de la biblioteca oriental y occidental, etc.* Cap. XII, ii.

Meléndez (Juan). *Tesoros verdaderos de las Indias en la*

[Meléndez (Juan): *cont.*]

historia de la gran provincia de S. Juan Bautista del Perú. 3 vols. Rome, 1681–2. [L]

— *Descripción de las fiestas hechas por la beatificación de Santa Rosa.* Lima, 1622. Cap. XII, v. Cap. XIV, i.

Memoria del virrey del Perú, Marqués de Avilés, desde 1801 hasta 1806. Publ. by C. A. Romero. Lima, 1901. [L] Cap. XV, iv.

Memorias de los virreyes que han gobernado el Perú durante el tiempo del coloniaje. See Fuentes (M.A.). Cap. XV, iv.

Méndez (Andrés). *Discursos sobre la centinela del reino de Chile.* Lima, 1641. Cap. IX, vii.

Mendiburu (Manuel de). *Diccionario histórico-biográfico del Perú.* 8 vols. Lima, 1874–90. [L]

— *Apuntes históricos del Perú.* Lima, 1902. [L]

Mendieta (Alonso) Ed. See Córdoba Salinas (D. de).

Mendoza Monteagudo (Juan de). *Las guerras de Chile.* Publ. by J. T. Medina in *Colección de poemas épicos relativos a Chile o escritos por chilenos durante el período colonial.* Vol. I, *q.v.* Cap. VI, ii.

Menéndez y Pelayo (Marcelino). *Historia de la poesía hispano-americana. Obras Completas* II.–III. Madrid, 1911–1913. [L]

— *Antología de poetas hispano-americanos.* 4 vols. Madrid, 1893–5. [L]

Mera (Juan León). *Ojeada histórico-crítica sobre la poesía ecuatoriana.* Quito, 1868. 2nd ed., Barcelona, 1893. [L] Cap. XVII, iii.

Mercurio peruano, de historia, literatura y noticias públicas que da a luz la Sociedad Académica de Amantes de Lima, 12 vols. Lima, 1791–95. [L].

NOTE.—The British Museum copy contains the number for June 23, 1791 which was suppressed. See Olavarrieta (A.).

— *Biblioteca peruana de historia, ciencias y literatura.* Reprints from the *Mercurio peruano,* by M. A. Fuentes. Lima, Poissy, 1861. [L] Cap. XIV, iv.

Mesía Venegas (Alonso). *Historia de los varones insignes de la provincia del Perú de la Compañía de Jesús.* Seville, 1632(?) Cap. X, vii.

NOTE.—This notice of publication is taken from *Bibliothèque de la Compagnie de Jésus, q.v.* Fr. Escudero y Perosso in *Tipografía hispalense* makes

[Mesía Venegas (Alonso): *cont.*]
no mention of such a book. But see Medina, *Bib. hisp. amer.*, and Torres Saldamando, *Los antiguos Jesuitas del Perú.*

Millaleubu (Pancho) (pseudonym). *La Tucapelina. Decadas heroicas sobre la restauración de su misión y estreno de su Iglesia.* (1786). MS. quoted at length by J. T. Medina in *Lit. col. de Chile*, vol. I, pp. 324-333. Cap. XVII, iii.

Mira Montes Suasola (Juan de). *Armas antárticas.* MS. in *Biblioteca Nacional de Madrid.* Analysis of the poem and copious quotations in four articles entitled *Tres poemas del coloniaje*, by Felix C. C. Zegarra, in *Revista peruana*, vol. III, *q.v.* Cap. XII, iv.

Molina (Cristóbal de) (de Cuzco). *Relación de las fabulas y ritos de los incas.* First printed in the *Revista chilena de historia y geografía*, vol. V, No. 9. Santiago de Chile, 1913.

— — Republ. in *Colección de libros y documentos referentes a la historia del Perú*, Vol. I, *q.v.*

— *The Fables and Rites of the Yncas.* Trans. from the original Spanish MS. by Sir C. R. Markham, and included in *Narratives of the Rites and Laws of the Yncas*, *q.v.* Cap. IV, iv.

Molina (Cristóbal de) (de Santiago). *Relación de la conquista y población del Perú.* First printed in *Sud-América.* Santiago de Chile, 1873.

— — Printed in *Colección de documentos inéditos para la historia de Chile* vol. VII, *q.v.*

— — Printed in *Colección de libros y documentos referentes a la historia del Perú*, vol. I, *q.v.*

— *Diario de la expedición de Almagro.* Cap. III, iv.

Molina (Juan Ignacio). *Compendio della storia geografica, naturale, e civile del regno de Chili.* Bologna, 1776. (A first sketch).

— *Saggio sulla storia naturale del Chili.* Bologna, 1782. [L]

— *Saggio sulla storia civile del Chile, etc.* Bologna, 1787.

— *Compendio de la historia civil del reino de Chile, etc.* Part II. Trans. into Spanish with additional notes by Nicolás de la Cruz y Bahamonde. Madrid, 1795.

— *Compendio de la historia geográfica, natural y civil del reino de Chile. etc.* Part I. Trans. into Spanish by Domingo Joseph de Arquellada y Mendoza. Madrid, 1788.

— — Another translation by Narciso Cueto publ. in *Colección de historiadores de Chile.* Vol. XI, *q.v.*

— *The geographical, natural and civil history of Chili*: translated from the original Italian. 2 vols. London, 1809. Cap. XVI, iv.

Mondschein (Johannes). *Ulrich Schmidel's Reise nach Süd-Amerika in den Jahren 1534–1554.* Straubing, 1893. [L]

Montalvo (Francisco Antonio de). *El sol del nuevo mundo etc.* Rome, 1683. [L] Cap. IX, v.

Montalvo (José Miguel). *El Zagal de Bogotá.* Play produced beginning of 19th cent. Bogotá. See Vergara y Vergara, *Hist. de la lit. en Nueva Granada.* Cap. XVII, iii.

Montesinos (Fernando). *Ofir de España. Memorias historiales y políticas del Péru. Vaticinios de su descubrimiento y conversión por los reyes católicos, etc.* First part containing 3 books. MS. lost.

— *Memorias antiguas historiales y políticas de Perú.* The 2nd book of above publ. by M. Jiménez de la Espada in *Colección de libros españoles raros o curiosos.* Vol. XVI, *q.v.*

— *Mémoires historiques sur l'ancien Pérou.* The above mentioned 2nd book trans. into French and published by H. Ternaux-Compans in *Voyages, relations, etc.* Vol. XVII, *q.v.*

— *Auto de la Fe celebrado en Lima a 23 de enero de 1639.* Madrid, 1640. [L] Cap. X, x.

Morelli (Cyriacus). See Muriel (Domingo).

Moreno (Gabriel). *Almanaque peruano y guía de forasteros.* 11 issues. Lima, 1799–1809.

— [Wrote also for *Mercurio peruano.* See Mendiburu, *Dic. hist. biog. del Perú*] Cap. XVII, v.

Moreno (José Ignacio). *Exhortación a la sumisión y concordia que hizo a sus feligreses en el día 10 de Mayo. . . . J. I. M. a consequencia de la proclama del . . . virrey del Perú, etc.* (With the proclamation). Lima, 1812. [L].

— *Refutación al papel titulado abuso del poder contra las libertades de la iglesia. Escrita por un verdadero católico.* Lima, 1831. [L]

— *Ensayo sobre la supremacía del Papa.* Lima (?), 1836. See Medina, *La imprenta en Lima*; also Mendiburu, *Dic. hist. biog. del Perú*; also *Mercurio peruano,* Vol. VIII, p. 280. Cap. XVII. v.

Moreno (René). *Bolivia y Perú; Notas históricas y bibliográficas.* 2nd edition. Santiago de Chile. 1905.

Moreno y Escandón (Francisco Antonio). *Historia del Nuevo Reino.* MS. lost. Cap. XVII, i.

Moreno y Pérez (Pedro de). *Explicación de la plaza y puerto de Valdivia.* (1731). See Medina (J. T.) *Diccionario biográfico colonial de Chile* and *Lit. Col. de Chile.* Cap. XVI, iv.

Mosaico (El). A literary miscellany, edited by J. M. Vergara y Vergara. (Vols. 1, 2, in British Museum). Bogotá 1858, etc.

Moses (Bernard). *The Spanish Dependencies in South America.* 2 vols. London, 1914. [L]

— *The Establishment of Spanish Rule in America.* New York, 1898. [L]

— *South America on the Eve of Emancipation.* New York, 1908. [L]

— *Spain's declining power in South America, 1730–1806.* University of California, 1919. [L]

Mosquera de Figueroa (Cristóbal). *Elogio de Alonso de Ercilla.* Prefixed to 1st edition of 3rd part of *La Araucana* (Madrid, 1589) and in many subsequent editions. See Ercilla y Zúñiga (A. de) Cap. V.

Muriel (Domingo). *Historia Paraquariensis Petri Francisci Xaverii de Charlevoix ex Gallico Latina, etc.* Venice, 1779.

— *Historia del Paraguay desde 1747 hasta 1767.* Trans. from the Latin by Pablo Hernández, and published in *Colección de libros y doc. ref. a la hist. de América.* Vol. XIX, *q.v.* See also Charlevoix (P. F. X.).

— *Fasti novi orbis et ordinationum apostolicarum ad Indias, etc.* Venice, 1776. (Publ. under the name *Cyriacus Morelli.*) Cap. XIII, v.

Mutis (José Celestino). *Observaciones y conocimientos de la quina.* Published in *Mercurio peruano, 1795,* Vol. XII, *q.v.* Cap. XVII, v.

— *El arcano de la quina.* Published in part in *Papel periódico de Santafé de Bogota,* Nos. 89 et seq (*q.v.*) ; discontinued after No. 128.

Nariño (José Antonio Ignacio Vicente). *Declaración de los derechos del hombre y del ciudadano.* Published by Eduardo Posada and Dr. Pedro M. Ibáñez in *El Precursor : Documentos sobre la vida . . . del General A. N., q.v.* Cap. XVII.

Navarrete (M. Fernández de). See Fernández de Navarrete (M).

Nieremberg (Juan Eusebio). *De la diferencia entre lo temporal y eterno . . . traducido en lengua guaraní por el Padre Joseph Serrano . . .* 1st book printed by Jesuit missions in Paraguay, Las Doctrinas, 1705.

— — New edition. Madrid, 1762. [L]

— — Printed in *Colección de los mejores autores españoles.* Vol. XLIV *q.v.* Cap. I.

Nouvelles annales des voyages. See *Annales des voyages, etc.*

Novísima recopilación de las leyes de España. 6 vols. Madrid, 1805–29. [L] Cap. I.

Nueva biblioteca de autores españoles. Ed. M. Menéndez y Pelayo and others. Madrid, 1900, etc. [L]

Nueva colección de documentos inéditos para la historia de España y de sus Indias. Edited by Francisco de Zabálburu and José Sancho Rayón. 6 vols. Madrid, 1892–1896. [L] A continuation of *Colección de documentos inéditos para la historia de España, q.v.*

Nuix (Giovanni). *Reflexiones imparciales sobre la humanidad de los españoles en las Indias, contra los pretendidos filósofos y políticos.* Trans. from the Italian, by Pedro Varela y Ulloa. Madrid, 1782. [L] Cap. II, i.

Núñez Cabeza de Vaca (Alvar). *La relación que dió Alvar Núñez Cabeza de Vaca de lo acaecido en las Indias en la armada donde iba por gobernador Pánfilo de Narváez, desde el año de veinte y siete hasta el año de treinta y seis, etc.* Zamora, 1542. [L] First edition very rare. The second edition appeared as *La relación y comentarios del gobernador Alvar Núñez Cabeza de Vaca de lo acaecido en las dos jornadas que hizo a las Indias.* Valladolid. 1555. [L]

— — Printed in *Bib. de aut. esp.* Vol. XXII, *q.v.*

— — Printed in *Colección de libros y documentos referentes a la historia de América.* Vols. V, IV, *q.v.*

— — Printed by González de Barcia in *Historiadores primitivos de Indias.* Vol. I, *q.v.*

— — [Paraphrase of the work appeared in *Purchas his Pilgrimes, q.v.*]

— *The Commentaries of A. Nuñez Cabeza de Vaca.* From the original Spanish edition, 1555. Trans. with notes, etc., by Luis L. Domínguez. Publ. in *The Conquest of the River Plate.* Hakluyt Society. London, 1891. [L]

— *Commentaires d'Alvar Núñez Cabeça de Vaca . . . rédigés por P. Hernandez.* Publ. by Ternaux-Compans in *Voyages, relations, etc.* Vols. V, VI, *q.v.*

— *Relatione di cio che intervenne nelle Indie alla armata della quale era governator Pamphilo Narvaez, etc.* Translation publ. by G. B. Ramusio in *Navigationi et viaggi.* Vol. III, *q.v.* Cap. XIII, i.

Núñez de Pineda y Bascuñán (Francisco). *Cautiverio feliz y razón de las guerras dilatadas de Chile.* First publ. by D. Barros Arana in his *Colección de historiadores de Chile.* Vol. III. *q.v.* Cap. IX, ii. Cap. XI, i. Cap. XVII, iii.

Odriozola (Manuel de). *Documentos literarios del Perú.* 10 vols. Lima, 1863–77. [L]

— *Documentos históricos del Perú en las épocas del coloniaje después de la conquista y de la dependencia hasta el presente.* 2 vols. Lima, 1863–4. [L]

— *Terremotos: Colección de las relaciones de los más notables que ha sufrido esta capital y que la han arruinado.* Lima, 1863. [L]

Ojeda Gallinato (Diego). *Grandezas de Lima.* Quoted by Diego Andrés Rocha in *Origen de los indios del Peru, etc.* (*q.v.*). See Mendiburu. *Dic. hist. biog. del Perú.*

— *Fiestas de la Ciudad de los Reyes al nacimiento del príncipe, D. Felipe Andrés Próspero.* Lima, 1659. Cap. XI, iii.

Olavarría (Tomás de). *Relación, etc.* (1607). MS. Cap. IX, vii.

Olavarría (Miguel de). *Informe sobre el reino de Chile, sus indios y guerras* (1594). Printed in Claudio Gay's *Documentos.* Vol. II, *q.v.* Cap. IX, vii.

Olavarrieta (Antonio), Ed. *Semanario crítico.* Lima, 1791 (etc ?). See Medina, *La imprenta en Lima,* and Mendiburu, *Dic. hist. biog. del Perú*; see also *Mercurio peruano*: original number for June 23, 1791, immediately suppressed owing to a violent attack on Olavarrieta which it contained.

NOTE.—The British Museum copy of the *Mercurio peruano* contains (Vol. II, p. 159) this original number. Cap. XVII, v.

Oliva (Anello de la). *Vidas de los varones ilustres de la Compañía de Jesús de la Provincia del Perú.* 4 Books. The British Museum has an autograph MS. of Book I (*Libro primero y Introducción a las vidas etc.*) with the *Elogios y catálogo de algunos varones insignes en santidad de la provincia del Perú de la Compañía de Jesús . . . sacados de las vidas que van escritas en estos cuatro libros de la historia.*

— *Catálogo de algunos varones ilustres en santidad en la Provincia del Perú de la Compañía de Jesús, etc.* Seville, 1632.

— *Libro primero del manuscrito original del R. P. Anello Oliva, S.J.: Historia del reino y provincias del Perú, de sus Incas reyes, descubrimiento y conquista por los españoles de la Corona de Castilla, etc.* Published by J. F. Pazos Varela and L. Varela y Orbegoso from a MS. in the library of Dr. D. F. Varela y Valle, of Lima. Lima, 1895. [L].

See Torres Saldamando, *Los antiguos Jesuitas del Perú,* Medina, *Bib. hisp. amer.,* and *Bibliothèque de la Compagnie de Jésus.*

[Oliva (Anello de la) : *cont.*]

— *Histoire du Pérou, traduite de l'espagnol sur le manuscrit inédit par H. Ternaux-Compans.* Based on MS. in British Museum. Paris, 1857. [L]. Cap. XI, iii; Cap. XIV, iv.

Olivares (Miguel de). *Historia militar, civil y sagrada de lo acaecido en la conquista y pacificación del reino de Chile.* Pt. I. (Pt. II lost.). Publ. by Barros Arana in *Colección de hist. de Chile.* Vol. IV. *q.v.*

— *Breve noticia de la provincia de la Compañía de Jesús de Chile.* Publ. by Barros Arana in *Colección de hist. de Chile.* Vol. VII, *q.v.* Cap. XVI, ii.

Olmos (Juan de). *La vida de la Madre Jerónima del Espíritu Santo.* See Vergara y Vergara, *Hist. de la lit. en Nueva Granada.* Cap. XII, ii.

Ondegardo (Juan Polo de). See Polo de Ondegardo (J.).

Oña (Pedro de). *Canción real . . . en que se recogen las excelencias del Santo* (Francisco Solano). *Río Lima al río Tibre.* First printed in A. Mendieta's edition of *D. de Córdoba's life of San Francisco Solano, q.v.* Also quoted in full by J. T. Medina, in *Hist. de la lit. col. de Chile.* Vol. I, p. 228, *q v.*

— *Arauco domado.* Primera parte, Lima, 1596. Madrid, 1605. [L]. Valparaiso, 1849. [L]

— — *Edición crítica de la Academia Chilena . . . anotada por José Toribio Medina.* Santiago de Chile, 1917.

— *El Ignacio de Cantabria. Primera parte.* Seville, 1639. [L] Cap. VI, i.

Oré (Luis Jerónimo de). *Símbolo católico indiano etc.* Lima, 1598. [L]

— *Relación de los mártires que ha habido en la Florida.* Printed 1604–1612.(?).

— *Rituale seu manuale peruanum etc.* Naples, 1607. [L]

— *Relación de la vida y milagros del venerable padre Fr. Francisco Solano etc.* Printed apparently without title page. Madrid,(?) 1613.(?)

— *Corona de la sacratísima Virgen María.* Madrid, 1619. Cap. XIV, ii.

Orosz (Ladislaus). *Decades quatuor virorum illustrium Paraquariae.* Tyrnau, 1759.

— *Decades quatuor aliae . . . virorum illustrium Paraquariae,* Printed but not circulated. Cap. XIII, v.

Orozco (José). *La conquista de Menorca.* See Mera (J. L.) *Ojeada histórico-crítica sobre la poesía equatoriana*, where four cantos of the poem are printed. Cap. XVII, iii.

Orozco (Manuel). [XVIII Cent. Ecuadorian poet. See Mera (J. L.), *Ojeada . . . sobre la poesía equatoriana.*] Cap. XVII, iii.

Ortega Texada y Contreras (José de). *Método para auxiliar y fomentar a los indios de los reinos del Perú y Chile.* Cadiz, 1789. Cap. IX., vii.

Ortiguera (Toribio de). *Jornada del río Marañón con todo lo acaecido en ella, y otras cosas notables dignas de ser sabidas, acaecidas en las Indias Occidentales.* Printed in *Nueva bib. de aut. esp.* Vol. XV. (*Historiadores de Indias II.*) *q.v.* Cap. X, ii.

Ortiz de Morales (José). *Coronas de oro del patriarca San José, deducidas y sacadas de cuanto dijeron los evangelistas y doctores de la Iglesia.* 1713. Cap. XII, ii.

Ossorio de Paz (José). *Quinquenio sacro, las cinco palabras del Apóstol San Pablo en cinco instrumentos de David, en veneración de las llagas de Cristo, Señor Nuestro, predicados en cinco sermones sobre los evangelios de las cuatro domínicas de la cuaresma y de la domínica de pasión, etc., etc.* Madrid, 1712. Cap. XII. ii.

Ovalle (Alonso de). *Histórica relación del reino de Chile, y de las misiones y ministerios que ejercita en él la Compañía de Jesús.* Rome, 1646. [L]

NOTE.—The British Museum copy has a set of portraits entitled *Gubernatores illustres, etc.*, several other engravings, and two sets of large woodcuts numbered 1–6 and 1–12 respectively.

— — Reprinted with a biographical introduction by J. T. Medina. 2 vols. Santiago de Chile, 1897.(?)

— *Historica relatione del regno de Cile, etc.* Rome, 1646. [L]

— *An historical relation of the kingdom of Chile.* Trans. from the Spanish and publ. by Churchill (A.) and (J.), in *A Collection of Voyages and Travels, etc.* Vol. III, *q.v.*

— *Relación verdadera de las paces que capituló con el araucano rebelado el marqués de Baides, etc.* Madrid. 1642. (A continuation of the *Histórica relación*).

— — Reprinted in *Colección de libros españoles raros o curiosos.* Vol. XIII, *q.v.*

— *Memorial y carta en que el padre A. del Valle . . , representa . . . la necesidad que sus misiones tienen de sujetos, etc.* Seville, 1642. Cap. IX, v.

Oviedo (Basilio Vicente de). *Pensamientos y noticias para utilidad de curas.* 11 vols. MS. See Vergara y Vergara. *Hist. de la lit. en Nueva Granada.* Cap. XII, ii.

Oviedo (Gonzalo). See Fernández de Oviedo y Valdés (Gonzalo).

Oviedo Herrera y Rueda (Luis Antonio de). Conde de la Granja. *Vida de Sta Rosa de Santa María . . . poema heroico.* Madrid, 1711. [L]. Lima, 1867.]L]

— *Poema sacro de la Pasión de N.S. Jesu Cristo.* Lima, 1717. Cap. XI, i.

Oviedo de Baños y Sotomayor (Diego de). [Wrote an appendix in two volumes to *Recopilación castellana* with explanatory notes and a digest of cases . . . Vergara believes the book was printed. See *Hist. de la lit. en N. Granada.*]

Oviedo y Baños (José de). *Historia de la conquista y población de la provincia de Venezuela.* Part I. Madrid, 1723. [L]

— — Printed in *Biblioteca de los americanistas.* Vols. III, IV. *q.v.* Cap. XII, ii.

Padilla y Pastrana (Juan de). *Memorial del Perú.* Lima, 1660. Cap. XV, iii.

— See also León Pinelo (Diego de).

Palma (Manuel Ricardo) Ed. *Anales del Cuzco. 1600–1750.* Lima, 1901. [L] Cap. XI, vi.

Papel periódico de la Ciudad de Santafé de Bogotá. 7 vols. Bogotá, Feb. 9, 1791—Jan. 6, 1797. [L]

Pastells (Pablo). *Historia de la Compañía de Jesús en la provincia del Paraguay según los documentos originales del Archivo General de Indias, etc.* Madrid, 1912. [L]

Pastrana (Antonio José). *Jardín ameno de San José.* Lima, 1666(?).

— *Empeños del poder y amor a Dios en la admirable y prodigiosa vida del Santísimo Patriarca Joseph, esposo de la Madre de Dios.* Madrid, 1696. Cap. XIV, iv.

Pauke (Florian). *Padre Florian Pauke's Reise in die Missionen nach Paraguay, etc.* Vienna, 1829.

— *Padre Florian Baucke* (sic) *ein Jesuit in Paraguay.* Regensburg, 1870. Cap. XIII, v.

Peñafiel (Leonardo). *Disputationum theologicarum, in primam partem Divi Thomae, Tomus primus: De Deo Uno.* Lyons, 1663.

[Peñafiel (Leonardo): *cont.*]

— *Disputationes scholasticae et morales de virtute fidei divinae, deque infidelitate, haeresi, et poenis haereticorum.* Lyons, 1673.

— *Tractatus de incarnatione Verbi divini. . . . Prima editio.* Lyons, 1678. Included in *Opera*, v. infra.

— *Opera.* Vols. I–IV. Lyons, 1678. [L]. Vol. III contains *Disputationes scholasticae, etc.* Vol. IV contains *Tractatus de incarnatione Verbi Divini* here printed for first time. Cap. XIV., iv.

Peñalosa Mondragón (Benito). *Libro de las cinco excelencias del español, etc.* Pamplona, 1629. [L] Cap. III, iii.

Peña Montenegro (Alonso de la). *Itinerario para párrocos de Indios, en que se tratan las materias más particulares tocantes a ellos, para su buena administración.* Madrid, 1668. Lyons, 1678. [L]. Antwerp, 1754. [L] Cap. XV.

Peralta Barnuevo Rocha y Benavides (Pedro de). *Desvíos de la naturaleza y origen de los monstruos* (?) 1695. [L]

— *Lima triunfante.* Lima, 1708. [L]

— *Imagen política, o gobierno del virrey-obispo de Quito.* Lima, 1714. [L].

— *Observationes astronomicae, habitae Limae.* Lima, 1717

— *El Jupiter olímpico (ascribed to Peralta).* Lima, 1720(?)

— *El templo de la fama, vindicado.* Lima, 1720 (?). [L]

— *El teatro heroico.* Lima, 1720.

— *Júbilos de Lima y fiestas reales, etc.* Lima, 1723.

— *Lima fundada, o conquista del Perú. Poema heroico, etc.* 2 pts. Lima, 1723. [L]

— — Printed by Odriozola in *Colección de documentos literarios del Peru.* Vol. I. *q.v.*

— *Historia de España vindicada.* Lima, 1730. [L]

— *Pasión y triunfo de Cristo.* Lima, 1738.

— Ed. *El conocimiento de los tiempos* (*q.v.*) for, with some exceptions, the years 1721–1742.

Note.—For an account of other works see Medina, *La imprenta en Lima* and Mendiburu, *Dic. hist. biog. del Perú.* Cap. XII, iv.

Peramás (José Manuel). *De vita et moribus sex sacerdotum paraguaycorum.* Faenza, 1791. [L]

— *De vita el moribus tredecim virorum paraguaycorum.* Faenza, 1793. [L]

[Peramás (José Manuel): *cont.*]

— *Annus patiens, etc.* MS.

— *L'anno di patimenti ossia diario in cui si racconta il viaggio del P.P., etc.* Publ. by J. Boéro in *Menologio della Compagnia di Gesu.* Appendix. Vol. II. Rome, 1859.

— *Journal du P. Joseph Péramas contenant le récit des choses arrivées aux Jesuites du Paraguay en l'année de leur expulsion.* Printed by A. Carayon in *Documents inéditis concernant la Compagnie de Jésus.* Vol. XVI, *q.v.*

See Hernández (P.). *El extrañamiento de los Jesuitas del Río de la Plata.* Cap. XIII, v.

Pérez (Rafael). *La Compañía de Jesús restaurada en la República Argentina y Chile, el Uruguay y el Brasil.* Barcelona, 1901. [L]

Pérez de Menacho (Juan). *Prima summa theologiae Sancti Thomae.* 6 vols.

— *Theologiae moralis tractatus.* 2 vols.

— *Tractatus de praeceptis ecclesiae.*

— *Privilegios de la Compañía de Jesus.* 2 vols.

— *Privilegios de los Indios.*

— *Rentas eclesiásticas.*

— *Preeminencias de las iglesias catedrales respecto de sus sufragáneas.*

See Mendiburu, *Dic. hist. biog. del Perú.* Cap. XIV, iv.

Pérez García (José). *Historia general, natural y militar, civil y sagrada del reino de Chile, etc.* Published with a biographical notice by J. T. Medina. 2 vols. Santiago de Chile, 1900. [L] Cap. XVI, iii.

Pietas (Jerónimo). *Informe al rey sobre las diversas razas de indios que pueblan el territorio araucano, etc.* (1729). MS. See Medina, *Lit. col. de Chile.* Cap. IX, vii.

Pinuer (Ignacio) *Relación de las noticias adquiridas sobre una ciudad grande de españoles, que hay entre los indios, al sur de Valdivia . . . 1774.* Publ. by P. Angelis in *Colección de obras y doc. ref. a la hist. . . . del Río de la Plata.* Vol. I, *q.v.* Cap. XVI, iv.

Pizarro (Pedro). *Relacíon del descubrimiento y conquista de los reinos del Perú, hecha . . . año 1571.* Printed in *Colección de documentos inéditos para la historia de España.* Vol. V, *q.v.* Cap. III, iv.

Plaza (José Antonio de). *Memorias para la historia de la Nueva Granada.* Bogotá, 1850. [L]

Polanco de Santillana (Nicolás). *De las obligaciones de los jueces y gobernadores en los casos fortuitos.*

— *Comentario a las leyes del título primero del libro primero de la recopilación.*

Both MSS. probably lost, written circa 1647. See Medina, *Lit. col. de Chile.* Cap. XV, ii.

Polo de Ondegardo (Juan). *Relación de los fundamentos acerca del notable daño que resulta de no guardar a los indios sus fueros.* MS. in Biblioteca Nacional de Madrid. Publ. by Torres de Mendoza in *Colección de documentos inéditos del archivo de Indias.* Vol. XVII. *q.v.*

— *Los errores y supersticiones de los indios, sacados del tratado y averiguación que hizo el Licenciado Polo.* Publ. for first time in *Confesionario para los curas de indios, q.v.*

— *Relación de los adoratorios en los cuatro caminos (zeques) que salían del Cuzco.* Inserted by Bernabé Cobo in his *Historia del Nuevo Mundo, q.v.*

— *Relación del linaje de los incas y como extendieron ellos sus conquistas* (written between 1560 and 1572).

NOTE.—All these works have been published by C. A. Romero in *Colección de libros y documentos referentes a la historia del Perú.* Vols. III and IV, *q.v.*

— *Report by Polo de Ondegardo. Of the Lineage of the Yncas; and how they Extended their Conquests.* Trans. by Sir C. R. Markham and published in *Narratives of the Rites and Laws of the Yncas, q.v.*

— *Informe.* (Report made at request of Viceroy, the Count of Nieva, as to value of "encomiendas" in the kingdom of Peru, in form of a letter dated in Lima, Dec. 12th, 1561). MS.

— *De l'état du Pérou avant la conquête.* French version of above publ. by M. Ternaux-Compans in *Nouvelles annales des voyages.* Vol. CIII, *q.v.* Cap. IV, iii.

Ponce de León (Francisco). *Descripción del reino de Chile, de sus puertos, caletas, y sitio de Valdivia.* Madrid, 1644. [L]

— *Relación de los servicios que ha hecho a su majestad en los reinos del Perú el presentado Fray Ponce de León.* Madrid(?), 1632(?). [L]

— *Memorial al Rey por el reino de Chile.* MS.

— *Conquistas y poblaciones del Marañón.* MS.

See Medina, *Lit. col. de Chile.* Cap. IX, vii. Cap. XI, vii. Cap. XVI, iv.

Posada (Eduardo). See *Biblioteca de historia nacional* and *Relaciones de mando.*

— and Ibáñez (Pedro M.) *El Precursor: Documentos sobre la vida pública y privada del general Antonio Nariño.* Bogotá, 1903. [L]. See Nariño (J. A. I. V.).

Pragmática sobre los diez días del año. Lima. La Ciudad de los Reyes, 1584. First publication to be printed in S. America.

— — For facsimile reproduction see *La primera muestra tipográfica salida de las prensas de la América del sur . . . con un breve prólogo de J. T. Medina.* Santiago de Chile, 1916. [L] Cap. I.

Pragmáticas (Las) del reino; recopilación de algunas bulas . . . con todas las pragmáticas, y algunas leyes, hechas para la buena gobernación del reino, etc. Seville, 1620. [L] Cap. I.

Prescott (William Hickling). *History of the Conquest of Mexico.* 3 vols. London, 1843. [L]

— *Historia de la conquista de Méjico.* Transl. by J. Navarro. 3 vols. Mexico, 1844–46. [L]

— *History of the Conquest of Peru.* 2 vols. London, 1847. [L]

— *Historia de la conquista del Perú.* Transl. by J. García Icazbalceta and containing *Relación de la conquista del Perú* by P. Sancho (*q.v.*). 2 vols. Mexico, 1850. [L]

Primera parte de comedias escogidas de los mejores de España. Madrid, 48 pts., 1652–1704. [L]

Purchas (Samuel), the Elder. *Purchas his Pilgrimes.* In five bookes. 4 Pts. London, 1625. [L]

NOTE.—To this collection is usually added, as a fifth volume, the 4th edition of *Purchas his Pilgrimage.* London, 1626. [L]

— *Hakluytus Posthumus,* or *Purchas his Pilgrimes.* 20 vols. Glasgow, 1905–07. [L]

Quesada (Vicente G.). *La vida intelectual en la América española durante los siglos XVI, XVII, y XVIII.* Printed in *Revista de la Universidad* (Buenos Aires). Vol. XI, *q.v.*

— *Crónicas potosinas: costumbres de la edad medioeval hispano-americana.* 2 vols. Paris, 1890. [L]

Quintana (Manuel José). *Vidas de españoles célebres.* 3 vols. Madrid, 1807–33. [L]

— — Printed in *Colección de los mej. aut. esp.* Vol. XXXIV, *q.v.*

Quiroga (Jerónimo de). *Memoria de las cosas de Chile.* Extract from 1st part published in the *Semanario erudito,* Vol. XXIII (*q.v.*), under title *Compendio histórico de los más principales sucesos de la conquista y guerras del reino de Chile hasta el año de 1656.*

[Quiroga (Jerónimo de): *cont.*]

— — Printed in *Colección de historiadores de Chile*. Vol. XI, *q.v.* Cap. XI, iii.

Quiroga (José). *Observaciones astronómicas para determinar el curso del río Paraguay.* Publ. by Fernando Franceschelli. Rome, 1753.

— *Compendio del viaje Paraguay arriba hasta el Taurú que hizo y escribió el P.I.Q.* (José Quiroga). Printed in *Historia del Paraguay* in *Colección de lib. y doc. ref. a la hist de América.* Vol. XIX. p. 241, etc. *q.v.*

— See also Lozano (Pedro). Cap. XIII, v.

Ramírez (Francisco Javier). *Cronicón sacro-imperial de Chile, desde el descubrimiento y adquisición de esta gran belicosa provincia por los reyes católicos, etc.* (1805). MS. See Medina, *Lit. col. de Chile.* Cap. XII, vi.

Ramírez de Arellano (Feliciano), Marqués de la Fuensanta del Valle. See *Colección de libros españoles raros o curiosos.*

Ramusio (Giovanni Battista). *Navigationi et viaggi.* Vol. I., Venice, 1550. [L]. Vol. II., Venice, 1583. [L] Vols. I–III, Venice, 1606. [L]

Rayón (José Sancho). See *Colección de libros españoles raros o curiosos* and *Nueva colección de documentos inéditos para la historia de España.*

Rebelión de Francisco Hernández Girón en el Perú en 1553. Published in *Coleccion de libros españoles raros o curiosos.* Vol. XIII, *q.v.*

Recabarren (Martín de). *Informe al rey sobre los medios de reducir a los indios y conservar la quietud del reino.* (1739). MS. See Medina, *Lit. col. de Chile.* Cap. IX, vii.

Recopilación de leyes de los reinos de las Indias. Madrid, 1681. [L]

Relación del sitio del Cuzco y principio de las guerras civiles del Perú hasta la muerte de Diego de Almagro, 1535 a 1539. Published in *Colección de libros españoles raros o curiosos.* Vol. XIII, *q.v.*

Relaciones de los virreyes del Nuevo Reino de Granada. Ed. by José Antonio García y García. New York, 1869.

— — Reprinted with additions in *Relaciones de mando*, *q.v.* Cap. XV, iv.

Relaciones de los virreyes y audiencias que han gobernado el Perú 3 vols. Lima, 1867–72. Cap. XV, iv.

Relaciones de mando: memorias presentadas por los gobernantes del Nuevo Reino de Granada. Compiled and published by E. Posada and P. M. Ibáñez in *Biblioteca de historia nacional.* Vol. VIII. *q.v.* Cap. XV, iv.

Relaciones geográficas de Indias. Ed. by M. Jiménez de la Espada, and publ. by the Ministerio del Fomento. 4 vols. Madrid 1881–1897. [L]

Repertorio colombiano. Vols. I–XI. Bogotá, 1878–79. [L]

Revista chilena. Edited by M. L. Amunátegui and D. Barros Arana. Vols. I–IV, Santiago de Chile, 1875–79. [L]

Revista chilena de historia y geografía. Santiago de Chile, 1912, etc.

Revista del archivo general de Buenos Aires. Founded and edited by Manuel Ricardo Trelles. Vols. I–III. Buenos Aires, 1869–71. [L]

Revista de la Universidad. Buenos Aires, 1898, etc.

Revista de Quito. Quito, 1898.

Revista peruana. Founded by Mariano Felipe Paz Soldán. Lima, 1879–1880. [L]

Rezabal y Ugarte (José). *Tratado del real derecho de las medias anatas seculares y del servicio de lanzas a que están obligados los titulos de Castilla.* Madrid, 1792.

— *Biblioteca de los escritores que han sido individuos de los seis colegios mayores, etc.* Madrid, 1805. [L] Cap. XV, iv.

Ribadeneira (Pedro de). *Bibliotheca scriptorum Societatis Jesu.* Rome, 1676. [L] Cap. XIV, iv.

Rivero (Juan). *Historia de las misiones de los llanos de Casanare y los ríos Orinoco y Meta.* Bogotá. 1883. Cap. XII, v.

Rocha (Diego Andrés). *Origen de los indios del Perú, Méjico, Santa Fe y Chile.* Lima, 1681.

— — Reprinted in *Colección de libros raros o curiosos que tratan de América,* Vols. III and IV, *q.v.*

Rodríguez (Francisco Antonio). [Poems, one of which entitled *Felicitación al señor oidor doctor Nicolás Prieto y Dávila* is given in full by J. M. Vergara y Vergara in *Hist. de la lit. en Nueva Granada,* pp. 277–281.] Cap. XVII, iii.

Rodríguez (Manuel). *El Marañón y Amazonas; historia de los descubrimientos, entradas y reducción de naciones, trabajos . . . así temporales, como espirituales en las*

[Rodríguez (Manuel): *cont.*]
dilatadas montañas y mayores ríos de la América, etc. Madrid, 1684. [L] Cap. XI, vii.

Rodríguez (Manuel del Socorro). *Historia de la fundación de la enseñanza.* MS.

— [Many manuscript poems in the Biblioteca Nacional de Bogotá and other collections. Three stanzas from one of these poems, *El triunfo del patriotismo,* quoted by J. M. Vergara y Vergara in *Hist. de la lit. en Nueva Granada,* pp. 229, 230]

— Ed. *Gaceta de Santafé.* Bogotá, 1785.

— Ed. *Papel periódico de Santafé de Bogotá, q.v.*

— Ed. *El redactor americano.* Bogotá, 1806.

— Ed. *Constitución feliz.* Bogotá, 1810. Cap. XVII, iii.

Rodríguez de León (Juan). See León Pinelo (Juan de).

Rodríguez de Ocampo (Diego). *Descripción y relación del estado eclesiástico del obispado de San Francisco de Quito. . . . Año de 1650.* Printed in *Relaciones geográficas de Indias.* Vol. III Appendix I, *q.v.* Cap. X, ix.

Rodríguez Fresle (Juan). (Also known as El Carnero de Bogotá). *Conquista y descubrimiento del Nuevo Reino de Granada de las Indias occidentales del mar océano, y fundación de la Ciudad de Santa Fe de Bogotá, etc.* Publ. by F. Pérez, as part of *Semana literaria del comercio.* Bogotá, 1859. [L]. New edition. Bogotá, 1884 [L] Cap. X, ix.

Rojas (Arístides). *Historia patria; Estudios históricos; Origenes venezolanos.* Caracas, 1891, etc. [L]

— *Historia patria; Legendas históricas de Venezuela.* 2 Series. Caracas, 1890–91. [L]

— *Capítulos de la historia colonial de Venezuela.* Madrid, 1919. [L]

Rojas y Fuentes (José Basilio de). *Apuntes de lo acaecido en la conquista de Chile, desde sus principios hasta el año de 1672.* Printed in *Colección de historiadores de Chile.* Vol. XI. *q.v.* Cap. XVI, ii.

Romana y Herrera (Felipe). *Tractatus de poenitentia.* (Collection of oral lessons given in 1737 by don Antonio Joseph de Guzmán in the Colegio del Rosario of Bogotá). See Vergara y Vergara, *Hist. de la lit. en Nueva Granada.* Cap. XII, ii.

Romero (Carlos A.). Ed. *Colección de libros y documentos referentes a la historia del Perú.* Lima, 1916, etc. [L]

Rosa (José Nicolás de la). *Floresta de la Santa Iglesia Catedral de Santa Marta.* Seville, 1756. (Dedicatory preface, 1741). 2nd edition. Valencia del Cid, 1833. Cap. XII, vi.

Rosales (Diego de). *Historia general del reino de Chile, Flandes indiano.* Edited . . . by B. Vicuña Mackenna. 3 vols. Valparaiso, 1877–78. [L]

— *Historia general del reino de Chile, desde la época aborigen hasta la gran rebelión del siglo XVII.* Published by B. Vicuña Mackenna. Valparaiso, 1877. [L]

— *Conquista espiritual de Chile.* MS. Cap. IX, viii.

Ruiz (Pedro). [A pamphlet on the art of flying. Lima, 1879 See Mendiburu, *Dic. hist. biog. del Perú.*] Cap. XVII, viii.

Ruiz de Montoya (Antonio). *Conquista espiritual hecho por los religiosos de la Compañía de Jesús en las provincias del Paraguay, Paraná, Uruguay y Tape.* Madrid, 1639. [L]

— *Arte de la lengua guaraní.* Containing also *Vocabulario de la lengua guaraní*; *Tesoro de la lengua guaraní.* 2 pts. Madrid, 1639. [L]

— *Arte de la lengua guaraní . . . con los escolios, anotaciones del P. Paulo Restivo, etc.* (Without *Vocabulario* and *Tesoro*). Jesuit Missions, S. María la Mayor. Paraguay, 1724.

— *Vocabulario de la lengua guaraní.* Publ. separately by P. Restivo. Jesuit Missions, S. María la Mayor. Paraguay, 1722. Cap. I. Cap. XIII, ii.

Ruiz López (Hipólito). *Quinología, o tratado del árbol de la quina o cascarilla, con su descripción y la de otras especies de quinos nuevamente descubiertas en el Perú, etc.* Madrid, 1792. [L]

— *Memoria de las virtudes y usos de la raíz de la planta llamada yallhoy en el Perú.* Madrid, 1805. [L]

— *Memoir on the virtue and uses of the plant called Yallhoy in Peru.* Published by Lambert (A. B.) in *An illustration of the genus Chinchona, etc.* London, 1821. [L]

— *Memoria sobre la legítima calaguala y otros dos raíces que con el mismo nombre nos vienen de la América meridional.* Madrid, 1805. [L]

— *Memoir on the genuine Calaguala, etc.* Published by Lambert (A. B.) in *An illustration of the genus Chinchona, etc.* London, 1821.

— and Pavón (José). *Suplemento a la quinología, en el qual se aumentan las especies de quina nuevamente*

[Ruiz López (Hipólito) and Pavón (José): *cont.*]
descubiertas en el Perú por Don Juan Tafalla, etc. Madrid, 1801. [L]

— *Flora peruviana, et chilensis, etc.* 3 vols. Madrid, 1798–1802. [L]. (The copy in the British Museum contains 28 plates from Vol. IV, the text of which was not published.) Cap. XVII, v.

Salazar (José María). *Sacrificio de Idomeneo.*

— *Soliloquio de Eneas.*
Both produced beginning of 19th century in Bogotá. See Vergara y Vergara, *Hist. de lit. en Nueva Granada.* Cap. XVII, ii.

Sánchez (Juan Bautista). *Curso de filosofía antigua y moderna.*

— *Historia eclesiástica.*

— *De matrimonio.*

— *De la voluntad divina.*

— *La obra de los seis días.*

— *Historia de la renovación del templo de Jerusalén.*

— *Lecciones parafrásticas sobre el maestro de las sentencias.*

— *Oraciones latinas.*

— *Panegíricos y sermones morales*
See Mendiburu, *Dict. hist. biog. del Perú.* Cap. XII, vi.

Sánchez Labrador (José). *El Paraguay católico.* Pts. II and III 2 vols. Buenos Aires, 1910. [L]
(Parte segunda :—*Relación fragmentaria de los viajes desde la reducción de Nuestra Señora de Belén hasta las misiones en los chiquitos y de regreso.* Parte tercera :—*Que contiene las nociones siguientes* I. *La de los Eyiguayeguis.* II. *La de los chonas, varios viajes y diarios y una breve noticia de Cuyaba.*)

— *Paraguay natural ilustrado.* 4 parts. MS.

— *Paraguay cultivado.* 4 vols. MS. Cap. XIII, v.

Sancho (Pedro). *Relatione d'un capitano spagnuolo della conquista del Peru.* Trans. from the original Spanish MS. and publ. by Ramusio (G. B.) in *Navigationi et viaggi.* Vol. III, *q.v.*

— *Relación de la conquista del Perú.* Trans. into Spanish from the Italian by J. G. Icazbalceta and publ. by him at the end of Vol. II of his translation of Prescott's *History of the Conquest of Peru. q.v.*

— *Rescate de Atahualpa. Testimonio de la acta de repartición del rescate de Atahualpa, otorgada por el escribano P. S.* Printed in *Vidas de españoles célebres* by M. J. Quintana, *q.v.*

[Sancho (Pedro) : *cont.*]
— — Printed in *Bib. de aut. esp.*, Vol. XIX, pp. 499–501, *q.v.*
— — Printed by Mendiburu in *Dic. hist. biog. del Perú*, Vol. III, pp 377–383, *q.v.*
— *Report on the distribution of the ransom of Atahuallpa.* Translated by Sir C. R. Markham in *Reports in the Discovery of Peru, etc, q.v.*

San Martín (Tomás de). *Parecer de D. Fr. Matías* (sic) *de San Martín, obispo de Charcas, sobre si son bien ganados los bienes adquiridos por los conquistadores, pobladores y encomenderos de Indias.* Published in *Colección de documentos inéditos del Archivo de Indias q.v.*

NOTE.—The first Bishop of Charcas who wrote this memorial, the MS. of which is in Seville, is Tomás de San Martín. Owing to a copyist's error the memorial, as printed, begins : " Visto por nos Fr. *Matías* de San Martín, maestro en santa teología y obispo de Charcas, el gran escrúpulo, etc." A reply by B. de Las Casas is printed with it. Cap. III, iii.

San Nicolás (Andrés de). *Historia general de los religiosos descalzos del orden de los ermitaños . . . de San Agustín de la congregación de España y de las Indias, etc.* Vol. I. Madrid, 1664.
— — Continued by others. Three volumes more appearing as follows :—Vol II, Madrid, 1681 ; Vol. III, Barcelona, 1743 ; Vol. IV, Saragossa, 1756. See Medina, *Biblioteca hispano-americana.*
— *Imagen de N. S. de Copacabana, portento del nuevo mundo, etc.* Madrid, 1663. Cap. IX, vi.

Santa y Silva (Juan José). *El mayor regocijo en Chile para sus naturales y españoles poseedores de él.* MS. See Medina, *Lit. col. de Chile.* Cap. IX, vii.

Santistevan Osorio (Diego de). *La Araucana, cuarta y quinta partes en que se prosigue y acaba la historia de D. Alonso de Ercilla.* Salamanca, 1597. Barcelona, 1598. [L]. Madrid, 1735. [L]
— *Primera y segunda parte de las guerras de Malta, y toma de Rodas.* Madrid, 1599. [L] Cap. VI, iv.

Sarmiento de Gamboa (Pedro). *Viaje al estrecho de Magallanes . . . en los años 1579 y 1580, etc.* Madrid, 1768. [L]
— *Narratives of the voyages of P. S. de G. to the Straits of Magellan.* Transl. etc., by Sir Clements Markham. Hakluyt Society, London, 1895. [L]
— *Segunda parte de la historia general llamada índica,*

[Sarmiento de Gamboa (Pedro): *cont.*]

etc. First printed from the Original MS. in Göttingen University Library and published with introduction and notes by Richard Pietschmann. Berlin, 1906. [L]

— *History of the Incas, etc.* Trans. by Sir Clements Markham, Hakluyt Society, London, 1907. [L]

— *Sumaria relación de P. S. de G., gobernador y capitán general del estrecho de la Madre de Dios, antes nombrado de Magallanes, y de las poblaciones en él hechas y que se han de hacer por V. M.* Published in *Colección de dócumentos inéditos del Archivo de Indias*, Vol. V, *q.v.* Cap. IV, iii.

Schirmbeck (Adam). *Messis paraquariensis a patribus Societatis Jesu per sexennium in Paraquaria collecta* etc. Munich, 1649. [L] Cap. XIII, ii.

Schmidel (Ulrich). *Warhafftige und liebliche Beschreibung etlicher fürnemen Indianischen Landtschafften und Insulen, die vormals in keiner Chronicken gedacht, und erstlich in der Schiffart Ulrici Schmidts von Straubingen mit grosser Gefahr erkündigt, und von ihm selber auffs fleissigst beschrieben und dargethan.* First printed in *Neuwe Welt: Das ist Wahrhafftige Beschreibunge, etc.* Frankfort-on-Main, 1567. [L]

— — Publ. as 2nd pt. of a book of travels, edited by Sebastian Franck, under title *Erst Theil dieses Weltbuchs von newen erfundenen Landtschafften; Ander Thiel dieses Weltbuchs etc.* 2 pts. Frankfort-on-Main 1567. [L]

— — 2nd edition in Theodor de Bry's collection of voyages (*America VIIter Theil*). 1597. [L]

— — Latin trans. by Gothard Artus issued in Latin version of de Bry's Collection (*Americae Pars VII.*). Nüremberg, 1599. [L]

— *Wahrhafftige Historien einer wunderbaren Schiffart welche U.S. . . in Americam . . . gethan.* Revised and abridged edition issued by Levinus Hulsius in his collection of voyages. Nüremberg 1599. [L]

— *Vera historia admirandae cujusdam navigationis quam U.S. . . . in Americam confecit, etc.* Translation of Hulsius' revised text. Nüremberg, 1599. [L]

— *Viaje al Río de la Plata etc.* Transl. of the Hulsius text by Gabriel Cárdenas (Z. Cano) a pseudonym of Andrés González de Barcia (note the anagram), ?1731. (There is a question whether this was published separately.)

— — Printed by A. González de Barcia in *Historiadores primitivos de las Indias occidentales* (*q.v.*).

— — Printed with some corrections by P. de Angelis in *Colección de*

[Schmidel (Ulrich): *cont.*]

obras y documentos rel a la hist. . . del Río de la Plata, Vol. III, *q.v.*

— *Histoire véritable d'un voyage curieux, fait par U. S. . . . dans l'Amérique* A transl. of Hulsius' version in H. Ternaux-Compans' *Collection de voyages, relations, etc.* Vol. V, (*q.v.*).

— *Voyage of U. S. to the rivers of La Plata and Paraguay, etc.* Trans. from the original (1567) German edition by L. L. Domínguez. and published in *The Conquest of the River Plate.* Hakluyt Society, London, 1891. [L]

— *Viaje al Río de la Plata . . . notas bibliográficas por B. Mitre; prólogo, traducción y anotaciones por S. A. Lafone Quevedo*, Buenos Aires, 1903. [L]

— See also Mondschein (J.). Cap. XIII, i.

Schumacher (Hermann A.). *Juan de Castellanos. Ein Lebensbild, aus der Conquista-Zeit.* Published in *Hamburgische Festschrift zur Erinnerung an die Entdeckung Amerikas.* Hamburg, 1892. [L]

Segurola (Sebastián de). *Diario de los sucesos del cerco de la ciudad de La Paz en 1781.* Letters written in 1782, publ. in *Archivo boliviano.* Vol. I, 268–278. *q.v.* Cap. XVI, v.

Semanario de agricultura, industria y comercio. Buenos Aires, Sept. 1., 1802 to Feb. 11, 1807.

Facsimile of front page of Num. I. and an analysis of contents in years 1802–3–4–5–6–7, given in J. T. Medina, *La imprenta en Buenos Aires.* p. 165, etc., *q.v.* Cap. XVII., vi.

Semanario erudito. 34 vols. Ed. by A. Valladares de Sotomayor. Madrid, 1788. [L] Cap. XI, iii.

Serrano y Sanz (M.) Ed. *Historiadores de Indias.* Vols. I. and II. publ. in *Nueva biblioteca de autores españoles.* Vols. XIII, XV. *q.v.*

Silva (José). *Storia critica dell' origine, progressi, e stato attuale del Giansenismo.*

— *Storia critica dell' opinioni filosofiche sulla causa fisica de terremoti.*

— *Allarme della vera religione, e della sana politica contra gli odierni attentati dell' irreligione e dell' anarchia.* Cap. XIV, iv.

Simón (Pedro). *Noticias historiales de las conquistas de Tierra Firme en las Indias occidentales.* Primera parte. Cuenca, 1627. [L]

— — *Primera parte; edición hecha sobre la de Cuenca de 1626. Segunda-tercera parte; publícase por vez primera*

[Simón (Pedro): *cont.*]

sobre los manuscritos de la Biblioteca Nacional. Edited by Medardo Rivas. 5 vols. Bogotá, 1882–92. [L].

— *The Expedition of Pedro de Ursúa and Lope de Aguirre in search of El Dorado and Omagua in 1560-61.* Translated from Fray P. S.'s *Sixth Historical Notice*. . .by W. Bollaert. Hakluyt Society, London, 1861. [L] Cap. X, viii.

Solís y Ribadeneira (Antonio de). *Historia de la conquista de Méjico, población, y progresos de la América septentrional, conocida por el nombre de Nueva España.* Madrid, 1684. [L]

— — Printed in *Historia de la conquista del Nuevo Mundo.* Vol. I. *q.v.*

— — Printed in *Bib. de aut esp.* Vol. XXVIII, *q.v.*

Solís y Valenzuela (Pedro de). *Epítome de la vida y muerte del ilustrísimo doctor don Bernardino de Almansa . . . arzobispo de Santafé de Bogotá, etc.* Lima, 1646. [L]

— *Panegírico sagrado, en alabanza del Serafín de las soledades, San Bruno.* Lima, 1646. [L] Cap. XIV, iii.

Solórzano Pereira (Juan de). *De Indiarum jure: sive de justa Indiarum occidentalium inquisitione, acquisitione et retentione, etc.* 2 vols. Madrid, 1629–1639. [L]

— *Política indiana, sacada en lengua castellana de los dos tomos del derecho y gobierno municipal de las indias occidentales que más copiosamente escribió en la latina . . . J. d. S. P. Por el mismo autor . . . añadidas muchas cosas que no están en los tomos latinos.* Madrid, 1648. [L]

— — *Corrigida e ilustrada con notas por . . . F. Ramiro de Valenzuela.* 2 vols. Madrid, 1776. [L]

— *Memorial o discurso informativo, jurídico, histórico, político de los derechos, honores . . . que se deben dar, y guardar a los consejeros honorarios, y jubilados, etc.* Madrid, 1642. [L] Cap. XV, ii.

Sosa (Pedro de). *Memorial del peligroso estado espiritual y temporal del reino de Chile.* Madrid (?), 1616 (?). [L]

NOTE.—The copy in the British Museum has MS. notes by the author. Cap. IX, vii.

Suárez (Francisco). *Commentariorum ac disputationum in tertiam partem Divi Thomae.* Vol. I, Alcalá, 1590. Vol. II. Alcalá, 1592. Vol. III, Salamanca, 1595. Vol. IV, Coimbra, 1602.

[Suárez (Francisco): *cont.*]

— *Metaphysicarum disputationum, in quibus et universa naturalis theologia ordinate traditur, etc.* 2 vols. Mainz, 1605. [L]

— *Opus de virtute et statu religionis.* Vol. I. Coimbra, 1608. Vol. II, Coimbra, 1609. Vol. III (Vols. II and III), Lyons, 1623. Vol. IV, Lyons, 1625.

— *Tractatus de legibus, ac Deo Legislatore in decem libros distributus.* Coimbra, 1611. Antwerp, 1613. [L]

— *Defensio Fidei Catholicae . . . adversus Anglicanae sectae errores, cum responsione ad apologiam pro juramento fidelitatis, et praefationem monitoriam . . . Jacobi Angliae Regis, etc.* Coimbra, 1613. [L]

— *Operis de religione tomus primus (—quartus et ultimus). Editio novissima, etc.* Lyons, 1630–34. [L]

— *Opera omnia: hactenus edita.* 23 vols. Venice, 1740–51. [L]

— — *Editio nova a D. M. André; etc.* 9 vols. Paris, 1856–58. [L]. Cap. XI, ii.

Suárez de Figueroa (Cristóbal de). *El pasajero.* Madrid. 1617. Cap. V.

— *Hechos de Don García de Mendoza, el Marqués de Cañete.* Madrid, 1613. [L]

— — Printed by Barros Arana in *Colección de historiadores de Chile.* Vol. V, *q.v.* Cap. V.

Tafalla (Juan). See Ruiz López (H) and Pavón (J.) *Suplemento a la quinología.* Cap. XVII, v.

Techo (Nicolás de). *Historia provinciae Paraquariae Societatis Jesu.* Lille, 1673. [L]

— *The history of the provinces of Paraguay, Tucuman, Rio de la Plata, Parana, Guaira and Urvaica, etc.* Trans. from the Latin, and publ. by Churchill (A.) and (J.) in *A Collection of Voyages and Travels.* Vol. IV. *q.v.* Cap. XIII, ii.

Telégrafo mercantil (El). Buenos Aires, April 1st, 1801–Oct. 17th, 1802.

Facsimile of front page of first issue and an account of other numbers given by J. T. Medina in *La imprenta en Buenos Aires.* p. 138, etc. *q.v.* Cap. XVII, vi.

Ternaux-Compans (Henri). *Recueil de documents et mémoires originaux sur l'histoire des possessions espagnoles dans l'Amérique, etc.* Paris, 1840. [L]

— *Voyages, relations et mémoires originaux pour servir à*

[Ternaux-Compans (Henri): *cont.*]
l'histoire de la découverte de l'Amérique. 20 vols. Paris, 1837–41. [L]

— *Bibliothèque américaine, ou catalogue des ouvrages relatifs à l'Amérique qui ont paru depuis sa découverte jusqu'à l'an 1700.* Paris, 1837. [L]

— See also Oliva (Anello).

Tesillo (Santiago de). *Guerra de Chile, causas de su duración, medios para su fin.* Madrid, 1647.

— — Printed in *Colección de hist. de Chile.* Vol. V, *q.v.*

— *Restauración del estado de Arauco y otros progresos militares, etc.* Lima, 1665.

— — Printed in *Colección de hist. de Chile.* Vol. XI, *q.v.* Cap. IX, ix.

Thayer Ojeda (Tomás). *Las antiguas ciudades de Chile. Apuntes históricos sobre su desarrollo y listas de los funcionarios que actuaron en ellas hasta el año 1565.* Publ. in *Anales de la Universidad.* Santiago de Chile, 1911. [L]

— *Memoria histórica sobre la familia Álvarez de Toledo en Chile.* Santiago de Chile, 1902. [L].

— *Santiago durante el siglo XVI, etc.* Published in *Anales de la Universidad de Chile* of Jan. and Feb., 1905, *q.v.* Cap. IV, iv.

Tobar y Buendía (Pedro). *Verdadera histórica relación del origen . . . y milagros de la imagen de Chiquinquira.* Madrid, 1695. Cap. XII, ii.

Toro (Juan Bautista). *El secular religioso, para consuelo y aliento de los que viviendo en el siglo, pretenden lograr el cielo.* Madrid, 1721. 2nd ed., 1722. 3rd, ed. Madrid, 1778.

— — See also article by Caro (M. A.), entitled *Curiosidades literarias,* in *Repertorio colombiano.* Vol. XII. No. 2. Cap. XIV, iv.

Torres (Bernardo de). *Crónica de la provincia peruana del Orden de los Ermitaños de S. Agustín nuestro padre.* 8 books, Lima, 1657. This contains as its 2nd part a summary of the 1st vol. of Calancha's *Crónica moralizada, q.v.* Continued by Juan Teodoro Vásquez, up to year 1721. MS. Cap. XII, vi; Cap. XIV, iii.

Torres (Cristóbal de). *Lengua eucarística del hombre bueno, etc.* Madrid, 1665. Cap. XIV, iv.

Torres (José). *Privilegios y prerrogativas del Esposo de la Madre de Dios.* Printed in Italian (?). See Medina, *Lit. col. de Chile.* Cap. XIV, iv.

Torres Bollo (Diego de). *Relatio historica rerum apud Indos in Provincia Peruana gestarum.* Rome, 1603.
— *Breve relatione . . .del Peru, circa il frutto che si raccoglie con gli Indiani di quel regno, etc.* Rome and Milan, 1603 (?). Venice, 1604. [L]
— *Comentarios del Perú. Breve relación del fruto que se recoge de los Indios.* Rome (?), 1603 (?).
— *Brevis relatio historica regum in provincia peruana apud indos, etc.* Transl. from the Italian. Maguntia, 1604. [L]
— *La nouvelle histoire du Pérou . . . touchant les choses notables . . . et le fruit qui se recueille avec les Indiens, etc* Paris, 1604. [L]
— *De rebus peruanis.* Another translation from the Italian. Antwerp, 1604. [L] Cap. X, iv.

Torres Saldamando (Enrique). *Los antiguos Jesuitas del Perú.* Lima, 1882.
— *Libro primero de los cabildos de Lima.* Lima, 1888. [L]

Tula Bazán (Pedro de). *Informe al obispo don Manuel de Alday sobre tres puntos tocantes al uso que las mujeres hacían en Santiago de los trajes con cola.* MS. See Medina, *Lit. col de Chile.* Cap. XIV, iv.

Ullauri (Juan). [For account of his works, see Juan León Mera's *Ojeada histórico-crítica sobre la poesía ecuatoriana.*] Cap. XVII, iii.

Ulloa (Antonio de). *Relación histórica del viaje a la América Meridional . . . con otras varias observaciones, etc., por D. Jorge y Santacilla.* Madrid, 1748. [L]
— *A voyage to South America . . . undertaken by A. de U. and J. J.* y *S.* London, 1758. [L]
— *Noticias americanas: entretenimientos físicos históricos sobre la América meridional, y la septentrional oriental.* Madrid, 1772. [L]
— *Mémoires philosophiques historiques, physiques concernant la découverte de l'Amérique.* Trans. by M. . . . Paris, 1787. [L] Cap. XII, i.
— See also Juan y Santacilla (J.) and Ulloa (A. de): *Noticias secretas.*

Unánue (José Hipólito). *Observaciones sobre el clima de Lima, y sus influencias en los seres organizados,*

[Unánue (José Hipólito): *cont.*]

en especial el hombre. Lima, 1806. [L]. Madrid, 1815. [L]

— — Printed in M. de Odriozola's *Documentos liter. del Perú.* Vol. VI. *q.v.* Cap. XVII, v.

— *Disertación sobre el aspecto, cultivo, comercio, y virtudes de la famosa planta del Perú nombrada coca.* Published in *Mercurio peruano,* 1794, Vol. XI, p. 205, *q.v.*

— See also other contributions to *Mercurio peruano.*

Urquiza (Juan de). *Tractatus de profundissima sciencia* MS. in Library at Lima.

— *Relación de la fundación de la real audiencia del Cuzco.* Madrid, 1795. Cap. X, vii.

Urrea (Jerónimo de). *Orlando Furioso . . . traducido en romance castellano por don I. de Urrea.* Antwerp, 1549. [L] Cap. V

Valderrama (Adolfo). *Bosquejo histórico de la poesía chilena.* Santiago de Chile, 1866. [L]

Valdés (José María). [Occasional poems, mostly lost. One quintilla quoted by J. M. Vergara y Vergara in *Hist. de la lit. en Nueva Granada.*] Cap. XVII, iii.

Valdivia (Luis de). *Arte y gramática general de la lengua que corre en todo el reino de Chile, con un vocabulario, y confesionario . . . Juntamente con la doctrina cristiana y catecismo del concilio de Lima en español, y dos traducciones de él en la lengua de Chile, etc.* Lima, 1606. [L]. Seville, 1684. [L]

— *Doctrina cristiana y catecismo en la lengua allentiac . . . con un confesionario, arte y vocabulario breves.* Lima, 1607.

— *Historia de la provincia castellana de la Sociedad de Jesús.* MS.

— *Varones ilustres de la Sociedad de Jesús.* MS. Cap. IX, vii.

Valdivia (Pedro de). *Cartas.* Five printed in Claudio Gay's *Documentos.* Vol. I, *q.v.* and in *Colección de historiadores de Chile.* Vol. I. *q.v.* Two more are printed in *Proceso de Pedro de Valdivia* by D. Barros Arana *q.v.* Cap. IV, v.

Valera (Blas). [Wrote a history of the Incas in Latin. MS. partly destroyed at the sacking of Cadiz in 1596. The sheets saved were used by Garcilaso de la Vega in the compilation of his *Comentarios reales.*] Cap. IV, ii.

Valle y Caviedes (Juan del). *Diente del Parnaso.*
— *Poesías serias y jocosas.*
Both published by M. Odriozola in *Documentos literarios del Perú.* Vol. V, *q.v.* Cap. XI, i.
Varela y Ulloa. See Nuix (J.).
Vargas Machuca (Bernardo de). *Apologías y discursos de las conquistas occidentales.* First publ. by A. M. Fabié in *Col. de doc. inéd para la hist. de Esp.* Vol. LXXI, *q.v.*
— *Milicia y descripción de las Indias.* Madrid, 1599.
— — Printed in *Colección de libros que tratan de Amér. raros o curiosos* Vols. VIII and IX, *q.v.*
— Several MSS. in British Museum Cap. II, i.
Vásquez (Francisco). *Relación verdadera de todo lo que sucedió en la jornada de Omagua y Dorado. . . .Trátase ansimismo del alzamiento de don Fernando de Guzmán, y Lope de Aguirre, y de las crueldades destos perversos tiranos.* Printed in *Nueva biblioteca de autores españoles* XV. (*Historiadores de Indias II.*) *q.v.* Cap. X, ii.
Vásquez (Juan Teodoro). *Crónica de la provincia peruana* etc. Continuation up to 1721. 2 vols. MS. See Torres (Bernardo). Cap. XII, vi.
Vásquez de Contreras (Diego). *Orlando Furioso . . . traducido en prosa castellana por D. V. de C.* Madrid, 1585. [L] Cap. V.
Vega Carpio (Lope Felix de). *Arauco domado.* ff. 77–101 of a collection entitled: *Parte veinte de las comedias de Lope de Vega.* Barcelona, 1630. [L] Cap. VI, iv.
Velasco (Juan de). *Historia del reino de Quito en la América meridional. Año de 1789.* 3 pts: i., *La historia natural,* ii. *La historia antigua,* iii. *La historia moderna.* First publ. Quito, 1841–44. [L]
— *Histoire du royaume de Quito.* A transl. of pt. ii of the above publ. in 1840 by H. Ternaux-Compans in his *Voyages, relations et mémoires etc.* Vols. XVIII, XIX, *q.v.*
— *Description du royaume de Quito.* Extracts from pt. iii of the above publ. in 1840 by H. Ternaux-Compans in his *Recueil de documents et mémoires, etc. q.v.*
— *Viaggi, relazioni e memorie relative al regno de Quito.* Transl. of Pt. ii. of the above publ. in 1840. in F. C. Marmoocchi's *Raccolta di viaggi, etc.* Vol. X. *q.v.* Cap. XVII, iii.
— [For specimens of his verse, see Mera (J. L.), *Ojeada histórico-crítica sobre la poesía ecuatoriana*].
Velasco (Martín). *Arte de sermones.* Cadiz, 1675. Cap. XI, iii.

Velásquez Altamirano (Gutierre). *Del oficio y potestad del vicario del príncipe, y gobierno universal de las Indias* MS. in Library of D. Lorenzo Ramírez de Prado. Cap. XV, iii.

Venegas (Alonso Mesía). See Mesía Venegas (A.).

Ventura Travada (Diego). *El suelo de Arequipa convertido en cielo.* First published by M. Odriozola in *Documentos literarios del Perú.* Vol. X, *q.v.*

Vergara Azcárate (José de). *El sacerdote instruido.*
— *Historia de las capellanías fundadas por laicos y religiosos en este arzobispado.*
— *Sermones morales y doctrinales.*
— *Historia de Gedeón, Ester y la casta Susana.*
— *De las reliquias y veneración de los santos.*
— *Cuestiones del cabildo de Santafé.*
— *Reparos dignos de atención en la erección de parroquias.* See Vergara y Vergara, *Hist. de lit. en Nueva Granada.* Cap. XIV, iv.

Vergara Azcárate (Fernando de). *Resoluciones morales, o explicación de los contratos en común y en particular.*
— *Cuestiones canónicas.*
— *Sermones de la Santísima Virgen y de los Santos.*
— *Breve noticia de la congregación de Nuestra Señora del Socorro.*
— *Dictamen de prudencia de nuestro padre San Ignacio de Loyola.*
— *Novena de San Agustín, doctor de la Iglesia.* See Vergara y Vergara, *Hist. de lit. en Nueva Granada.* Cap. XIV, iv.

Vergara y Caycedo (Felipe). *Vindicación del angélico Dr. Tomás de Aquino sobre el misterio de la concepción de María.*
— *Elementos de filosofía natural que contienen los principios de la física, demostrados por las matemáticas, y confirmados con observaciones y experiencias.*
— [Many other works all in MS. See Vergara y Vergara, *Hist. de lit. en Nueva Granada.*] Cap. XVII, i.

Vergara y Vergara (José María). *Historia de la literatura en Nueva Granada.* Bogotá, 1895. Sec. ed. Bogotá, 1905. [L]

Vicuña Mackenna (Benjamín). *Historia crítica y social de la ciudad de Santiago, 1541–1868.* 2 vols. Valparaiso, 1869. [L]

[Vicuña Mackenna (Benjamín): *cont.*]

— *Chile. Relaciones históricas.* Santiago de Chile, 1877–1878. [L]

— *Bibliografía americana, estudios y catálogo . . . de la biblioteca americana coleccionada por el Sr. G. Beeche.* Valparaiso, 1879. [L]

— *Obras completas.* 40 vols. Santiago de Chile, 1876. [L]

Viescas (Ramón). [Wrote lyric poetry. See Mera (J. L.), *Ojeada histórico-crítica sobre la poesía ecuatoriana*, where several poems are printed.] Cap. XVII, iii.

Villagra (Gaspar de). *Historia de la Nueva Méjico.* (Poem in 34 cantos). Alcalá de Henares, 1610. [L]

Villamor (Pablo de). *La vida de la Madre Francisca del Niño Jesús.* Madrid, 1723. Cap. XII, ii.

Villarroel (Gaspar de). *Gobierno eclesiástico-pacífico, y unión de los dos cuchillos pontificio y regio.* 2 vols. Madrid 1656–7. [L]. Madrid, 1737, [L]

— *Primera parte de las historias sagradas y eclesiásticas morales.* 3 vols. Madrid, 1660.

— *Judices comentariis literalibus cum moralibus aphorismis illustrati.* Madrid, 1626. [L]

— *Semana Santa : tratado de los comentarios, dificultades y discursos literales y místicos sobre los evangelios de la Cuaresma.* Vol. I, Lisbon, 1631; vol. II, Lisbon, 1632; Vol. III, Seville, 1634.

— — Complete edition 3, vols. Madrid, 1662. Cap. XIV, iii. Cap. XV.

Xuárez (Gaspar). See Juárez.

Xerés (Francisco de). See Jerez.

Xeréz (Francisco de). See Jerez.

Xufré del Águila (Melchor). See Jufré del Águila.

Yapaguay, Nicolás. *Explicación del catecismo en lengua guaraní.* (*con dirección del P. Pablo Restivo*) 3 pts. Printed by Jesuit Mission. Pueblo de S. María la Mayor. Paraguay, 1724. [L]

— *Sermones y ejemplos en lengua guaraní.* Printed by the Jesuit Mission in Pueblo de St. Francisco Javier. Paraguay, 1727. Cap. I.

Yupangui. See Castro Tito Cusi Yupangui (Diego de).

Zabálburu (Francisco). See *Nueva colección de documentos inéditos para la historia de España y de sus Indias.*

Zamacola (Juan Domingo de). *Derrotero desde Buenos Aires a Arequipa.*
— *Historia de Nuestra Señora de Cayma.*
— *Sucesos de las revoluciones de las provincias del Perú desde 1780 hasta 1785.*
— *Relación del terremoto experimentado en Arequipa el 13 de Mayo de 1780, y una descripción del volcán Misti.*
— *Diario de la visita del obispo D.P.T. Chávez de la Rosa, por las provincias de Tarapacá, Tacna y Moquegua.*
— *Relación de la fundación del pueblo de San Fernando en el valle de Socabaya.*
— *Historia descriptiva y geográfica de Arequipa y territorio de su comprensión desde el emperador Inca, Mayta Capac, que la fundó.*
— *El porque de los médicos.*
— *El peor es nada* (satire on idleness).
— *Arte de chupar tabaco* (satire on women who smoke, reproving luxury and the use of artificial colours on the face). See Mendiburu, *Dic. hist. biog. del Perú.* Cap. XVI, v.

Zamora (Alonso de). *Historia de la provincia de S. Antonino del Nuevo Reino de Granada del orden de Predicadores compuesta por el M. R. P. M. F. Alonso de Zamora.* Barcelona, 1701. [L] Cap. XII, ii.

Zárate (Agustín de). *Historia del descubrimiento y conquista de la provincia del Perú.* Antwerp, 1555. [L] 2nd edition Seville, 1577. [L]
— — Printed by A. González Barcia in *Colección de hist primit. del Perú.* Vol. III, *q.v.*
— — Printed in *Bib. aut esp.* Vol. XXVI, *q.v.*
— *Le historie del Signor A. de Z. dello scoprimento et conquista del Peru, etc.* Trans. by S. A. Ulloa. Venice, 1563. [L]
— The strange and delectable history of the discoverie and conquest of Peru. Trans. by T. Nicholas. London, 1581. [L]
— *Histoire de la découverte et de la conquête du Perú.* Trans. by Seigneur de Citry et de la Guette. Paris, 1716. [L] Cap. III, vi.

Zea (Francisco Antonio). *Avisos de Hebéfilo a los jóvenes de los dos colegios sobre la inutilidad de sus estudios*

[Zea (Franciso Antonico): *cont.*]

presentes, etc. Published in *Papel periódico de Santafé* de Bogotá. Nos. 8 and 9 (for April 1 and 8, 1791). *q.v.*

— [Poem on the *Dos de Mayo 1808*, quoted by Vergara y Vergara in *Hist. de la lit. en Nueva Granada*, pp. 273–4.]

— *Colombia constituida.* Poem in blank verse. Paris, 1822.

— *Varios discursos.* Caracas, 1825. [L]

— [Various official documents on Colombian affairs. [L]]

— Ed. *El semanario de agricultura.*

— Ed. *El mercurio de España.* Cap. XVII., i, ii.

Zinny (Antonio). *Historia de los gobernadores de las provincias argentinas desde 1535 hasta 1810.* 3 vols. Buenos Aires, 1879–82. [L] Cap. XV, iv.

INDEX

Date Due